NATIONAL 4 & 5

COMPUTING SCIENCE

John Walsh

HODDER
GIBSON
AN HACHETTE UK COMPANY

Acknowledgements

Dedication

To Helen, Peter John, Mary, Sarah, Siobhan and Cecilia.

With thanks to Jane Paterson.

Although every effort has been made to ensure that website addresses are correct at time of going to press, Hodder Gibson cannot be held responsible for the content of any website mentioned in this book. It is sometimes possible to find a relocated web page by typing in the address of the home page for a website in the URL window of your browser.

Hachette UK's policy is to use papers that are natural, renewable and recyclable products and made from wood grown in sustainable forests. The logging and manufacturing processes are expected to conform to the environmental regulations of the country of origin.

Orders: please contact Bookpoint Ltd, 130 Park Drive, Abingdon, Oxon OX14 4SE. Telephone: (44) 01235 827720. Fax: (44) 01235 400454. Lines are open 9.00–5.00, Monday to Saturday, with a 24-hour message answering service. Visit our website at www.hoddereducation.co.uk. Hodder Gibson can be contacted direct on: Tel: 0141 848 1609; Fax: 0141 889 6315; email: hoddergibson@hodder.co.uk.

© John Walsh 2014
First published in 2014 by
Hodder Gibson, an imprint of Hodder Education,
An Hachette UK Company
2a Christie Street
Paisley PA1 1NB

Impression number   5 4 3
Year   2018 2017 2016 2015

Cover photo © Bellenixe – Fotolia.com
Illustrations by Tony Wilkins, DC Graphic Design Limited, Peter Lubach at Redmoor Design and Integra Software Services Pvt. Ltd.
Typeset in Bembo Regular 12.5/14.5 by Integra Software Services Pvt. Ltd., Pondicherry, India
Printed in Dubai

A catalogue record for this title is available from the British Library

ISBN: 978 1444 182 200

Contents

Preface

This book is based upon the National 4 and National 5 statements of knowledge and understanding set out in Appendix 2 of the National 5 Computing Science Course Support Notes version 1.1 dated July 2013. It should be noted that this book is the author's own interpretation of the content of this document.

The chapters match the grouping of the content as described in the above document. Hence, Chapters 1 to 5 cover the Software Design and Development Unit and Chapters 6 to 16, Information System Design and Development.

Short revision questions designed to focus students' learning have been placed at the end of each chapter, together with some suggested practical activities. Answers to all end of chapter questions are available to download (free of charge) from **www.hoddergibson.co.uk/updatesandextras**.

An extensive glossary and a comprehensive index of terms are included. Glossary terms are in red in the main text.

The programming languages Scratch®, LiveCode®, C, Visual Basic®, True BASIC® and COMAL® are used to illustrate computational constructs. Other languages used in the book include HTML, JavaScript® and AppleScript®. Screenshots from both Access® and FileMaker® Pro database applications are provided.

Note that this book is *not* an instruction manual for any particular package. Your teacher or lecturer will provide support material tailored to the programming languages and application packages that you will use in your centre.

Note that the order of the Chapters does not constitute a recommended teaching order.

John Walsh

February 2014

Unit 1

Software Design and Development

This chapter and the four which follow, each form part of the Software Design and Development Unit.

Each chapter is designed to cover the contents statements as they are grouped within the Unit and Course descriptions for National 4 and National 5 Computing Science; namely Low-level operations and computer architecture, Computational constructs, Data types and structures, Testing and Documenting solutions, Algorithm specification and Design notations. The examples given in each chapter are based upon a range of hardware and software, which is current at the time of writing.

The unifying themes of both National 4 and National 5 Computing Science courses are:

- technological progress and trends
- the relationship between software, hardware and system performance
- information representation and transfer as a core component of any computation.

CHAPTER 1 Low-level operations and computer architecture

This chapter explains what **binary** is and how a computer system uses binary to store different types of data. The basic building blocks or **architecture** of a computer are also described here. Along the way, we consider how it is possible for a computer to carry out our instructions. We examine the following topics.

- the use of binary to represent and store:
  - positive integers
  - characters
  - instructions (machine code)
- units of storage (bit, byte, Kb, Mb, Gb, Tb, Pb)

- the use of binary to represent and store:
  - real numbers
  - graphics (bit-mapped and vector)
- translation of high-level program code to binary (machine code): interpreters and compilers
- basic computer architecture:
  - processor (registers, ALU, control unit), memory, buses (data and address), interfaces

Whatever the type of **data**, it is all eventually stored inside the computer as binary numbers.

Let's have a look at what binary is and what it has to do with computers before we go any further.

The two-state machine

A computer system is known as a **two-state machine** because the processing and **storage devices** in a computer system have one feature in common – their components only have two states. These two states are 'on' and 'off' and are represented using the digits 1 for 'on' and 0 for 'off'. This system of using only two numbers is called the **binary system** because the word binary means 'two states'. In the same way as a light bulb can have two states, 'on' or 'off', a binary number has two values 1 or 0, 'on' or 'off'.

The two-state system is one of the main reasons why computers use the binary system to store data.

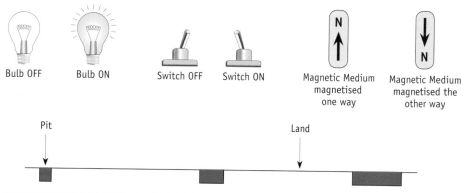

0000111000000000000000000001111100000000000000000011111110000

Figure 1.01 Some examples of two-state systems

Use of binary to represent and store positive integers

Bits

A single unit in binary is called a **bit**. The word bit is made up from the two words **BI**nary digi**T**.

Unlike computers, people use the decimal system. Decimal means ten, so people count in units, followed by tens, hundreds, thousands, and so on.

For example, the number 2407 is made up like this:

Th	**H**	**T**	**U**	
1000	100	10	1	these are the place values
2	4	0	7	these are the digits

This means $(2 \times 1000) + (4 \times 100) + (0 \times 10) + (7 \times 1)$.

This is very easy for us to understand because we are familiar with the decimal system. Thinking about place values in this way will help us to understand the binary system.

Binary works in a similar way, except that binary place values do not go up in tens, they go up in twos. Let's look at a binary number made up of four bits:

8	4	2	1	these are the place values
1	1	0	1	these are the bits

Each bit has its own place value, starting with units, then twos, fours, eights, and so on.

The binary number in the example is 1101.

This means $(1 \times 8) + (1 \times 4) + (0 \times 2) + (1 \times 1)$ which is 13 in decimal.

Bytes

A binary number which is made up of eight bits (for instance 1101 0110) is called a **byte**. What is the largest number a byte can hold? Let's work it out. A byte has eight bits, so if each bit had the value 1, this would give 1111 1111.

Now consider the place values for eight bits:

128	64	32	16	8	4	2	1	these are the place values
1	1	1	1	1	1	1	1	these are the bits

So we have 128 + 64 + 32 + 16 + 8 + 4 + 2 + 1 which is 255 in decimal.

Note that a byte can have the value zero, so a byte can hold a range of values from zero (0000 0000) to 255 (1111 1111), making a total of 256 different numbers.

Where do the place values come from?

The place values come from the number base, which, in the case of the binary system, is the number 2. Each different place value can be created by starting from 2^0, like this:

Power of 2	8	7	6	5	4	3	2	1	0
Place value	256	128	64	32	16	8	4	2	1

Figure 1.02 A binary wristwatch, model 'Samui Moon' by Time Technology, displaying 3:25

Note that the leftmost bit in a binary number is called the **most significant bit** (MSB) because it has the highest place value and that the rightmost bit with the smallest place value (1) is called the **least significant bit** (LSB).

Changing between binary and decimal representations

Binary to decimal

It is easy to change a binary number into its decimal value; just write down the place values and add them up like this:

Place values	128	64	32	16	8	4	2	1	
Binary number	0	1	0	0	0	0	1	1	
Decimal	0	+64	+0	+0	+0	+0	+2	+1	= 67

Decimal to binary

The easiest way to change a decimal number into a binary number is to write down the place values and then subtract each place value from the number in turn, like this:

Suppose the number is 99, then look at the place values: 128 is larger than 99, so put a 0 at place value 128.

Now subtract 64 from 99, so that $99 - 64 = 35$, put a 1 at place value 64.

Now subtract 32 from 35, so that $35 - 32 = 3$, put a 1 at place value 32.

Fill in the place values larger than 3 with 0, and then move to the next suitable place value which is 2, $3 - 2 = 1$, so put a 1 at place value 2.

Now we are left with $1 - 1 = 0$, so put a 1 at place value 1.

Result:

Place values	128	64	32	16	8	4	2	1	
Binary number	0	1	1	0	0	0	1	1	= 99

Quick Tip

Binary numbers using place values

Place values	128	64	32	16	8	4	2	1
Binary number	0	0	0	1	1	1	1	1

Instead of adding all of the place values to find the decimal equivalent of 11111, just go to the next place value upwards and subtract 1, so, in this example, binary 11111 is $32 - 1 = 31$ ... easy!

Check Your Learning

Now answer questions 1–10 (on page 31) on use of binary to represent and store positive integers (National 4).

Use of binary to represent and store real numbers

More about representing numbers

Numbers may be classified as **real numbers** or **integer** numbers. Real numbers include ALL numbers, both whole and fractional. Integer numbers are a subset of real numbers, which include only whole numbers, either positive or negative, for example 7 or −20.

Floating point representation

Real numbers are represented in binary by using a system called **floating point representation**.

Let's start by looking at real numbers in decimal. Any decimal number can be represented with the decimal point in a fixed position and a multiplier, which is a power of 10.

For example:

$$214 = .214 \times 1000 = .214 \times 10^3$$

point moves three places

This is a decimal number and so uses powers of ten. 10 is the **base**.

Any number can be represented in any number base in the form:

$$\mathbf{m \times base^e}$$

where *m* is called the **mantissa** and *e* is the **exponent**. The mantissa is the actual digits of the number and the exponent is the power (to which the base is raised). If we are only working in decimal (base 10), then the base need not be stored, since the base is always the same. Therefore we need only store the mantissa (214 in the above example) and the exponent (3 in the above example).

For the binary system, the base would be 2. Again, since the base is *always* 2, the base can be ignored and does not need to be stored in the computer alongside each number.

Taking the above example of decimal 214, let's work out how this would be represented in binary using floating point:

Decimal 214 may be represented in binary as 1101 0110:

$$1101\ 0110 = .1101\ 0110 \times 2^8 = .1101\ 0110 \times 2^{1000}$$

point moves eight places

Reminder

! Remember: 1000 in binary = 8 in decimal.

So in this case, the mantissa would be 1101 0110 and the exponent would be 1000.

Let's look at another example, this time changing a binary number into floating point representation.

Suppose the binary number is 1100.001 This gives:

$$1101.001 = .1100001 \times 2^4 = .1100001 \times 2^{100}$$

point moves four places   100 in binary = 4 in decimal

The mantissa in this case would be 1100001 and the exponent 100.

Figure 1.03 Numbers

Use of binary to represent and store negative integers

It is also possible to store negative numbers in binary. The name of the system that is used to store negative integers is the **two's complement**.

Method 1

It is easy to obtain the two's complement of a number by following these steps:

positive number in 8 bits	0000 0111	+7
change all the ones to zeros and	1111 1000	
vice versa, then add 1	+1	
negative number	1111 1001	−7

To change a number back from the two's complement you just repeat the same process as you followed to create it.

Example

negative number in 8 bits	1111 1001	−7
change all the ones to zeros and	0000 0110	
vice versa, then add 1	+1	
positive number	0000 0111	+7

Method 2

Another method of obtaining the two's complement of a number is to have the leftmost (or the most significant) bit represent **–128**, for example:

–128	64	32	16	8	4	2	1	
1	0	0	0	0	0	0	0	= –128

Note that the rest of the place values are *positive*.

Again, taking the same example of –7, this method gives:

–128	64	32	16	8	4	2	1
1	1	1	1	1	0	0	1

So, we have:

–128 +64 +32 +16 +8 +0 +0 +1 = –7

Table 1.01 shows how some positive and negative integers are stored.

Decimal	Two's complement
127	0111 1111
64	0100 0000
2	0000 0010
1	0000 0001
0	0000 0000
–1	1111 1111
–2	1111 1110
–64	1100 0000
–127	1000 0001
–128	1000 0000

Table 1.01 Comparing positive and negative integers

Check Your Learning

Now answer questions 11–16 (on page 32) on use of binary to represent and store integers and real numbers (National 5).

Units of storage

So far, we have only looked at bits and bytes as units of **storage**. Computers store very large amounts of data, and so it is helpful to be able to use larger units of storage to represent these.

The larger units of storage that you should know about in your course include **Kilobytes**, **Megabytes**, **Gigabytes**, **Terabytes** and **Petabytes**.

One Kilobyte is 1024 bytes (because $2^{10} = 1024$). One Kilobyte is also called one **Kb** for short.

In the same way, one Megabyte (**Mb**) is 1024 Kilobytes (2^{20} bytes).

One Gigabyte (**Gb**) is 1024 Megabytes (2^{30} bytes).

A Terabyte (**Tb**) is 1024 Gigabytes (2^{40} bytes).

A Petabyte (**Pb**) is 1024 Terabytes (2^{50} bytes).

Have a look at Table 1.02, which compares units of storage and provides some examples of how much data may be stored by each unit.

1 bit	1 or 0
1 byte	Numbers 0 to 255 or a single character
1 Kilobyte	One side of a page of text
1 Megabyte	A 500-page book
1 Gigabyte	One hour of standard-definition video
1 Terabyte	2 000 hours of CD-quality audio
1 Petabyte	The storage requirements for rendering the CGI effects for the movie *Avatar* (2009)

Table 1.02 Comparing units of storage

The quantity of **memory** (**RAM**) in a computer is typically measured in Gigabytes. The computer's **backing storage capacity** is measured in either Gigabytes or Terabytes.

Check Your Learning

Now answer questions 17–20 (on page 32) on units of storage (National 4).

Use of binary to represent and store characters

Representing characters

A **character** is a symbol, number or letter on the computer **keyboard**. Characters include the digits 0 to 9 (these are the *numeric* characters), letters (these are the *alphabetic* characters) and punctuation marks (these are the *special* characters).

Character set

The computer must be able to represent all the characters we may wish to use. A list of all the characters, which a computer can process and store, is called its **character set**. Different types of computer may have slightly different character sets. To allow a computer to represent all the characters, a different code number is given to each character.

The most popular form of this code is the **American Standard Code for Information Interchange** or **ASCII**. ASCII is a seven-bit code. Using a seven-bit code allows 2^7 or 128 different codes, so ASCII can represent 128 characters. If more than 128 characters are required, then eight bits can be used, giving 2^8 or 256 possible characters. This is called **extended ASCII**, and allows additional characters, such as those with accents (for example é and ç) or special symbols, like ™ and ©, to be represented.

Character	Binary	Decimal	Character	Binary	Decimal
Space	0010 0000	32	K	0100 1011	75
!	0010 0001	33	L	0100 1100	76
'	0010 0010	34	M	0100 1101	77
0	0011 0000	48	N	0100 1110	78
1	0011 0001	49	O	0100 1111	79
2	0011 0010	50	P	0101 0000	80
3	0011 0011	51	Q	0101 0001	81
?	0011 1111	63	R	0101 0010	82
@	0100 0000	64	S	0101 0011	83
A	0100 0001	65	T	0101 0100	84
B	0100 0010	66	U	0101 0101	85
C	0100 0011	67	V	0101 0110	86
D	0100 0100	68	W	0101 0111	87
E	0100 0101	69	X	0101 1000	88
F	0100 0110	70	Y	0101 1001	89
G	0100 0111	71	Z	0101 1010	90
H	0100 1000	72	a	0110 0001	97
I	0100 1001	73	b	0110 0010	98
J	0100 1010	74	c	0110 0011	99

Table 1.03 Sample of ASCII

Many different computers use ASCII to represent **text**. This makes it easier for text to be transferred between different computer systems. ASCII is an example of a **standard file format** – you can read more about standard file formats in Chapter 8.

Unicode (Universal Character Set)

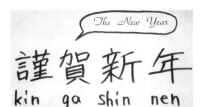

Figure 1.04 A seasonal greeting from Japan

This book is written in English, and uses characters from the Roman or Latin character set. Many other languages, such as Japanese, use completely different types of characters.

The **Unicode** character set is designed to represent the writing schemes of all of the world's major languages. The first 128 characters of Unicode are identical to ASCII. This allows for compatibility between Unicode and ASCII. Unicode (UTF-16) is a 16-bit code and can represent 65 536 different characters.

It's not just computers that use Unicode. Your phone may also use Unicode when sending characters like the wide variety of emoticons now in use. The Unicode standard continues to be developed, and is at version 6.03 at the time of writing this book.

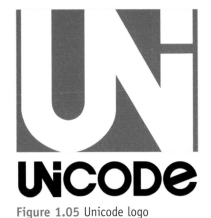

Figure 1.05 Unicode logo

The advantage that Unicode has over ASCII is that many more characters (or every possible character) may be represented. A disadvantage is that Unicode takes up at least twice as much space as ASCII (16 bits compared to 8 bits) in the computer's memory and in **backing storage**.

There is a great deal more to Unicode than can be described in a few lines in this book. You can find out more about Unicode at www.unicode.org/ and http://en.wikipedia.org/wiki/unicode.

Check Your Learning

Now answer questions 21–26 (on page 32) on use of binary to represent and store characters (National 4).

Use of binary to represent and store instructions (machine code)

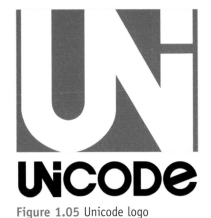

Figure 1.06 Binary numbers

Instructions are used to tell a computer what to do. Just now, my computer is following a set of instructions which are telling it to display the characters which I am typing on the **screen**.

A set of instructions that a computer can understand is called a **program**. Programs are written in **computer languages**. Here are two programs, each written in a different computer language:

©1997 Kania

Real programmers code in binary.

Figure 1.07 Programming in machine code

Program 1	Program 2
PRINT "HELLO"	1000 1101 1101 1101
PRINT "PLEASE TELL ME YOUR NAME"	1110 0011 1110 0011
INPUT YOUR_NAME	1000 1000 1101 1101

Which one is easier for you to understand? Program 1 is written in a language very like English. A computer language that uses normal or everyday language is called a **high-level language**.

The second example is not at all easy for most people to understand. This is because it is written in the computer's own language. The computer's own language is called **machine code**.

If you were able to write an instruction for a computer in machine code, then the computer would be able to understand it straight away, but nobody else would! Most **computer programs** are not written directly in machine code for this reason. Instead, they are written in high-level languages, which are then changed or *translated* into machine code.

You can read more about **translation of high-level program code to binary (machine code)** later in this chapter.

Check Your Learning

Now answer questions 27–33 (on pages 32–33) on use of binary to represent and store instructions (machine code) (National 4).

National 5

Use of binary to represent and store graphics

Representing graphics

Graphics or pictures on the computer screen are made up from tiny dots called **pixels**. The term pixel is short for **picture element**. The whole of the computer screen is made up of many thousands of pixels. Each pixel may be 'on' or 'off' depending on whether the value of the pixel in memory is 1 (on – so you can see it) or 0 (off – so you can't see it). These graphics are called **bit-mapped graphics** because there is a direct relationship between the bits in the computer's memory and the picture displayed on the computer screen.

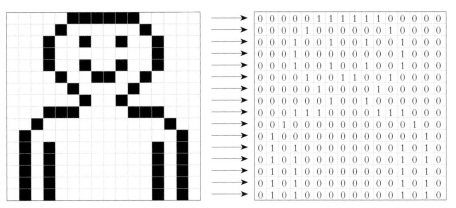

Figure 1.08 How bit-mapped graphics are stored in a computer

Look at Figure 1.08, which shows how graphics are stored in the computer's memory. The picture is drawn on a 16×16 grid. Grid squares which are 'on' are represented by a '1' and grid squares which are 'off' are represented by '0'. The amount of memory required to store this graphic would be 16×16 bits, which is 256 bits.

Graphics resolution

The **quality** of the picture is determined by the **resolution** of the graphics available. The resolution is the amount of detail which can be shown on a screen or on a printout. The smaller the size of the pixels, the finer the detail that can be displayed on the screen. Small pixels mean high resolution. See Figure 1.09 (a high-resolution graphic). Large pixels mean low resolution. One way of describing the resolution of the screen is to give the number of pixels horizontally and vertically. For instance, a screen display operating at 800×600 pixels (SVGA) is a lower resolution than 1024×768 pixels (**XGA**). Another way of describing the resolution is to give the total number of pixels available, although this description is usually applied to **devices** such as **digital cameras**, as in 'a 10 **Megapixel** camera'. Table 1.04 shows some screen resolutions for comparison.

Standard	Width × height	Total number of pixels
iPod nano®, iPod classic®	320 × 240	76 800
VGA	640 × 480	307 200
SVGA	800 × 600	480 000
iPhone®, iPod touch® (3.5 inch screen – 2012)	960 × 640	614 400
XGA	1024 × 768	786 432
DVD	720 × 576 (PAL)	414 720
HDTV , Blu-ray™ (720p)	1280 × 720	921 600
HDTV (full), Blu-ray™ (1080p, 1080i)	1920 × 1080	2 073 600 (approx. 2 Megapixels)
iPad® (9.7 inch screen – 2012)	2048 × 1536	3 145 728 (approx. 3 Megapixels)

Standard	Width × height	Total number of pixels
iMac® (27 inch screen – 2011)	2560 × 1440	3 686 400 (approx. 3.5 Megapixels)
MacBook Pro® (15.4 inch screen – 2012)	2880 × 1800	5 184 000 (approx. 5 Megapixels)
4K UHDTV (2160p)	3840 × 2160	8 294 400 (approx. 8.3 Megapixels)
Full aperture 4K (film)	4096 × 3112	12 746 752 (approx. 12.1 Megapixels)
8K UHDTV (4320p)	7680 × 4320	33 177 600 (approx. 33 Megapixels)

Table 1.04 A comparison of some screen resolutions

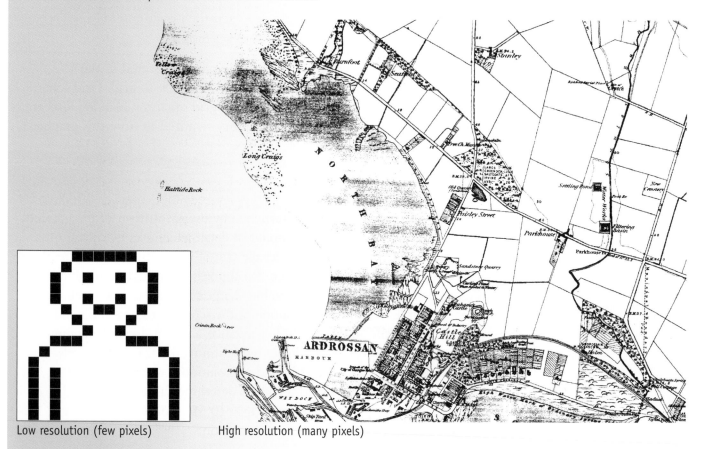

Low resolution (few pixels)   High resolution (many pixels)

Figure 1.09 Resolution of black and white bit-mapped graphics

Bit-mapped and vector graphics

Graphics packages can be classified into two main types, bit-mapped and **vector**. Both types of package are used to produce pictures, but they store the graphics in a different way. Bit-mapped packages **paint** pictures by changing the colour of the pixels which make up the screen display. Vector packages work by drawing objects on the screen. Bit-mapped packages and vector graphics packages are commonly known as paint and **draw packages** respectively. Vector packages are sometimes also called *object-oriented* graphics.

Other differences between bit-mapped and vector graphics

1 When two shapes overlap on the screen in a bit-mapped package, the shape which is on top rubs out the shape underneath. When the same thing is

done in a vector graphics package, the shapes remain as separate objects. They can be separated again and both shapes stay the same. See Figure 1.10.

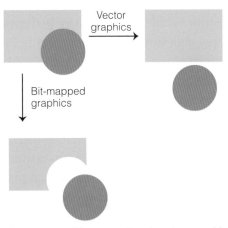

Vector graphics

Bit-mapped graphics

Figure 1.10 Bit-mapped and vector graphics

2 When you save a **file** created by a bit-mapped package, then the whole screen is saved, whether or not it contains any images. This results in a relatively large **file size** being produced. The objects produced by a vector graphics package have their descriptions stored as a file of data called **object attributes**. These object attributes take up far less **backing storage** space than a file created by a bit-mapped package, since only the object attributes rather than the whole screen need be stored. Figure 1.11 shows an object and its attributes. Note that a more complex vector graphics image will have an increased file size due to the fact that more objects must be stored.

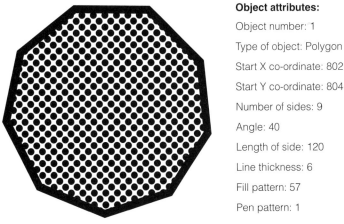

Object attributes:

Object number: 1

Type of object: Polygon

Start X co-ordinate: 802

Start Y co-ordinate: 804

Number of sides: 9

Angle: 40

Length of side: 120

Line thickness: 6

Fill pattern: 57

Pen pattern: 1

Figure 1.11 Object attributes

3 When you create a picture using a bit-mapped package, its resolution is fixed at that time. If you then go on to print the picture, the original resolution will be maintained in the printout. The resolution of a **printer** is measured in dots per inch (dpi). For the purpose of comparison, we will also refer to screen resolution as dots per inch rather than pixels. Suppose the resolution of the computer screen is 72 dpi in two dimensions and the printer which you are using is an ink jet, set at its default value of 360 dpi. When your picture is printed it will be at the screen resolution of 72 dpi, because in order to print, the **processor** sends the bit map to the printer. This feature is called **resolution dependence**.

When a picture is created using a vector graphics package, the resolution of the screen has no effect on the resolution of the printout. The picture will be printed out at the full resolution available on the printer. This feature is called **resolution independence**. Resolution independence is possible using vector graphics because when the picture is printed, the processor sends the file of object attributes, which represent the picture, to the printer.

4 When editing a picture created by a bit-mapped graphics package, it is possible to zoom in as far as the individual pixels and make changes. When the editing is complete, then the magnification should be reset to normal. Over-enlarging a bit-mapped image will eventually result in **pixelation**, when the individual pixels become visible. This is sometimes done intentionally for special effects purposes. When editing a picture produced by a vector graphics package, it is possible to zoom in to enlarge portions of the picture on the screen, but it is not possible to edit any pixels. It is possible to edit the individual objects which make up the picture, and alter any of the attributes, such as line width.

Calculation of storage requirements of bit-mapped graphics

It is easy to calculate the storage requirements of black and white bit-mapped graphics. You begin by working out the total number of pixels in the graphic. Multiplying the height in pixels by the width in pixels gives the total number. Each pixel requires one bit of storage, so the answer is given in bits. To change bits into bytes, divide by eight, because there are eight bits in a byte. To change bytes into Kilobytes, divide by 1024, and to change Kilobytes into Megabytes, divide by 1024.

Look at Figure 1.08, which shows how graphics are stored in the computer's memory. The picture is drawn on a grid 16 pixels across and 16 down. A '1' represents grid squares which are 'on', and a '0' represents grid squares which are off. The amount of memory needed to store this picture would be 16×16 bits – which is 256 bits or <u>32 bytes</u>.

The picture would be more clearly defined, or less rough, if we used more, smaller, pixels to make it up. You can see how reducing the size and increasing the number of pixels affects a picture by looking at the two graphics shown in Figure 1.09. By doing this we can put more detail into the picture. This is called increasing the resolution of the graphics.

Think about the amount of memory used to store the picture on the right in Figure 1.09.

It is 2666 pixels wide by 1764 pixels high.

The total number of pixels is therefore 2666 × 1764 = 4 702 824 pixels

= 4 702 824 bits (in black and white)

= 4 702 824 / 8 bytes

= 587 853 bytes

= <u>574.075 Kilobytes</u>

Figure 1.12 A high-resolution colour graphic

More calculations on bit-mapped graphics

Sometimes the question you are asked may give the size of the image in inches and the number of dots per inch (dpi). In this case, we use the formula:

Total number of pixels used in the image = height in inches × dots per inch (dpi) × breadth in inches × dots per inch (dpi).

Example 1

Suppose the size of the graphic to be stored is 1 inch by 2 inches, and the resolution is 90 dpi.

The total number of pixels used in the image is (1 × 90) × (2 × 90) = 16 200 pixels

The storage requirements would therefore be 16 200 bits = 2 025 bytes = 1.98 Kilobytes.

Example 2

An A4 page (10 × 8 inches) is to be scanned at 300 dpi.

The total number of pixels used in the image is (10 × 300) × (8 × 300) = 7 200 000 pixels.

The storage requirements would therefore be 7 200 000 bits = 900 000 bytes = 878.9 Kilobytes.

Comparing these two examples shows clearly the effect that increasing the size and resolution of a graphic has on its memory and backing storage requirements.

You should also now understand why a computer system which is used for high-resolution graphics may require a large amount of **main memory** and backing storage capacity.

Colour graphics

Calculating the memory requirements for the storage of colour or greyscale graphics requires just one more step compared to the formula on the previous page:

> Storage requirements = total number of pixels used in the image × number of bits used to represent colours or shades of grey for each pixel.

The number of bits used to represent colours or shades of grey used in the graphic is known as the **bit depth** or the **colour depth** of the image. Table 1.05 shows the relationship between the colour depth and the number of colours or shades of grey that may be represented.

Colour depth (bits)	Number of colours or shades of grey that may be represented
1	2
2	4
3	8
4	16
5	32
6	64
7	128
8	256
16	65 536
24	16 777 216

Table 1.05 Colour depth

Let's look again at the examples on page 17, but this time involving colour graphics.

Example 1　　　　　**Colour**

Suppose the size of the graphic to be stored is 1 inch by 2 inches, and the resolution is 90 dpi in 256 colours.

The total number of pixels used in the image is $(1 \times 90) \times (2 \times 90) = 16\,200$ pixels.

The number of bits used to represent 256 colours would be 8 bits because 256 is 2^8.

The storage requirements would therefore be $16\,200 \times 8$ which is $129\,600$ bits, $16\,200$ bytes or 15.82 Kilobytes.

Example 2　　　　　**Colour**

An A4 page (10×8 inches) is to be scanned at 300 dpi in $65\,536$ colours.

The total number of pixels used in the image is $(10 \times 300) \times (8 \times 300) = 7\,200\,000$ pixels.

The number of bits used to represent $65\,536$ colours would be 16 bits because $65\,536$ is 2^{16}.

The storage requirements would therefore be $7\,200\,000 \times 16$ which is $115\,200\,000$ bits, $14\,400\,000$ bytes or 13.73 Megabytes.

Try some calculations for yourself, using the figures supplied in Table 1.04 earlier in this chapter. Do the calculations for both **monochrome** (black and white) and colour graphics. Look back at Table 1.05 to show the number of bits required for different colours.

Calculation of storage requirements of vector graphics

We compared vector graphics and bit-mapped graphics on pages 14–16. What must be stored in this case is a set of numbers, called object attributes, for each vector graphic object in the image. It is unlikely that you will be required to carry out *calculations* involving vector graphics, but you should understand that for simple vector graphics, the storage requirements are much less than for bit-mapped graphics.

Scalable vector graphics (SVG)

Scalable vector graphics is one method of representing vector graphics on a computer system. **SVG** works in two dimensions (2D). SVG was developed to allow vector graphics to be used on **web pages**. SVG files are plain text files, written in **mark-up language**, and, just like **HTML**, they may be edited using a **text editor** like *Textedit* or *Notepad*. When SVG files are saved, they use filenames ending in .svg. SVG graphics may be displayed in a **web browser**.

Figure 1.13 Vector graphics

A listing of some code in SVG and the resulting graphic image is shown below:

Figure 1.14

```
<?xml version="1.0"?>
<!DOCTYPE svg PUBLIC "-//W3C//DTD SVG 1.1//EN"
"www.w3.org/Graphics/SVG/1.1/DTD/svg11.dtd">
<svg xmlns="www.w3.org/2000/svg">
<circle cx="200" cy="200" r="100" fill="green"/>
</svg>
```

The part of the code which draws the graphic is highlighted in green. The purpose of the rest of the code is to tell the browser to expect some SVG code. Look at Figure 1.15. The part of the screen on the left shows the storage requirements of the SVG code which draws the green circle, namely 230 bytes. Storing the same graphic as a bit-mapped image requires 172 649 bytes, approximately 750 times more storage space.

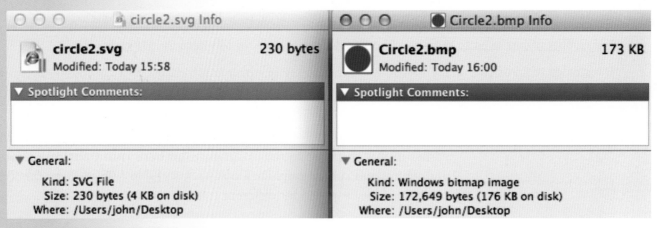

Figure 1.15 Comparing storage requirements of bit-mapped and vector graphics

The storage requirements of the tiger image in Figure 1.13 are 98 Kilobytes for the SVG code and 995 Kilobytes if bit-mapped graphics are used. Try writing some SVG, or modifying some existing code, and check out the storage requirements. One reason why code takes up much less storage than bit-mapped images is that each character in the code only requires one byte of storage, whereas a single pixel in a bit-map graphic may require as much as three bytes (24 bits).

Check Your Learning

Now answer questions 34–45 (on pages 33–34) on use of binary to represent and store graphics (bit-mapped and vector) (National 5).

Translation of high-level program code to binary (machine code): interpreters and compilers

What is a program?

A set of instructions that a computer can understand is called a program. Programs are written in computer languages. The types of computer language we will look at in this chapter are machine code and high-level language.

What is machine code?

Machine code is the computer's own language. Here is a small part of a program written in machine code:

```
1000  1101  1101  1101
1110  0011  1110  0011
1000  1000  1101  1101
```

You can see that machine code is written using only the numbers 1 and 0. These numbers are called binary because there are only two of them. Programs written in machine code are very difficult for us to understand because they are just made up of 1s and 0s and nothing else. We looked at binary numbers earlier in this chapter. A machine code program will only run on a certain processor, that is, it is not **portable**. A portable program will run on different processors without having to be changed.

What is a high-level language?

A computer language that uses normal or everyday language is called a high-level language. Here is an example of a program written in a high-level language:

```
PRINT "HELLO"
PRINT "PLEASE TELL ME YOUR NAME"
INPUT YOUR_NAME
```

High-level language programs are easy for us to understand because they are written in an everyday language very like English. High-level languages are used to write portable programs.

Examples of high-level languages

Table 1.06 gives some examples of high-level languages and what they are used for.

High-level language	What the language is used for
SCRATCH®	Learning programming
VISUAL BASIC®	Learning programming
COMAL®	Learning programming
C++	Creating applications, operating systems and games
HTML	Creating web pages
JAVA™	Internet programming

Table 1.06 Some high-level languages and their uses

Do you know any other computer languages not shown in the table? What are these other languages used for?

Checklist for computer languages

High-level languages	Machine code
Uses everyday English words	Uses only numbers 1 and 0
Easy to understand	Difficult to understand
Easy to edit	Difficult to edit
Easy to find mistakes in a program	Difficult to find mistakes in a program
Easy to run on different computers (portable)	Programs linked to certain processors are not portable

Table 1.07 Comparing high-level languages and machine code

The need for translation

When you give an instruction to a computer in a high-level language (like this: PRINT 'Hi There!') the computer changes the high-level language into machine code before the processor can carry out or execute the instruction. Execution in this case just means carrying out an instruction.

The instruction 'PRINT' in the example becomes '11110001' inside the computer. Only when the computer changes the instruction into machine code, will the processor be able to carry out the instruction.

Like changing a sentence from Gaelic into English, changing a program from one computer language into another computer language is called translation. Programs that carry out translations are called **translator programs**.

A translator program is a computer program used to convert program code from one language to another, for example from a high-level language to machine code. Translator programs are used because it is very difficult to write programs directly in machine code. It is much easier for the **programmer** to write the program in a high-level language and then have it changed into machine code by a translator program. The two types of translators that we will look at are **compilers** and **interpreters**.

What is a compiler and what does it do?

A compiler is a program that can translate a high-level language program into machine code in a single **operation**. The original high-level language program is called the **source code** and the machine code program produced by the translation is called the **object code**. Once the object code has been created, then the compiler program is no longer required.

The object code runs very fast because it is in the computer's own language, machine code. The object code program may be saved separately from the original source code. However, the source code should also be saved because, without it, it is impossible to edit the program since the object code, once produced, cannot be easily changed. The operation of a compiler is shown in Figure 1.16.

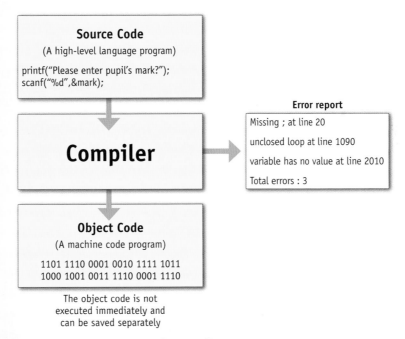

Figure 1.16 The operation of a compiler

What is an interpreter and what does it do?

An interpreter is a translator program, which changes one line of a high-level language program into machine code and then executes it, before moving on to the next line. *Interpreted programs* run much more slowly than *compiled programs* because the interpreter must *translate and execute* each instruction every time the program is run. Unlike compilers, there is no object code produced by an interpreter, and the interpreter must be present in order for the program to be translated and run. You can see how an interpreter works in Figure 1.17.

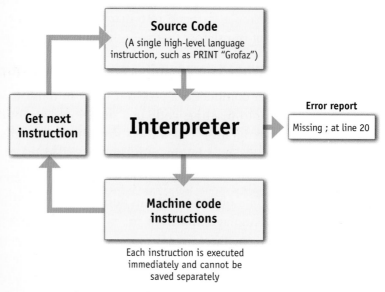

Figure 1.17 The operation of an interpreter

An interpreter can report any mistakes in the program code as it is being developed, rather than waiting until the program is complete the way compilers do. For this reason, interpreted programming languages are popular with students and others who are learning how to write programs.

Using an interpreter is a single process, unlike using a compiler, which requires the program to be compiled separately and then run.

Sometimes an interpreter will be used while developing a program because of the ease of finding mistakes, and then a compiler will be used after all of the mistakes have been found. The program will then be compiled, so that the finished program will run as fast as possible.

Figure 1.18

Here is another example which helps to explain the difference between the two types of translators. Let's compare how they work when translating the following high-level program code:

```
FOR counter:= 1 TO 100 DO
    PRINT "Hello"
NEXT counter
```

The main difference is in the number of times the code must be translated. When using a compiler, the code is translated once and then never again unless the program is changed. When using an interpreter, the code must be translated each time the program is run. Table 1.08 summarises the differences between the two translators.

Compiler	Interpreter
Compiler program in computer's memory.	Interpreter program AND source code in computer's memory.
Translates WHOLE of source code into object code.	Translates source code ONE line at a time.
Reports errors at end of translation.	Reports errors as you go.
Object code saved and run on its own.	Each line is run as soon as it is translated.
ONLY object code remains in memory.	Both translator and source code MUST remain in memory while program is run.
Total number of lines of code translated = **3**.	Total number of lines of code translated = **300**.

Table 1.08 Comparing translators

Always remember that it is the *compiled program* which runs faster than the *interpreted program*. It is the speed of execution of the translated programs that we are comparing, rather than the speed of the translation process.

Checklist for translator programs

Interpreted programs	Compiled programs
Run slow	Run fast
Report mistakes immediately	Report mistakes at end of compilation
Are translated (interpreted) one line at a time	Whole program is translated (compiled) at once
Translate and run is a single process	Translate and run are separate processes
Cannot save translated version	Can save object code
Interpreter required to run the code	Compiler not required to run the code

Table 1.09 Comparing interpreted programs and compiled programs

Check Your Learning

Now answer questions 46–55 (on page 34) on translation of high-level program code to binary (machine code): interpreters and compilers (National 5).

Basic computer architecture: processor, memory, buses, interfaces

Computer architecture

How something is made up, such as a building or a computer, is often referred to as its **architecture**. So in this case, **computer architecture** means the structure of a computer system.

All the physical parts of a computer system (the bits you can see and touch) are called the **hardware**. A single item of hardware is called a device. A computer system is made up of a processor and memory together with **input**, **output** and storage **devices**.

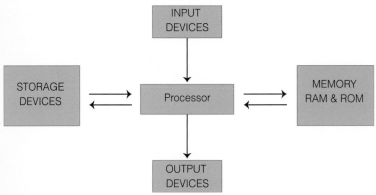

Figure 1.19 The structure of a computer system

Figure 1.20 A typical desktop computer system

A typical **desktop computer** system may include a processor, memory, a **monitor**, a keyboard, a **mouse**, a printer and one or more disk drives, such as a **solid-state drive**, a **hard disk drive** and a **DVD-Rewriter drive**. A typical desktop computer system is shown in Figure 1.20.

Processor

This is the part of the computer where all the sorting, searching, calculating and decision-making goes on. In many computers nowadays all these processes are carried out by a single **chip**. A chip is a specially treated piece of silicon and is very small, only a few millimetres across. You can see a photograph of a processor chip in Figure 1.21.

Figure 1.21 A processor chip
(Intel® Core™ i7 Haswell)

A computer can carry out any process if it is given a set of instructions to tell it what to do. The set of instructions that control how a computer works is called a program. Another name for computer programs is **software**. It may help you to think of the processor as the 'brain' of the computer system – but it isn't like a real brain because a computer can't think or act for itself. It can only carry out the instructions programmed into it. Computers can carry out instructions very quickly because the processor can process several billions of instructions every second.

In order for the computer to carry out a process, it must be supplied with instructions from its memory, one at a time, in the correct order. By changing the program, a computer can carry out a completely different process. The purpose of a processor, therefore, is to carry out the instructions supplied to it in the form of a computer program.

The parts of a processor

The processor is the main part of the computer. It is made up of the **control unit**, the **arithmetic and logic unit (ALU)** and the **registers**.

The control unit controls all the other parts of the processor and makes sure that the program instructions of the computer are carried out in the correct order. The control unit makes sure everything happens in the correct place and at the correct time. Each instruction is passed into the control unit to be carried out.

The arithmetic and logic unit or ALU carries out the calculations (arithmetic) and makes the decisions. When a computer makes a decision, it is known as a logical operation. Deciding whether one number is the same as, larger than, or less than another number is an example of a logical operation.

The registers are a group of storage locations in the processor. The registers are used to hold data being processed, program instructions being run, and **memory addresses** to be accessed. Compared to the computer's main memory, registers have only a small amount of storage space since they do not have to hold a whole program at once, just a few instructions.

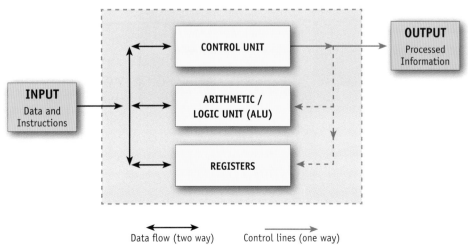

Figure 1.22 The processor

Memory

Do you have a good memory? Having a poor memory may be inconvenient or embarrassing for a person, but for a computer a poor memory would be a disaster. If it doesn't have a perfect memory the computer can't work properly, because it needs its memory to **store programs** and data before and after processing. A single error in memory would mean that a program wouldn't work.

The place where each item is stored in a computer's memory is important because the processor has to be able to find any item of data. Each item of data is stored in memory in a **storage location**.

The memory of a computer system is made up of a set of memory chips. There are two types of memory chip. Each type of memory chip is used for a different purpose in a computer system. These two types of memory chip are **Random Access Memory (RAM)** and **Read Only Memory (ROM)**.

Figure 1.23 Random Access Memory (RAM) chips

Random Access Memory (RAM)

RAM is a type of computer memory which holds its data as long as the computer is switched on. RAM can only store programs and data *temporarily* because anything stored in RAM is *lost* when the computer is switched off.

Read Only Memory (ROM)

ROM is used to store programs and data permanently. The contents of a ROM chip are *not* lost when you switch the computer off. ROM is **permanent memory**. The contents of ROM are fixed when the chip is manufactured.

Figure 1.24 Read Only Memory (ROM) chip

You can read more about RAM and ROM in Chapter 11.

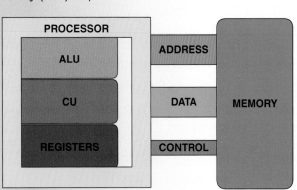

Figure 1.25 Processor, memory and buses

Buses

Buses is the term used for the sets of wires which connect the processor to the other parts *inside* the computer system, such as the memory and input/output devices. The **address bus**, the **data bus** and the **control bus** are three of the buses in a computer system. These buses are shown in Figure 1.25.

Address bus

An **address** is a binary number used to identify a storage location in main memory. The address bus carries the address information from the processor to the memory and any other devices attached to the bus. The address bus is *unidirectional* or one-way only.

Data bus

The data bus carries data to and from the processor, memory and any other devices attached to the data bus. The data bus is therefore *bi-directional* or two-way.

Control bus

The control bus is unlike the other buses because it is made up of a number of separate wires or lines, each with its own function.

Figure 1.26 shows how the buses connect to the other internal parts of the computer system.

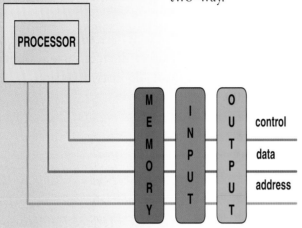

control

data

address

Figure 1.26 Some other bus connections

Interfaces

An **interface** is the hardware and associated software needed to allow communication between the processor and its **peripheral** devices. A peripheral is a device which may be connected to the outside of a computer system, for input, **output** or backing storage.

Interfaces also compensate for any differences between the computer and the peripheral, such as speed and differences in **data** format (which may require **conversion**).

Interfaces can compensate for *differences in speed* by storing data temporarily, for example characters entered at a keyboard or data which is being sent to a printer.

Interfaces can compensate for *differences in data format* by converting the data, for example from **analogue** to **digital**. Look back at Figure 1.01 at the beginning of this chapter to see what a digital signal looks like. An audio CD player contains a Digital to Analogue Converter to change the digital data on the CD into analogue data – that is, music – so that we can hear it.

A **scanner** converts an image from a photograph or drawing into digital form that a computer can process. This is an example of **Analogue to Digital Conversion**.

Types of interface

The **Universal Serial Bus** (**USB**) is the most common interface used on current computer systems. USB 3 (**SUPERSPEED**) is the latest version of this interface. Earlier versions include USB 1 and USB 2. All new desktop and **laptop** computers have at least one USB connector. A wide variety of peripherals, from scanners, printers, cameras and **card readers** to fairy lights and cup warmers, all use the USB interface.

IEEE 1394 / **Firewire**® (Apple®) / **i.Link** (Sony) are used on computer systems, some **digital video cameras** and other devices such as digital video recorders. Firewire® is commonly available in two versions, Firewire® 400 and Firewire® 800.

Figure 1.27 Firewire® logo

Figure 1.28 Thunderbolt® logo

Thunderbolt® (Intel® / Apple®) is a high-speed interface for data and display (video) signals.

Figure 1.29 Ethernet logos

Ethernet is a standard for **Local Area Networking** (**LAN**). To use Ethernet, a computer must be fitted with a **Network Interface Card** (**NIC**). There are several versions, including **Gigabit Ethernet**, which is used on most current desktop and laptop computers.

Figure 1.30 WiFi and Bluetooth® logos

Wireless Network Interface: to use **wireless** networking, a computer must be fitted with a Wireless Network Interface Card (WNIC). Wireless interfaces include **WiFi** and **Bluetooth**®.

You can read more about interfaces in Chapter 12.

Check Your Learning

Now answer questions 56–83 (on pages 34–35) on basic computer architecture (National 5).

Practical Tasks

1 Use a search engine to find out the cost of a binary wristwatch in the UK.

2 Use the school email system to send a 'secret' message, written in ASCII, to another student in your Computing class.

3 Choose one programming language from table 1.06 on page 22 (or use one of the languages you have learned about in class) and answer these questions:
   a) When was it invented?
   b) Who invented it?
   c) What was it invented to do?
   d) How did it get its name?
   e) Was it named after a famous person?

f) Is its name short for something else?

g) Is the language normally compiled or interpreted?

Use the information at: http://en.wikipedia. org/wiki/List_of_programming_languages to help you answer the questions.

4 Contribute to a class Wiki on current interfaces, for example Ethernet, USB, Firewire®, Thunderbolt®, WiFi, Bluetooth®. State which devices use these interfaces.

5 Use one of your school's desktop computers to find out the
   a) name and manufacturer of the processor used.
   b) quantity of RAM installed.
   Repeat this exercise for the Raspberry Pi computer.

Questions

Use of binary to represent and store positive integers (National 4)

1 Why is a computer system often called a two-state machine?

2 How many digits are used to represent numbers in the
   a) binary system?
   b) decimal system?

3 What is a
   a) bit?   b) byte?

4 a) What is the largest number that may be represented in 8 bits in the binary system?
   b) What is this number in decimal?

5 Convert the following binary numbers into decimal:
   a) 0000 1011   b) 1001 1111
   c) 1010 1010   d) 1111 1110
   e) 0101 0101   f) 1100 1100
   g) 0011 0011   h) 1001 1001
   i) 1110 0100   j) 1001 1011

6 Convert the following decimal numbers into binary. Use 8 bits to store the binary number:
   a) 122   b) 193

   c) 255   d) 56
   e) 14   f) 78
   g) 127   h) 250
   i) 179   j) 112

7 Write your age as a binary number.

8 Write the number of your house as a binary number.

9 a) What's the time?

Figure 1.31 Time Technology watch

   b) This is a 12-hour watch. Explain why all of the lights in both rows would never be lit up at once.

10 a) State the first eight place values of the binary system, in order, from high to low.
   b) How may these place values be calculated?

Questions *continued*

Use of binary to represent and store integers and real numbers (National 5)

11 What is
   a) an integer?
   b) a real number?

12 Describe how real numbers may be represented in a computer system.

13 Which part of a real number may be represented by
   a) a mantissa?
   b) an exponent?

14 Convert these numbers to floating point representation:
   a) 111.0001
   b) 1000010.1

Units of storage (National 4)

17 Put the following terms in decreasing order of size, largest first:

   Megabyte, bit, Terabyte, Petabyte, Kilobyte, byte, Gigabyte

18 How many
   a) bits in a byte?
   b) bytes in a Kilobyte?
   c) Terabytes in a Petabyte?
   d) bits in a Megabyte?

19 Approximately how much storage space is taken up by
   a) one side of a page of text?
   b) one hour of standard definition video?

20 Which units are commonly used to measure a computer's
   a) backing storage capacity?
   b) main memory capacity?

Use of binary to represent and store characters (National 4)

21 What is a
   a) character?
   b) character set?

22 a) What does ASCII stand for?
   b) How many characters can ASCII represent?
   c) Give a reason for your answer to part b).

Snapshots

"Wait a minute -- that's important. Is it *praying mantis* or *preying mantis*?"

15 Name the system that is used to represent and store negative integers.

16 Convert these numbers to binary:
   a) –6   b) –25
   c) –92   d) –120

   d) What is the ASCII for
      i) 'e'?
      ii) 'E'?

   Express your answers in decimal or binary.

23 a) Write your class in ASCII.
   b) Write your name in ASCII.
   c) Write your birthday in ASCII.
   d) Write the name of your school in ASCII.

24 Use the ASCII table on page 10 to help you 'decode' this message.
   87 69 76 67 79 77 69 32 84 79 32 67 79 77 80
   85 84 73 78 71 32 83 67 73 69 78 67 69 33

25 State one advantage of Unicode compared to ASCII.

26 State one advantage of ASCII compared to Unicode.

Use of binary to represent and store instructions (machine code) (National 4)

27 What is a program?

28 What is a program written in?

29 Name two types of computer language.

30 What name is given to the computer's own language?

31 Which two numbers are used to write machine code programs?

32 Why is a program written in machine code difficult to understand?

33 What name is given to a computer language which uses normal or everyday English words?

Use of binary to represent and store graphics (bit-mapped and vector) (National 5)

34 Why are bit-mapped graphics so called?

35 What is a pixel?

36 Which type of graphics package draws objects on the screen?

37 With respect to graphics, what is resolution?

38 Roldan is playing his favourite computer game when he achieves a high score. He takes a screenshot so that he can put it on his social networking page.
   a) Which type of graphic is a screenshot (bit-mapped or vector)?
   b) Roldan's friend, Allan, sends an email message with an attached graphic file. Describe two tests Roldan could carry out on the graphic in order to find out if it is bit-mapped or a vector image.

39 The character shown in Figure 1.32 has been stored using
   a) a bit map.
   b) ASCII.

In each case calculate (or show) the number of bits required for representing the character by each method.

   c) Which method is most efficient (uses least backing storage space)?

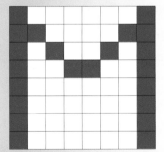

Figure 1.32

40 Draw an 8 × 8 grid on squared paper. Use it to decode these bit patterns:
   a) 11111111
      01000010
      00100100
      00011000
      00011000
      00100100
      01000010
      11111111

   b) 00111100
      01000010
      01000010
      01000010
      00111100
      00100100
      01000010
      10000001

41 Calculate the backing storage requirements for the following bit-mapped images, assuming all are in black and white.
   a) A 640 × 480 screen shot of a web page.
   b) A 2440 × 1892 image from a digital camera.
   c) A scan of a 10 × 8 inch page at 150 dpi.
   d) A 14 × 20 inch image at 1200 dpi.

Express your answers in Kilobytes or Megabytes as appropriate.

Now assume that the following colours were used in the bit-mapped images whose sizes are described above.

   e) Image 'a' at 256 colours.
   f) Image 'b' in 24-bit colour.
   g) Image 'c' in 65 536 colours.
   h) Image 'd' in 16 colours.

Calculate the new storage requirements for the colour images.

42

Figure 1.33 A picture created with ASCII

This picture is approximately 100 × 50 characters in size. Calculate the backing storage requirements of this picture.

43 a) What are object attributes?
   b) State four attributes which could apply to a circle.

Questions *continued*

44 Complete the following table of SVG code, by using your own knowledge or referring to a suitable website, e.g. www.w3schools.com.

Object	SVG code
Rectangle	
Circle	<circle cx="300" cy="76" r="90" stroke="black" stroke-width="1" fill="blue"/>
Ellipse	
Line	
Polygon	
Text	

45 Explain why vector graphics usually have lower storage requirements than bit-mapped ones.

Translation of high-level program code to binary: interpreters and compilers (National 5)

46 Name two high-level languages and what they are used for.

47 What is a translator program?

48 Name two types of translator.

49 Why must programs written in high-level languages be translated before they can be run?

50 What is
 a) an interpreter?
 b) a compiler?
 c) source code?
 d) object code?

51 Which translator program does not produce object code?

52 Why does a compiled program run faster than an interpreted program?

53 What type of computer language (high-level or machine code) will be found in
 a) object code?
 b) source code?

54 A programmer has to write a program that will run fast. Which type of translator software should she choose?

55 Why should a programmer keep the source code for a program, even after it has been translated into object code?

Basic computer architecture (National 5)

56 What is computer architecture?

57 What is hardware?

58 What is a device?

59 What is software another name for?

60 Why is a computer system sometimes called a 'very fast idiot'?

61 Name five parts of a computer system.

62 In which part of the computer is the calculating and decision-making done?

63 What name is given to the set of instructions that controls how a computer works?

64 Name one current computer processor manufacturer.

65 Name one processor chip from the manufacturer Intel®.

66 What is a computer's memory
 a) used for?
 b) made up of?

67 Name two types of memory chip.

68 What are computer buses made of?

69 What do computer buses do?

70 Name three computer buses.

71 Name three parts of the processor.

72 Which part of a processor carries out the logical operations and makes the decisions?

73 Which part of a processor makes sure that the program instructions are carried out in the correct order?

74 Which part of the processor holds data while it is being processed?

75 What is an interface?

76 What is a peripheral?

77 Name one common type of interface used on a computer system.

78 Look at the photograph of the Raspberry Pi computer in Figure 1.34. Which interfaces can you spot?

Figure 1.34 Raspberry Pi computer

79 Copy and complete the following diagram of a computer system.

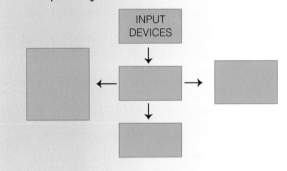

80 Jemima visits a computer shop to buy a new computer. She knows that a computer system is made up of input, output and storage devices, but when she asks for these, the shopkeeper tells her that she has forgotten about two very important parts of the computer. What else does Jemima need to buy?

81 A computer chip factory uses lots of metals, such as copper, silver and gold, in order to make the connections inside the chips. What other substance is used to make computer chips?

82 Many stories have been written, and films made, showing what might happen if computers were able to take over the world and control it. Why is it unlikely that this will really happen?

83 James wants to connect his digital video camera to his computer in order to download movie clips he has filmed. His mum says that he should use an interface to allow him to do this.
a) Is his mum correct?
b) Why does James need to use an interface for this task?
c) Name one interface that would help James to connect his video camera.

Key Points

- Data inside a computer system is held in binary form.
- The binary number system uses two numbers, 0 and 1.
- A single unit in binary is called a bit.
- A byte has eight bits.
- One Kilobyte has 1024 bytes.
- One Megabyte has 1024 Kilobytes.
- One Gigabyte has 1024 Megabytes.
- One Terabyte has 1024 Gigabytes.
- One Petabyte has 1024 Terabytes.
- Types of data which may be represented in a computer system include numbers, text and graphics.
- Numbers may be stored as integer or floating point (real numbers).
- Floating point uses a mantissa and an exponent.

- The mantissa holds the number and the exponent holds the power.
- Negative numbers are stored using two's complement.
- To change
  - bits to bytes, divide by 8.
  - bytes to bits, multiply by 8.
  - bytes to Kilobytes, divide by 1024.
  - Kilobytes to bytes, multiply by 1024.
  All larger units are multiples of 1024.
- Text may be stored as integer values using the American Standard Code for Information Interchange (ASCII).
- ASCII is a seven-bit code which can represent 128 characters.
- A character is a symbol or letter on the computer keyboard.

- The Unicode character set is designed to represent the writing schemes of all of the world's major languages.
- Unicode (UTF-16) is a 16-bit code and can represent 65 536 different characters.
- A set of instructions that a computer can understand is called a program.
- A computer language that uses normal or everyday language is called a high-level language.
- The computer's own language is called machine code.
- Graphics are made up of tiny dots called pixels.
- The quality of the picture is determined by the resolution of the graphics available.
- The smaller the size of the pixels, the finer the detail that can be displayed on the screen.
- Graphics packages can be classified into two main types, bit-mapped and vector.
- Bit-mapped packages paint pictures by changing the colour of the pixels which make up the screen display.
- Bit-mapped graphics have a direct relationship between the bits in the computer's memory and the picture displayed on the computer screen.
- Vector packages work by drawing objects on the screen.
- Scalable Vector Graphics is one method of representing vector graphics on a computer system.
- Storage requirements of black and white bit map = total number of pixels (bits) used in the image.
- Total number of pixels used in the image = height in inches × dots per inch × breadth in inches × dots per inch.
- Storage requirements of colour or greyscale bit map = total number of pixels used in the image × number of bits used to represent colours or shades of grey for each pixel
- The number of bits used to represent colours or shades of grey used in the graphic is known as the bit depth or the colour depth of the image.

- A translator program is a computer program used to convert program code from one language to another.
- A compiler is a program that can translate a high-level language program into machine code in a single operation.
- The original high-level language program is called the source code and the machine code program produced by the translation is called the object code.
- An interpreter changes one line of a high-level language program into machine code, and then executes it, before moving on to the next line, each time the program is run.
- Computer architecture means the structure of a computer system.
- All the physical parts of a computer system are called the hardware.
- A single item of hardware is called a device.
- A computer system is made up of a processor and memory together with input, output and storage devices.
- The processor is the part of the computer where all the sorting, searching, calculating and decision-making goes on.
- The processor is the main part of the computer. It is made up of the control unit, the arithmetic and logic unit (ALU) and the registers.
- The control unit controls all the other parts of the processor and makes sure that the program instructions of the computer are carried out in the correct order.
- The arithmetic and logic unit or ALU carries out the calculations (arithmetic) and makes the decisions.
- The registers are used to hold data being processed, program instructions being run, and memory addresses to be accessed.
- Each item of data is stored in memory in a storage location.
- An address is a binary number used to identify a storage location in main memory.

- Two types of memory chip are Random Access Memory (RAM) and Read Only Memory (ROM).
- RAM can only store programs and data temporarily because anything stored in RAM is lost when the computer is switched off.
- The contents of a ROM chip are not lost when you switch the computer off.
- Buses is the term used for the sets of wires which connect the processor to the other parts inside the computer system.
- The address bus, the data bus and the control bus are three of the buses in a computer system.

- An interface is the hardware and associated software needed to allow communication between the processor and its peripheral devices.
- A peripheral is a device which may be connected to the outside of a computer system, for input, output or backing storage.
- Interfaces also compensate for any differences between the computer and the peripheral, such as speed and differences in data format.
- Types of interfaces include USB, Firewire®, Thunderbolt®, Ethernet and Wireless.

CHAPTER 2 | Computational constructs and data types and structures

National 5

This chapter describes the exemplification and implementation of the following constructs and data types.

- expressions to assign values to variables
- expressions to return values using arithmetic operations (+, -, *, /, ^)
- execution of lines of code in sequence demonstrating input–process–output
- use of selection constructs including simple conditional statements
- iteration and repetition using fixed and conditional loops
- string, numeric (integer) variables, graphical objects

- expressions to return values using arithmetic operations (MOD)
- use of selection constructs including simple and complex conditional statements and logical operators
- expressions to concatenate strings and arrays using the & operator
- pre-defined functions (with parameters)
- character, numeric (integer and real) variables, Boolean variables
- 1-D arrays

Remember that this book is not a programming manual. Your teacher or lecturer will provide you with material to suit your chosen software development environment(s).

Computational constructs

We looked at **computer programs** in Chapter 1 – here is a brief reminder.

A computer can carry out any process if it is given a set of instructions to tell it what to do. The set of instructions that control how a computer works is called a program. Programs are written in computer languages. Two types of computer language are **machine code** and **high-level language**. Machine code is the computer's own language. Machine code is written in **binary** using only the numbers 1 and 0. A computer language that uses normal or everyday language is called a high-level language. The examples which we will look at in this chapter are all written in high-level languages.

What are computational constructs?

Computational means using computers. To *construct* something is to build it or put it together out of a set of parts. **Computational constructs** are therefore the parts of a programming language which are used to create a computer program.

What is computational thinking?

Computational thinking is thinking of a problem in such a way that makes it possible to solve it by using a computer system. We have to do the thinking for the computer because it cannot think for itself – it can only carry out the instructions programmed into it. We use computational thinking when we are able to look at and understand a problem and then work out a series of steps to solve it. This is called an **algorithm**.

Looking at and understanding a problem is called **analysis**. Working out a series of steps to solve a problem is called **design**. Once a solution to a problem has been worked out, it needs to be turned into instructions for the computer (a program). This is **implementation**. The program must then be **tested** to make sure that it does not contain any mistakes which would prevent it from working properly. A description of what each part of the program does, or **documentation**, should also be included. This **sequence** of steps, beginning with analysis, is known as the **software development process**. You can find out more about testing and documentation in Chapter 3, algorithms in Chapter 4 and design in Chapter 5.

Pseudocode

The **design notation** which we will use to describe these features is **pseudocode**. Pseudocode uses normal or everyday language to describe the design of a program. Pseudocode is particularly useful for designing high-level language programs because each line of pseudocode translates directly into a single line of code in a high-level language. You can find out more about pseudocode and other design notations in Chapter 5.

Note that when example algorithms are given, the details are limited to cover the structure being shown. None of the algorithms in this chapter necessarily represents a complete program design.

Figure 2.01

Data types and structures

What is a variable?

Data is stored in a computer's **memory** in **storage locations**. Each storage location in the computer's memory has a unique **address** (see Chapter 1). A **variable** is the name that a **programmer** uses to identify the contents of a storage location. (This is much more convenient than using a **memory address** – compare *number* with *90987325*.) By using a variable name, a programmer can store, retrieve and handle data without knowing what the data will be.

Data types

The **data types** stored by a program may be a number, a **character**, a string, a date, an **array**, a **sound** sample, a **video** clip or indeed, any kind of data. Characters, strings, integer numbers and **graphical objects** data are described below.

Real numbers and **Boolean** data are also described below.

The **(1-D) array** data structure is explained later in this chapter.

Character data

A character is a symbol, letter or number on the computer **keyboard**. Some languages allow single characters to be declared, for instance, in **Visual Basic®**:

```
Dim ThisCharacter As Char
```

In **Java™**:

```
char capitalJ = 'J';
```

String data

String data is a list of characters, for example a word in a sentence. Depending upon the programming language in use, it may or may not be necessary to state or **declare** the type of variable at the start of the program, for example, in Visual Basic®:

```
Dim name As String
```

In **COMAL®** or **TrueBASIC®**, a dollar ($) sign is added to the end of the variable name to denote a string, like this:

```
name$
word$
```

Numeric (integer) data

Numeric (integer) data includes whole numbers. In Visual Basic®:

```
Dim score As Integer
```

is used at the beginning of the program to show that the variable *score* is to be used for holding a whole number or integer.

Numeric (real) data

Numeric (real) data – includes *all* numbers, both whole and fractional. Again, in Visual Basic®:

```
Dim price As Single
```

is used at the beginning of the program to show that the variable price is to be used for holding a real number.

Boolean data

Boolean data has only two values, TRUE and FALSE. Again, in Visual Basic®:

```
Dim found As Boolean
found = False
```

is used at the beginning of the program to show that the variable found is to be used for holding a Boolean value. Boolean values are sometimes represented by numbers, for instance False = 0 and True = –1 (in Visual Basic® and +1 in some languages).

Graphical objects data

A graphical object is an image which is displayed on the **screen** as part of a computer program. Another name for a graphical object is a **sprite**. Sprites are commonly used for characters and other animated objects in games. Figure 2.02 shows some sprites in the **Scratch**® programming language.

Crab   Starfish

Robot1   Dinosaur3

Diver1   Diver2

Figure 2.02 Sprites (graphical objects) in the Scratch® programming language

41

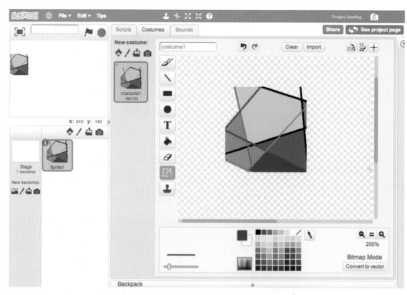

Figure 2.03 It is easy to create a new sprite in Scratch®

Figure 2.04 Graphical objects in the Alice programming language

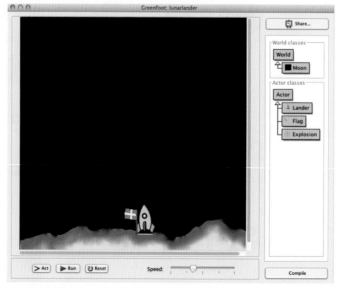

Figure 2.05 Graphical objects in the Greenfoot programming language

Input and output

Data which is to be processed by a computer program must first be **input,** or taken into that program. High-level languages use a variety of instructions in order to take data into a computer program. Here are some examples:

```
(BASIC)           INPUT number
(Visual Basic)    number = InputBox("Please enter the
                  number")
(Pascal)          Readln (number);
```

Figure 2.06 Input in Scratch[®]

After the data has been processed, it is useful to see the results. The **output** feature may be used to display these. Here are some examples:

```
PRINT "The total is "; total
picDisplay.Print Tab(20); "The total is "; total
Writeln('The total is ',total);
```

Figure 2.07 Output in Scratch[®]

Expressions to assign values to variables

Assignment

An **assignment statement** is used to give a value to a variable. Assignment statements are often used at the beginning of a program to give an initial value to a variable, for example 0.

```
number = 0
name$ = "Mark"
```

This means that the variable number is given the value 0, and the variable name$ is given the **text** 'Mark'. Later on in the program, another assignment statement may be used to **update** the value of the variable number to contain a different value, for example:

```
number = 10
number = number + 1
```

What value does the variable number now contain?

Figure 2.08 shows an example of assignment from Scratch®.

Figure 2.08 Assignment in Scratch®

Expressions to return values using arithmetic operations

Objects and operations

What is an operation?

An **operation** is a process which is carried out on an item of data. There are several types of operations used in programming. These include **arithmetical**, **relational** and **logical** (N5) **operations**.

What is an object?

An **object** is the item of data which is involved in the process.

Arithmetical operations

Arithmetical operations are calculations involving numbers. The set of arithmetic operators includes add, subtract, multiply, divide and **exponent** (power of). These operators are represented in many programming languages by using the symbols $+, -, *, /, ^$ and **MOD** (N5).

Examples of arithmetical operations

`number_one + number_two`	the objects are number_one and number_two, the operation is **add**
`profit = sale_price - cost_price`	the objects are profit, sale_price and cost_price, the operation is **subtract**
`storage_space = number_of_pixels × colour_depth`	the objects are storage_space, number_of_pixels and colour_depth, the operation is **multiply (times)**
`Kilobytes = bytes / 1024`	the objects are **Kilobytes** and **bytes**, the operation is **divide**

National 5

```
area_of_circle = PI × radius^2
```
the objects are area_of_circle and radius, the operation is **exponent (power of)**

```
remainder = dividend MOD divisor
```
the objects are dividend, divisor and remainder, the operation is **MOD (MODULO/US)**

Relational operations

Relational operations use relational operators to compare data and produce an answer of true or false. The set of relational operators includes:

=   equals

>   greater than

<   less than

>=   greater than or equal to

<=   less than or equal to

≠ or <>   is not equal to

Relational operators may be used in program **control structures** such as **selection** and **repetition**.

Examples of relational operations

```
IF value >= 7 THEN .....
WHILE month < 12 .....
```

> ### Reminder
>
> ! Remember: When entering a relational operator like >= into a program, there is **no** space between the two characters > and =.

Logical operations

The set of logical operators includes **AND**, **OR** and **NOT**. Logical operations are usually combined with relational operations in program control structures, like those involving an **IF** condition.

Examples of logical operations

```
number > 3 AND number < 10
answer$ = "N" OR answer$ = "n"
```

National 5

Expressions to concatenate strings and arrays using the & operator

String operations can process string data. String operations include joining strings, known as **concatenation**, and selecting parts of strings, known as **substrings**.

Examples of string operations

```
PRINT "house" & "boat"
```
would produce the result 'houseboat'. This is **concatenation**.

```
word$ := "mousetrap"
PRINT word$ (: 5)
```
would produce the result 'mouse'. This is selecting a **substring**.

```
PRINT LEN (word$)
```
would produce the result 9 (the length of the string "mousetrap").

Note that some languages use '+' instead of '&' for concatenation.

Some other string operations include:

- changing strings to numbers and numbers to strings
- changing characters into their **ASCII** values and ASCII values into characters
- changing case – 'j' to 'J' and vice versa
- removing blank spaces from a string.

(Some languages may not contain specific **keywords** for all of these operations.)

Check Your Learning   Now answer questions 1–10, 14–20, 24 and 25 (on pages 108 and 109) on computational constructs and data types and structures (National 4).

Check Your Learning   Now answer questions 11-13, 21–23 and 26–28 (on page (109) on computational constructs and data types and structures (National 5).

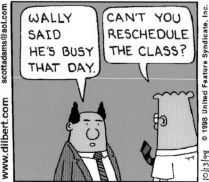

Figure 2.09

Control structures

The control structures used in programming are sequence, selection and repetition (**iteration**). Examples of the use of these control structures are given here.

Execution of lines of code in sequence demonstrating input–process–output

Figure 2.10 Sequence is important!

Sequence

Sequence means the order in which things are done. For example, remove clothes, take shower, dry off, put on clothes, is a sequence of operations. Putting these operations into the wrong order could cause a few problems. Just so with programming, the sequence or order in which you give instructions to the computer is important.

The purpose of sequence is to ensure that instructions given to the computer in the form of a computer program are carried out (or executed) in the correct order.

Consider the following example algorithm, given in pseudocode:

```
algorithm to add two numbers
1.    SEND "Enter first number" TO DISPLAY
2.    RECEIVE first_number FROM KEYBOARD          ← INPUT
3.    SEND "Enter second number" TO DISPLAY
4.    RECEIVE second_number FROM KEYBOARD         ← INPUT
5.    SET total TO first_number + second_number   ← PROCESS
6.    SEND total TO DISPLAY                        ← OUTPUT
```

This example will work correctly if, and only if, the steps are followed in the correct sequence, and none of the steps is missed out.

What would happen if the following algorithm were used?

```
1.    SEND "Enter first number" TO DISPLAY
2.    RECEIVE first_number FROM KEYBOARD
3.    SET total TO first_number + second_number
4.    SEND "Enter second number" TO DISPLAY
5.    SEND total TO DISPLAY
```

Use of selection constructs including simple and complex conditional statements

Figure 2.11 Ballot box

Selection

Selection means making a choice, or deciding something. Selection is based on one or more conditions, used together with a control structure such as IF. Conditions have values, they may be either true or false. The control structure IF is also known as a **conditional statement**.

Examples of conditions

```
age = 18
```
is a **simple condition**

```
month >= 1 AND month
<= 12
```
is a **complex condition** (two or more simple conditions linked by the logical operators AND, OR, NOT)

These conditions may be used together with a suitable control structure, like an IF statement, in order to carry out selection, like this:

```
IF age >= 18 THEN
      SEND "I can vote" TO DISPLAY
ELSE
      SEND "I can't vote" TO DISPLAY
END IF
```

```
IF Month >= 1 AND Month <= 12 THEN
      process date
ELSE
      SEND error message TO DISPLAY
END IF
```

In each case, the condition is tested, and if true, then the appropriate action is carried out. Selection allows the sequence of execution of program statements to be changed. This has the effect of increasing the number of possible pathways that may be followed through a program.

The control structure commonly used to allow selection is IF ... THEN ... ELSE ... END IF.

The IF structure is suitable for use when a single selection (or a limited number of selections) is to be made.

National 5

National 5

The general form of the IF structure is:

```
IF condition is true THEN
     do something
ELSE
     do something different
END IF
```

Example of an algorithm which uses the IF structure

```
pass or fail algorithm
1.    IF pupil's test mark is greater than or equal to
      50 THEN
2.        SEND pass message TO DISPLAY
3.    ELSE
4.        SEND fail message TO DISPLAY
5.    END IF
```

Iteration and repetition using fixed and conditional loops

Figure 2.12 Repetition

A **loop** is a programming construct, which is used to allow a process to take place over and over again. Loops may be either **fixed** or **conditional**. Repetition and iteration are terms which are both used to refer to a loop in programming. This book makes no distinction between repetition and iteration.

Fixed loops

The purpose of a fixed loop is to repeat a set of program statements for a predetermined number of times. Fixed loops are controlled by a variable called a **loop counter**. The purpose of a loop counter is to count up the number of times the loop structure is to be repeated between the two limits set at the start of the loop. The loop counter may also be used for calculations inside the loop or be displayed in order to count entries, for example.

The general form of a fixed loop is:

```
FOR counter FROM start number TO finish number ... DO
     ............
     ............
END FOR
```

Note .... stands for lines of program code inside the loop.

Examples of algorithms which use fixed loops

```
algorithm to display a name five times
1.    FOR counter FROM 1 TO 5 DO
2.        SEND "name" TO DISPLAY
3.    END FOR
```

this loop counts between the two fixed limits (1 and 5)

```
algorithm to display one name a number of times
1.    SEND "Enter number of times" TO DISPLAY
2.    RECEIVE number _ of _ times FROM KEYBOARD
3.    FOR counter FROM one TO number _ of _ times
4.        SEND "name" TO DISPLAY
5.    END FOR
```

this loop counts for a variable number of times depending on the value stored in the variable "number_of_times"

One feature of fixed loops in some programming languages is that they can increase or decrease in steps other than one. The keyword STEP is used for this. The purpose of the next example is to display all the even numbers from 2 to 30.

```
algorithm showing a fixed loop with steps
1.    FOR counter FROM 2 TO 30 STEP 2
2.        SEND counter TO DISPLAY
3.    END FOR
```

Loops may occur inside other loops: these are called **nested loops**.

```
tab algorithm showing nested loops
1.    FOR down FROM 1 TO 5 DO
2.        FOR across FROM 10 TO 20 DO
3.            SEND "*" TO DISPLAY
4.        END FOR
5.    END FOR
```

(using down and across in TAB)

One form of fixed loop is particular to structured data types or arrays (see later in this chapter for more detail). This is the FOR … EACH loop.

```
1.    FOR EACH element FROM the array DO
2.            SEND element TO DISPLAY
3.    END FOR EACH
```

Only some high-level languages use the keywords FOR … EACH. One such language is **LiveCode**®. An example implementation is shown in that section.

Figure 2.13

Conditional loops

The purpose of a conditional loop is to manage the situation where the number of times repetition must take place is not known in advance. Statements inside this type of loop may be carried out once, many times or not at all, depending upon one or more test conditions which are attached to the control structure of the loop.

The difference between a fixed loop and a conditional loop is that a fixed loop always repeats the same number of times, but a conditional loop could repeat any number of times, or not at all.

The advantages of using conditional loops are:

- the amount of data to be processed need not be known in advance
- a mathematical calculation can continue until an answer is found
- more than one exit condition may be used, for example the loop could continue until the result is obtained or an error is found.

There are two types of conditional loop, each taking its name from the position of the test condition, either at the start or at the end of the loop. These are called test at start and test at end.

The program statement(s) inside a conditional loop with test at start *may not be run at all* if the test condition is not met. The program statement(s) inside a conditional loop with test at end *is always run at least once*. When this type of loop (conditional with test at end) is used for repeated data entry, like taking in a list of names or numbers, a **terminating value** or **sentinel value** is often used. The terminating value should be carefully chosen to be different from the actual data which is being entered.

The general form of a conditional loop with test at start is:

```
WHILE condition is true DO
    ..........

    ..........
END WHILE
```

51

The general form of a conditional loop with test at end is:

```
REPEAT
    ............
    ............
UNTIL condition is true
```

Note: .... stands for lines of program code inside the loops.

Examples of algorithms which use conditional loops

take in a word algorithm with test at end
```
1.    REPEAT
2.        SEND "Enter a word" TO DISPLAY
3.            RECEIVE word FROM KEYBOARD
4.        UNTIL word = "end"
```
the word "end" is called the terminating value which tells the loop when to stop

Press space bar to continue algorithm
```
1.    REPEAT
2.        SEND "Press space bar" TO DISPLAY
3.            RECEIVE character FROM KEYBOARD
4.        UNTIL character = " "
```

Calculation algorithm using a running total
```
1.    SET total TO 0
2.    SET number TO 0
3.    REPEAT
4.    SET total TO total + number
5.    SEND "Enter a number" TO DISPLAY
6.    RECEIVE number FROM KEYBOARD
7.        UNTIL number = -999
8.    SEND total TO DISPLAY
```
in this case the number -999 is the terminating value

algorithm with test at start
```
1.    SEND "Enter a word" TO DISPLAY
2.    RECEIVE word FROM KEYBOARD
3.    WHILE NOT ((word = "end") OR (word = "END")) DO
4.    SEND "Enter a word" TO DISPLAY
5.    RECEIVE word FROM KEYBOARD
6.    END WHILE
```

```
input validation algorithm with test at start
1.    SEND "Please enter data" TO DISPLAY
2.    RECEIVE data FROM KEYBOARD
3.    WHILE data is outwith range
4.    SEND "Please re-enter data" TO DISPLAY
5.    RECEIVE data FROM KEYBOARD
6.    END WHILE
```

see Chapter 4 for more about **input validation**

More about data types and structures

1-D arrays (one-dimensional arrays)

An array is a list of data items *of the same type* grouped together using a single variable name. Each part of an array is called an **element**. Each element in an array is identified by the **variable name** and a **subscript** (**element number** or **index**), which identifies the position of the element in the array. Indexing may start from 0 (zero) depending upon the language in use, but this explanation will start from 1 to make it easier to understand. An array is an example of a structured data type. Note that a string is an array of character data.

An array of names might look like this:

> name (1) – John – this is the first element of the name array
>
> name (2) – Helen – this is element number 2 of the name array
>
> name (3) – Peter – this element has the subscript 3
>
> name (4) – Mary – this element has the index 4

This array has four parts. Element number 3 of this array is the name 'Peter'.

Arrays which have one number as their subscript are called one-dimensional arrays.

When programming using arrays, it is always necessary to **declare** the name of the array and its size at the start of the program, so that the computer may set aside the correct amount of memory space for the array.

Here is the code to set aside space for an array called *apples* with a size of *15*, in four different programming languages:

```
DIM apples% (15)
VAR apples : array [1..15] of integer;
int apples [15];
Dim apples(15) As Integer
```

Example of an algorithm which makes use of arrays for data storage

```
algorithm to read names and marks into two arrays
1.    SET size_of_list TO 9
2.    SET array_counter TO 0
3.    SET names TO ["Harjinder", "Paul", "Jennifer", "David",
      "Siobhan", "Cecilia", "Angus", "Sarah", "Anwar"]
4.    SET marks TO [76, 68, 56, 52, 89, 75, 61, 93, 92]
5.    REPEAT
6.        SET array_counter TO array_counter + 1
7.        SET names [array_counter] TO value
8.        SET marks [array_counter] TO value
9.    UNTIL array_counter = size_of_list
```

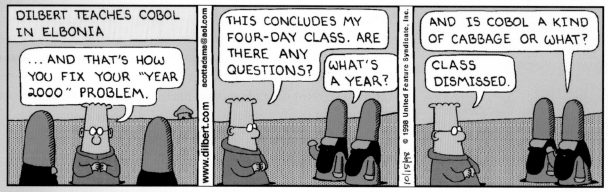

Figure 2.14

Procedures and functions

When a program is designed and written, it is divided into smaller sections called subprograms. Subprograms may be called in any order in a program, and they may be reused many times over. Each subprogram performs a particular task within the program. Subprograms may be written at the same time as the rest of the program or they may be prewritten. High-level procedural languages use two types of subprograms. These are **procedures** and **functions**.

Procedures

Before a procedure may be used in a program, it must be *defined*. Defining a procedure gives it a name. Using a procedure in a program is known as calling the procedure. A procedure *produces an effect* in a program. An example of a procedure definition and a procedure call are shown below and opposite.

Example of a procedure definition

```
PROC sum
total := number_one + number_two
PRINT total
ENDPROC sum
```

Example of a procedure call in a program

```
// main steps
setup
sum
END
```

Functions

A function is similar to a procedure, but *returns a single value* to a program. Like a procedure, a function must be defined and given a name before it can be used in a program.

Pre-defined functions (with parameters)

The functions described in this unit are already written as part of the programming language. These are known as **pre-defined functions**. A pre-defined function is a calculation which is built in to, or part of, a programming language. A **parameter** is **information** about a data item being supplied to a subprogram (function or procedure) when it is called into use. When the subprogram is used, the calling program must pass parameters to it. This is called parameter passing.

Example of a pre-defined function

The SQR function returns the square root of a number. In the example below, the variable **number** is the parameter.

```
number := 4
root := SQR (number)
PRINT root
```

> ● **Sample Output**
>
> 2

The INT function changes a number with a decimal point into a whole number, removing the decimal part.

```
PRINT INT(3.141)
```

> ● **Sample Output**
>
> 3

The LEN function returns the number of characters in a string.

```
PRINT LEN("John")
```

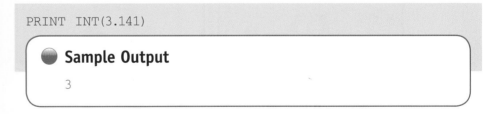

> ● **Sample Output**
>
> 4

```
town$ = "Ardrossan"
PRINT LEN(town$)
```

town$ is the parameter

● **Sample Output**

9

If you study the documentation for the particular programming language that you are using, you can find many other examples of pre-defined functions.

In the following sections A to F, we will look at the means of implementing some of the algorithms listed earlier in this chapter, and give examples in a variety of different high-level languages. You should compare each of the following examples with its related algorithm in the previous section.

Check Your Learning

Now answer questions 29–32(a) and 33–44 (on page 109) on computational constructs and data types and structures (National 4).

Check Your Learning

Now answer questions 32(b) and 45–54 (on page 109) on computational constructs and data types and structures (National 5).

Figure 2.15

Section A: COMAL® implementations

Program implementation based on algorithm to add two numbers

```
// Title : COMAL Example 1
// Author : John Walsh
// Date : 15 April 2000
//
PRINT "Please enter the first number ";    ← OUTPUT
INPUT number_one                           ← INPUT
PRINT "Please enter the second number ";
INPUT number_two
total := number_one + number_two           ← ASSIGNMENT
PRINT "The total is "; total
END
```

● **Sample Output**

```
Please enter the first number ? 19
Please enter the second number ? 54
The total is 73
```

Program implementation based on pass or fail algorithm

```
// Title : COMAL Example 2
// Author : John Walsh
// Date : 15 April 2000
//
PRINT "Please enter pupil's mark ";
INPUT mark
     IF mark >= 50 THEN    ← CONDITIONAL STATEMENT
         PRINT "Pass"
     ELSE
         PRINT "Fail"
     ENDIF
END
```

● **Sample Output**

```
Please enter pupil's mark ? 49
Fail
Please enter pupil's mark ? 50
Pass
Please enter pupil's mark ? 51
Pass
```

Note that this example shows a simple condition.

Program implementation based on algorithm to display a name five times

```
// Title : COMAL Example 3
// Author : John Walsh
// Date : 15 April 2000
//
FOR loop_counter := 1 TO 5 DO      ← FIXED LOOP
      PRINT "John"
NEXT loop_counter
END
```

🔵 **Sample Output**

```
John
John
John
John
John
```

Program implementation based on algorithm to display one name a number of times

```
// Title : COMAL Example 4
// Author : John Walsh
// Date : 15 April 2000
//
PRINT "Please enter the number of times a name is required"
INPUT number_of_times
FOR loop_counter := 1 TO number_of_times DO    ← FIXED LOOP
      PRINT "John"
NEXT loop_counter
END
```

🔵 **Sample Output**

```
Please enter the number of times a name is required
? 3
John
John
John
```

Program implementation based on algorithm showing a fixed loop with steps

```
// Title : COMAL Example 5
// Author : John Walsh
// Date : 15 April 2000
//
FOR loop_counter := 2 TO 30 STEP 2 DO    ← LOOP WITH STEPS
      PRINT loop_counter
NEXT loop_counter
END
```

● Sample Output

```
2
4
6
8
10
12
14
16
18
20
22
24
26
28
30
```

Program implementation based on tab algorithm showing nested loops

```
// Title : COMAL Example 6
// Author : John Walsh
// Date : 15 April 2000
//
FOR down := 1 TO 5 DO                    ← LOOP 1
      FOR across := 10 TO 20 DO              ← LOOP 2
            PRINT TAB (across, down); "*"        ← TAB
      NEXT across
NEXT down
END
```

⬤ Sample Output

```
**********
**********
**********
**********
**********
```

Program implementation based on take in a word algorithm with test at end

```
// Title : COMAL Example 7
// Author : John Walsh
// Date : 1 May 2000
//
timesinloop := 0
REPEAT
        timesinloop := timesinloop + 1
        PRINT "Please enter a word (or END to finish) ";
        INPUT word$// word$ is a string variable
UNTIL word$ = "END" OR word$ = "end"      ← TEST AT END
PRINT "Program ended"
PRINT "The number of times in the loop is "; timesinloop
END
```

⬤ Sample Output

Run 1

```
Please enter a word (or END to finish) ? Conditional
Please enter a word (or END to finish) ? loop
Please enter a word (or END to finish) ? with
Please enter a word (or END to finish) ? test
Please enter a word (or END to finish) ? at
Please enter a word (or END to finish) ? end
Program ended
The number of times in the loop is 6
```

Run 2

```
Please enter a word (or END to finish) ? end
Program ended
The number of times in the loop is 1
```

*Note that the code in a conditional loop with test at end is always run at least once.

*Note that this example shows a complex condition.

Program implementation based on calculation algorithm using a running total

```
// Title : COMAL Example 8
// Author : John Walsh
// Date : 15 April 2000
//
total := 0
number := 0
REPEAT
      total := total + number
      PRINT "Please enter a number (-999 to finish)";
      INPUT number
UNTIL number = -999                          ← TEST AT END
PRINT "The total of the numbers entered is "; total
PRINT "Program ended"
END
```

● Sample Output

Run 1

Please enter a number (-999 to finish)? -999
The total of the numbers entered is 0
Program ended

Run 2

Please enter a number (-999 to finish)? 6
Please enter a number (-999 to finish)? 7
Please enter a number (-999 to finish)? 1
Please enter a number (-999 to finish)? -999
The total of the numbers entered is 14
Program ended

*Note that this example shows a simple condition.

Program implementation based on algorithm with test at start

```
// Title : COMAL Example 9
// Author : John Walsh
// Date : 1 May 2000
//
timesinloop := 0
PRINT "Please enter a word ";
INPUT word$ // word$ is a string variable
WHILE NOT ((word$ = "end") OR (word$ = "END")) DO   ← TEST AT START
      timesinloop := timesinloop + 1
      PRINT "Please enter a word ";
      INPUT word$
ENDWHILE
PRINT "Program ended"
PRINT "The number of times in the loop is "; timesinloop
END
```

⬤ Sample Output

Run 1
```
Please enter a word ? Conditional
Please enter a word ? loop
Please enter a word ? with
Please enter a word ? test
Please enter a word ? at
Please enter a word ? start
Please enter a word ? end
Program ended
The number of times in the loop is 6
```
Run 2
```
Please enter a word ? end
Program ended
The number of times in the loop is 0
```

*Note that the code in a conditional loop with test at start need not be run at all if the condition is not met.

*Note that this example shows a complex condition.

Program implementation based on algorithm to read names and marks into two arrays

```
// Title : COMAL Example 10
// Author : John Walsh
// Date : 16 April 2000
//
array_counter := 0
DIM pupil_name$ (9)
DIM pupil_mark% (9)
REPEAT
       array_counter := array_counter + 1
       READ pupil_name$ (array_counter)
       READ pupil_mark% (array_counter)
UNTIL EOD
END
//
DATA Harjinder, 76, Paul, 68, Jennifer, 56
DATA David, 52, Siobhan, 89, Cecilia, 75
DATA Angus, 61, Sarah, 93, Anwar, 92
```

*Note that there is no output from this program.

Figure 2.16

Section B: Visual Basic® implementations

Program implementation based on algorithm to add two numbers

```
'Title : Visual Basic Example 1
'Author : John Walsh
'Date : 25 May 2000
'

Option Explicit
Dim number_one As Integer, number_two As Integer, total As Integer

Private Sub cmdEnd_Click()
End
End Sub

Private Sub cmdEnterNumbers_Click()
number_one = InputBox("Please enter the first number")  ← INPUT
number_two = InputBox("Please enter the second number")
total = number_one + number_two                         ← ASSIGNMENT
picDisplay.Print Tab(20); "The total is "; total        ← OUTPUT
End Sub
```

● **Sample Output**

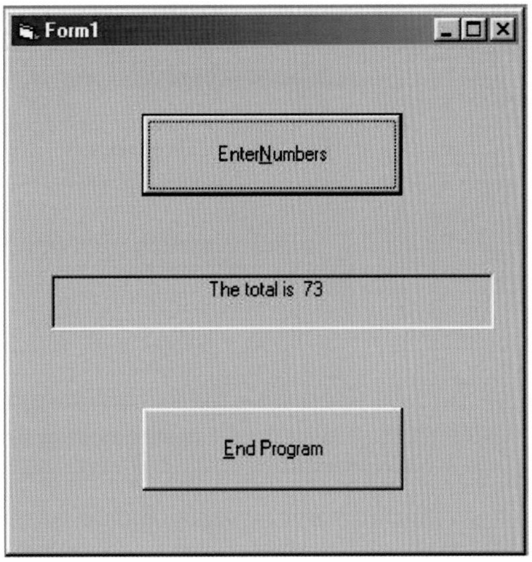

Figure 2.17 Sample output of Visual Basic® Example 1

Program implementation based on pass or fail algorithm

```
'Title : Visual Basic Example 2
'Author : John Walsh
'Date : 25 May 2000
'
Option Explicit
Dim mark As Integer

Private Sub cmdEnterMark_Click()
picDisplay.Cls
mark = InputBox("Please enter the mark")
If mark >= 50 Then     ← CONDITIONAL STATEMENT
        picDisplay.Print Tab(25); "Pass"
Else
        picDisplay.Print Tab(25); "Fail"
End If
End Sub

Private Sub cmdEnd_Click()
End
End Sub
```

● Sample Output

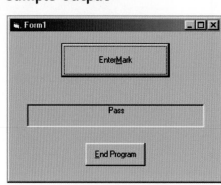

Figure 2.18 Sample output of Visual Basic® Example 2

Note that this example shows a simple condition.

Program implementation based on algorithm to display a name five times

```
'Title : Visual Basic Example 3
'Author : John Walsh
'Date : 26 May 2000
'
Option Explicit
Dim loop_counter As Integer

Private Sub cmdStartLoop_Click()
picDisplay.Cls
For loop_counter = 1 To 5       ← FIXED LOOP
        picDisplay.Print "John"
Next loop_counter
End Sub

Private Sub cmdEnd_Click()
End
End Sub
```

Sample Output

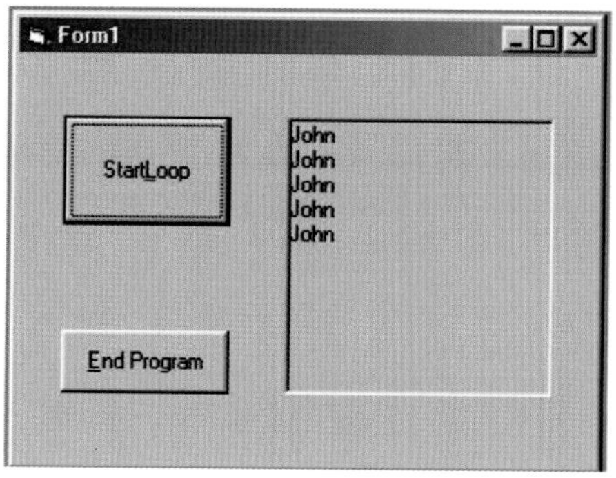

Figure 2.19 Sample output of Visual Basic® Example 3

Program implementation based on algorithm to display one name a number of times

```
'Title : Visual Basic Example 4
'Author : John Walsh
'Date : 27 May 2000
'
Option Explicit
Dim loop_counter As Integer, number_of_times As Integer

Private Sub cmdTakeNames_Click()
picDisplay.Cls
number_of_times = InputBox("Please enter the number of times a name is required")
For loop_counter = 1 To number_of_times          ← FIXED LOOP
      picDisplay.Print "John"
Next loop_counter
End Sub

Private Sub cmdEnd_Click()
End
End Sub
```

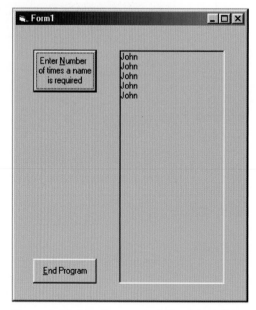

● **Sample Output**

Figure 2.20 Sample output of Visual Basic® Example 4

Note that this example shows a fixed loop.

Program implementation based on algorithm showing a fixed loop with steps

```
'Title : Visual Basic Example 5
'Author : John Walsh
'Date : 27 May 2000
'
Option Explicit
Dim loop_counter As Integer

Private Sub cmdDisplayNumbers_Click()
picDisplay.Cls
For loop_counter = 2 To 30 Step 2      ← STEPS
        picDisplay.Print loop_counter
Next loop_counter
End Sub

Private Sub cmdEnd_Click()
End
End Sub
```

Sample Output

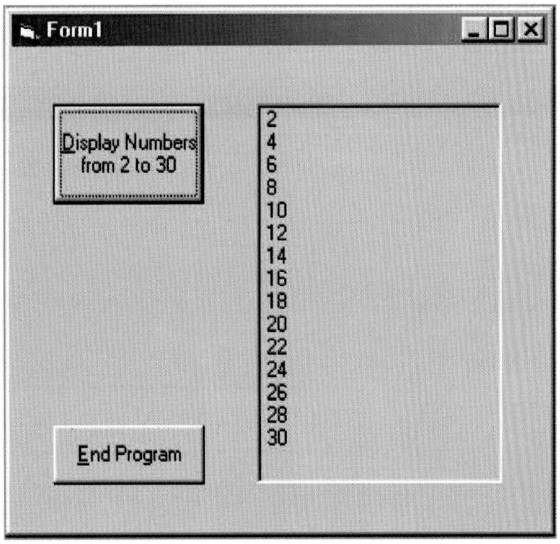

Figure 2.21 Sample output of Visual Basic® Example 5

Program implementation based on tab algorithm showing nested loops

```
'Title : Visual Basic Example 6
'Author : John Walsh
'Date : 27 May 2000
'
Option Explicit
Dim across As Integer, down As Integer

Private Sub cmdPrintStars_Click()
picDisplay.Cls
For down = 1 To 5
    For across = 10 To 20
        picDisplay.Print Tab(across); "*"; ← TAB
    Next across '
Next down
End Sub

Private Sub cmdEnd_Click()
End
End Sub
```

Sample Output

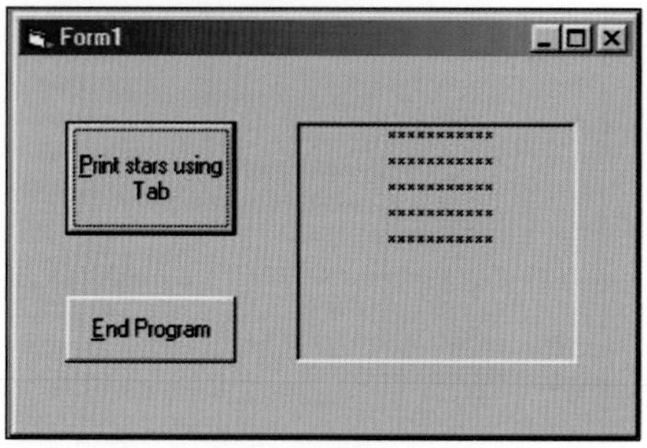

Figure 2.22 Sample output of Visual Basic® Example 6

Note that only one TAB parameter is allowed so this example is not directly equivalent.

Program implementation based on take in a word algorithm with test at end

```
'Title : Visual Basic Example 7
'Author : John Walsh
'Date : 27 May 2000
'
Option Explicit
Dim word As String, timesinloop As Integer

Private Sub cmdEnterWords_Click()
'picDisplay.Cls - is disabled for the Sample Output timesinloop = 0
Do
        timesinloop = timesinloop + 1
        word = InputBox("Please enter a word (or END to finish)")
        picDisplay.Print word
Loop Until word = "END" Or word = "end"        ← TEST AT END
picDisplay.Print "Loop ended"
picDisplay.Print "The number of times in the loop is "; timesinloop
End Sub

Private Sub cmdEnd_Click()
picDisplay.Cls
End
End Sub
```

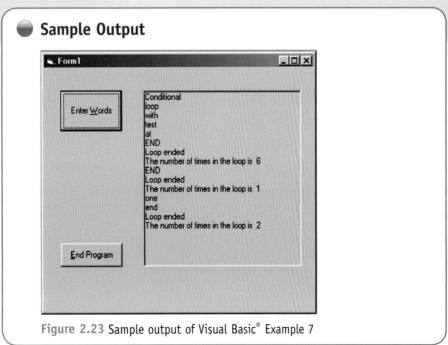

Sample Output

Figure 2.23 Sample output of Visual Basic® Example 7

*Note that the code in a conditional loop with test at end is always run at least once.

*Note that this example shows a complex *condition*.

Program implementation based on calculation algorithm using a running total

```
'Title : Visual Basic Example 8
'Author : John Walsh
'Date : 28 May 2000
'
Option Explicit
Dim total As Integer, number As Integer

Private Sub cmdEnterNumbers_Click()
'picDisplay.Cls
total = 0
number = 0
Do
        total = total + number
        number = InputBox("Please enter a number (-999 to finish)")
        picDisplay.Print number
Loop Until number = -999            ← TEST AT END
picDisplay.Print "The total of the numbers entered is "; total
End Sub

Private Sub cmdEnd_Click()
picDisplay.Cls
End
End Sub
```

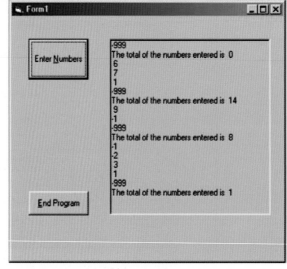

Sample Output

Figure 2.24 Sample output of Visual Basic® Example 8

*Note that this example shows a simple condition.

Program implementation based on algorithm with test at start

```
'Title : Visual Basic Example 9
'Author : John Walsh
'Date : 28 May 2000
'
Option Explicit
Dim word As String, timesinloop As Integer

Private Sub cmdEnterWords_Click()
'picDisplay.Cls - is disabled for the Sample Output
timesinloop = 0
word = InputBox("Please enter a word (or END to finish)")
picDisplay.Print word
Do While Not ((word = "end") Or (word = "END"))     ← TEST AT START
        timesinloop = timesinloop + 1
        word = InputBox("Please enter a word (or END to finish)")
        picDisplay.Print word
Loop
picDisplay.Print "Loop ended"
picDisplay.Print "The number of times in the loop is "; timesinloop
End Sub

Private Sub cmdEnd_Click()
picDisplay.Cls
End
End Sub
```

Sample Output

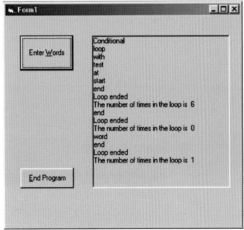

Figure 2.25 Sample output of Visual Basic® Example 9

*Note that the code in a conditional loop with test at start need not be run at all if the condition is not met.

*Note that this example shows a complex condition.

73

Program implementation based on algorithm to read names and marks into two arrays

```
'Title : Visual Basic Example 10
'Author : John Walsh
'Date : 29 May 2000
'
Option Explicit
Option Base 1 " makes array index start at 1
Dim array_counter As Integer
Dim pupil_name(10) As String
Dim pupil_mark(10) As Integer

Private Sub cmdFillArray_Click()
array_counter = 0
LstNames.AddItem "Harjinder"
LstMarks.AddItem 76
LstNames.AddItem "Paul"
LstMarks.AddItem 68
LstNames.AddItem "Jennifer"
LstMarks.AddItem 56
LstNames.AddItem "David"
LstMarks.AddItem 52
LstNames.AddItem "Siobhan"
LstMarks.AddItem 89
Do
        array_counter = array_counter + 1
        pupil_name(array_counter) = LstNames.List(array_counter)
        'Val changes a string into an integer value
        pupil_mark(array_counter) = Val(LstMarks.List(array_counter))
        'ListCount is the number of items in the list
Loop Until array_counter = LstNames.ListCount
End Sub

Private Sub cmdEnd_Click()
End
End Sub
```

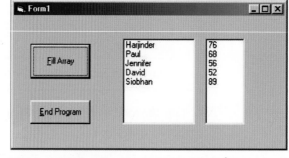

Figure 2.26 Sample output of Visual Basic® Example 10

Section C: TrueBASIC® implementations

Program implementation based on algorithm to add two numbers

```
! Title : TrueBASIC Example 1
! Author : John Walsh
! Date : 19 May 2000
!
PRINT "Please enter the first number ";
INPUT number_one                          ←  INPUT
PRINT "Please enter the second number ";
INPUT number_two
LET total = number_one + number_two       ←  ASSIGNMENT
PRINT "The total is "; total              ←  OUTPUT
END
```

⬤ **Sample Output**

```
Please enter the first number ? 19
Please enter the second number ? 54
The total is 73
```

Program implementation based on pass or fail algorithm

```
! Title : TrueBASIC Example 2
! Author : John Walsh
! Date : 19 May 2000
!
PRINT "Please enter pupil's mark ";
INPUT mark
IF mark >= 50 THEN          ←  CONDITIONAL STATEMENT
        PRINT "Pass"
ELSE
        PRINT "Fail"
END IF
END
```

⬤ **Sample Output**

```
Please enter pupil's mark ? 49
Fail
Please enter pupil's mark ? 50
Pass
Please enter pupil's mark ? 51
Pass
```

*Note that this example shows a simple *condition*.

Program implementation based on algorithm to display a name five times

```
! Title : TrueBASIC Example 3
! Author : John Walsh
! Date : 19 May 2000
!
FOR loop_counter = 1 TO 5          ← FIXED LOOP
        PRINT "John"
NEXT loop_counter
END
```

🔘 **Sample Output**

```
John
John
John
John
John
```

Program implementation based on algorithm to display one name a number of times

```
! Title : TrueBASIC Example 4
! Author : John Walsh
! Date : 19 May 2000
!
PRINT "Please enter the number of times a name is required"
INPUT number_of_times
FOR loop_counter = 1 TO number_of_times  ← FIXED LOOP
        PRINT "John"
NEXT loop_counter
END
```

🔘 **Sample Output**

```
Please enter the number of times a name is required
? 3
John
John
John
```

Note that this example shows a fixed loop.

Program implementation based on algorithm showing a fixed loop with steps

```
! Title : TrueBASIC Example 5
! Author : John Walsh
! Date : 19 May 2000
!
FOR loop_counter = 2 TO 30 STEP 2        ← STEPS
       PRINT loop_counter
NEXT loop_counter
END
```

⬤ **Sample Output**

```
2
4
6
8
10
12
14
16
18
20
22
24
26
28
30
```

Program implementation based on tab algorithm showing nested loops

```
! Title : TrueBASIC Example 6
! Author : John Walsh
! Date : 19 May 2000
!
FOR down = 1 TO 5
      FOR across = 10 TO 20
            PRINT TAB (across, down); "*"        ← TAB
      NEXT across
NEXT down
END
```

● Sample Output

```
**********
**********
**********
**********
**********
```

Program implementation based on take in a word algorithm with test at end

```
! Title : TrueBASIC Example 7
! Author : John Walsh
! Date : 19 May 2000
!
LET timesinloop = 0
DO
        LET timesinloop = timesinloop + 1
        PRINT "Please enter a word (or END to finish) ";
        INPUT word$
LOOP UNTIL word$ = "END" OR word$ = "end"   ← TEST AT END
PRINT "Program ended"
PRINT "The number of times in the loop is "; timesinloop
END
```

⬤ Sample Output

Run 1

```
Please enter a word (or END to finish) ? Conditional
Please enter a word (or END to finish) ? loop
Please enter a word (or END to finish) ? with
Please enter a word (or END to finish) ? test
Please enter a word (or END to finish) ? at
Please enter a word (or END to finish) ? end
Program ended
The number of times in the loop is 6
```

Run 2

```
Please enter a word (or END to finish) ? end
Program ended
The number of times in the loop is 1
```

*Note that the code in a conditional loop with test at end is always run at least once.

*Note that this example shows a complex condition.

Program implementation based on calculation algorithm using a running total

```
! Title : TrueBASIC Example 8
! Author : John Walsh
! Date : 19 May 2000
!
LET total = 0
LET number = 0
DO
        LET total = total + number
        PRINT "Please enter a number (-999 to finish)";
        INPUT number
LOOP UNTIL number = -999          ← TEST AT END
PRINT "The total of the numbers entered is "; total
PRINT "Program ended"
END
```

⬤ Sample Output

Run 1

Please enter a number (-999 to finish)? -999
The total of the numbers entered is 0
Program ended

Run 2

Please enter a number (-999 to finish)? 6
Please enter a number (-999 to finish)? 7
Please enter a number (-999 to finish)? 1
Please enter a number (-999 to finish)? -999
The total of the numbers entered is 14
Program ended

Note that this example shows a simple condition.

Program implementation based on algorithm with test at start

```
! Title : TrueBASIC Example 9
! Author : John Walsh
! Date : 20 May 2000
!
LET timesinloop = 0
PRINT "Please enter a word (stop to finish) ";
INPUT word$
DO WHILE NOT ((word$ = "end") OR (word$ = "END"))    ← TEST AT START
        LET timesinloop = timesinloop + 1
        PRINT "Please enter a word ";
        INPUT word$
LOOP
PRINT "Program ended"
PRINT "The number of times in the loop is "; timesinloop
END
```

Sample Output

Run 1
```
Please enter a word ? Conditional
Please enter a word ? loop
Please enter a word ? with
Please enter a word ? test
Please enter a word ? at
Please enter a word ? start
Please enter a word ? end
Program ended
The number of times in the loop is 6
```
Run 2
```
Please enter a word ? end
Program ended
The number of times in the loop is 0
```

*Note that the code in a conditional loop with test at start need not be run at all if the condition is not met.

*Note that this example shows a complex condition.

Program implementation based on algorithm to read names and marks into two arrays

```
! Title : TrueBASIC Example 10
! Author : John Walsh
! Date : 20 May 2000
!
LET array_counter = 0
DIM pupil_name$ (10)
DIM pupil_mark (10)
DO while more data
        LET array_counter = array_counter + 1
        READ pupil_name$ (array_counter)
        READ pupil_mark (array_counter)
LOOP
!
DATA Harjinder, 76, Paul, 68, Jennifer, 56
DATA David, 52, Siobhan, 89, Cecilia, 75
DATA Angus, 61, Sarah, 93, Anwar, 92
END
```

*Note that there is no output from this program.

Section D: C implementations

Program implementation based on algorithm to add two numbers

```c
/*Title : C Example 1 */
/*Author : John Walsh */
/*Date : 19 April 2000 */

#include <stdio.h>

int main(void)
{
int numberOne, numberTwo, total;

numberOne = numberTwo = total = 0;

printf ("Please enter the first number ? ");
scanf("%d",&numberOne);                    ← INPUT
printf ("Please enter the second number ? ");
scanf("%d",&numberTwo);

total = numberOne + numberTwo;             ← ASSIGNMENT

printf ("The total is %d",total);          ← OUTPUT

return 0;
}
```

● **Sample Output**

```
Please enter the first number ? 19
Please enter the second number ? 54
The total is 73
```

Program implementation based on pass or fail algorithm

```c
/*Title : C Example 2 */
/*Author : John Walsh */
/*Date : 19 April 2000 */

#include <stdio.h>

int main(void)
{
int mark;

mark = 0;

printf ("Please enter pupil's mark ? ");
scanf("%d",&mark);

if (mark >= 50)                    ← CONDITIONAL STATEMENT

printf ("Pass \n");

else

printf ("Fail \n");

return 0;
}
```

⬤ **Sample Output**

```
Please enter pupil's mark ? 50
Pass
```

Program implementation based on algorithm to display a name five times

```
/*Title : C Example 3 */
/*Author : John Walsh */
/*Date : 24 April 2000 */

#include <stdio.h>

int main(void)
{
int loopCounter;

for ( loopCounter = 1; loopCounter <=5; loopCounter++ )  ← FIXED LOOP
printf("John\n");

return 0;
}
```

Sample Output

```
John
John
John
John
John
```

Program implementation based on algorithm to display one name a number of times

```
/*Title : C Example 4 */
/*Author : John Walsh */
/*Date : 24 April 2000 */

#include <stdio.h>

int main(void)
{
int loopCounter, numberOfTimes;

printf("Please enter the number of times a name is required \n");
scanf("%d",&numberOfTimes);

for ( loopCounter = 1; loopCounter <= numberOfTimes; loopCounter++ )
printf("Cecilia\n");                                    ↑ FIXED LOOP

return 0;
}
```

Sample Output

```
Please enter the number of times a name is required
? 3
Cecilia
Cecilia
Cecilia
```

Program implementation based on algorithm showing a fixed loop with steps

```c
/*Title : C Example 5 */
/*Author : John Walsh */
/*Date : 24 April 2000 */

#include <stdio.h>

int main(void)
{
int loopCounter;

for ( loopCounter = 2; loopCounter <= 30 ; loopCounter+=2 )    ← STEPS

printf("%d\n",loopCounter);

return 0;
}
```

Sample Output

```
2
4
6
8
10
12
14
16
18
20
22
24
26
28
30
```

Program implementation based on tab algorithm showing nested loops

```
/*Title : C Example 6 */
/*Author : John Walsh */
/*Date : 24 April 2000 */

#include <stdio.h>

int main(void)
{
int across, down;

for ( down = 1; down <= 5 ; down++ )

{
printf("\n");

for ( across = 10; across < 20 ; across++ )

printf("*");/* "\t" gives a tab in C but without parameters */
}       /* so this example is not directly equivalent  */

return 0;
}
```

Sample Output

```
**********
**********
**********
**********
**********
```

Program implementation based on take in a word algorithm with test at end

```c
/*Title : C Example 7 */
/*Author : John Walsh */
/*Date : 1 May 2000 */

#include <string.h>
#include <stdio.h>

int main( void )

{
char word [20];
int timesInLoop;

timesInLoop = 0;

do

{
timesInLoop ++;
printf( "Please enter a word (or END to finish) ");
scanf("%s",word);
}

while (strcmp(word, "end") != 0 && strcmp(word, "END") != 0);   ← TEST
printf( "Program ended\n");                                        AT END
printf ("The number of times in the loop is %d \n",timesInLoop);

return 0;

}
```

● Sample Output

Run 1

```
Please enter a word (or END to finish) ? Conditional
Please enter a word (or END to finish) ? loop
Please enter a word (or END to finish) ? with
Please enter a word (or END to finish) ? test
Please enter a word (or END to finish) ? at
Please enter a word (or END to finish) ? end
Program ended
The number of times in the loop is 6
```

Run 2

```
Please enter a word (or END to finish) ? end
Program ended
The number of times in the loop is 1
```

*Note that the code in a conditional loop with test at end is always run at least once.

*Note that this example shows a complex condition.

Program implementation based on calculation algorithm using a running total

```c
/*Title : C Example 8 */
/*Author : John Walsh */
/*Date : 19 April 2000 */

#include <stdio.h>

int main(void)
{
int number, total;

number = total = 0;

do
{
total = total + number;
printf("Please enter the number (-999 to finish)? ");
scanf("%d",&number);
}
while (number != -999);                          ← TEST AT END

printf("The total of the numbers entered is %d \n",total);
printf( "Program ended\n");

return 0;
}
```

> ⬤ **Sample Output**
>
> **Run 1**
> Please enter a number (-999 to finish)? -999
> The total of the numbers entered is 0
> Program ended
>
> **Run 2**
> Please enter a number (-999 to finish)? 6
> Please enter a number (-999 to finish)? 7
> Please enter a number (-999 to finish)? 1
> Please enter a number (-999 to finish)? -999
> The total of the numbers entered is 14
> Program ended

*Note that this example shows a simple condition.

Program implementation based on algorithm with test at start

```c
/*Title : C Example 9 */
/*Author : John Walsh */
/*Date : 1 May 2000 */

#include <string.h>
#include <stdio.h>

int main( void )

{

char word [20];
int timesInLoop;

timesInLoop = 0;

printf( "Please enter a word (or END to finish) ");
scanf("%s",word);

while (strcmp(word, "end") != 0 && strcmp(word, "END") != 0)   ← TEST
                                                                 AT START

{
timesInLoop ++;
printf( "Please enter a word ");
scanf("%s",word);
}

printf ( "Program ended\n" );
printf ("The number of times in the loop is %d \n",timesInLoop);

return 0;
}
```

● Sample Output

Run 1
```
Please enter a word ? Conditional
Please enter a word ? loop
Please enter a word ? with
Please enter a word ? test
Please enter a word ? at
Please enter a word ? start
Please enter a word ? end
Program ended
The number of times in the loop is 6
```
Run 2
```
Please enter a word ? end
Program ended
The number of times in the loop is 0
```

*Note that the code in a conditional loop with test at start need not be run at all if the condition is not met.

*Note that there is no example code for Program implementation based on algorithm to read names and marks into two arrays in this section.

Section E: LiveCode® implementations

Program implementation based on algorithm to add two numbers

```
// Title : LiveCode Example 1
// Author : John Walsh
// Date : 11 May 2013

global number_one, number_two, total
on mouseUp
    put 0 into number_one
    put 0 into number_two
    ask "Please enter the first number"
    put it into number_one                              ← INPUT
    ask "Please enter the second number"
    put it into number_two
    put (number_one + number_two) into total            ← ASSIGNMENT
    put "The total is" &&total into field "output"      ← OUTPUT
end mouseUp
on mouseUp
    put empty into field "output"
end mouseUp
```

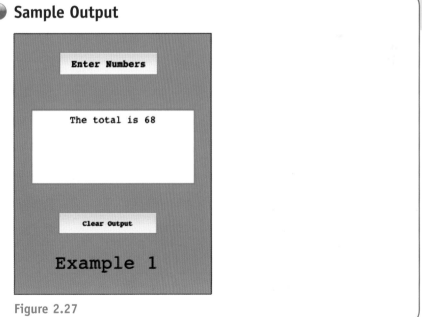

Sample Output

Enter Numbers

The total is 68

Clear Output

Example 1

Figure 2.27

Program implementation based on pass or fail algorithm

```
// Title : LiveCode Example 2
// Author : John Walsh
// Date : 11 May 2013

global score
on mouseUp
    put 0 into score
    ask "Please enter the mark"
    put it into score
    if score >= 50 then          ← CONDITIONAL STATEMENT
        put "Pass" into field "output"
    else
        put "Fail" into field "output"
    end if
end mouseUp
on mouseUp
    put empty into field "output"
end mouseUp
```

Sample Output

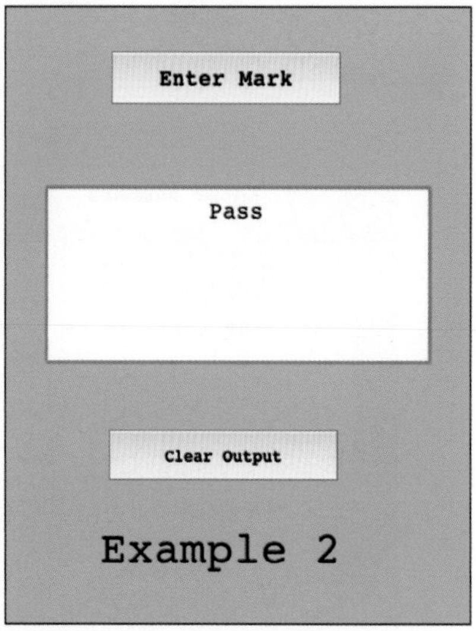

```
        Enter Mark


              Pass




        Clear Output

      Example 2
```

Figure 2.28

*Note that this example shows a simple condition.

Program implementation based on algorithm to display a name five times

```
// Title: LiveCode Example 3
// Author: John Walsh
// Date: 11 May 2013

global loop_counter
on mouseUp
    put 0 into loop_counter
    repeat with loop_counter = 1 to 5        ← FIXED LOOP
        put "John" into line loop_counter of field "output"
    end repeat
end mouseUp
on mouseUp
    put empty into field "output"
end mouseUp
```

● **Sample Output**

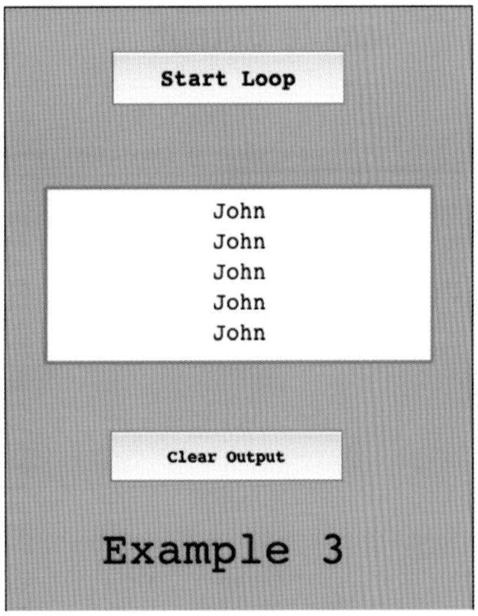

Start Loop

John
John
John
John
John

Clear Output

Example 3

Figure 2.29

Program implementation based on algorithm to display one name a number of times

```
// Title: LiveCode Example 4
// Author: John Walsh
// Date: 11 May 2013

global loop_counter, number_of_times
on mouseUp
    put 0 into loop_counter
    put 0 into number_of_times
    ask "Please enter the number of times a name is required"
    put it into number_of_times
    repeat with loop_counter = 1 to number_of_times  ← FIXED LOOP
        put "John" into line loop_counter of field "output"
    end repeat
end mouseUp
on mouseUp
    put empty into field "output"
end mouseUp
```

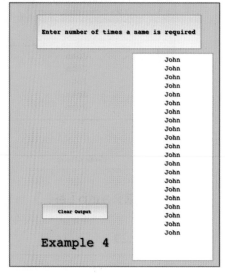

● **Sample Output**

Enter number of times a name is required

John
John
John
John
John
John
John
John
John
John
John
John
John
John
John
John
John
John
John
John

Clear Output

Example 4

Figure 2.30

Program implementation based on algorithm showing a fixed loop with steps

```
// Title: LiveCode Example 5
// Author: John Walsh
// Date: 11 May 2013

global loop_counter
on mouseUp
    put 0 into loop_counter
    repeat with loop_counter = 2 to 30 step 2          ← STEPS
      put loop_counter into line loop_counter of field "output"
    end repeat
end mouseUp
on mouseUp
    put empty into field "output"
end mouseUp
```

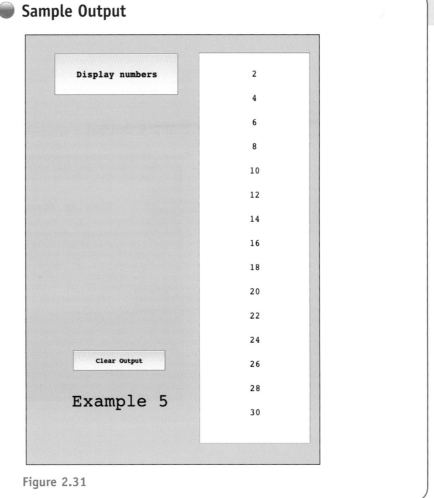

Sample Output

Display numbers

2
4
6
8
10
12
14
16
18
20
22
24
26
28
30

Clear Output

Example 5

Figure 2.31

Program implementation based on tab algorithm showing nested loops

```
// Title: LiveCode Example 6
// Author: John Walsh
// Date: 12 May 2013

global across, vert, line_of_stars
on mouseUp
    put 0 into across
    put 0 into vert
    put empty into line_of_stars
    repeat with vert = 1 to 10
        repeat with across = 1 to 10
        put "*" & " " after line_of_stars
        end repeat
      put line_of_stars into field "output"
      put return after line_of_stars
    end repeat
end mouseUp
on mouseUp
    put empty into field "output"
end mouseUp
```

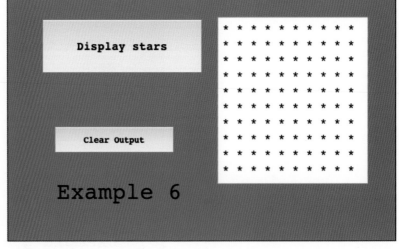

Sample Output

Figure 2.32

Program implementation based on take in a word algorithm with test at end

```
// Title: LiveCode Example 7
// Author: John Walsh
// Date: 12 May 2013

global times_in_loop, word_entered
on mouseUp
    put 0 into times_in_loop
    put empty into word_entered
    repeat until word_entered="END" or word_entered = "end"
        add 1 to times_in_loop
        ask"Please enter a word (or END to finish)"
        if the result = "Cancel" then exit to top
        put it into word_entered
        put word_entered & return into line times_in_loop of field "output"
    end repeat
    put "Loop ended" & return & "The number of times in the loop is "
    &times_in_loop into line times_in_loop + 1 of field "output"
end mouseUp
on mouseUp
    put empty into field "output"
end mouseUp
```

Sample Output

```
                    Conditional
  Enter Words       loop
                    with
                    test
                    at
                    END
                    Loop ended
                    The number of times in the loop is 6




  Clear Output

  Example 7
```

Figure 2.33

*Note that the code in a conditional loop with test at end is always run at least once.

*Note that this example shows a complex condition.

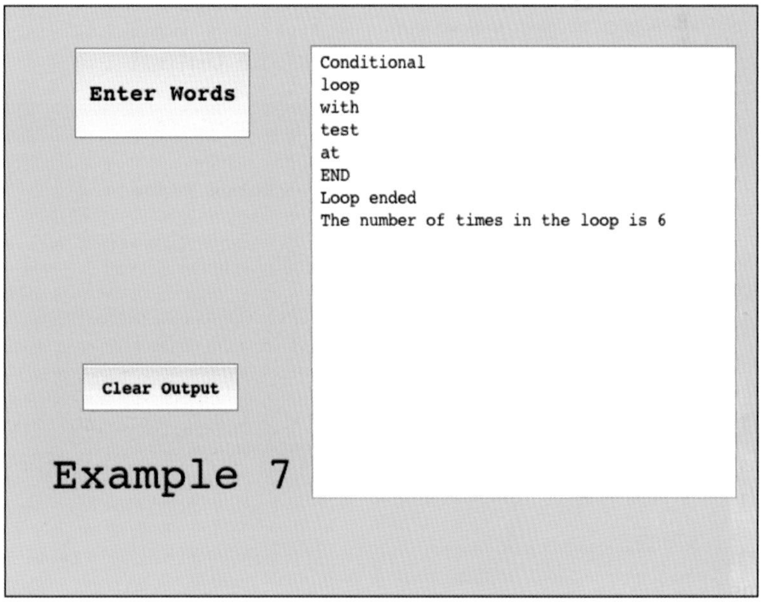

Program implementation based on calculation algorithm using a running total

```
// Title: LiveCode Example 8
// Author: John Walsh
// Date: 12 May 2013

global total, number_entered, line_counter
on mouseUp
    put 0 into total
    put 0 into number_entered
    put 0 into line_counter // use for formatting output
    repeat until number_entered=-999
        add 1 to line_counter
        add number_entered to total
        ask"Please enter a number (-999 to finish)"
        if the result = "Cancel" then exit to top
        put it into number_entered
        put number_entered & return into line line_counter of field "output"
    end repeat
    put "The total of the numbers entered is " &total & return into line line_
    counter + 2 of field "output"
end mouseUp
on mouseUp
    put empty into field "output"
end mouseUp
```

Note that this example shows a simple condition.

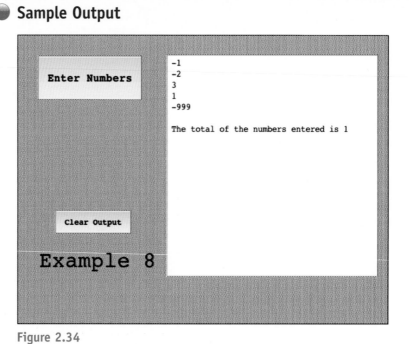

Sample Output

```
-1
-2
3
1
-999

The total of the numbers entered is 1
```

Enter Numbers

Clear Output

Example 8

Figure 2.34

Program implementation based on algorithm with test at start

```
// Title: LiveCode Example 9
// Author: John Walsh
// Date: 12 May 2013

global times_in_loop, word_entered
on mouseUp
    put 0 into times_in_loop
    put empty into word_entered
    ask"Please enter a word (or END to finish)"
    if the result = "Cancel" then exit to top
    put it into word_entered
    put word_entered & return into line 1 of field "output"
    repeat while not ((word_entered="END") or (word_entered = "end"))
        add 1 to times_in_loop
        ask"Please enter a word (or END to finish)"
        if the result = "Cancel" then exit to top
        put it into word_entered
        put word_entered & return into line times_in_loop+1 of field "output"
    end repeat
    put "Loop ended" & return &"The number of times in the loop is " &times_in_
    loop into line times_in_loop + 2 of field "output"
end mouseUp
on mouseUp
    put empty into field "output"
end mouseUp
```

*Note that the code in a conditional loop with test at start need not be run at all if the condition is not met.

*Note that this example shows a complex condition.

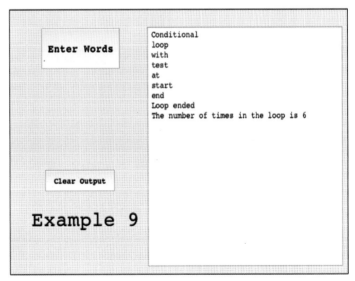

Sample Output

```
Conditional
loop
with
test
at
start
end
Loop ended
The number of times in the loop is 6
```

Enter Words

Clear Output

Example 9

Figure 2.35

Program implementation based on algorithm to read names and marks into two arrays

```
// Title: LiveCode Example 10
// Author: John Walsh
// Date: 12 May 2013

global arrayname, arrayscore, loop
on mouseUp
    put empty into field "output name"
    put empty into field "output score"
    put "Harjinder", "Paul", "Jennifer", "David", "Siobhan", "Cecilia", "Angus",
    "Sarah", "Anwar" into arrayname
    split arrayname by comma
    put 76, 68, 56, 52, 89, 75,61, 93, 92 into arrayscore
    split arrayscore by comma
    put "NAME" into line 1 of field "output name"
    put "SCORE" into line 1 of field "output score"
    repeat with loop = 1 to 9

        put arrayname[loop] into line loop+2 of field "output name"
        put arrayscore[loop] into line loop+2 of field "output score"
    end repeat
end mouseUp
on mouseUp
    put empty into field "output"
end mouseUp
```

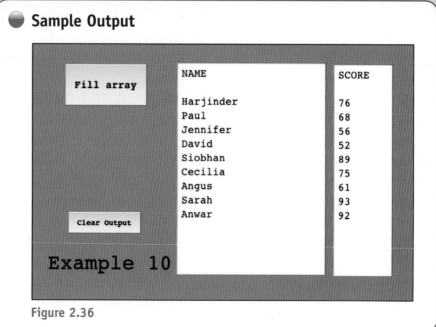

Sample Output

	NAME	SCORE
Fill array		
	Harjinder	76
	Paul	68
	Jennifer	56
	David	52
	Siobhan	89
	Cecilia	75
	Angus	61
	Sarah	93
Clear Output	Anwar	92
Example 10		

Figure 2.36

```
// Title: LiveCode For Each Example
// Author: John Walsh
// Date: 19 May 2013
global arrayname, loop
on mouseUp
    put empty into field "output name"
    put 0 into loop
    put "Harjinder", "Paul", "Jennifer", "David", "Siobhan", "Cecilia", "Angus",
    "Sarah", "Anwar" into arrayname
    split arrayname by comma
    repeat for each element test in arrayname
        add 1 to loop
        put test into line loop of field "output name"
    end repeat
end mouseUp
on mouseUp
    put empty into field "output"
end mouseUp
```

● **Sample Output**

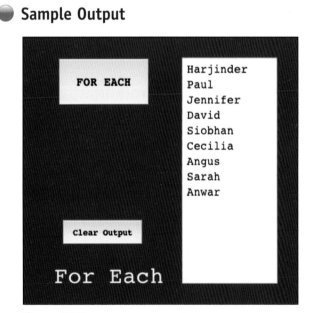

Figure 2.37

Section F: Scratch® implementations

Program implementation based on algorithm to add two numbers

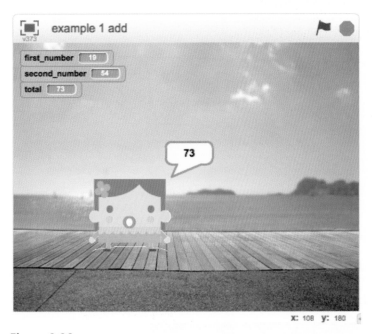

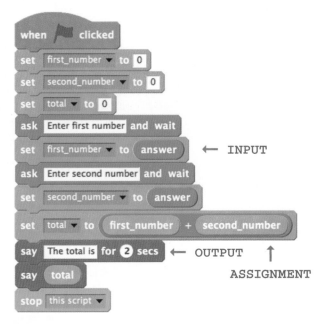

Figure 2.38

Program implementation based on pass or fail algorithm

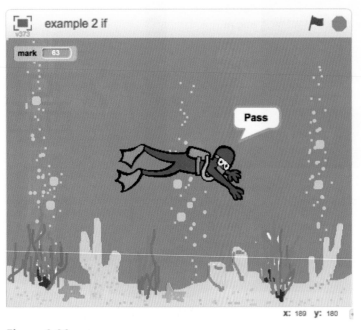

Figure 2.39

Note that this example shows a simple condition.

Program implementation based on algorithm to display a name five times

Figure 2.40

X: 240 y: 180

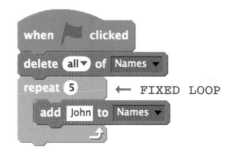

Program implementation based on algorithm to display one name a number of times

Figure 2.41

X: 44 y: 180

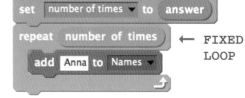

Program implementation based on algorithm showing a fixed loop with steps

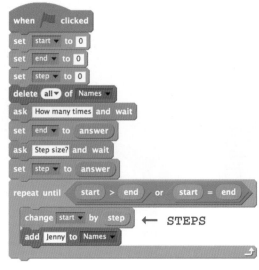

Figure 2.42

Program implementation based on tab algorithm showing nested loops

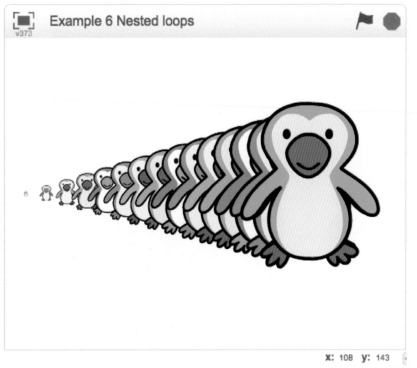
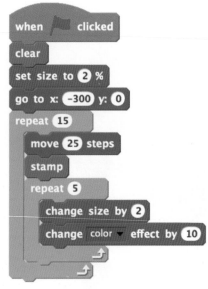

Figure 2.43

Program implementation based on take in a word algorithm with test at end

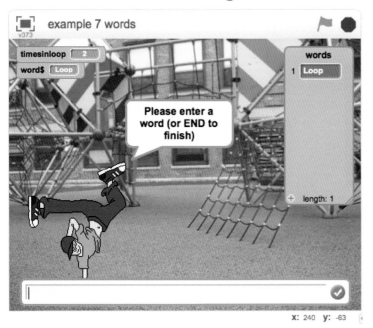
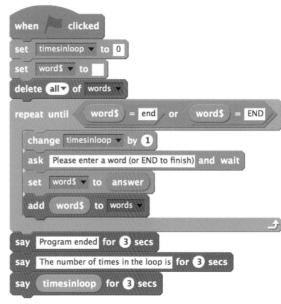

Figure 2.44

Note that the code in a conditional loop with test at end is always run at least once.

Note that this example shows a complex condition.

Program implementation based on calculation algorithm using a running total

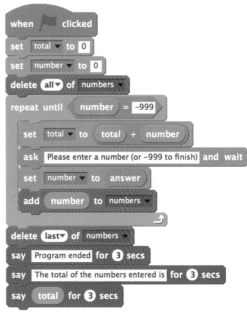

Figure 2.45

Note that this example shows a simple condition.

Program implementation based on algorithm with test at start

 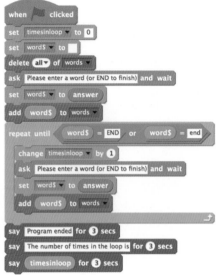

Figure 2.46

*Note that the code in a conditional loop with test at start need not be run at all if the condition is not met.

*Note that this example shows a complex condition.

Scratch® example 9 is comparable to the other examples in different languages because the output produced from the same given input is identical. The loop structure looks different because the keywords used in the Scratch® language are different. The condition contained in the 'repeat until' block is tested at the start because the 'set' and 'add' blocks provide a value for the variable 'word$' before the loop begins.

Program implementation based on algorithm to read names and marks into two arrays

There is no DATA or EOD in Scratch, so this code simply puts the required data into the two lists as shown. Unlike some other languages, Scratch lists and their contents are visible on screen while the program is running.

Figure 2.47

Practical Tasks

1 Look back at the code examples on pages 57–96. Choose one of the languages and rewrite the code as suggested below.

Example numbers (correspond to text)

1) Change the code to allow three numbers to be added.

2) Change the pass mark to 12.

3) Change the loop counter to 10.

4) Change the code so that the user is asked to enter a name at the start.

5) Change the step value to 4.

6) Change the values in the loop to create a larger rectangle.

7) Change the terminating value to 'stop' instead of 'end'.

If none of the examples shown in the book matches the computer language that you are familiar with, try changing the examples into your preferred language before attempting the changes suggested above.

2 Write algorithms for the following problem outlines, showing refinements as appropriate:

a) Take in a first name and a second name and display them.

b) Calculate the area of a circle given the radius as input (πr^2).

c) Take in 10 test marks and calculate the average mark.

d) Take in a sentence and display it 50 times.

e) Take in a name and ask the user how many times the name is to be displayed, and then display the name.

f) Take in five names using a loop with a terminating value.

g) A pass or fail algorithm for up to 20 pupils' marks.

h) Input validation for months 1–12 with a suitable message.

i) A quiz with 10 questions and a score at the end.

j) Calculate the result of doubling a number 10 times. The number should start at 1.

k) The number of weeds on a football pitch doubles every month. If there are 200 weeds today, how many weeds will there be in a year?

l) You have a bank account with £100 in it. How much money will you have in 10 years if the annual interest is 5%?

3 Make a translation table for one of the examples shown in this chapter. Choose one language that you are familiar with and one that you are not. Use pseudocode in the first column and write your explanation of what is happening in another column.

Over the page is a table comparing three languages used in the *Program implementation based on algorithm to add two numbers* example on page 57.

PSEUDOCODE	C	LiveCode®	My explanation
	int numberOne, numberTwo, total;	global number_one, number_two, total	tells the computer the types of variables in use
SET number_one TO 0 SET number_two TO 0 SET total TO 0	numberOne = numberTwo = total = 0;	put 0 into number_one put 0 into number_two	puts the starting values into each of the variables
SEND "Enter first number" TO DISPLAY	printf ("Please enter the first number ? ");	ask "Please enter the first number"	asks for a number
RECEIVE **first_number** FROM KEYBOARD	scanf("%d",&numberOne);	put it into number_one	stores the number in one variable
SEND "Enter second number" TO DISPLAY	printf ("Please enter the second number ? ");	ask "Please enter the second number"	asks for another number
RECEIVE **second_ number** FROM KEYBOARD	scanf("%d",&numberTwo);	put it into number_two	stores the number in a second variable
SET **total** TO first_ number + second_ number	total = numberOne + numberTwo;	put (number_one + number_two) into total	adds the contents of the two variables and places the answer in a third variable
SEND **total** TO DISPLAY	printf ("The total is %d",total);	put "The total is" &&total into field "output"	displays the contents of the third variable (total) on the screen

Questions

Computational constructs and data types and structures (National 4 and 5)

1 What is a program?

2 Name two types of computer languages.

3 What are computational constructs?

4 What is computational thinking?

5 What is an algorithm?

6 State the term used for
  a) looking at and understanding a problem.
  b) working out a series of steps to solve a problem.

  c) changing a design into a program.
  d) checking to find whether a program contains mistakes.
  e) describing what each part of a program does.
  f) using everyday language to describe the design of a program.

7 What is a variable?

8 Name two data types.

9 What is string data?

10 What is numeric (integer) data?

11 What is character data?

12 What is numeric (real) data?

13 What is Boolean data?

14 What is a graphical object?

15 State one example of a programming language which uses graphical objects.

16 State one example of an input statement and one example of an output statement using any programming language with which you are familiar.

17 What is an assignment statement used for?

18 Write assignment statements for your name and age using a high-level language.

19 What is an
a) operation?
b) object?

20 Name two operations used in programming.

21 Which types of operations produce an answer of true or false?

22 Which type of operation uses 'NOT'?

23 Which type of operation uses 'MOD'?

24 State two relational operators.

25 Write a condition which tests
a) if the word "test" is entered
b) if a mark is at least 20
c) if a counter is 0

using any programming language with which you are familiar.

26 What is concatenation?

27 What name is given to selecting parts of strings?

28 Look at the following statement in a programming language:

   total = first_number + second_number

What would the value total hold if first_number = 18, second_number = 20, and
a) first_number, second_number and total are numeric variables?
b) first_number, second_number and total were all string variables?

29 Name three control structures.

30 Which control structure means
a) the order in which things are done?
b) making a choice?
c) doing something over and over again?

31 State one example of a conditional statement.

32 a) State one example of a simple *condition*.
b) State one example of a complex *condition*.

33 Explain why a *condition* and a *control structure* are both necessary for selection.

34 Which construct is used to allow a process to be repeated?

35 Which type of loop has no limits?

36 Which type of loop has limits?

37 Explain the purpose of a fixed loop.

38 Explain how a fixed loop may be controlled.

39 What is the purpose of the STEP command?

40 What name is given to a loop which is inside another loop?

41 What is the purpose of a conditional loop?

42 State one advantage of using a conditional loop structure instead of a fixed loop.

43 State one advantage of using *test at start* as opposed to *test at end* in a conditional loop structure.

44 a) What is the purpose of a *terminating value*?
b) Give an example of an algorithm where such a value is used.

45 What is an array?

46 Each part of an array is called an element. Explain how each element in an array may be identified.

47 Explain how you could tell if an array is one-dimensional (1-D).

48 Why is it necessary to declare the use of an array at the start of a program?

49 What is a subprogram?

50 Name two types of subprogram.

51 What is the difference between a *procedure* and a *function*?

52 What is a pre-defined function?

53 State one example of a pre-defined function.

54 What is a parameter?

Key Points

- The set of instructions that control how a computer works is called a program.

- Programs are written in computer languages.

- Two types of computer language are machine code and high-level language.

- Machine code is the computer's own language.

- Machine code is written in binary using only the numbers 1 and 0.

- A computer language that uses normal or everyday language is called a high-level language.

- Computational constructs are the parts of a programming language, which are used to create a computer program.

- Computational thinking is thinking of a problem in such a way that makes it possible to solve it by using a computer system.

- A series of steps to solve a problem is called an algorithm.

- Analysis is looking at and understanding a problem.

- Design is working out a series of steps to solve a problem.

- Implementation is turning a design into a computer program.

- Testing makes sure that a computer program does not contain any mistakes.

- Documentation is a description of what each part of the program does.

- Pseudocode uses normal or everyday language to describe the design of a program.

- A variable is the name that a programmer uses to identify the contents of a storage location.

- A character is a symbol, letter or number on the computer keyboard.

- String data is a list of characters, for example a word in a sentence, or someone's name.

- Numeric (real) data – includes *all* numbers, both whole and fractional.

- Integer data includes only whole numbers.

- Boolean data has only two values, TRUE and FALSE.

- A graphical object is an image which is displayed on the screen as part of a computer program.

- Data which is to be processed by a computer program, must first be input, or taken into that program.

- The output feature may be used to display the results from a program.

- An assignment statement is used to give a value to a variable.

- An operation is a process which is carried out on an item of data.

- An object is the item of data which is involved in the process.

- Arithmetical operations are calculations involving numbers.

- The set of arithmetic operators includes: add (+), subtract (−), multiply (∗), divide (/), exponent (^) and modulus (MOD).

- Relational operations use relational operators to compare data and produce an answer of true or false.

- The set of relational operators includes: equals (=), greater than (>), less than (<), greater than or equal to (>=), less than or equal to (<=) and is not equal to (≠ OR <>).

- The set of logical operators includes: AND, OR and NOT.

- String operations include joining strings, known as concatenation, and selecting parts of strings, known as substrings.

- Sequence means the order in which things are done.

- Selection means making a choice or deciding something.

- Selection is based on one or more conditions, used together with a control structure such as IF.

- The control structure IF is known as a conditional statement.

- The IF structure is suitable for use when a single selection (or a limited number of selections) is to be made.

- A loop is a programming construct, which is used to allow a process to take place over and over again.

- Loops may be either fixed or conditional.
- The purpose of a fixed loop is to repeat a set of program statements for a predetermined number of times.
- The purpose of a conditional loop is to manage the situation where the number of times repetition must take place is not known in advance.
- There are two types of conditional loop: test at start and test at end.
- The program statement(s) inside a conditional loop with test at start *may not be run at all* if the test condition is not met.
- The program statement(s) inside a conditional loop with test at end *is always run at least once*.
- A terminating value or sentinel value is often used to end a conditional loop.
- An array is a list of data items *of the same type* grouped together using a single variable name.
- Each part of an array is called an element.
- Each element in an array is identified by the variable name and a subscript.
- Arrays which have one number as their subscript are called one-dimensional arrays.
- When a program is designed and written, it is divided into smaller sections called subprograms.
- High-level procedural languages use two types of subprograms: procedures and functions.
- A procedure produces an effect in a program.
- A function is similar to a procedure, but returns a single value to a program.
- A pre-defined function is a calculation which is built in to a programming language.
- A parameter is information about a data item being supplied to a subprogram when it is called into use.

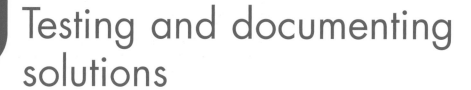

CHAPTER 3 Testing and documenting solutions

This chapter describes:

- normal, extreme and exceptional test data
- readability of code (internal commentary, meaningful variable names)

- syntax, execution and logic errors in programs
- readability of code (internal commentary, meaningful identifiers, indentation).

Normal, extreme and exceptional test data

To make sure that your program actually solves the problem it is supposed to, you have to **test** it. Testing a program means that you have to run it to see whether or not it behaves as expected.

Test data

One method of testing a program is to use a set of **data** called **test data**. It would take far too long to test a program for all possible sets of test data, so you have to choose a representative set of data. If the program works correctly for the test data, then you can be reasonably certain that the program will work for other similar data.

There are three different types of test data: **normal**, **extreme** and **exceptional**.

The best way to use test data is to calculate what the answer will be if your program works properly, *before* you run the program. Then, run the program with the test data. If the results from the program match the answers you got from your manual calculation, the program is probably correct.

Another way of testing a program is to get someone else to do it for you! By the time you've finished writing your program, you're usually so familiar with the program code you've written that you can't see any mistakes. Someone else looking at it might be able to spot mistakes that you've missed.

Let's look at a problem which will help you to understand what is meant by normal, extreme and exceptional test data.

Average problem

Write a program which takes in up to 10 integers (or whole numbers), ranging in value from 0 to 100 and then calculates the average correct to two decimal places.

Suppose you have written a program, which solves this problem, and you are getting ready to test your program.

Examples of test data

Normal – the program should accept this data:

Data	Expected Output
45,86,93,4,23,67,43	Average = 51.57
90,10,78,89,54,34,17,66,98	Average = 59.56

Normal data is data which is within the limits that your program should be able to deal with.

Extreme – the program should accept this data:

Data	Expected Output
1,100,0	Average = 33.67
1,100	Average = 50.50
100,100	Average = 100.00
1,1	Average = 1.00
0,0	Average = 0.00
1	Average = 1.00
0	Average = 0.00

Extreme data is data which is at the ends of the acceptable **range** of data, on the limit(s) or boundaries of the problem.

Exceptional – the program should reject this data:

Data	Possible error message
-1	Out of range, please enter a whole number between 0 and 100
101	Out of range, please enter a whole number between 0 and 100
0.2	Not a whole number, please enter a whole number between 0 and 100
number	Not a number, please enter a whole number between 0 and 100

Exceptional data is data which is invalid. A well-written program should be able to detect any exceptional data, warn the user of the error, and give them another chance to enter the data. Sometimes it is possible to reduce the chance of error messages caused by invalid data appearing in your program. A well-written program should **validate** all user input. See Chapter 4 for some examples of **input validation**.

Depending on the problem you've been asked to solve, you might be given a set of test data to use, or you might have to make up your own. If you have to make up your own test data, you should try to choose a set of test data which includes normal, extreme and exceptional data. If your program doesn't produce the results you expect, you'll have to check through each line of the code for errors.

Figure 3.01 Test data

Creating a **table of test data** is a useful way of planning and recording the results of testing your program.

Test data	Type of test data	Expected output	Actual output	Action required
45,86,93,4,23,67,43	normal	Average = 51.57	Average = 51.57	None
90,10,78,89,54,34,17, 66,98	normal	Average = 59.56	Average = 59.56	None
1,100,0	extreme	Average = 50.50	Average = 50.50	None
100,100	extreme	Average = 100.00	Average = 100.00	None
1,1	extreme	Average = 1.00	Average = 1.00	None
0,0	extreme	Average = 0.00	Average = 0.00	None
1	extreme	Average = 1.00	Average = 1.00	None
0	extreme	Average = 0.00	Average = 0.00	None
−1	exceptional	Out of range, please enter a whole number between 0 and 100	Out of range, please enter a whole number between 0 and 100	Re-enter

Test data	Type of test data	Expected output	Actual output	Action required
101	exceptional	Out of range, please enter a whole number between 0 and 100	Out of range, please enter a whole number between 0 and 100	Re-enter
0.2	exceptional	Not a whole number, please enter a whole number between 0 and 100	Not a whole number, please enter a whole number between 0 and 100	Re-enter
number		Not a number, please enter a whole number between 0 and 100	Not a number, please enter a whole number between 0 and 100	Re-enter

Check Your Learning

Now answer questions 1–7 (on page 121) on test data (National 4).

Syntax, execution and logic errors in programs

Many different types of error can occur when you are programming.

Syntax errors

Syntax errors occur when the **syntax**, or rules of the programming language, are broken.

A statement syntax error is misspelling a **keyword**, like typing *PRUNT* instead of *PRINT* or *WRITLEN* instead of *WRITELN*.

A program or structure syntax error happens when you have made a mistake in the structure of your program, such as incorrect use of a **control structure**. This type of syntax error may be detected by examining or proofreading a structured listing.

Example of incorrect use of a control structure

```
FOR counter := 1 to 10 DO
      For times:= 1 to 7 DO
        PRINT times, counter
      NEXT times
```

Can you spot the mistake?

If you are using a **compiled language**, you will find that it reports both types of syntax errors only when the program is about to be compiled. An **interpreted language** usually reports statement syntax errors when the line containing the mistake is entered.

Execution or run-time errors

Execution or run-time **errors** are errors which show up during program execution. **Overflow**, rounding and **truncation** are types of error which are caused by a limited amount of **memory** either in the computer (e.g. a fixed amount of space to store numbers) or decided by the **programmer** (e.g. a DIM statement). **Division by zero** is another typical run-time error.

Overflow is a general term which describes what happens when something becomes too large to be processed accurately. For example, the result of a calculation may become too large to be stored in the space the computer has for numbers. The error which caused the loss of the Ariane space rocket on 4 June 1996 was an example of an overflow error. The program tried to put a 64-**bit** number into a memory location capable of holding only 16 bits.

Rounding happens when a number is reduced to a given number of decimal places, for instance 3.89 may be rounded up to 3.9. A rounding error is an error caused by rounding (+0.01) in this case.

Truncation means shortening a number to a given number of decimal places. If the number 3.89 in the example above was truncated to one decimal place it would become 3.8. The truncation error would amount to −0.09 in this case.

Division by zero may be caused by incorrect validation of an input variable or a result of a calculation. Division by zero will normally cause a program to **crash** if it is allowed to occur.

Logic(al) errors

Logical errors are mistakes in the design of the program. Logical errors only show up when you run the program and you can spot them because the program does not do what it is supposed to do, for instance, it produces the wrong results.

Example of a logic error in part of a program written in the COMAL® language

```
counter := 0
REPEAT
        counter := counter+1
UNTIL counter = 0
```

Can you explain what will happen when this part of the program is run?

Check Your Learning   Now answer questions 8–14 (on page 121) on program errors (National 5).

Readability of code

Internal commentary / documentation

Internal commentary or **documentation** is so-called because it is contained inside the program itself, as part of the language statements.

For example:

> REM This is a REMark in the BASIC language
>
> // This is an example of a comment statement in COMAL and in LiveCode
>
> { PASCAL comments have curly brackets }
>
> /* Allows comments in the **C** programming language */

Internal documentation is sometimes called internal commentary because the programmer is commenting or remarking on what the code is doing at different stages throughout the program. You can put as many comment lines as you like in your program – they don't have any effect when the program is run.

Adding internal commentary to your programs can be a chore, especially if you are in a hurry to get the program finished and working. However, it is very useful if you, or someone else, has to look back at your program at any time in the future.

All of the programs which you write should have internal commentary. At the very least, there should be several statements at the beginning of each program which tell the user the program name, the filename under which the program is stored, the author's name and the date when the program was written, like this:

> { Average program }
>
> { Saved as AVERAGE }
>
> { Written by Cecilia }
>
> { 3 March 2019 }

In general, the more detailed the internal commentary, the easier it will be for you (or someone else) to revisit your program at some time in the future (perhaps in order to **update** the program) and understand what each line of program code is actually doing.

Meaningful variable names

A **variable** is the name that a program uses to identify a **storage location** in the computer's memory. A variable name may be as short as a single letter of the alphabet. Most **high-level languages** do not allow variable names to *begin with* numbers or symbols, although the names may contain symbols (but not spaces). For instance, a $ sign is used at the end of a variable name to identify it as a **string variable** (such as name$) in some languages.

One other general rule for variable names is that they must not be the same as any of the keywords in the high-level language that is being used. For instance, a program in the BASIC language could not use the word PRINT as the name of a variable.

Look at the following program:

```
x := 0
y := 0
REPEAT
x := x + y
INPUT y
UNTIL y = 0
PRINT x
```

It is not easy to understand what this program is doing because the variables in the program are all single letters. A **meaningful variable name** contains one or more words which describe it.

If this program had meaningful variable names, then it would look like this one:

```
total := 0
number := 0
REPEAT
total := total + number
INPUT number
UNTIL number = 0
PRINT total
```

Using meaningful variable names is a good way of improving the **readability** of a program. Other examples of meaningful variable names use underscore **characters** (_) or so-called CamelCase to link more than one word together, like this:

number_of_mini_beasts = area_of_quadrat * density_of_observers

WholeName = FirstName && SecondName

One other advantage of the use of meaningful variable names is that the programmer is less likely to make mistakes when writing a program using words (which could easily become mixed up) compared to single letters.

Check Your Learning

Now answer questions 15–19 (on page 122) on readability of code (National 4).

Meaningful identifiers

An identifier is a name used for any part of a program, such as the name of a subprogram or sub-routine (**procedure** or **function**) and not just limited to variable names. Here are some examples:

> *PROC initialise*
>
> *Private SUB Button_To_Press*
>
> *FUNC area_of_circle*

The advantages of the use of **meaningful identifiers** are the same as those described for meaningful variable names.

Indentation

A **program listing** is a printout or **hard copy** of the program code. A structured listing is a program listing which uses **indentations** (formatting) to show some of the structure of the program. Program structures such as the beginning and end of procedures, control structures such as **loops** and decisions are usually all indented in a structured listing.

In addition to this, a structured listing may also highlight language keywords and variable names in some way. One form of highlighting keywords and variable names is to put the keywords into upper-case lettering (capitals) and the variable names into lower-case letters. Some software development environments, for instance **LiveCode**® uses different colours in its structured listings.

Indenting program structures in this way has two main advantages:

1 You can see at a glance where each of the program control structures begins and ends. This makes it easy to understand the structure of each part of the program.
2 You are more likely to be able to spot mistakes in the program when you examine a structured listing as opposed to one which is unstructured. The indentations which form the control structures move to the right at the start of each control structure, and return to the same relative position at the end of the control structure. The highlighting of keywords and variables also helps you to spot mistakes, since you can see at a

glance if the keywords and variables have been entered correctly. You can see some examples of structured listings in Figure 3.02.

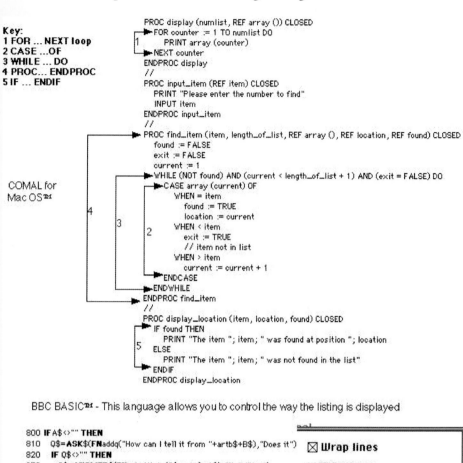

```
Key:
1 FOR ... NEXT loop
2 CASE ... OF
3 WHILE ... DO
4 PROC... ENDPROC
5 IF ... ENDIF
```

COMAL for Mac OS™

```
PROC display (numlist, REF array ()) CLOSED
  FOR counter := 1 TO numlist DO
    PRINT array (counter)
  NEXT counter
ENDPROC display
//
PROC input_item (REF item) CLOSED
  PRINT "Please enter the number to find"
  INPUT item
ENDPROC input_item
//
PROC find_item (item, length_of_list, REF array (), REF location, REF found) CLOSED
  found := FALSE
  exit := FALSE
  current := 1
  WHILE (NOT found) AND (current < length_of_list + 1) AND (exit = FALSE) DO
    CASE array (current) OF
      WHEN = item
        found := TRUE
        location := current
      WHEN < item
        exit := TRUE
        // item not in list
      WHEN > item
        current := current + 1
    ENDCASE
  ENDWHILE
ENDPROC find_item
//
PROC display_location (item, location, found) CLOSED
  IF found THEN
    PRINT "The item "; item; " was found at position "; location
  ELSE
    PRINT "The item "; item; " was not found in the list"
  ENDIF
ENDPROC display_location
```

BBC BASIC™ - This language allows you to control the way the listing is displayed

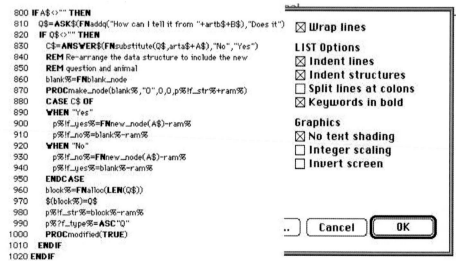

```
800  IF A$<>"" THEN
810    Q$=ASK$(FNaddq("How can I tell it from "+artb$+B$),"Does it")
820    IF Q$<>"" THEN
830      C$=ANSWER$(FNsubstitute(Q$,arta$+A$),"No","Yes")
840      REM Re-arrange the data structure to include the new
850      REM question and animal
860      blank%=FNblank_node
870      PROCmake_node(blank%,"O",0,0,p%!f_str%+ram%)
880      CASE C$ OF
890        WHEN "Yes"
900          p%!f_yes%=FNnew_node(A$)-ram%
910          p%!f_no%=blank%-ram%
920        WHEN "No"
930          p%!f_no%=FNnew_node(A$)-ram%
940          p%!f_yes%=blank%-ram%
950      ENDCASE
960      block%=FNalloc(LEN(Q$))
970      $(block%)=Q$
980      p%!f_str%=block%-ram%
990      p%?f_type%=ASC"Q"
1000     PROCmodified(TRUE)
1010   ENDIF
1020 ENDIF
```

☒ **Wrap lines**

LIST Options
☒ **Indent lines**
☒ **Indent structures**
☐ **Split lines at colons**
☒ **Keywords in bold**

Graphics
☒ **No text shading**
☐ **Integer scaling**
☐ **Invert screen**

(..) (Cancel) (OK)

Figure 3.02 Structured listings

Check Your Learning

Now answer questions 20–23 (on page 122) on meaningful identifiers and indentation (National 5).

Practical Tasks

1 a) Use a word-processing (or other suitable application) package to create a table of test data, like this one.

Type of test data	Data	Expected result	Actual result	Action required
Normal	5,6	30	11	Check arithmetic formula in program
Extreme	1,10	10	11	Check arithmetic formula in program
Exceptional	0	Number outwith range	Number outwith range	None

b) Look at the column headings in the table you have created. Which of these columns should you complete

i) before testing a program?

ii) after testing a program?

c) Look at the example test data and the results of testing in the table in part a), and see if you can spot what is wrong with the part of the program which is being tested.

d) Choose one of the Practical Tasks questions on page 107 in Chapter 2 and use a table to help create test data for the problem.

Questions

Test data (National 4)

1 Why does a program need to be tested?

2 State one method of testing a program.

3 Why should you choose only a representative set of test data?

4 Name the three different types of test data.

5 What should be done before testing a program with test data?

6 Name the test data which a program should
a) accept.
b) reject.

7 What does creating a table of test data help a programmer to do?

Program errors (National 5)

8 What is a syntax error?

9 State one example of a syntax error.

10 When are syntax errors usually reported in
a) an interpreted language?
b) a compiled language?

11 When do execution errors show up in a program?

12 Name two execution errors.

13 What name is given to mistakes in program design?

14 State one example of a logical error (use code or pseudocode for your answer).

Questions *continued*

Readability of code (National 4)

15 What is internal commentary?

16 Why is internal commentary useful?

17 What is a variable?

Meaningful identifiers and indentation (National 5)

20 What is the difference between a variable name and an identifier?

21 What is the purpose of indentation?

18 What is a meaningful variable name?

19 State one advantage of using meaningful variable names compared with using single letters.

22 What type of listing shows indentation?

23 State two advantages of using indentation in program listings.

Key Points

- Programs should be tested to check that they work properly with no mistakes.
- Test data is used to test a program.
- There are three different types of test data: normal, extreme and exceptional.
- Normal data is data which is within the limits that a program should be able to deal with.
- Extreme data is data which is at the ends of the acceptable range of data, on the limit(s) or boundaries of the problem.
- Exceptional data is data which is invalid.
- To use test data correctly, the answer should be calculated before running the program and the results compared.
- Using a table of test data is a useful way of planning and recording the results of testing a program.
- Syntax errors occur when the syntax, or rules of the programming language are broken.
- Execution or run-time errors are errors which show up during program execution.
- Execution errors include overflow, rounding, truncation and division by zero.
- Logical errors are mistakes in the design of the program.

- Internal commentary or documentation is so called because it is contained inside the program itself, as part of the language statements.
- Internal commentary has no effect on the running of a program.
- Internal commentary helps to explain what the code is doing throughout the program.
- A variable is the name that a program uses to identify a storage location in the computer's memory.
- A meaningful variable name contains one or more words which describe it.
- Using meaningful variable names is a good way of improving the readability of a program.
- An identifier is a name used for any part of a program, such as the name of a subprogram or sub-routine (procedure or function) and not just limited to variable names.
- A program listing is a printout or hard copy of the program code.
- A structured listing is a program listing which uses indentations (formatting) to show some of the structure of the program.
- Indenting program structures can help to show where each of the program control structures begins and ends and makes it easier to spot mistakes.

CHAPTER 4

Algorithm specification

This chapter describes exemplification and implementation of algorithms, including input validation.

What is an algorithm?

An **algorithm** is a **sequence** of instructions that can be used to solve a problem. Algorithms which are in common use in programming are known as **standard algorithms**.

Some examples of standard algorithms include **input validation**; finding maximum and minimum; counting occurrences and various types of **search**.

This chapter is all about the input validation algorithm. You should know about it in some detail, and be able to implement it in a **high-level language**.

What is input validation?

Input validation is the process of checking that the input is acceptable or within a certain **range**. Some form of **validation** is required when checking user input to a program.

For example:

- valid dates in the year 2019 could range from 1/1/2019 to 31/12/2019
- ages of students in the fourth year at school might have a range of 14 to 16 years
- checking that numbers in a list are all within a certain range, e.g. 0 to 100 marks in a test
- checking that **text** input is correct, only accepting "Y" OR "y" OR "N" OR "n".

A well-written program should validate all user input.

Input validation algorithms

There is a variety of possible input validation algorithms:

```
1.    REPEAT
2.        SEND "Please enter data" TO DISPLAY
3.        RECEIVE data FROM KEYBOARD
4.    UNTIL data is within range
```

This is not very **user friendly**, since it does not give any indication to the user of what might be wrong with any rejected input. The user may think that they are entering a list of **data** rather than being repeatedly asked to re-enter an invalid item. Adding an **IF** statement makes this algorithm more useful.

```
1.    REPEAT
2.       SEND "Please enter data" TO DISPLAY
3.       RECEIVE data FROM KEYBOARD
4.         IF data is outwith range THEN SEND "Please re-enter data" TO DISPLAY
5.    UNTIL data is within range
```

Or, alternatively, enter the data first, and if the user correctly **inputs** the valid data on the first occasion, the validation **loop** need not be entered at all:

```
1.    SEND "Please enter data" TO DISPLAY
2.    RECEIVE data FROM KEYBOARD
3.    WHILE data is outwith range
4.        SEND "Please re-enter data" TO DISPLAY
5.        RECEIVE data FROM KEYBOARD
6.    END WHILE
```

It is this last version of the algorithm which is implemented in this chapter.

Some high-level languages automatically provide some form of input validation. For instance, entering a string (text value) into a **variable** designed to accept a numeric input will provide the user with an error message, like this:

```
Please enter a number
? w
Bad value.
? 1.2
```

The input validation algorithm is implemented in **COMAL**®, **True BASIC**®, **Visual Basic**® and **LiveCode**®.

COMAL® implementation

```
// Title : COMAL Example 1.1
// Author : John Walsh
// Date : 14 June 2000
//
PRINT "Please enter a number in the range 1-10"
INPUT number
WHILE number < 1 OR number > 10 DO
    PRINT "The number you have entered is outwith the range 1-10 Please re-enter"
    INPUT number
ENDWHILE
PRINT "The number entered was "; number
END
```

Sample Output

```
Please enter a number in the range 1-10
? 1
The number entered was 1
Please enter a number in the range 1-10
? 10
The number entered was 10
Please enter a number in the range 1-10
? 5
The number entered was 5
Please enter a number in the range 1-10
? 0
The number you have entered is outwith the range 1-10 Please re-enter
? 3
The number entered was 3
```

TrueBASIC® implementation

```
! Title : TrueBASIC Example 1.1
! Author : John Walsh
! Date : 14 June 2000
!
PRINT "Please enter a number in the range 1-10"
INPUT number
DO WHILE (number < 1) OR (number > 10)
    PRINT "The number you have entered is outwith the range 1-10 Please re-enter"
    INPUT number
LOOP
PRINT "The number entered was "; number
END
```

● Sample Output

```
Please enter a number in the range 1-10
? 1
The number entered was 1
Please enter a number in the range 1-10
? 10
The number entered was 10
Please enter a number in the range 1-10
? 5
The number entered was 5
Please enter a number in the range 1-10
? 0
The number you have entered is outwith the range 1-10 Please re-enter
? 3
The number entered was 3
```

Visual Basic® implementation

```
'Title : Visual Basic Example 1.1
'Author : John Walsh
'Date : 14 June 2000
'

Option Explicit
Dim number As Integer

Private Sub cmdEnterNumbers_Click()
'picDisplay.Cls
number = InputBox('Please enter a number in the range 1–10')
Do While (number < 1) Or (number > 10)
number = InputBox("The number you have entered is outwith the range 1–10 Please
re-enter")
Loop
picDisplay.Print "The number entered was "; number
End Sub

Private Sub cmdEnd_Click()
picDisplay.Cls
End
End Sub
```

Sample Output

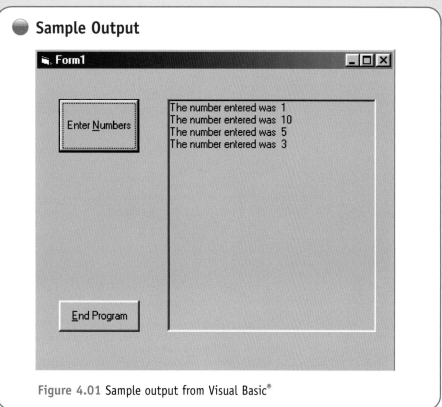

Figure 4.01 Sample output from Visual Basic®

LiveCode® implementation

```
// Title: LiveCode Input Validation
// Author: John Walsh
// Date: 11 June 2013

global number_entered
on mouseUp
    put 0 into number_entered
    ask"Please enter a number in the range 1-10"
    if the result = "Cancel" then exit to top
    put it into number_entered
    put number_entered & return into line 1 of field "output"
    repeat while (number_entered<1) or (number_entered>10)
        put"The number you entered was outwith the range 1-10 Please re-enter"
        into line 1 of field "output"
        ask"Please enter a number in the range 1-10"
        if the result = "Cancel" then exit to top
        put it into number_entered
    end repeat
    put "The number entered was "&& number_entered & return into line 1 of
    field "output"
end mouseUp
```

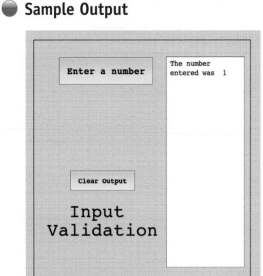

Sample Output

Enter a number

The number entered was 1

Clear Output

Input Validation

Figure 4.02 Sample output from LiveCode®

Check Your Learning

Now answer questions 1–4 (on page 129) on algorithm specification (National 5).

Practical Tasks

1 Look back at the first two algorithms at the beginning of this chapter, whose implementations are not shown here. Implement these algorithms using a high-level programming language.

2 Create a new program which only allows the words: "Yes" or "No" to be entered.

3 Choose one of the examples shown in this chapter and add a counter to the program which adds up the number of times the user had to enter a number before it was valid.

Questions

Algorithm specification (National 5)

1 At which stage in software development is an algorithm produced?

2 Why does the input validation algorithm use a conditional (REPEAT / WHILE) rather than an unconditional (FOR) loop structure?

3 a) Which design notation is used to represent the algorithms in this chapter?

b) Suggest why this design notation was chosen.

4 Choose one of the input validation algorithms from this chapter and show how it would be represented using a graphical design notation.

Key Point

- An input validation algorithm is used to check that data input is within a certain (acceptable) range.

Design notations

This chapter describes the following design notations.

- graphical to illustrate selection and iteration
- other contemporary design notations

- pseudocode to exemplify programming constructs
- other contemporary design notations

What is design?

Program design is the process of planning the solution. The design of the program is very important for its success. Time spent at this stage is very worthwhile and can reduce the chance of errors appearing later on in the solution. What the program designer is trying to achieve is to produce an **algorithm**, which is the name given to a set of instructions used to solve a problem. Design is the second step in the **software development process**, following **analysis**.

What is design notation?

The way of representing the program design or algorithm is called the **design notation**. The **programmer** has a choice of design notations.

We will use the Average problem from Chapter 3 to provide examples of design notation. Here is a quick reminder:

Write a program which takes in up to 10 integers (or whole numbers), ranging in value from 0 to 100 and then calculates the average correct to two decimal places.

Graphical design notation to illustrate selection and iteration

What is graphical design notation?

Graphical design notations (GDN) use shapes to describe a design. Graphical design notations include **flow charts**, **structure diagrams** and **storyboards**. You can see some examples of **selection** and **iteration/repetition** opposite. Note that repetition and iteration are terms which are both used to refer to a **loop** in programming. This book makes no distinction between repetition and iteration.

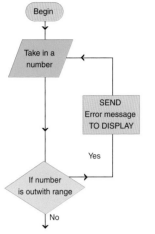

Figure 5.01 Flow chart example

Flow charts

A flow chart may be used to represent a program or a system. Flow charts use diagrams made up of differently shaped boxes connected with arrows to show each step in a program.

The flow chart on the left uses a graphical design notation to show selection and iteration. In this case, the program keeps taking in a number until the number is within a range. If the number is outwith the range, an error message is displayed.

Structure diagrams

Structure diagrams, like flow charts, use linked boxes to represent the different sub-problems within a program. The boxes in a structure diagram are organised to show the level of each sub-problem within the solution.

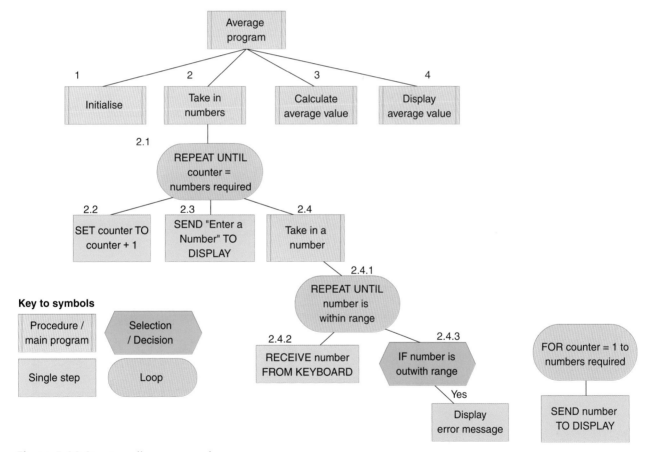

Figure 5.02 Structure diagram examples

Storyboards

A storyboard is a series of still drawings that maps out a proposed story over a number of separate panels. Storyboards are widely used in film and **animation** as well as **software** and information system development. You can see examples of different storyboards in Figure 5.03.

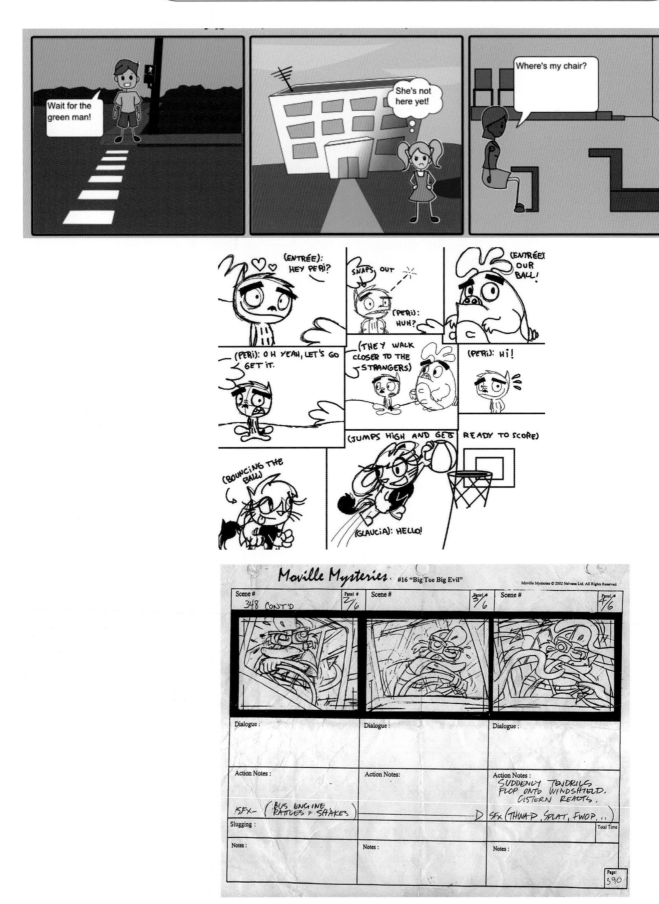

Figure 5.03 Storyboard examples

Storyboards have several advantages over other graphical design notations. They are an effective way of showing users how software will work once it has been written. It is possible to check the proposed navigational links on a storyboard. It is also much less expensive to edit a storyboard than a completed software application.

However, a storyboard does not relate directly to, or help to explain the function of, any code required to operate the software, apart from **hyperlinks**.

Other contemporary design notations

Wireframe

A **wireframe** is a diagram or sketch used to represent the appearance and function of a **website**. A wireframe contains details on the position of each element of the page content, such as placeholders for text and **graphics**, **navigation** buttons or hyperlinks. Wireframes are an important part of the design process for a website.

A wireframe may consist of just a basic outline which is hand-drawn (so-called low-fidelity) or a more detailed diagram, often created using dedicated software (high-fidelity), which closely resembles the **web page** in appearance and function. You can see a low-fidelity wireframe and the finished website below.

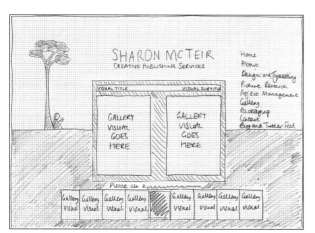
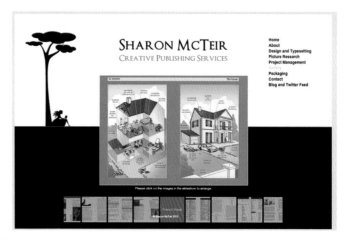

Figure 5.04 Wireframe examples

Check Your Learning

Now answer questions 1–10 (on page 137) on design notation (National 4).

Pseudocode design notation to exemplify programming constructs

What is Pseudocode?

Pseudocode is the name given to the language used to define problems and sub-problems before they are changed into code in a **high-level computer language**. Pseudocode uses ordinary English terms rather than the special programming language **keywords** used in high-level languages. Pseudocode is a form of **textual design notation** (**TDN**).

Here is some pseudocode showing part of the design of one possible solution to the Average problem. Compare this pseudocode with the structure diagram in Figure 5.02, which shows the design of a solution to the same problem.

Algorithm or main steps

```
1.    initialise
2.    take in numbers
3.    calculate average value
4.    display average value
```

Refine sub-problem 2

```
2.1    REPEAT
2.2        SET counter TO counter + 1
2.3        SEND "Enter a number" TO DISPLAY
2.4        take in a number
2.5    UNTIL counter = numbers required
```

Refine sub-problem 2.4

```
2.4.1  REPEAT
2.4.2  RECEIVE number FROM KEYBOARD
2.4.3     IF number is outwith range THEN display error message
2.4.4  UNTIL number is within range
```

Pseudocode is very useful when you are programming in languages like BASIC®, COMAL® or LiveCode®, because it fits in neatly with the structure of the code. The **main steps** in the algorithm relate directly to (in fact become) the main program and the **refinements** of each sub-problem become the code in the **procedures**. Table 5.01 shows the standardised pseudocode terms which are used in this book. You can look at many more examples of pseudocode in Chapter 2.

Table of standardised pseudocode terms

TERM	REFERS TO
INTEGER	whole number
REAL	whole or fractional number
BOOLEAN	true or false
CHARACTER	letter, symbol or number
ARRAY	set of data items of the same type/structured
STRING	array of characters
DISPLAY	output device
KEYBOARD	input device
SET ... TO ...	assign value
IF ... THEN ... ELSE ... END IF	conditional statement
WHILE ... DO ... END WHILE	conditional loop
REPEAT ... UNTIL	conditional loop
REPEAT ... TIMES ... END REPEAT	fixed loop/unconditional
FOR ... FROM ... TO ... DO ... END FOR	fixed loop/unconditional
FOR ... EACH ... FROM ... DO ... END FOREACH	fixed loop/unconditional
RECEIVE ... FROM ...	input from device, e.g. keyboard
SEND ... TO ...	output to device, e.g. display
ARITHMETICAL OPERATIONS	(-, +, *, /, ^, mod, &)
RELATIONAL OPERATIONS	(=, ≠, <, <=, >, >=)
LOGICAL OPERATIONS	(AND, OR, NOT)
id/identifier	variable name or subprogram
parameter	value to be supplied to a subprogram
length	subprogram returning the length of a string

Table 5.01 Standardised pseudocode terms

Other contemporary design notations

Unified Modelling Language (UML)

Figure 5.05 UML logo

Unified Modelling Language is a general purpose modelling language used to describe complete systems and not just software design. UML includes a variety of diagrams, known as structural and behavioural diagrams. Structural diagrams show the parts of a system being modelled. Behavioural diagrams show how the objects in a system interact with each other. There is a great deal more to UML than may be described in a single paragraph in this book. Two examples of UML diagrams are shown in Figures 5.06 and 5.07.

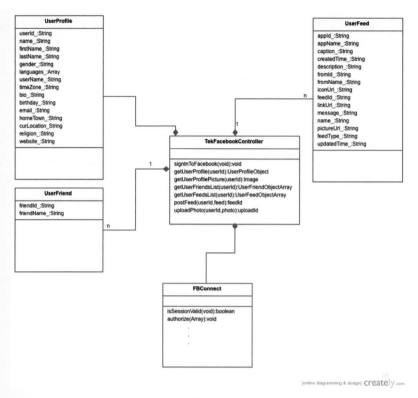

Figure 5.06 UML Structural (class) diagram example

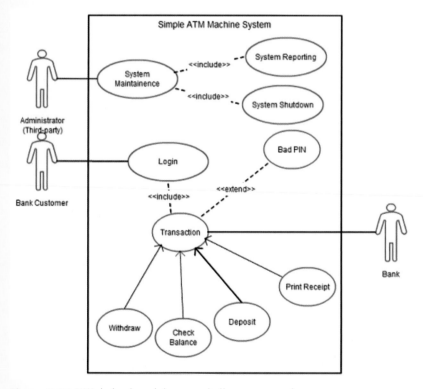

Figure 5.07 UML behavioural (use case) diagram example

Check Your Learning

Now answer questions 11–16 (on page 138) on design notation (National 5).

Practical Tasks

1 Using a graphical design notation of your own choice, write algorithms for the following problem outlines, showing refinements as appropriate:

   a) Calculate the square root of a number between 1 and 20.

   b) Calculate the circumference of a circle given the radius as input ($2\pi r$).

   c) Input validation for days 1–31 with a suitable message.

   d) A quiz with four questions and a second chance to get the correct answer after a hint is given.

   (Chapter 2 has more of the same type of question in the Practical Tasks section.)

2 Investigate online tools for creating design notations. Here are some URLs to get you started: www.storyboardthat.com and http://creately.com.

3 Have a look at www.wirify.com/, which uses a bookmark to turn any web page into a wireframe.

Questions

Design notation (National 4)

1 What is design?

2 What is an algorithm?

3 What is design notation?

4 Name and describe one design notation with which you are familiar.

5 What is Graphical Design Notation?

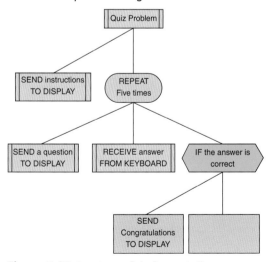

Figure 5.08 One type of design notation

6 a) Identify the type of design notation shown in Figure 5.08.
   b) Copy the design shown in Figure 5.08 and
      i) complete the empty box with a suitable message.
      ii) amend the design to include a score (of correct answers).

7 What is a storyboard?

8 If you were asked to design a software application, which design notation would you choose? Explain why you chose this design notation.

9 What is a wireframe?

10 What details may be contained in a wireframe?

National 5

Design notation (National 5)

11 What is pseudocode?

12 What language is used in pseudocode?

13 What makes pseudocode so useful when describing the design of a program?

14 Which pseudocode term is used to represent
   a) a variable containing a whole number?
   b) a variable containing true or false?
   c) an array of characters?
   d) a conditional statement?
   e) conditional repetition with test at start?
   f) conditional repetition with test at end?
   g) fixed repetition: iteration?
   h) input from a keyboard?
   i) assign a value?

15 What is UML?

16 Name two types of diagrams used in UML.

Key Points

- Program design is the process of planning the solution.

- The way of representing the program design or algorithm is called the design notation.

- Graphical design notations (GDN) use shapes to describe a design.

- Graphical design notations include flow charts, structure diagrams and storyboards.

- Flow charts use diagrams made up of differently shaped boxes connected with arrows to show each step in a program.

- Structure diagrams, like flow charts, use linked boxes to represent the different sub-problems within a program.

- The boxes in a structure diagram are organised to show the level of each sub-problem within the solution.

- A storyboard is a series of still drawings that maps out a proposed story over a number of separate panels.

- Storyboards have several advantages over other graphical design notations.

  - They show how software will work.

  - They may be used to check the links.

  - It is cheaper to edit a storyboard than a completed application.

- A wireframe is a diagram or sketch used to represent the appearance and function of a website.

- Pseudocode is the name given to the language used to define problems and sub-problems before they are changed into code in a high-level computer language.

- Pseudocode fits neatly with the structure of the code.

- The main steps in the algorithm become the main program and the refinements of each sub-problem become the code in the procedures.

- Unified Modelling Language is a general purpose modelling language used to describe complete systems and not just software design.

Unit 2

Information System Design and Development

The following eleven chapters each form part of the Information System Design and Development Unit.

Each chapter is designed to cover the contents statements as they are grouped within the Unit and Course descriptions for National 4 and National 5 Computing Science; namely Structures, links and testing, User interface, Media types, Coding, Purpose, features and functionality, users, Hardware and software requirements, Storage, Networking and Connectivity, Security risks and precautions, Legal implications and Environmental impact.

The topics described in this unit may be applicable to a range of information system types and contexts including databases, websites, games, mobile applications and kiosk systems.

The examples given in each chapter are based upon a range of hardware and software, which is current at the time of writing.

CHAPTER 6

Structures, links and testing

This chapter looks at structures, links and testing in database and web environments. The following topics are covered.

Database structures and links

- database structure: field, record, file
- field types (text, numbers, date, time, graphics, calculated)
- database operations (search, sort)

- database structure: flat file, linked tables, primary keys and foreign keys
- field types: object, link, Boolean
- database operations: search and sort on multiple fields
- validation (including presence check, restricted choice, field length and range)
- good design to avoid data duplication and modification errors (insert, delete, update)

Web-based structures and links

- website, page, URL
- hyperlinks

- hyperlinks: internal, external
- relative and absolute addressing
- navigation
- web browsers and search engines
- good design to aid navigation, usability and accessibility

Testing

- links and navigation
- matches user interface design

Note that this chapter is not an instruction manual for a particular database package. Your teacher or lecturer will provide you with material to suit the software you will be using.

What is a database?

Any large amount of **information** must be stored in some sort of order so that it can be accessed easily and quickly – a filing system is ideal for the job. Everyone uses filing systems, but they may not always be aware of them – cups, saucers and plates are probably 'filed' in a kitchen cupboard, newspapers might be 'filed' under a coffee table, socks might be 'filed' in a drawer in your bedroom.

A **database** is a structured collection of similar information, which you can **search** through. Databases can be stored *manually* (in a filing cabinet, or on index cards) or *electronically* using a computer system. Keeping your database on computer means that you can access the information much more easily and quickly than if you used the manual system – but the data must be organised in a way that allows speed of access. A program that is used for organising data on a computer system is called a **database package** or **database management system**.

The difference between **data** and information and the advantages of using computer-based information systems are discussed in Chapter 10.

Database structure

Data in a database is organised into **files, records** and **fields**. A file is a collection of structured data on a particular topic. Individual files are made up of records. A record is a collection of structured data on a particular person or thing. Each record is made up of one or more fields. A field is an area on a record, which contains an individual piece of data. Figure 6.01 shows more clearly how a database is structured.

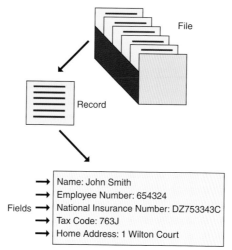

Figure 6.01 An example of a manual database. Computer databases use the same principles, storing individual items in fields, which together make up a record. A group of records is a file.

Example of a database

Look at a telephone directory. Each separate area in the directory – name, address, town and telephone number – is a *field*. The set of fields (that is, the whole address and phone number) for one person is a *record*. The set of records together – the whole **directory** – is a *file*. There are now many computer databases, which you can access to obtain telephone numbers, for example uk.yell.com.

Figure 6.02 Yell.com

Field types (data types)

When you open a database application, the first thing you must do is to create one or more fields to hold the information which you want to store. You should then choose the **field type** to suit the type of information that you wish to store. Field types include: **text**, numbers, **date**, **time**, **graphics**, **object** (N5), **calculated**, **link** (N5) and **Boolean** (N5). You may also specify the size of the field, for example the number of **characters** or digits.

Text

A text field is used to hold letters, numbers and symbols.

Numbers

A numeric field only stores numbers. The difference between storing a number in a numeric field and storing it in a text field is that a number in a text field may not be used in a calculation as part of a calculated field.

Date

Date fields can only contain dates. When the field is created, you can decide how the date is to be displayed, for example 18/02/54 or 18 February 2054.

Time

Time fields can hold hours, minutes and seconds. Note that the time is held as a time of day rather than a time interval. For instance, 17:28:00 instead of 55 minutes.

Graphics

A graphic field holds a picture. Some databases allow a graphic field to hold a **multimedia** file like a movie.

Object

An object field may contain a variety of different types of data, such as a presentation, **video**, spreadsheet, or a **bit-mapped graphic** file.

Calculated

A calculated field will carry out a calculation on another field or fields and give you an answer, like a formula in a spreadsheet. To explain this, think of a database that contains two fields, called *total pay* and *total deductions*. You could set up a third field, called *net pay*, with the formula (= *total pay* − *total deductions*). This is a calculated field. You can see other examples of calculated fields in Figure 6.03.

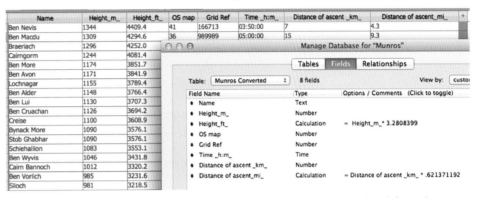

Figure 6.03 Calculated fields in a database. The height in feet is calculated from the height in metres. The distance in miles is calculated from the distance in kilometres.

Link

A link field contains a **hyperlink**, or **URL (Uniform Resource Locator)**. The hyperlink may be to another file, a document or a **web page**. Not all types of database package are capable of containing link fields.

Boolean

A Boolean field contains only two values, for instance, true or false, yes or no.

Database operations

Add and update records

Once you have created the basic record structure by deciding on the fields, the next step is to use the database package to enter information. At this point the database is empty, and you must add a new record for each item that you are going to enter. After the database has been completed, you may wish to **update** it if the information changes. In order to do this, you will have to update a record. Once you have located and altered the record, always remember to save the new version of the file.

Searching and sorting

Searching and **sorting** records are the two main reasons for using a database package. Depending on the database package in use, the commands **query** or find may be used instead of **search**. As far as this book is concerned, we will stick with 'search', since that is the term used by the SQA.

Search

Searching on one field

The search facility allows you to look through the database for information. To do this, you must enter the field that you want to search and the details that you want to find. This is called to 'search on a field' using whatever conditions you require. To give an example, you might be looking for items on your database with 'Height in metres greater than 5000'; here the field that you would be searching on is 'Height in metres' and the condition you want is 'greater than 5000'. Searching on one field using a single condition is called a simple search.

Relational operators are used to create search conditions. These are the same relational operators that we first met in Chapter 2.

Relational operators include:

<	less than
<=	less than or equal to
=	equal to
>	greater than
>=	greater than or equal to
≠ (or < >)	not equal to

Figure 6.04 shows how a simple search on one field can be carried out.

Figure 6.04a A (simple) search on one field in a database (Filemaker® Pro)

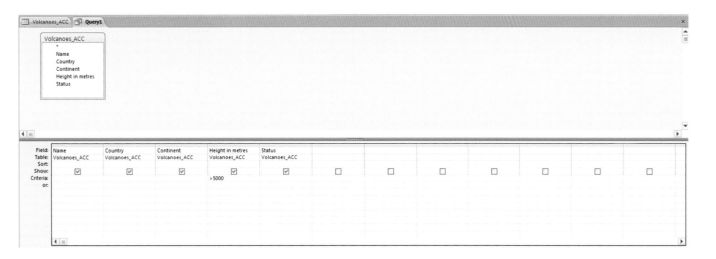

Figure 6.04b A (simple) search on one field in a database (Access®)

Wildcard search

If you are not sure of the exact wording of the data to be found in a search, then it is possible to use the **wildcard character** '*'. For example, searching a database of mountains for Name equals 'Ben*' would find all of the mountains which had names beginning with "Ben". The wildcard character may be used at any position in a search.

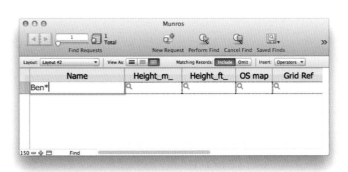

Figure 6.05a A wildcard search on one field in a database (Filemaker® Pro)

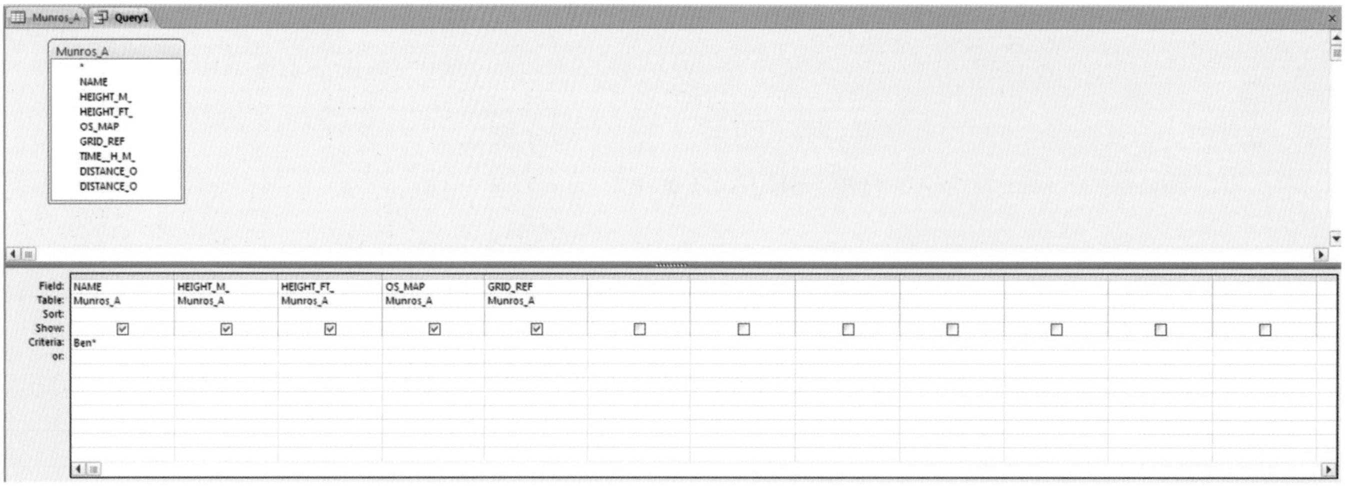

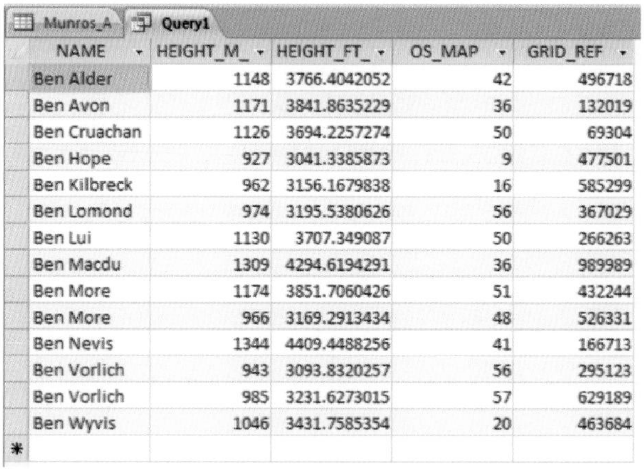

NAME	HEIGHT_M_	HEIGHT_FT_	OS_MAP	GRID_REF
Ben Alder	1148	3766.4042052	42	496718
Ben Avon	1171	3841.8635229	36	132019
Ben Cruachan	1126	3694.2257274	50	69304
Ben Hope	927	3041.3385873	9	477501
Ben Kilbreck	962	3156.1679838	16	585299
Ben Lomond	974	3195.5380626	56	367029
Ben Lui	1130	3707.349087	50	266263
Ben Macdu	1309	4294.6194291	36	989989
Ben More	1174	3851.7060426	51	432244
Ben More	966	3169.2913434	48	526331
Ben Nevis	1344	4409.4488256	41	166713
Ben Vorlich	943	3093.8320257	56	295123
Ben Vorlich	985	3231.6273015	57	629189
Ben Wyvis	1046	3431.7585354	20	463684

Figure 6.05b A wildcard search on one field in a database (Access®)

National 5

Searching on more than one field (multiple fields)

You can link the conditions of search in a field. At the end of the search all the records which match the set of conditions you have put in will be displayed. If no records match the required conditions, then you can choose to change the conditions or abandon the search. *Searching on more than one field* or *searching on multiple fields* or *searching on a single field using multiple conditions* is called a **complex search**.

The conditions which you can use in a complex search are usually joined by the words **AND** or **OR**. These are the same **logical operators** which we read about in Chapter 2. Joining two conditions with AND means that *both* of the conditions must be met for a search to be successful. Joining two conditions with OR means that either condition can be met for the search to succeed. **NOT** is the other logical operator which indicates that the condition should not be met.

Figure 6.06 shows a search through three fields on a database. The fields are *occupation*, *sex* and *age*, and the conditions are *scholar* AND *female* AND *greater than 12*. A successful search provides a list of girls on the database over 12 who are still at school.

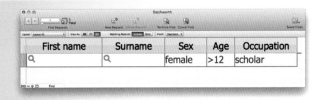

First name	Surname	Sex	Age	Occupation
Dinah	Cutts	Female	13	scholar
Jane	Brownsell	Female	13	scholar
Mary J	Shadbolt	Female	13	scholar
Lucy M	Chalkley	Female	13	scholar
Philadelphia	Colborn	Female	13	scholar
Emma M	Collins	Female	14	scholar
Charlotte	Page	Female	14	scholar
Louisa	Skeggs	Female	15	scholar

Figure 6.06a A search on multiple fields in a database (using AND) (Filemaker® Pro)

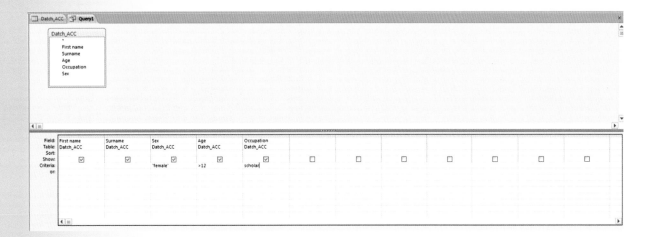

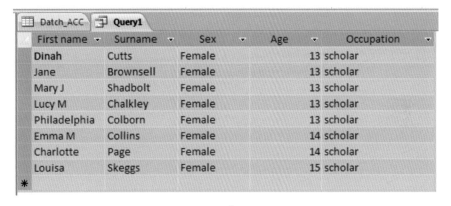

Figure 6.06b A search on multiple fields in a database (using AND) (Access®)

Figure 6.07 shows another search, this time using OR. The field is *Continent* and the conditions are *Continent equals South America* OR *Continent equals Central America*. A successful search provides a list of volcanoes on your database in both Central and South America. Although this search uses only one field, it is still a complex search because it uses two conditions.

Name	Country	Continent	Height in metres	Status
		South America		
		Central America		

Name	Country	Continent	Height in metres	Status
Cotopaxi	Ecuador	South America	5978	active
Popocatapetl	Mexico	Central America	5452	active
Sangay	Ecuador	South America	5410	active
Tungurahua	Ecuador	South America	5033	active
Cotacachi	Ecuador	South America	4937	active
Purace	Columbia	South America	4756	active
Tajmulco	Guatemala	Central America	4210	active
Tacana	Guatemala	Central America	4064	active
Acatenango	Guatemala	Central America	3960	active
Colima	Mexica	Central America	3850	active
Fuego	Guatemala	Central America	3835	active
Santa Maria	Guatemala	Central America	3768	active
Atitlan	Guatemala	Central America	3525	active
Irazu	Costa Rica	Central America	3432	active
Misti	Peru	South America	5801	dormant
Pichincha	Ecuador	South America	4789	dormant
Paricutin	Mexico	Central America	2774	dormant
Aconcagua	Argentina/Chile	South America	6960	believed extinct
Chimborazo	Ecuador	South America	6282	believed extinct
Orizaba	Mexico	Central America	5700	believed extinct

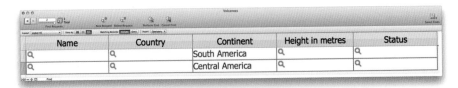

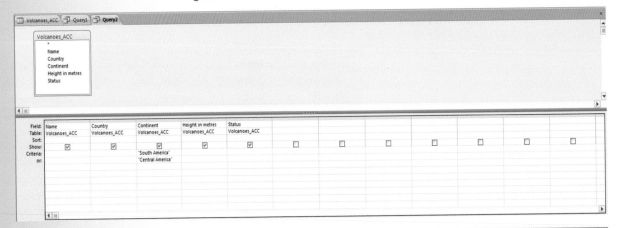

Figure 6.07a A search on multiple fields in a database (using OR) (Filemaker® Pro)

Field:	Name	Country	Continent	Height in metres	Status
Table:	Volcanoes_ACC	Volcanoes_ACC	Volcanoes_ACC	Volcanoes_ACC	Volcanoes_ACC
Sort:					
Show:	☑	☑	☑	☑	☑
Criteria:			"South America"		
or:			"Central America"		

Name	Country	Continent	Height in metres	Status
Cotopaxi	Ecuador	South America	5978	active
Popocatapetl	Mexico	Central America	5452	active
Sangay	Ecuador	South America	5410	active
Tungurahua	Ecuador	South America	5033	active
Cotacachi	Ecuador	South America	4937	active
Purace	Columbia	South America	4756	active
Tajmulco	Guatemala	Central America	4210	active
Tacana	Guatemala	Central America	4064	active
Acatenango	Guatemala	Central America	3960	active
Colima	Mexica	Central America	3850	active
Fuego	Guatemala	Central America	3835	active
Santa Maria	Guatemala	Central America	3768	active
Atitlan	Guatemala	Central America	3525	active
Irazu	Costa Rica	Central America	3432	active
Misti	Peru	South America	5801	dormant
Pichincha	Ecuador	South America	4789	dormant
Paricutin	Mexico	Central America	2774	dormant
Aconcagua	Argentina/Chile	South America	6960	believed extinct
Chimborazo	Ecuador	South America	6282	believed extinct
Orizaba	Mexico	Central America	5700	believed extinct

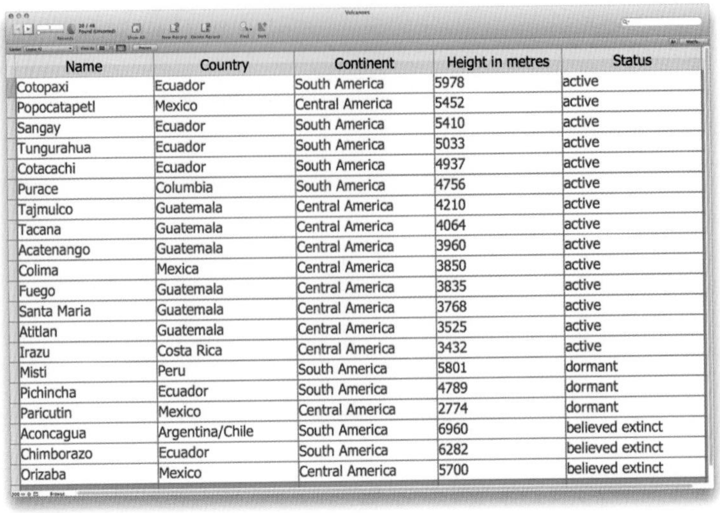

Figure 6.07b A search on multiple fields in a database (using OR) (Access®)

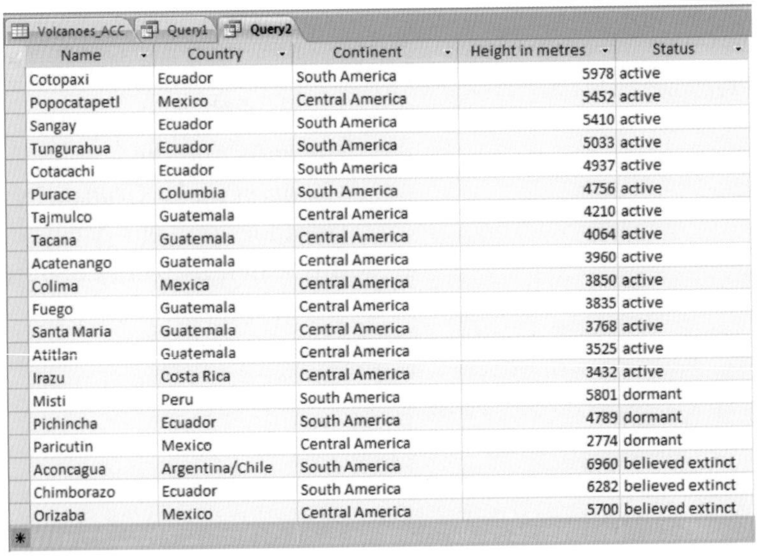

Here is a simple sentence you can learn which will help you when answering theory questions about searching.

Search the file _____ on the field _____ for records which match the condition _____ .

You can fill in the blanks with the *file name*, the *field name* and the *condition* to match any search. You can add more fields and conditions. Even if you don't know the correct answer, you should still get some marks, because you have used the terms *search*, *file*, *field* and *record* in the correct manner.

Sort

Sorting allows you to arrange the records in a database in alphabetic or numeric and ascending or descending order. Ascending numeric order would be 1, 2, 3, 4 … , descending alphabetic order would be Z, Y, X, W … . To start the sort you must choose a field (like '*Height in metres*' in the previous example) on which to sort the database, or the records will stay in the order in which you typed them, not the order you want.

You should use sorting whenever you have changed the database by adding or deleting information. For example, a club membership list is stored in a database. The list is stored in alphabetical order by member's name and a new person joins the club. Once the new member's details have been added the database must be sorted to make sure that the records are still in alphabetical order.

Sort on one field

In the example in Figure 6.08, the database has been sorted in order of 'Atomic Number'.

 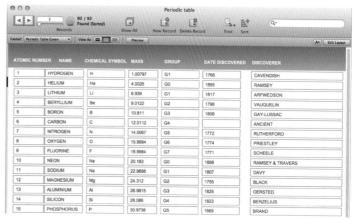

Figure 6.08 Records in a database sorted on one field

Sort on more than one field (multiple fields)

You can **sort on more than one field**. For example, the database in Figure 6.09 is sorted on *surname* and then *age*.

Figure 6.09 Records in a database sorted on two fields

Here is a simple sentence you can learn which will help you when answering theory questions about sorting.

Sort the file _____ on the field _____ in _____ order.

You can fill in the blanks with the *file name*, the *field name* and the order such as *alphabetical* or *ascending numerical*. You can add more fields and orders. Even if you don't know the correct answer, you should still get some marks, because you have used the terms *sort*, *file* and *field* in the correct manner.

Check Your Learning

Now answer questions 1–13 (on page 168) on databases (National 4).

Database structure

What is a flat file?

The databases that we have looked at so far in this chapter have one feature in common. They are all **flat files**. A flat file is a database which is contained in a single **table**. Table 6.01 shows another example of a flat file.

Forename	Surname	Guidance class	Guidance teacher	Room	Period
Asafa	Ghofu	1.5	Mrs Mercer	F12	Monday 7
Mark	Shanks	1.5	Mrs Mercer	F12	Monday 7
Sarah	Smith	1.5	Mrs Mercer	F12	Monday 7
Jemima	Bales	1.3	Ms Connelly	S59	Monday 7
Siobhan	Creasey	1.3	Ms Connelly	S59	Monday 7
Tracy	McGurk	1.3	Ms Connelly	S59	Monday 7

National 5

Forename	Surname	Guidance class	Guidance teacher	Room	Period
Cecilia	Bone	1.1	Mrs Allahan	G98	Thursday 2
Janice	Robson	1.1	Mrs Allahan	G98	Thursday 2
Hazel	Seton	1.1	Mrs Allahan	G98	Thursday 2
George	Seton	1.1	Mrs Allahan	G98	Thursday 2
David	Banks	1.2	Mr Simmons	F23	Tuesday 2
Gerard	Herard	1.2	Mr Simmons	F23	Tuesday 2
Cameron	Walsh	1.2	Mr Simmons	F23	Tuesday 2
Miklos	Apczak	1.6	Mr Grofaz	S26	Tuesday 3
Indiana	MacSeveney	1.6	Mr Grofaz	S26	Tuesday 3
Charmaine	Plant	1.6	Mr Grofaz	S26	Tuesday 3
John	Service	1.7	Ms Patrick	G67	Wednesday 5
Harjinder	Singh	1.7	Ms Patrick	G67	Wednesday 5
Mary	Timmons	1.7	Ms Patrick	G67	Wednesday 5
Fiona	Black	1.2	Mr Simmons	F23	Tuesday 2
Devonia	Crumble	1.4	Mr Byers	S30	Friday 6
Helen	McCarroll	1.1	Mrs Allahan	G98	Thursday 2
Robert	Leo	1.1	Mrs Allahan	G98	Thursday 2
Mary	Stuart	1.5	Mrs Mercer	F12	Monday 7
Peter	John	1.3	Ms Connelly	S59	Monday 7
James	Joseph	1.6	Mr Grofaz	S26	Tuesday 3

Table 6.01 A flat file is made up of a single table

Flat files have some disadvantages. For instance, a lot of the data stored in Table 6.01 is duplicated. **Data duplication** is wasteful of time because the same data must be entered many times instead of just once. Data duplication also wastes space on **backing storage** and in the computer's **memory (RAM)** when the database is open. It is easy to make a mistake when entering the same data over and over again. Typing errors can cause other mistakes when the database is searched or sorted, causing incorrect results to be obtained. A database which contains these types of errors is said to be **inconsistent**.

Modification errors may occur when **inserting**, deleting from or **updating** a database. In order to add a new student's details to Table 6.01, the teacher's name, room and period would need to be inserted. Deleting or updating a teacher's name would mean changing every occurrence of the name throughout the whole table. If the table contained the details of all of the students in the first year in a large school, then it is more likely that mistakes would be made. A well-designed database should be free from modification errors.

It would be much more efficient if the single table was split into two tables, each containing only a single instance of the data. This process of splitting the table involves removing repeating items of data. There would be no duplication of data. Students' and teachers' details would be held separately and could be modified much more quickly and accurately than when held in a flat file database. Adding a student to the school, for example, would only require their name and class to be entered. Changing a teacher's name would only have to be done once instead of twenty or thirty times.

Forename	Surname	Class
Sarah	Smith	1.5
Jemima	Bales	1.3
Mark	Shanks	1.5
Asafa	Ghofu	1.5
Siobhan	Creasey	1.3
Tracy	McGurk	1.3
Mary	Stuart	1.5
Janice	Robson	1.1
Hazel	Seton	1.1
George	Seton	1.1
David	Banks	1.2
Gerard	Herard	1.2
Cameron	Walsh	1.2
Miklos	Apczak	1.6
Indiana	MacSeveney	1.6
Charmaine	Plant	1.6
John	Service	1.7
Harjinder	Singh	1.7
Mary	Timmons	1.7
Fiona	Black	1.2
Devonia	Crumble	1.4
Helen	McCarroll	1.1
Robert	Leo	1.1
Cecilia	Bone	1.1
Peter	John	1.3
James	Joseph	1.6

Table 6.02 Student table

Class	Guidance teacher	Room	Period
1.1	Mrs Allahan	G98	Thursday 2
1.2	Mr Simmons	F23	Tuesday 2
1.3	Ms Connelly	S59	Monday 7
1.4	Mr Byers	S30	Friday 6
1.5	Mrs Mercer	F12	Monday 7
1.6	Mr Grofaz	S26	Tuesday 3
1.7	Ms Patrick	G67	Wednesday 5

Table 6.03 Teacher table

Linked tables, primary keys and foreign keys

Looking again at the two tables shows that they can be used together to provide all of the data required. The student table is **linked** to the teacher table by the class field, which is common to both tables. The class field is an example of a **key field** which is a field used to link tables.

When a database contains links between tables, it is referred to as a **relational database**.

The class field (column) in the teacher table is known as a **primary key**, because it has a **unique value** which may be used to identify a record. Any field in a database which is used as a primary key must always contain a value, that is, it cannot be **empty** (or **null**).

The class field in the student table is known as a **foreign key**. A foreign key is a field in a table which links to the primary key in a related table. Establishing a relationship creates a link between the primary key in one table and the foreign key in another table. This relationship may then be used to find all of the information contained in both tables.

Table 6.04 shows that the *Class* relation may be used to find the students' names from the teachers' table. Similarly, in the other direction, the *Class* relation allows the teacher's name, room and period to be determined.

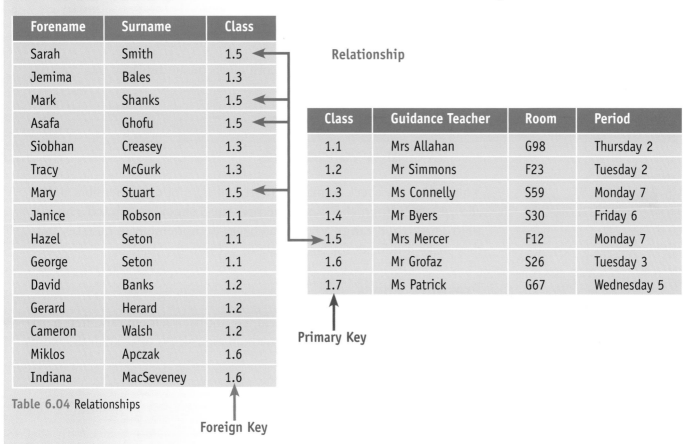

Forename	Surname	Class
Sarah	Smith	1.5
Jemima	Bales	1.3
Mark	Shanks	1.5
Asafa	Ghofu	1.5
Siobhan	Creasey	1.3
Tracy	McGurk	1.3
Mary	Stuart	1.5
Janice	Robson	1.1
Hazel	Seton	1.1
George	Seton	1.1
David	Banks	1.2
Gerard	Herard	1.2
Cameron	Walsh	1.2
Miklos	Apczak	1.6
Indiana	MacSeveney	1.6

Table 6.04 Relationships

Relationship

Class	Guidance Teacher	Room	Period
1.1	Mrs Allahan	G98	Thursday 2
1.2	Mr Simmons	F23	Tuesday 2
1.3	Ms Connelly	S59	Monday 7
1.4	Mr Byers	S30	Friday 6
1.5	Mrs Mercer	F12	Monday 7
1.6	Mr Grofaz	S26	Tuesday 3
1.7	Ms Patrick	G67	Wednesday 5

Primary Key

Foreign Key

Figure 6.10 shows how the relationship would be set up in a relational database package. Different database programs have their own methods of sharing these relationships.

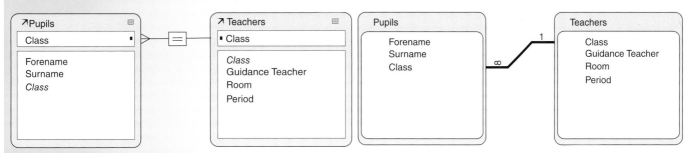

Figure 6.10 Setting up a relationship

Forename	Surname	Class	::Guidance Teacher	::Room	::Period
Cecilia	Bone	1.1	Mrs Allahan	G98	Thursday 2
Janice	Robson	1.1	Mrs Allahan	G98	Thursday 2
Hazel	Seton	1.1	Mrs Allahan	G98	Thursday 2
George	Seton	1.1	Mrs Allahan	G98	Thursday 2
Helen	McCarroll	1.1	Mrs Allahan	G98	Thursday 2
Robert	Leo	1.1	Mrs Allahan	G98	Thursday 2
David	Banks	1.2	Mr Simmons	F23	Tuesday 2
Gerard	Herard	1.2	Mr Simmons	F23	Tuesday 2
Cameron	Walsh	1.2	Mr Simmons	F23	Tuesday 2
Fiona	Black	1.2	Mr Simmons	F23	Tuesday 2

Figure 6.11 Data from both tables

Figure 6.11 shows the data from both tables being displayed in a database report.

What is validation?

Validation is a check to make sure that an item of data is sensible and allowable. Validation checks include **presence check**, **restricted choice**, **field length** and **range**. Validation checks do not eliminate mistakes, but they make it difficult for wrong data to get into the database.

Presence check

This checks to make sure that a field has not been left empty. Often, a required field will be highlighted with an asterisk (*) or contain the word 'required'.

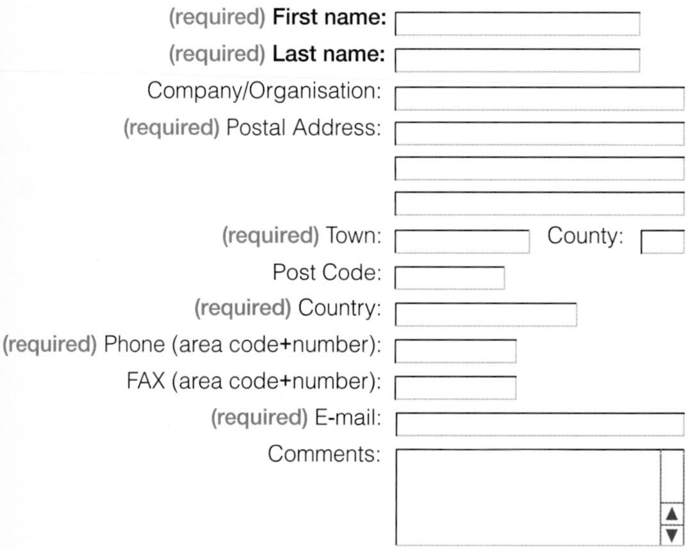

Figure 6.12 Presence check during data entry

Restricted choice

This gives users a list of options to choose from and so limits the input to pre-approved answers.

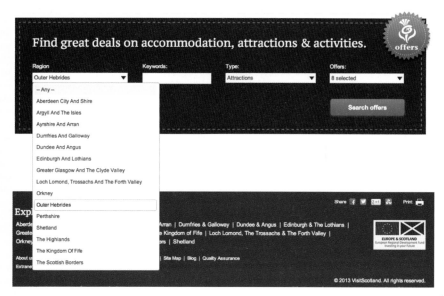

Figure 6.13 Restricted choice (Image by permission of VisitScotland.)

Field length

This ensures the correct number of numbers or characters has been entered in a field. For example, UK postcodes are between 6 and 8 characters long (including the space). 'KA21 5NT' would be allowed, but IV342 7HY would be rejected.

If the entry has more characters than will fit in the field, then an error message should appear. Limiting the size of a field also helps to reduce the amount of storage space required for the database file. A smaller file will be quicker to load and quicker to send over a **network**.

Range

This keeps the data within given limits. A range check can be made on fields that contain numbers, like ages, money or dates, to check that the numbers are sensible. For example:

- an age of more than 120 or less than 0
- a total on a bill of £0.00
- a month of greater than 31 or less than 1.

Field type

This makes sure the correct type of data is entered. A field for a credit card number would not allow letters or symbols to be entered, so typing a letter O instead of a number 0 would not be allowed. A number field would also have to permit the entry of a . (decimal point).

Calculation of backing storage requirements in a database

It is easy to calculate the amount of **backing storage** required to hold data in a database. Look at each field in one record and count or estimate the maximum number of characters, which are likely to be in each field. Remember that spaces between words count as characters! Add these together to give the maximum size of a record.

Now multiply the size of one record by the number of records in the database. This will give you the total number of characters in the database. Each character requires a storage space of one **byte**, so this gives the answer in bytes.

To change the answer into **Kilobytes**, remember that 1 Kilobyte is 1024 bytes, so divide the total number of bytes by 1024. If the answer is required in **Megabytes**, divide the number of Kilobytes by 1024, because there are 1024 Kilobytes in a Megabyte.

Figure 6.14

Check Your Learning   Now answer questions 14–31 (on pages 169–170) on databases (National 5).

Web-based structure

What is the World Wide Web?

The **World Wide Web** (WWW) is a collection of information held in multimedia form on the **internet**. This information is stored at locations called **websites** in the form of web pages. Each web page is a single document, although it may be too large to display on a **screen** without **scrolling**. A screenshot of a web page is shown in Figure 6.15.

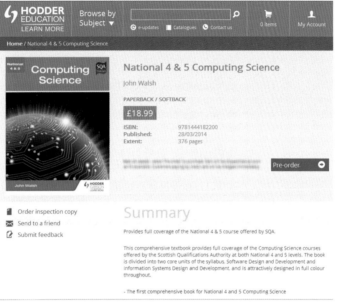

Figure 6.15 A web page

Web pages are permanently available to any user of the internet. Each organisation, or individual, who provides information organises this information as a website, often consisting of many pages. Websites are a very effective way of distributing information. To make it easier to find information, each website has its own **home page**. The home page provides a starting point for the user to explore the site. It's like a main **menu**, and may also provide hyperlinks to other sites.

What is a hyperlink?

Hyperlinks are links between World Wide Web pages, documents or files. They are activated by clicking on **text** which acts as a button, or on a particular area of the screen like a **hotspot**.

An **internal hyperlink** takes the user to another page within the same website. An **external hyperlink** takes the user to a different website, either on the same **server** or on a different server.

HTML or **HyperText Mark-up Language** is the language used to create web pages. The following example shows how the HTML language may be used to create an internal hyperlink using the **href attribute** and the <a> (**anchor**) **tag**.

```
<a href="home.htm"> Home Page </a>
```

An external hyperlink may be created by using HTML in a similar manner.

```
<a href="www.bbc.co.uk/news/scotland/ "> BBC </a>
```

In both of these cases, the href attribute is used to hold the URL of the link.

If the URL points to an external website, then the URL is said to be **absolute** (**absolute addressing**).

If the URL points to a page within the same website (i.e. internal), then it is known as a **relative** URL (**relative addressing**).

You can read more about HTML, tags and attributes in Chapter 9.

What is a URL?

URL stands for Uniform Resource Locator. Any web page can be accessed directly if its full **web address** or URL is known. The URL is a unique address for a specific file available on the internet. A typical URL looks like this:

http://www.stmatthewsacademy.sch.uk/departments/Computing/index.htm

The first part (**http**) is the **protocol**, in this case HyperText Transfer Protocol.

The second part (www.stmatthewsacademy.sch.uk) is the **domain name**.

The last part (departments/Computing/index.htm) is the **pathname**, which leads to the file, in this case the index page.

Note that not all domain names begin with www, for example http://doit.ort.org. You can find out more about protocols in Chapter 14.

Check Your Learning   Now answer questions 32–39 (on page 171) on web-based structure (National 4).

What is navigation?

Navigation is how the user finds their way around the information system. The **navigation structure** is the way in which the pages or screens in the information system are arranged. Types of navigation structure include **linear**, **hierarchical** and **web**. You can find out more detail about navigation structure and **navigation methods** in Chapter 7.

Web browsers and search engines

What is a web browser?

A **web browser** is a program that allows the user to browse or surf through the World Wide Web. When browsing the World Wide Web, a browser loads web pages from another computer on the internet and displays them. Related pages may be easily loaded by clicking on hyperlinks, which are shown in a different colour on the web page. A browser may also provide other facilities such as **file transfer** or **email**. In the same way that a website has a home page, a browser may be set to access a specific web page when it starts up. This is the browser's home page and browsers have a **home button** or menu choice to make it easy to return to this page at any time. Browser menu bars are shown in Figures 6.16 and 6.17.

Figure 6.16 Firefox® menu bar

A browser allows pages to be saved or printed, and can move backward and forward through pages already accessed. Some browsers can store the contents of web pages in a reading list so that they may be read **offline**. A **browser** also stores a **history** of recently viewed pages and can remember web page addresses or URLs by using **bookmarks** or **favourites**. When you bookmark a page, the web address of the page is stored. Clicking on a bookmark or selecting from a menu will cause the page to be found and displayed. **Tabbed browsing** allows many different web pages to be easily accessed from a single screen **window** by using a tabbed document interface. Browser applications include **Internet Explorer®**, **Firefox®**, **Safari®**, **Chrome™** and **Opera™**.

Figure 6.17 Tabbed browsing in Chrome

What is a search engine?

The internet contains millions of pages of information on every subject. The best way of finding the information you want is to use a **search engine**. A search engine is a special site on the World Wide Web, which is designed to help you to find information.

> Wolfram|Alpha (www.wolframalpha.com) introduces a fundamentally new way to get knowledge and answers – not by searching the web, but by doing dynamic computations based on a vast collection of built-in data, algorithms, and methods.

Figure 6.18 Some search engines

Search engines work in various different ways, but they all:

- search the internet for different words
- build up an **index** of these words, and where they can be found
- allow users to search for particular words in their indexes
- provide hyperlinks to where these words may be found on the internet.

Most search engines allow the user to carry out two different types of **searches** or queries, **basic** and **advanced**.

Basic search

A basic search allows the user to enter one or more **keywords** into an entry box, and then click a button or press return on the **keyboard** to start the search. A keyword is the text which is used to search a file for a given entry or part of an entry. On some systems the term **search string** is used instead of keyword.

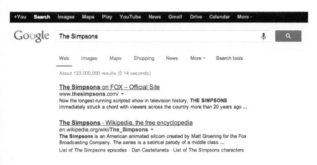

Figure 6.19 A basic search

A sensible choice of keywords can save a great deal of time when searching. The more detail you can give in the keywords the better. A search for *long nosed bandicoot* would be more likely to give a precise answer than *bandicoot* on its own.

Using **phrases** is very useful in a search engine. To use phrases they must be enclosed in quotation marks, like this – "St. Matthew's Academy", "Ardrossan Highland Games", "Ceud mille failte", and "Seann triubhas". The search engine will only give results that include the exact phrase. Using phrases is very useful, because it can help to narrow down a search, and is more likely to produce the desired results than by using separate keywords.

A successful search using a search engine will result in several matches. Each match is called a **hit**. The search engine displays the hits in what it considers to be the most appropriate order or rank.

If you try out the same search using the same keywords on two or more different search engines, you are likely to get different results, because all search engines have slightly different ways of indexing the information that they find. Sometimes the hits that the search engines find do not work when you click on the associated link. This is usually caused by the site having been moved to a different location, before the search engine has had a chance to update its indexes.

Quick Tip   **Search engines**

To get the best results from a particular search engine, you should read its associated help pages and try out various searches in order to familiarise yourself with how it works.

In addition to keyword searching for text, it is also possible to search only for particular types of data, such as music or images. You can also narrow the search by location or recent time interval or specify that the results should only come from websites in a particular country.

Some search engines allow you to enter **natural language queries** instead of single keywords. *"Where can I buy a Blu-ray™ drive?"*, *"What is the weather like in Grand Junction?"*. You should avoid making your sentences too long or complicated when using natural language queries.

Advanced search

An advanced search allows the user to refine their search in various ways, for example by restricting the search to only parts of the web, or by choosing different options from a menu.

Most search engines allow the use of AND, OR, NOT. Some search engines allow (+) to represent AND, and (–) instead of NOT.

AND means that all the terms linked by AND must appear, for instance: *national AND computing AND science*, *mountain AND munro AND Scotland*.

OR means that at least one term must appear, for example: *chips OR pakora*, *red kola OR irn bru*, *cidona OR club orange*.

NOT excludes a term, like: *CDROM NOT DVDROM*, *pool NOT swimming*

Figure 6.20a Google™ advanced search

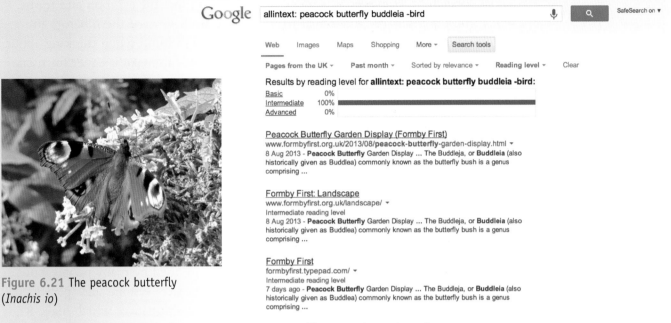

Figure 6.21 The peacock butterfly (*Inachis io*)

Figure 6.20b Google™ advanced search results

Good design to aid navigation, usability and accessibility

If a website is well designed, then it will have high-quality navigation, **usability** and accessibility. We will look at some of these characteristics in more detail in the next chapter, but here is an outline.

What is navigation?

Navigation is how the user finds their way around the information system. A web browser application contains features such as an **address bar** into which a URL may be entered to go directly to a particular web page. It also has **forward** and **backward buttons**, a home button or menu choice and is capable of remembering each page visited in its history. All of these features aid navigation. The web page itself will contain hyperlinks and hotspots. It may provide **breadcrumbs** to show your position in the website. **Guided navigation**, **tag clouds** and **site maps** are other popular features which can help users find their way around a website.

What is usability?

Usability is how easy it is to use and learn about an item, whether it be a **computer program**, website, tool or machine. A website, or any other item, may be regarded as having a degree of usability if it is satisfying to use and you can accomplish the task you set out to do with it.

Consider the **user interface** shown in Figure 6.23. Interfaces like this one are said to be 'intuitive' which means that you instinctively know how to operate it. However, it is more accurate to say that the symbols and **icons** on the interface are familiar to us because we have used them before in other situations. It is worthwhile keeping this in mind when thinking about design – sticking to familiar icons and symbols can make it easier for users.

Figure 6.22 Example user interface – iTunes®

What is accessibility?

An information system is **accessible** when it is usable by everyone, including people with disabilities. Mice and keyboards are used by many people, but they do not suit every person. **Speech recognition** systems and specialised pointing and selecting **devices** are examples of alternatives which make it possible for all users to interact with a computer system. The Accessiweb site holds a list of websites which satisfy its criteria for accessibility.

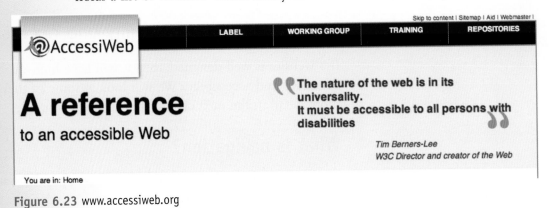

Figure 6.23 www.accessiweb.org

Check Your Learning

Now answer questions 40–56 (on page 171) on web-based structure (National 5).

Testing

The website or information system must be **tested** to make sure that it operates as intended (links and navigation) and that it meets the original specification for the design (matches user interface design).

National 5

Links and navigation

The hyperlinks are tested to ensure that they all work as expected, whether they link to another page in the same website (internal) or to a different website (external). Here are some other questions which could be used while testing them.

- Do all of the buttons, menus and input boxes work?
- Do they all provide appropriate feedback to the user?
- If the web page contains graphics, **audio** or video, do they open and play back correctly?
- Has the website been tested on different browsers or on different **operating systems**?
- Does the website require additional **software** such as a plugin to operate correctly?

(You can read more about links and navigation in Chapter 7.)

Matches user interface design

- Does the website match the original design for the user interface?
- Is the colour and size of the typeface appropriate?

(You can read more about **design notations** in Chapter 5.)

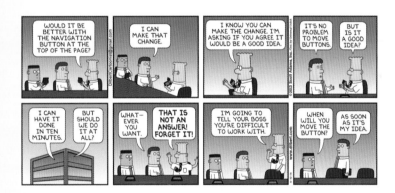

Figure 6.24 Navigation

Check Your Learning

Now answer questions 57–58 (on page 171) on testing (National 5).

Practical Tasks

1 a) Make up a manual database on at least one of the following:

    i) A list of people and their telephone numbers.

    ii) A Christmas card list.

    iii) Each person in the class's favourite pop group, movie, app and television programme

    iv) A birthday list.

b) Using a database package that you are familiar with, enter the details of the manual database(s) you created earlier. Carry out whichever of the following tasks applies to your database.

    i) Sort the entries in alphabetical or date order.

    ii) Find and display your own record in a form layout.

    ii) Display the records of any person whose name begins with the same letter as your name in a table layout.

    iii) Search for the people who were born in the same month as you.

    What other information could you find out from or include in this database?

c) Using a database package that you are familiar with, find out how to create fields which incorporate validation checks. Include presence check, restricted choice, field length and range in your answer.

2 Using a search engine, find out some statistics about the quantity of information added to the World Wide Web each day. Use the poster in Figure 6.25 as a starting point to give you some ideas. You can see a larger version of the poster at: http://blog.qmee.com/wp-content/uploads/2013/07/Qmee-Online-In-60-Seconds21.png.

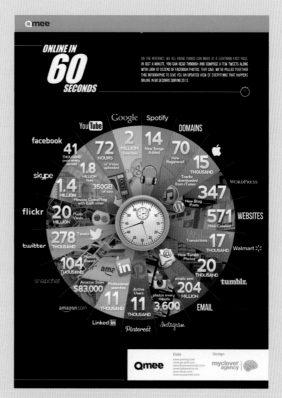

Figure 6.25

3 a) Find out about the UX or 'user experience' at www.usability.gov.

    Create a presentation on usability and deliver it to your group or class.

b) Have a look at www.accessiweb.org, www.w3.org/WAI/ and www.readspeaker.com. (You may need to use a browser with a translating feature.)

    Create a presentation on accessibility and deliver it to your group or class.

c) Use a search engine to find out why one type of website navigation is called 'breadcrumbs'.

4 a) Have a look at what Chapter 9 says about cookies. Use a search engine to find out some more about how cookies are used by websites and web browsers.

b) Write a paragraph about the advantages of cookies and one about any disadvantages associated with their use.

c) Find out how the settings on a browser may be used to manage cookies.

5 A plug-in is an item of software that adds a particular feature to an existing application. Plug-ins are frequently used to add features to web browsers.

a) Use a search engine to find out which web browser plug-ins are the most popular.

b) Create a table like the one below and add your findings to it.

Popularity	Name of plug-in	Purpose of plug-in
1	Adobe® Acrobat Reader®	Display of PDF files
2	Java™ Virtual Machine	
3	Microsoft Silverlight®	
4		
5		
6		
7		
8		
9		
10		

c) The latest version of HTML is HTML5. HTML5 is capable of providing features similar to certain plug-ins.

i) Have a look at one opinion about HTML5 here: http://zmags.com/getting-on-board-with-html5/. Search for other opinions about HTML5.

ii) Now write your own opinion, with evidence, stating whether or not you think that HTML5 will eventually replace many plug-ins, like those you have found and added to your table in b).

6 Look at the following tables containing information on music albums.

Tracks		
Track number	Track name	Disc reference
017	Clearly	AB678
019	Thrifty	JL900
005	Forever blue	JL900
009	Can't believe	UH678
010	When you are near	GH322
001	Why do flowers bloom in spring	JL900
003	Gone fishing	TH876
015	Sunshine	KL117
002	Citadel	KL117
007	After the day	PLF809
008	Careless lives	DG677
011	Meridian	AA313
013	Thoroughly	KL117
006	Tempered ivory	AA313
014	Scales of peace	TH876
008	Night-time	PLF809
019	Grandiose	GH322
017	Be that anyway	DG677

Discs			
Disc reference	**Album**	**Artist**	**Genre**
AB678	When are you	The Crafts	Soul
AA313	Keep loving	Tender	Contemporary
DG677	Then there was one	California	Alternative
GH322	Xylem	Treen	Dance
JL900	Farming	The Brand	Pop
KL117	Special edition	Cherries	Pop
PLF809	Greening	Lippi	Rock
TH876	Whale of a time	Baleen	Folk
UH678	Dream together	Jim Tholes	Rock

a) For each table, identify a field that may be used to link the tables.

b) Using a database package with which you are familiar, enter the data in both tables.

c) Using your answer to part a), link the tables and obtain a screenshot of the relationship that you have created.

d) Use your linked tables to produce reports containing

   i) Album, Artist, Track Name and Track Number.

   ii) Album, Genre and Track Name.

Questions

Databases (National 4)

1 What is a database?

2 What three items make up the structure of a database?

3 What is a field?

4 What is a record?

5 What is a file?

6 Name the part of a database which
   a) contains an individual piece of information.
   b) contains all of the data about one person or thing.
   c) is a collection of one or more of b).

7 Name six database field types.

8 Which database field type holds
   a) letters and numbers?
   b) only numbers?
   c) an image?
   d) a sum?

9 State the two main operations carried out in a database.

10 Name the process of searching using one field with a single condition in a database.

11 Name two relational operators.

12 State one example of a condition created by using a relational operator.

13 What is a wildcard operator and what is it used for?

Databases (National 5)

14 Copy and complete Table 6.04 to show the field types required to hold the data in each case.

Data	Field type
129.67	
August	
27 August 2015	
www.waddle.com	
True / False	
net price = price + vat	

Table 6.04

15 Name three logical operators.

16 Name the process of sorting using more than one field in a database.

17 Look at the database shown in Figure 6.26. It has been sorted into order on two fields. Identify the fields and the sort order.

18 The database in Figure 6.27 has been sorted on three fields. Which fields has this database been sorted on?

First name	Surname	Sex	Age	Occupation ▾
Mary A	Tingay	Female	15	barmaid
Alfred	Hornett	Male	14	boy carter
Benjamin	Hornett	Male	16	carpenter
Elizabeth	Brunton	Female	16	domestic
Charlotte	Ephgrave	Female	15	domestic
Maria	Taylor	Female	16	domestic
Edward	Allen	Male	13	farm boy
Alfred	Brunton	Male	14	farm boy
George	Chapman	Male	12	farm boy
William	Croft	Male	12	farm boy
John	Draper	Male	14	farm boy
John	Fletcher	Male	15	farm boy
Thomas	Fletcher	Male	12	farm boy
John	Gregory	Male	14	farm boy
Rueben	Gregory	Male	14	farm boy
William	Gregory	Male	12	farm boy
Edward	Hungrave	Male	13	farm boy

Figure 6.27

19 What is a table (in a database)?

20 Place the following terms in ascending order of size: table, field, file, record

21 State the name given to a database with only one table.

22 State the name given to a database containing linked tables.

23 Explain the purpose of a primary key.

24 State two properties of a primary key.

25 Explain the purpose of a foreign key.

26 Look at the two tables over the page.
   a) Name the key field used to link the tables.
   b) State how the key field is used in each table in order to create a link between the two tables.

Surname	Initials	Dept Code	Job Title	Location	Contract	Pay	Grade
Taylor	P	SE303	System Designer	Birmingham	PA	£3.09	U
Higson	VM	SE203	Help Desk Technician	Manchester	PD	£3.61	U
White	F	SE403	System Analyst	Portsmouth	PD	£3.65	U
Collins	MP	SE303	System Designer	Birmingham	PD	£3.69	U
Laird	EG	SE303	System Designer	Birmingham	PA	£3.69	U
Das	G	AD102	Programmer	London	PA	£3.71	U
Otis	RS	AD102	Programmer	London	PD	£3.71	U
Clancy	M	AD202	Programmer Analyst	Manchester	PA	£3.81	U
Davies	NR	AD202	Programmer Analyst	Manchester	PD	£3.81	U
Evans	JL	AD202	Programmer Analyst	Manchester	PA	£3.81	U
Miles	TM	SE203	Help Desk Technician	Manchester	PD	£3.81	U
Reekie	CA	SE203	Help Desk Technician	Manchester	PB	£3.81	U
Moore	BJ	AD402	Network Engineer	Portsmouth	PA	£3.85	U

Figure 6.26

Questions *continued*

Forename	Surname	Class
Sarah	Smith	1.5
Jemima	Bales	1.3
Mark	Shanks	1.5
Asafa	Ghofu	1.5
Siobhan	Creasey	1.3
Tracy	McGurk	1.3
Mary	Stuart	1.5
Janice	Robson	1.1
Hazel	Seton	1.1
George	Seton	1.1
David	Banks	1.2
Gerard	Herard	1.2
Cameron	Walsh	1.2

Class	Guidance teacher	Room	Period
1.1	Mrs Allahan	G98	Thursday 2
1.2	Mr Simmons	F23	Tuesday 2
1.3	Ms Connelly	S59	Monday 7
1.4	Mr Byers	S30	Friday 6
1.5	Mrs Mercer	F12	Monday 7
1.6	Mr Grofaz	S26	Tuesday 3
1.7	Ms Patrick	G67	Wednesday 5

27 Look the customer database shown in Figure 6.28. State
   a) one reason why this database could be said to be inefficient.
   b) what could be done to improve this database.
   c) why your answer to b) would improve the database.

DVD CODE	TITLE	COST	NAME	TELEPHONE NUMBER
008	The Pianist	2.5	Annette Kirton	384756
014	Prime Suspect	2	Annette Kirton	384756
003	American Pie	2.5	Fred Flintstone	817263
011	Notting Hill	2.5	Fred Flintstone	817263
003	American Pie	2.5	Isobel Ringer	293847
011	Notting Hill	2.5	Isobel Ringer	293847
002	Finding Nemo	2.5	John Silver	142536
015	Shrek	1.5	John Silver	142536

Figure 6.28

28 What is validation?

29 Name four types of validation check.

30 State three instances when a modification error is likely to occur.

31 a) Calculate the storage requirements for an address-book database containing 300 records. Use your own name and address as a typical entry.
   b) How large would the file be if you included each person's telephone number as well?

Web-based structure (National 5)

32 What is the World Wide Web?

33 Where is the information on the World Wide Web stored?

34 What are hyperlinks?

35 How may a hyperlink be activated?

Web-based structure (National 5)

40 Hyperlinks may be internal or external. Explain the difference between internal and external hyperlinks.

41 Which type of hyperlink uses
   a) absolute addressing?
   b) relative addressing?

42 What is navigation?

43 What is a web browser?

44 Name one browser that you have used.

45 What use are bookmarks or favourites in a browser?

46 What does a browser's home button or menu choice do?

47 What use is browser history?

48 What use are tabs in a browser?

49 What name is usually given to a website designed to help you to find information?

50 Describe how such a website operates.

51 What is the name given to the text used to carry out a search?

36 What computer language may be used to create web pages?

37 What does URL stand for?

38 Describe the structure of a URL.

39 How can a web page be accessed directly?

52 What name is given to each result of a successful search?

53 State one example of an advanced search.

54 Name two navigation features which a web page may contain.

55 What is usability?

56 What is accessibility?

Testing (National 5)

57 Name two features of an information system that should be tested.

58 Look at Figure 6.29, which shows an information system used for identifying wild flowers.
   a) How many flowers are in the database?
   b) To find a flower, the user selects one or more of the descriptions on the screen and then the show button at the bottom. What would be the search condition if the red button were selected?
   c) This information system does not require access to the Web while operating, although it contains hyperlinks. Are these hyperlinks internal or external?

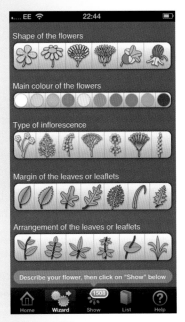

Figure 6.29

Key Points

- A database is a structured collection of similar information which you can search through.

- A database is made up of fields, records and files: this is the database structure.

- A file is a collection of structured data on a particular topic.

- Individual files are made up of records.

- A record is a collection of structured data on a particular person or thing.

- Each record is made up of one or more fields.

- A field is an area on a record, which contains an individual piece of data.

- Each field must have a field type.

- Field types include text, number, date, time, graphics, object, calculated, link and Boolean.

  - A text field is used to hold letters, numbers and symbols.

  - A numeric field only stores numbers.

  - Date fields can only contain dates.

  - Time fields can hold hours, minutes and seconds.

  - A graphic field holds a picture.

  - An object field may contain a variety of different types of data, such as a presentation, video, spreadsheet, or a bit-mapped graphic file.

  - A calculated field will carry out a calculation on another field or fields and give you an answer, like a formula in a spreadsheet.

  - A link field contains a hyperlink, or URL (Uniform Resource Locator).

  - A Boolean field contains only two values, for instance, true or false, yes or no.

- The two main operations in a database are search and sort.

- Search allows you to look for specific information in the database.

- A search can be simple or complex.

- A simple search is performed on only one field with a single condition.

- A complex search is searching on multiple fields or using multiple conditions.

- Relational operators may be used to create search conditions.

- Relational operators include: < less than; <= less than or equal to; = equal to; > greater than; >= greater than or equal to; ≠ (or < >) not equal to.

- Logical operators are used to join conditions in a complex search: AND – both conditions must be met; OR – one condition must be met.

- The wildcard operator* represents any information: this allows users to search for results with similar information, such as names beginning with Jo*.

- Sorting allows the user to arrange the records in a database into a certain alphabetic or numeric order, such as: ascending order (a ➡ z or 0 ➡ 9) or descending order (z ➡ a or 9 ➡ 0).

- A simple sort is performed on only one field; a complex sort on multiple fields.

- A table is a set of data items organised in rows and columns.

- A flat file is a database which is contained in a single table.

- A database may have more than one table.

- Linking tables allows access to the information in all of the tables.

- A database which contains linked tables is called a relational database because linking the tables creates a relationship between them.

- Key fields are used to link tables: they may be primary keys or foreign keys.

- A primary key has a unique value, which identifies individual records in a database.

- A primary key must contain an entry, it cannot be empty.

- A foreign key is a field in a table which links to the primary key in a related table.

- Validation is a check to make sure that an item of data is sensible and allowable.

  - Field length ensures the correct number of numbers or characters has been entered.

- Field type makes sure the correct type of data is entered.
- Range check keeps the data within given limits.
- Presence check checks to make sure that a field has not been left empty.
- Restricted choice gives users a list of options to choose from and so limits the input to pre-approved answers.
- A well-designed relational database will help to avoid errors such as:
  - data duplication where two entries are the same: data in a relational database should only require to be entered and stored once.
  - Data modification: data need only be entered, deleted or updated on one table.
- The World Wide Web (WWW) is a collection of information held in multimedia form on the internet.
- Hyperlinks are links between World Wide Web pages, documents or files.
- An internal hyperlink takes the user to another page within the same website.
- An external hyperlink takes the user to a different website, either on the same server or on a different server.
- URL stands for Uniform Resource Locator.
- The URL is a unique address for a specific file available on the internet.
- Any web page can be accessed directly if its full web address or URL is known.
- HTML or HyperText Mark-up Language is the language used to create web pages.
- If the URL points to an external website, then the URL is said to be absolute (absolute addressing).
- If the URL points to a page within the same website (i.e. internal), then it is known as a relative URL (relative addressing).
- A URL is made up of a protocol, a domain name and a pathname.

- A web browser is a program that allows the user to browse or surf through the World Wide Web.
- A browser also stores a history of recently viewed pages, and can remember web page addresses by using bookmarks or favourites.
- A search engine is a special site on the World Wide Web, which is designed to help you to find information.
- Search engines:
  - search the internet for different words
  - build up an index of these words, and where they can be found
  - allow users to search for particular words in their indexes
  - provide hyperlinks to where these words may be found on the internet.
- A basic search allows the user to enter one or more keywords.
- A keyword is the text which is used to search a file for a given entry or part of an entry.
- A successful search will result in one or more hits.
- An advanced search allows the user to refine their search.
- Most search engines allow the use of AND, OR, NOT in an advanced search.
- If a website is well designed, then it will have high-quality navigation, usability and accessibility.
- Navigation is how the user finds their way around the information system.
- Usability is how easy it is to use and learn about an item.
- An information system is accessible when it is usable by everyone, including people with disabilities.
- The website or information system must be tested to make sure that it operates as intended (links and navigation) and that it meets the original specification for the design (matches user interface design).

User interface

This chapter examines user requirements, which include:

- visual layout
- navigation
- selection
- consistency
- interactivity
- readability
- accessibility.

What is a user interface?

The **user interface** is the way in which the computer and the user communicate. The user interface is also called the **HCI** or **Human Computer Interface**. If a user interface is poor, then no matter how effective the **software**, no one will want to use it.

Figure 7.01 User interface design

The user can communicate with a computer in a variety of ways, for instance by using a **keyboard**, **mouse**, **track pad** or **touchscreen**. The computer can communicate with the user through **output devices**, for example **monitor**, **loudspeaker** or **printer**. You can read more about these **input** and output **devices** in Chapter 11, later on in this book.

Figure 7.02 Examples of different user interfaces

What is a target audience?

The **target audience** is the people who will use an **information** system. It is important that designers and **programmers** of information systems take the target audience into account. If the user interface is suitable for the skills and abilities of the target audience, then it is more likely that they will get the best out of the information system that they are using. The users in the target audience may be beginners (**novices**) or **experts**. They may vary widely in age – ranging from young children to teenagers and very much older adults. We will look more closely at the types of users who make up the target audience in Chapter 10.

Check Your Learning

Now answer questions 1–7 (on page 182) on user interface and target audience (National 5).

What are the user requirements?

The user requirements or **user interface requirements** are the features of the user interface which should be taken into account by the designer and the programmer of the information system.

The user requirements are **visual layout**, **navigation**, **selection**, **consistency**, **interactivity** and **readability**. **Accessibility** is one further user requirement which should also be included.

What is visual layout?

Visual layout is the appearance of the information system on the **screen** or how the display is organised. A screen which is crammed full of **text** and **graphics** is more difficult to read than one which makes effective use of **white space**. White space is the part of the screen which does not contain any content. Effective use of white space is a key element of visual layout design and it helps to focus the reader's attention upon what is important on the page. Figure 7.03 shows the **home page** for the Google™ search engine, which makes very effective use of white space in order to highlight the key feature, which is the search box.

Figure 7.03 The Google™ home page

Other key features of visual layout are:

- The number of different colours and typefaces used should be carefully considered and not overused. Use of a **colour wheel** and associated colour schemes can help when designing pages by showing which colours work best together. (See Figure 7.04.)
- Try to avoid overloading the user with information by reducing the amount presented at one time.
- Balance the graphics and the text so that there is a similar amount on each page.
- Reduce sound effects to essential only and allow the user to turn off background music.

Primary colours
Secondary colours
Tertiary colours

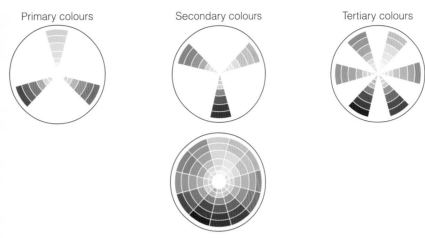

Figure 7.04 Colour wheels

What is navigation?

Navigation is how the user finds their way around the information system.

Navigation structure

The **navigation structure** is the way in which the pages or screens in the information system are arranged. Types of navigation structure include **hierarchical**, **linear** and **web**.

Hierarchical (or **tree**) navigation is shown in Figure 7.05. Hierarchical navigation is the most common and well-understood type of navigation used on the web. Hierarchical navigation allows fast movement between pages and can be easily expanded to allow more information to be added.

Level 1
Level 2
Level 2
Level 3
Level 3
Level 3
Level 3

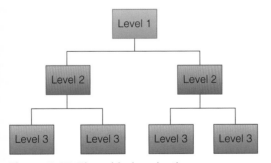

Figure 7.05 Hierarchical navigation

Linear (or **sequential**) **navigation** is shown in Figure 7.06. Linear navigation is useful for processes that may be followed in a set order, like reading a story or making a purchase by entering delivery details followed by payment information and then finally confirming the transaction. If required, linear navigation allows the user to go back to the previous page. Linear navigation can be time consuming, so it is better to keep such **sequences** short.

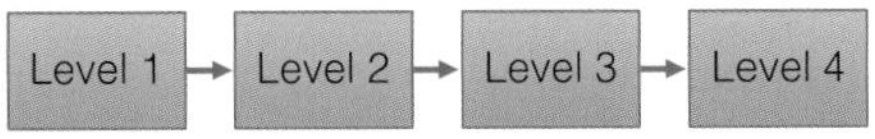

Level 1
Level 2
Level 3
Level 4

Figure 7.06 Linear navigation

Web navigation is shown in Figure 7.07. Web navigation allows multiple direct connections between **web pages**.

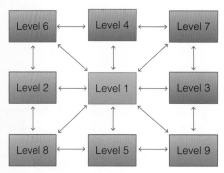

Figure 7.07 Web navigation

Navigation methods

The **navigation methods** which are in common use on computer-based information systems include:

- **Browser** features: making use of the built-in features of browser software, for instance, the **buttons – back**, **forward** and **home**. The back and forward buttons take you through the pages contained in your **browsing history** and the home button takes you to a pre-set page. The history feature remembers every page visited and it is possible to retrace your pathway through the web. Tabs may be used to allow multiple pages to be open in a single **window**. **Favourites** or **bookmarks** may be used to mark and find frequently accessed pages.
- **Menus**: many websites contain drop-down menus accessed via tabs on the web page itself.
- **Searching**: some browser programs have a dedicated search box; others allow the user to enter search **keywords** directly into the **address bar**.
- **Hyperlinks** take the user to other pages or screens in the same information system (**internal**) or to another website or program (**external**).
- Hyperlinks may be text-based or **hotspots**, which are linked to images or objects on the screen. The mouse **pointer** changes to a hand when placed over a hyperlink.
- **Context-sensitive navigation**: hiding those navigation features which are not needed and only displaying those required at a particular time.
- Breadcrumbs: breadcrumbs are a sequence of terms which show you where you are in a website, for example:
  mycloud > myschool > computing science > programming > haggis
  would be displayed as you moved through the website. Clicking on any of the levels would return you to that position.
- **Guided** or **faceted navigation**: filters containing different options are displayed and the user makes a selection which narrows the **search**. Guided navigation is often used on shopping websites as it allows users to easily find items. See Figure 7.08.

- **Tag clouds**: a tag cloud has a list of terms, either displayed with numbers or in differently sized typefaces to show popularity. See Figure 7.08.
- **Site maps** provide an overview of the whole website to the user, making it possible to navigate directly to a particular page. See Figure 7.09.

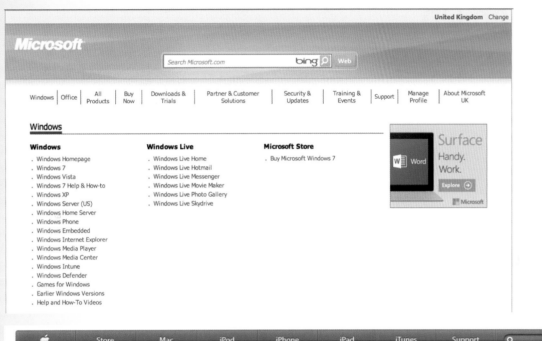

Figure 7.09 Microsoft® and Apple® site maps. You can see the full versions at www.microsoft.com/en/gb/sitemap.aspx and www.apple.com/uk/sitemap/.

Figure 7.08 Tag cloud (IBM) and guided navigation (Amazon™ © 2014 Amazon.com Inc. and its affiliates. All rights reserved.)

What is selection?

Selection is making a choice. Selection methods used in information systems include using a menu, filling in a form or clicking on a radio button or a hotspot.

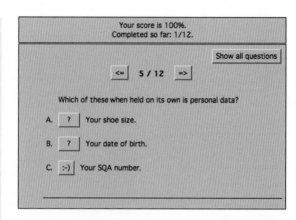

Figure 7.10 Form filling, radio buttons and hotspots

What is consistency?

A school uniform is consistent because it has the same set of colours and features, like the school badge. An information system is consistent if each page looks similar. Features which help a system to be consistent include:

- having the navigation buttons on the same place on each page
- using the same typeface, colours and styles
- maintaining the balance between text and graphics throughout.

What is interactivity?

Consistency is how a page looks compared to the other pages which make up the information system. Interactivity is the 'feel' of the page, for example the feedback that is received from selection. The most useful information systems always provide feedback to the user when a selection is made. For

Figure 7.11 Feedback

instance, if the user wishes to delete a **file**, then the system should ask for confirmation, such as in Figure 7.11.

Other examples of feedback include:

- providing more information on a topic
- displaying **audio** or **video**
- leading the user through a process by highlighting the next step.

What is readability?

An information system is readable when it is easy to read and understand. Readability may be tested by looking at the level of difficulty of the language used. One way of doing this is to measure the reading age of the text, by using **word-processing** software or a dedicated website. Using short words and sentences improves readability. This paragraph has a reading age of 14.

Be careful not to confuse the readability of an information system with readability of program code. Readability of program code may be improved by adding **internal commentary**. We looked at **readability of code** in Chapter 3.

What is accessibility?

An information system is **accessible** when it is **usable** by everyone, including people with disabilities. Mice and keyboards are used by many people, but they do not suit every person. Speech recognition systems and specialised pointing and selecting devices are examples of alternatives which make it possible for all users to interact with a computer system.

Methods of making a system accessible include:

- changing the typeface or the size and colour of the text
- magnifying the screen
- reading text aloud
- speech recognition
- adding sign language to video
- automatic **form-filling**, such as **auto-complete**.

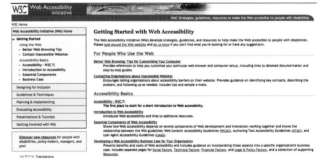

Figure 7.12 Making websites accessible (left). The Web Accessibility initiative: www.w3.org/WAI/gettingstarted/Overview.html (right)

Check Your Learning

Now answer questions 8–30 (on pages 182–183) on user requirements (National 5).

Practical Tasks

1 Choose two of the websites which you use regularly. Check the readability of the text contained in them. Here are two URLs to help you: www.read-able.com and www.readability-score.com.

2 Use the BBC website to find out more about making websites easier to use: www.bbc.co.uk/accessibility/.

3 Write a set of user interface requirements for one of the websites which you have designed.

4 Have a look at 'Gradybot' at www.bbc.co.uk/news/technology-22125682 and write a paragraph on what you think about its user interface. According to its users, how could the user interface of the 'Gradybot' be improved upon?

5 Go to http://appleinsider.com and search 'Microsoft backing off Metro, plans boot-to-desktop mode for windows 8.1'.

Read the article. What reason is given for the change to the user interface suggested by this article?

Questions

User interface and target audience (National 5)

1 What is a user interface?

2 What does the term HCI stand for?

3 Why is the quality of the user interface important?

4 State two ways in which the user can communicate with the computer.

5 State two ways in which the computer can communicate with the user.

6 What does the term target audience mean?

7 What can the designer of an information system do to help the target audience get the best out of it?

User requirements (National 5)

8 What are the user requirements?

9 List seven user requirements of an information system.

10 What is visual layout?

11 Match the correct features of the visual layout to the users in the table.

1 Step-by-step instructions on how to use the website

2 Bright and colourful screen which captures and holds the user's attention

3 Clear descriptions of the items displayed on the page

4 Large typeface or read aloud/text to speech

5 Essential information only, uncluttered

User	Visual layout
Young child	
Shopper	
Person with sensory impairment	
Expert	
Novice	

12 What is white space?

13 Describe one way in which white space improves visual layout.

14 What is navigation?

15 Explain the difference between hierarchical and linear navigation. You may draw a diagram to illustrate your answer.

16 State one advantage of
 a) hierarchical navigation.
 b) linear navigation.

17 Name three browser buttons or menu choices that may be used for navigation on a website.

18 Explain how a hotspot on a website may be identified.

19 a) What is context-sensitive navigation?
 b) What are breadcrumbs?
 c) What is guided navigation?
 d) What is a tag cloud?

20 What is selection?

21 State three methods of selection in an information system.

22 What is consistency?

23 State two features that will help pages have a consistent appearance throughout the information system.

24 What is interactivity?

25 State one example of interactive feedback that may be received from a web page.

26 What is readability?

27 How may readability be measured?

28 What is accessibility?

29 State two methods of improving the accessibility of a website.

30 Look at Figure 7.13, which shows an information system on a smartphone which is used for identifying birds.
 a) Starting from the screen of the left-hand side, describe what the user selected to finish up with the screen on the right.
 b) State two features of the user interface on this app that make it suitable for use on a smartphone.

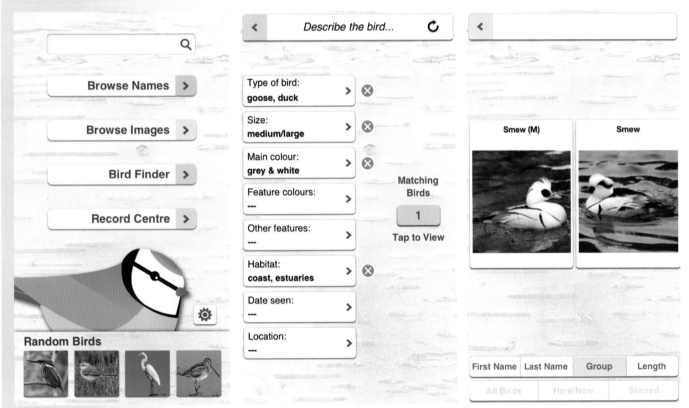

Figure 7.13 Information system for bird identification

Key Points

- The user interface is the way in which the computer and the user communicate.

- The user can communicate with a computer in a variety of ways, for instance by using a keyboard, mouse, track pad or touchscreen.

- The target audience is the people who will use an information system.

- It is important that designers and programmers of information systems take the target audience into account.

- The users in the target audience may be beginners (novices) or experts.

- The user requirements are the features of the user interface which should be taken into account by the designer and the programmer of the information system.

- The user requirements are visual layout, navigation, selection, consistency, interactivity, readability and accessibility.

- Visual layout is the appearance of the information system on the screen or how the display is organised.

- A screen which is crammed full of text and graphics, is more difficult to read than one which makes effective use of white space.

- Navigation is how the user finds their way around the information system.

- The navigation structure is the way in which the pages or screens in the information system are arranged.

- Types of navigation structure include hierarchical, linear and web.

- Hierarchical navigation allows fast movement between pages and can be easily expanded to allow more information to be added.

- Linear navigation is useful for processes that may be followed in a set order, like reading a story or making a purchase.

- Web navigation allows multiple direct connections between pages.

- Navigation methods used in information systems include browser features, menus, searching, hyperlinks, context-sensitive navigation, breadcrumbs, guided navigation, tag clouds and site maps.

- Selection is making a choice.

- Selection methods used in information systems include using a menu, filling in a form, clicking on a radio button or a hotspot.

- An information system is consistent if each page looks similar.

- Interactivity is the feel of the system when it is being used.

- The most useful information systems always provide feedback to the user when a selection is made.

- An information system is readable when it is easy to read and understand.

- Readability may be tested by looking at the level of difficulty of the language used.

- An information system is accessible when it is usable by everyone, including people with disabilities.

CHAPTER 8

Media types

This chapter describes types of media and covers the following topics.

- sound, graphics, video, text
- standard file formats:
  - text: TXT, RTF
  - audio: WAV, MP3
  - graphics: JPEG, BMP, GIF, PNG
  - video: MPEG (MP4), AVI
  - PDF
- factors affecting file size and quality, including resolution, colour depth, sampling rate; calculation of file size for colour bit map
- need for compression

Be very careful not confuse the media types in this chapter with the storage media in Chapter 12 or the transmission media in Chapter 13. These other types of media are forms of hardware. The media types dealt with in this chapter are software.

Media types

Computers use a range of **media** or **data types**. These include **sound**, **graphics**, **video** and **text**.

Computers store and handle **information**. Information is handled by a computer in the form of **data**. Computers control the storage of information and can change the way it is presented to the user. They can control the way data is moved from one place to another and they can change data from one form to another by using the rules that are stored in a **computer program**.

There are many different types of information stored on a computer as data.

Sound

This includes music or any other noise produced by a computer. Sound is also called **audio** data.

Graphics

The diagrams and other pictures in this book are graphics.

Video

Movies or videos are a type of data produced by a **digital video camera**, some **digital still cameras** and mobile phones. Video data is made up of a **sequence** of moving or 'live' action images.

Animation is data made up of moving graphics. Animation is the creation of apparent movement through the presentation of a sequence of slightly different still pictures. One method of producing animation is rapidly changing between two or more still images, like a flick book. Computer animation is used in the film and television industry to mix computer-generated images with 'live' action.

Text

Any **character** which appears on a computer **keyboard**, for example upper-case letters (ABCDEFGHIJKLMNOPQRSTUVWXYZ), lower case letters (abcdefghijklmnopqrstuvwxyz), numbers, punctuation marks and special characters, like the *octothorpe* (#), are text. Remember that numbers stored as text may not be used in calculations.

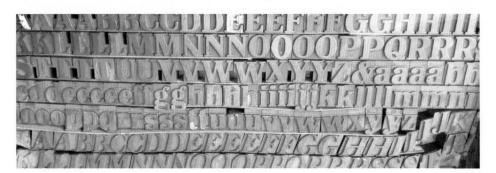

Figure 8.01

Multimedia

Multimedia is the presentation of information by a computer system using graphics, video, animation, sound and text.

Storage

Computers store data as a series of numbers, so any information that can be translated or coded as a series of numbers can be stored as data and processed by a computer. All of the different types of data described above are stored as a series of numbers inside a computer. You can read more about how numbers and other types of data are stored in Chapter 1.

Check Your Learning

Now answer questions 1–3 (on page 196) on media types (National 4).

Standard file formats

What is a standard file format?

A **standard file format** is a way of storing data so that it can be understood by and transferred between different **application packages**.

Why standard file formats are needed

All applications have their own particular file type. When you save data from an application into a **file**, additional information is saved which associates the file with the application that created it. This makes it easier for users, because opening the file (for example by clicking on the file **icon** with the **mouse**) will also automatically open the application.

If you wish to load the **data file** into a different application, then the other application program may not recognise the file and will not load it.

Sometimes there will be a variety of applications which can open the file. Simply clicking on the file may not open it in the user's *preferred* application. This may be avoided by using the *'open with'* feature (*right click*) on **Windows**® or Mac® **operating systems**.

Software companies know that users can increase their productivity and reduce their workload if it is possible to save files and data so that they may be transferred easily between different applications. For these reasons, various standard file formats have been developed. If two applications are able to save or load files in a standard file format, then it is easy to transfer data between them.

As an example, the **word-processing** package which I am using to write this book has 15 different file formats for saving its files. Each type of application software has its own set of standard file formats.

A (pre)cautionary tale

Students often write essays at home using a word-processing application, and then bring the files into school for further editing or printing. However, the students are sometimes dismayed to find that their files will not load into any of the applications on the school computers. This happens because the file types are not recognised by the applications.

This problem could have been avoided completely had the student taken some time to save a second copy of their work in a standard file format, such as **rich text format**.

Text: TXT, RTF

TXT (Text)

Text may be transferred between application packages, provided it is stored in a standard file format, which both packages can understand. The most common file format used for storing text is **ASCII**. ASCII is the **American Standard Code for Information Interchange**. An ASCII file consists of plain text, that is individual characters coded in ASCII. Each character in ASCII has its own unique code which is a number. For instance A = 65, B = 66 and so on. The representation of text in ASCII was dealt with earlier in this book in Chapter 1. An ASCII file has no formatting information and so the ASCII file type is readable by most applications. A plain text file may be identified by the suffix .TXT.

Feature summary: plain text, no formatting

RTF (Rich Text Format)

RTF is a complex format used to store data from a word-processing application. In addition to the text, RTF also holds information about the alignment, typefaces, sizes, colour and styles used in the document. RTF can be used to transfer data between most word-processing packages without losing the format. This can save a great deal of time because the user does not have to reformat the text after it has been transferred to the new application. A rich text file may be identified by the suffix .RTF.

Feature summary: formatted text

Audio: WAV, MP3

WAV (WAVeform audio file format)

WAV is the native sound format for Windows®. It is identified by, and gets its shortened name from, the suffix .WAV. WAV files are normally uncompressed and therefore have a larger **file size** than, for instance, **MP3** files. WAV files are used for high-quality sound applications, like CDs.

Feature summary: uncompressed, large file size, high quality

MP3 (MPEG-1 Audio Layer-3)

MP3 is currently the most popular file format on the web for distributing CD-quality sound. MP3 files are compressed to around one tenth of the size of the original file, yet preserve the **quality**. MP3 uses **lossy compression**. See later in this chapter for more about lossy compression. MP3 files can also be downloaded to portable players.

Feature summary: lossy compression, popular for downloads

Figure 8.02 WAV logo

Graphics: JPEG, BMP, GIF, PNG

JPEG

The **Joint Photographic Expert Group** has defined standards for still picture compression, and this format is called **JPEG**. JPEG files are compressed to save **backing storage** space, anywhere between 2:1 and 30:1. JPEG uses lossy compression, but has the advantage that the amount of compression is adjustable. This means that higher-quality JPEG images may be stored, but that they will take up more **storage** space, and vice-versa. The JPEG format is good for natural, real-life images. JPEG files do not allow transparency or animation.

Feature summary: 16.7 million colours, 24-bit, good for natural scenes, lossy compression

Figure 8.03 JPEG (16.7 million colours) and GIF (256 colours)

BMP

BMP is a bit-mapped image file format used on Windows® systems. BMP files are large, usually uncompressed. BMP files have **colour depths** of between 1 and 64 bits. 24-bit BMP files with 16.7 Million colours are common.

Feature summary: typically 16.7 Million colours, 1-64 bits, uncompressed

GIF (Graphics Interchange Format)

GIF is a format for storing graphics images. GIF files are compressed making them faster to load and transfer. GIF files may be **interlaced**, which means that a low-quality version of the image can be displayed whilst the rest of the data is still being downloaded. You can see an example of interlacing in Figure 8.04. Simple animations can also be held in GIF format by storing a sequence of images in a single GIF file. This is shown in Figure 8.05. GIF uses **lossless compression**, which means that no detail in the original image is lost when it is compressed. GIF files have a colour depth of 8 bits, meaning that they can have 256 colours (2^8). GIF files can have one transparent colour and work well for line drawings and pictures with solid blocks of colour, like cartoons.

Figure 8.04 Interlacing

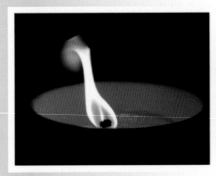 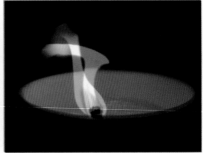 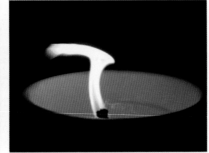

Figure 8.05 Animated sequence of images in a single GIF file

Feature summary: interlacing, animation, transparency, 256 colours, 8-bits, lossless compression, good for solid areas of colour

PNG (Portable Network Graphics)

PNG incorporates the advantages of GIF files, without the limitations. Like GIF files, PNG files use lossless compression. PNG files can have up to 48 bits colour depth. PNG images may also be partially transparent. **Partial transparency** is shown in Figure 8.06.

Figure 8.06 No transparency, partial transparency, full transparency

Feature summary: Interlacing, partial transparency, 48-bits, lossless compression

Figure 8.07 MPEG logo

Video: MPEG (including MP4), avi

MPEG

The **Motion (Moving) Picture Expert Group** has defined sets of standards for moving images, and this format is called **MPEG**. MPEG files are compressed to save backing storage space. MPEG is called a **container file** because it *contains* both video and audio in one file.

MPEG-1 was designed for lossy compression of video and audio. MPEG-1 is used worldwide to compress video and audio. It was the development of MPEG-1 which brought about digital TV and DAB radio. MPEG-1 Audio Layer-3 (MP3) has evolved from this standard.

MPEG-2 is used for digital TV, HDTV and **DVD**. MPEG-2 also uses lossy compression. **Devices** which can play MPEG-2 can also play MPEG-1.

MPEG-4 (MP4) is used for interactive video and **portable** devices. MPEG-4 files use lossless compression. MPEG-4 files use the suffix .mp4.

The .m4a suffix is used for MPEG-4 files which contain only audio, for example, as used by the iTunes® application. Similarly, .m4b allows **bookmarking** of audio and is used for **podcasts**; .m4p indicates that the audio file is protected by **DRM – Digital Rights Management**.

You can find out more about the MPEG standard at http://mpeg.chiariglione.org/.

Feature summary: (MPEG-1, MPEG-2 – lossy compression; MP4 – lossless compression)

AVI

Audio Video Interleave(d) (AVI) is the standard movie format for Windows®, and was designed by Microsoft®. AVI is the most popular video format. Many digital still cameras, when they are used to record video, store the files as AVI. Like MPEG, AVI is a multimedia *container* format. AVI files are large, and are intended for downloads rather than for streaming on the web.

Feature summary: (Standard Windows® movie format), large file size

PDF (Portable Document Format)

The **PDF** file type is a file format developed by Adobe Systems in order to exchange complete documents between different computer **platforms**, including Windows®, Mac OS® and mobile. PDF files may contain text, graphics, video, audio and clickable **hyperlinks**. Many different application packages may be used to create PDF files and programs like Adobe® Acrobat Reader® and Preview are used to view them. PDF became an open standard in 2008.

Many downloadable documents, such as past papers, are available in PDF. PDF is often used to create forms with spaces for responses.

PDF files are also widely used by publishers. When a book or a magazine is to be printed, the entire publication is saved as a PDF file or files, which are then sent to the printers.

PDF files may be both **encrypted** and **password** protected. See Figure 8.08. PDF files may also have **electronic signatures** added to them. Remember that any kind of signature, electronic or otherwise, may be forged.

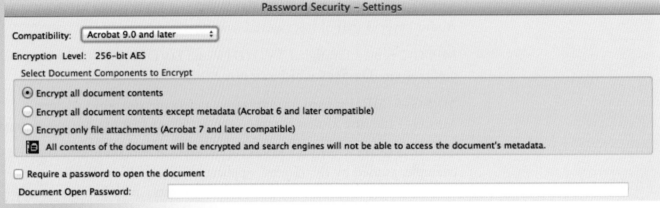

Figure 8.08 PDF security settings

Feature summary: format for exchanging complete documents between platforms

Factors affecting file size and quality

The factors which affect file size and quality are **resolution**, colour depth and **sampling rate**. Audio, graphics and video files are the only file formats to which these factors may be applied.

What is file size?

File size is the amount of space taken up by a file when it is being held on a **backing storage medium** such as **hard disk** or **flash ROM**. In the case of image files, the file size may be an indication of quality, but this is not the case for other types of data. For instance, an audio file may be large because of its length, but still may be of poor quality. We first looked at file size in Chapter 1.

What is quality?

Quality may be judged by comparing the original with its representation in a given file format. The closer the resemblance to the original, then the higher the quality of the data. So we can say that quality is how closely a file matches when compared to the original.

Image quality

If you look at Figure 8.03 and compare the JPEG image with the GIF image, then it is possible to see that the GIF **image** has a lower **quality** than the JPEG, mainly because of the reduced colour depth of the GIF file. It is not quite so easy to compare two JPEG images, which are identical apart from the amount of compression that has been used. In this case, it is often necessary to zoom into the image before any variation in quality may be noticeable. However, if the image files are displayed on the computer **screen**, then detailed information about the resolution and colour depth may be shown, giving a better guide to quality. The JPEG image has a file size of 207 **Kilobytes** and the GIF, 103 Kilobytes.

Resolution

The resolution is the amount of detail which can be shown on a screen or on a printout. The smaller the size of the **pixels**, the finer the detail that can be displayed on the screen. Small pixels mean high resolution. Large pixels mean low resolution. One way of describing the resolution of the screen is to give the number of pixels horizontally and vertically. Another way of describing the resolution is to give the total number of pixels available, for instance, 10 **Megapixels**. The greater the number of pixels in an image, the higher the quality and the larger the file size, since more data must be stored.

Colour depth

The colour depth is the number of bits used to represent colours or shades of grey used in a graphic. A one-bit colour depth allows two different colours to be represented, because one bit may have only two values, 0 or 1. GIF images are limited to 8-bit colour depth, which means that they may have 256 different colours. Most other image file formats in this chapter have a 24-bit colour depth, allowing 16 777 216 different colours to be shown. Increasing the **bit depth** increases the number of possible colours and therefore the quality and increases the file size. You can read more about resolution and colour depth in Chapter 1.

Video quality

The quality of a video file also depends on resolution and colour depth, since a video is a series of still images, displayed one after the other, in sequence. One other factor in determining **video quality** is the speed at which each of the still images, or frames, is displayed. This is known as the **frame rate**. A typical frame rate for video is 24 or 25 frames per second (fps). *The Hobbit* was the first film to be taken or *shot* at 48 fps.

Audio quality

Audio quality is difficult to gauge by listening – a lot depends on the **loudspeakers** or the **head/earphones** being used. High-quality audio can appear less so on poor equipment, although good equipment can easily show up a poor-quality sound. Measuring the sampling rate and the **sampling depth** of the audio is the best guide.

Sound is **analogue**. In order for it to be processed by a computer system, it must be changed into **digital**. This is done by measuring or **sampling**. The sampling rate is the number of times in one second that measurements of the sound are taken. A CD-quality sound has a sampling rate of 44 100 times per second or 44.1 Kilohertz. The sampling depth is the number of bits that are used for each measurement. A CD-quality sound has a sampling depth of 16 bits, allowing 65 536 different levels of sound. Increasing the sampling rate will increase the quality of the sound and increase the file size, since more data must be stored.

Calculation of file size for colour bit map

The file size of a colour bit-mapped image may be calculated by using the formula:

> Storage requirements = total number of pixels used in the image × number of bits used to represent colours or shades of grey for each pixel

You can read more about and see examples of the calculation of the file size of a colour bit-mapped image in Chapter 1.

Calculation of file size for video

The file size of a video may be calculated by using the formula:

> Storage requirements = total number of pixels used in each frame × number of bits used to represent colours or shades of grey for each pixel (colour depth) × number of frames per second × time in seconds

Calculation of file size for audio

The file size of an audio file may be calculated by using the formula:

> Storage requirements = sampling rate (Hz) × sampling depth (bits) × time in seconds × number of channels (2 for stereo)

Figure 8.09 Compression

Need for compression

File **compression** is the process of reducing the size of a file. File compression is needed in order to save backing storage space or to shorten the time taken to send a file between two computer systems. If you send a file via the **internet**, or download a file, then it will most likely be compressed. Many audio, video and graphics file formats use compression.

No matter what type of compression is used, it will be either lossy or lossless. Lossy compression involves sacrificing some of the data in order to reduce the file size. This may mean that the resolution of an image is reduced, or that a sound file has a reduced frequency range. Lossless compression means that no data is lost. As you might expect, lossy compression will result in the greater reduction in file size. The use of lossy compression with image files may cause unwanted flaws or **artefacts** to appear in the image. Some artefacts are shown in Figure 8.10.

Figure 8.10 Artefacts may be seen in the compressed image on the left

Check Your Learning

Now answer questions 4–44 (on page 196) on media types (National 5).

Practical Tasks

1 Create a text file in a word-processing application or text editor. Format the text as coloured and italics. Save the file as plain text (TXT) and rich text (RTF). What do you expect will happen to the text formatting in each file?

2 If you have a smartphone, portable media player or tablet, find out which audio and video formats are supported by the device. Record your answers in a table.

3 Find out what the song called 'Tom's diner' has to do with MP3 files.

Questions

Media types (National 4)

1 Name four types of media (data).

2 Which type of media is
   a) music?   b) pictures?
   c) movies?   d) characters?

Media types (National 5)

4 What is a standard file format?

5 Explain why standard file formats are needed.

6 Name two standard file formats for
   a) text.
   b) audio.
   c) graphics.
   d) video.

7 Which standard file format allows complete documents to be exchanged between different computer systems?

8 Explain how you can use your computer's operating system to choose which application package may be used to open a file.

9 What is ASCII?

10 Which file format uses ASCII?

11 Explain how ASCII is used on a computer system.

12 State one advantage of using RTF instead of TXT.

13 What does the suffix WAV stand for?

14 Why is it normal for WAV files to have a large file size?

15 What does the suffix MP3 stand for?

16 If a WAV file of size 30 Megabytes was stored as MP3, what would the MP3 file size be?

17 From where does JPEG take its name?

18 To which type of image is the JPEG file format suited?

19 Why do BMP files usually have a large file size?

20 What does the suffix GIF stand for?

21 Explain how GIF files may hold simple animations.

22 State one type of image to which GIF is suited.

23 What is the maximum number of colours that may be used in a GIF image?

3 Explain how it is possible for a computer to store and process many different media (data) types.

24 What does the suffix PNG stand for?

25 State three of the numbers used in MPEG video.

26 Which MPEG format is used in
   a) DVD?
   b) DAB radio?
   c) portable devices?

27 Name the group who invented the MPEG standard.

28 Which company created the AVI standard?

29 What does AVI stand for?

30 What does PDF stand for?

31 What software is required to be able to view PDF documents?

32 State three factors which affect file size and quality.

33 What is file size?

34 What is quality?

35 What is resolution?

36 What is colour depth?

37 What is sampling rate?

38 State two methods of increasing the quality of a graphic.

39 State one method of increasing audio quality.

40 Explain what happens to the file size when the quality of an image is increased.

41 State the formula used for the calculation of the file size of a colour bit map.

42 What is compression?

43 Why is compression needed?

44 Explain the difference between lossy and lossless compression.

Key Points

- Computers use a range of media or data types. These include sound, graphics, video and text.

- Sound includes music or any other noise produced by a computer.

- Graphics includes diagrams, photographs and any other images.

- Video data is made up of a sequence of moving or 'live' action images.

- Any character which appears on a computer keyboard is text.

- Multimedia is the presentation of information by a computer system using graphics, video, animation, sound and text.

- All data in a computer is stored as a series of numbers.

- A standard file format is a way of storing data so that it can be understood by and transferred between different application packages.

- **Text:**
  - The most common file format used for storing text is ASCII.
  - ASCII is the American Standard Code for Information Interchange.
  - Rich Text Format (RTF) also holds information about the alignment, typefaces, sizes, colour and styles used in the document.

- **Audio:**
  - WAVeform audio file format (WAV) is the native sound format for Windows®.
  - MP3 (MPEG-1 Audio Layer-3) files are compressed to around one tenth of the size of the original file, yet preserve the quality.

- **Graphics:**
  - The Joint Photographic Expert Group (JPEG) is good for natural, real-life images.
  - BMP is a bit-mapped image file format used on Windows® systems.
  - GIF (Graphics Interchange Format) works well for line drawings and pictures with solid blocks of colour, like cartoons.
  - GIF is limited to 256 colours.

- Portable Network Graphics (PNG) incorporates the advantages of GIF files, without the limitations, i.e. more than 256 colours may be represented.

- **Video:**
  - The Motion Picture Expert Group video format is called MPEG.
  - MPEG-1, MPEG-2 and MPEG-4 (MP4) are all standards used to store video.
  - Audio Video Interleave(d) (AVI) is the standard movie format for Windows®.

- PDF (Portable Document Format) is a file format developed by Adobe® Systems Inc. in order to exchange complete documents between different computer platforms, including Windows®, Mac OS® and mobile. PDF files may contain text, graphics, video, audio and clickable hyperlinks.

- The factors which affect file size and quality are resolution, colour depth and sampling rate.

- Audio, graphics and video files are the only file formats to which these factors may be applied.

- File size is the amount of space taken up by a file when it is being held on a backing storage medium such as hard disk or flash ROM.

- Quality is how closely a file matches when compared to the original.

- The resolution is the amount of detail which can be shown on a screen or on a printout.

- The colour depth is the number of bits used to represent colours or shades of grey used in a graphic.

- The sampling rate is the number of times in one second that measurements of the sound are taken.

- Increasing the resolution and colour depth of an image or the sampling rate of an audio file will improve the quality and also increase the file size, since more data must be stored.

- The file size of a colour bit-mapped image may be calculated by using the formula: Storage requirements = total number of pixels used in the image × number of bits used to represent colours or shades of grey for each pixel.

- The file size of a video may be calculated by using the formula: Storage requirements = total number of pixels used in each frame × number of bits used to represent colours or shades of grey for each pixel (colour depth) × number of frames per second × time in seconds
- The file size of an audio file may be calculated by using the formula: Storage requirements = sampling rate (Hz) × sampling depth (bits) × time in seconds × number of channels (2 for stereo)
- File compression is the process of reducing the size of a file.
- File compression is needed in order to save backing storage space or to shorten the time taken to send a file between two computer systems.

CHAPTER 9

Coding

This chapter describes the exemplification and implementation of coding to create and modify information systems, including the use of:

- scripting languages (including JavaScript®)
- mark-up languages (including HTML).

Scripting languages

What is a scripting language?

A **scripting language** is a programming language that allows the user to carry out or **automate tasks**, which would otherwise have to be done as a series of single steps. Scripting languages may be used to automate tasks in **application packages**, **web browsers** and **operating systems**.

Scripting languages are normally **interpreted**. You can read more about the operation of an **interpreter** in Chapter 1.

Examples of scripting languages include **JavaScript®**, **VBScript®** and **AppleScript®**.

JavaScript®

JavaScript® was invented for use in web browsers. It was created by **Brendan Eich** in 1995, while working at Netscape. The purpose of JavaScript® is to make **web pages** more dynamic and interactive. A simple example of this interaction is shown in the **script** below:

```html
<html>
<head>
<title></title>
<script type="text/javascript">
function Computing()
{alert ("Computing Science Rocks!");}
</script>
</head>
<body>
<a href="javascript:Computing()">ComputingScience</a>
</body>
</html>
```

ComputingScience

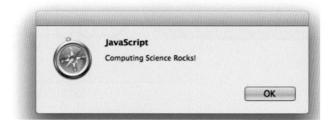

ComputingScience

Figure 9.01 Sample outputs from the JavaScript® example on the previous page

Advantages of JavaScript®

JavaScript® has a number of advantages. These include:

- it may be included in the **HTML** code of a web page
- the code will operate without an **internet** connection, without having to communicate with a **server** and is relatively fast
- it can load only the required content and the whole web page need not be reloaded
- it is a fully-featured programming language – you may be using JavaScript® as your main programming language for this course.

Disadvantages of JavaScript®

- **Security**: hackers can use JavaScript® to run malicious code or **malware** on a user's computer. However, users can disable the JavaScript® code from working by changing the settings in the browser.

- Advertising: JavaScript® may be used to create adverts and pop-up **windows**, which can annoy users.

- Layout: the **output** from JavaScript® may look different on different browsers.

Whether the following feature of JavaScript® is an advantage or a disadvantage, I leave it up to the reader to decide. JavaScript® can be used to write **cookies**, which are used to identify and track visitors to web pages, by storing **data** on the user's computer. This may be convenient for users who frequently visit a site, for instance, such as online shopping.

These websites have stored data that can be used to track your browsing. Removing the data may reduce tracking, but may also log you out of websites or change website behavior.

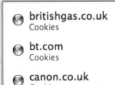

britishgas.co.uk
Cookies

bt.com
Cookies

canon.co.uk
Cookies

Figure 9.02 Cookies

VBScript®

VBScript® is a scripting language which is provided along with the Microsoft **Windows**® Operating System. VBScript® works in a variety of different Microsoft applications and is modelled on **Visual Basic**®. VBScript® is used in a similar manner to JavaScript®, when used with **Internet Explorer**®. However, VBScript® does not work on all web browsers. Have a look at the example VBScript® below. What do you think will be the output when this script is run?

```
<!DOCTYPE html>
<html>
<body>
<script type="text/vbscript">
Dim cars(2)
cars(0)="Bristol Fighter"
cars(1)="Gumpert Apollo"
cars(2)="Isdera Commendatore"
For Each x In cars
    document.write(x & "<br>")
Next
</script>
</body>
</html>
```

AppleScript®

AppleScript® is a scripting language provided with Apple® computers. It was invented in 1993 and works with the Macintosh Operating System and any scriptable applications. The AppleScript® Editor program is used to create scripts. Scripts may be run directly from the editor or they may be saved separately as stand-alone applications. An example script is shown below. Have a look at it and see if you can work out what it does.

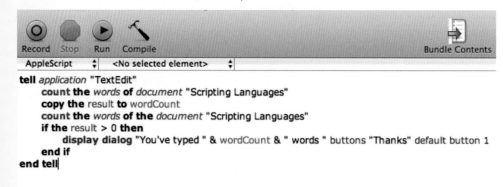

```
tell application "TextEdit"
    count the words of document "Scripting Languages"
    copy the result to wordCount
    count the words of the document "Scripting Languages"
    if the result > 0 then
        display dialog "You've typed " & wordCount & " words " buttons "Thanks" default button 1
    end if
end tell
```

Figure 9.03 AppleScript®

Mark-up languages

What is a mark-up language?

A **mark-up language** is a programming language used for describing how **text** and other media are presented to the user. The term 'mark-up' comes from the notations made on a paper manuscript which is being edited and prepared for publication. If you use a highlighter pen on your notes, then that is an example of mark-up.

Mark-up languages include SGML, XML, HTML, **VRML**, X3D and XHTML.

HyperText Mark-up Language (HTML)

HTML is used to create documents or web pages, which may be viewed by using a web browser. HTML uses **elements** to carry out the mark-up functions. An HTML document has three main elements, the document type declaration, the **head** and the **body**. Each part or element of an HTML document is separated or delimited by a **tag**. Each tag has a start like this <> and most tags require an end tag, like this </>. Start and end tags are also called open and closing tags.

The basic layout of some tags is shown opposite. Note that the tags are nested, for instance, the **<title>** tag is contained entirely between, or is surrounded by, the two <head> tags. The <p>aragraph tags are nested within the <body> tags in the same manner. Some tags, such as <style> and **<img>**, have **attributes**, like **color** and **alt**, which provide additional information about an element. Attributes can contain values and are enclosed in quotes, for instance, alt = "An image of a car".

```
<!DOCTYPE html>          ← Document type
<html>                   ← Mark-up language used
    <head>               ← Start of head
        <title>          ← Start of title
        My first web page ← text
        </title>         ← End of title
    </head>              ← End of head
<body>                   ← Start of body
    <p>First paragraph</p>
    <p>Second paragraph</p>
</body>                  ← End of body
</html>                  ← End of HTML
```

When a web page is created in a **text editor** such as NotePad or TextEdit, then the elements and tags, which describe the structure of the page, are visible. When the web page is displayed, the tags do not appear, only their effect may be seen. Care must be taken when opening and closing tags, otherwise the tag itself will appear on-screen.

When a web page is created in web page creation **software**, such as Adobe® Dreamweaver®, Freeway™ or Microsoft Expression®, the user enters the content of the web page directly onto the **screen** without having to include any tags. This type of software is called **WYSIWYG**, or What You See Is What You Get. The tags and other elements of the web page are created automatically by the software.

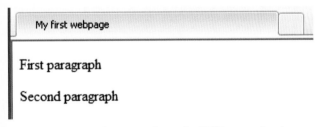

Figure 9.04 Sample output from the HTML example above

Table 9.01 contains a description of some html tags and attributes.

Tags and attributes	Description	Example
<html>	The html tag is used to show the beginning of mark-up.	
<head>	Shows the header, contains title and links to style sheets.	
<body>	The web page content is placed inside these tags.	
<title>	Puts a title in the browser title bar.	

Tags and attributes	Description	Example
<a>	The hypertext anchor tag.	
href	Used with <a> to indicate the URL. The text in between the tags provides a hyperlink.	
	If the URL points to an external website, then the URL is said to be absolute.	<a href="www.bbc.co.uk/news/scotland/ "> BBC </a>
	If the URL points to a page within the same website (i.e. internal), then it is known as a relative URL.	<a href="home.htm"> Home Page </a>
	An anchor URL points to a specific place on a web page.	<a href="#top"> Return to top </a>
<img>	Used to display an image.	<img src="logo.gif" alt="Company logo" height="100" width="59">
src	Filename of image. This can be a pathname or URL.	
alt	Text description of image. The text is also displayed if the image cannot be found.	
<p>	Paragraph tag.	
<h1> ... <h6>	Heading tags. Decreasing in size from <h1> to <h6>.	
<i>	Text in italics.	Also <em>
<b>	Text in bold typeface.	Also <strong>
<script>	The text inside this tag is an interactive script.	<script type="text/javascript">
type	Used with the <script tag> to tell the browser which scripting language is being used.	
<!--	Used to add comments to the document, which can help explain your code to others.	<!--This is a comment. Comments are not displayed in the browser-->

The <style> tag and some of its attributes	Description	Examples of attributes and their values
<style>	Inline style is placed in the tags.	<p style="color: red">text</p>
	Internal style is defined within the <head> tags.	<style> h2 {color:white;} </style>
	External style uses a separate CSS file, which is called by using a <link> tag.	<link rel="stylesheet" type="text/css" href="web.css" />
background-color	Controls the background colour of the page. May be used with a named colour or by using the RGB colour system†.	{background-color:#ff0000;} {background-color:rgb(255,0,0);} {background-color:red;} *Note US spelling

The <style> tag and some of its attributes	Description	Examples of attributes and their values
color	Controls the text colour. May be used with a named colour or by using the RGB colour system†.	{color:blue;} *Note US spelling*
margin-left	Size of the left margin measured in pixels (px).	{margin-left:10px}
font-family	Name of the font or typeface used for the text.	{font-family:"Times New Roman";}
font-size	Size of the text.	{font-size:24pt;}

†The RGB (Red Green Blue) colour system uses three values, one for each colour. The values may be written in decimal or hexadecimal (base 16), where a=10, b=11, c=12, d=13, e=14 and f=15. The smallest value is 0, written as 00 and the largest value is 255, written as ff. For example, #ff0000 is red, #00ff00 is green and #ffffff is white.

Table 9.01

Here is an example of internal html styling:

```
<html>
<head>
<style>
body {background-color:#07b030;}
h1 {color:orange;margin-left:10px;font-family:"Times New Roman";font-size:32pt;}
h2 {color:white;margin-left:20px;font-family:"Arial";font-size:18pt;}
p   {color:blue;margin-left:30px;font-family:"Courier";font-size:18pt;}
</style>
</head>

<body>

<h1>This html code shows style!</h1>
<h2>This header is coloured white</h2>

<p>This paragraph has a left margin of 10 pixels</p>

</body>
</html>
```

This html code shows style!

This header is coloured white

This paragraph has a left margin of 10 pixels

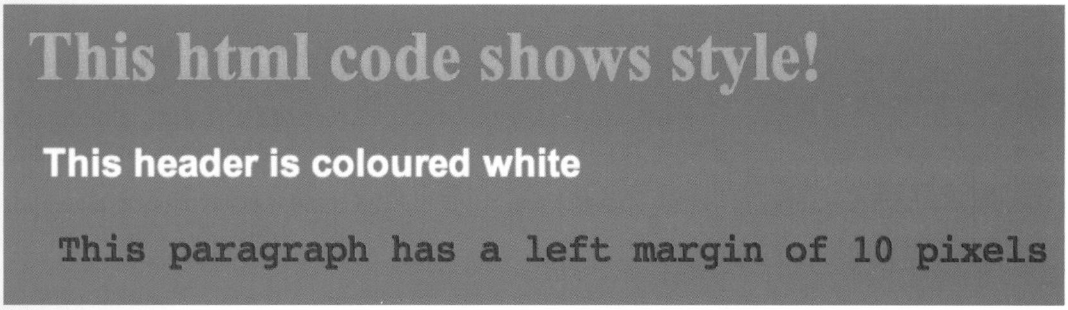

Figure 9.05 Sample output from the internal HTML styling example

Check Your Learning

Now answer questions 1–24 (at the bottom of the page) on coding (National 5).

Note: This chapter is not meant to be a comprehensive treatment of scripting or mark-up languages. Your teacher or lecturer will provide you with further examples and exercises.

Practical Tasks

1 The best way to learn coding is to practise it. Many websites provide free online tutorials in scripting and mark-up languages. Some suitable URLs are given here and you can find many others by using a search engine:
- www.w3schools.com
- www.codecademy.com/
- www.html.net

2 Look back at the examples of code shown in this chapter and try them out on a computer system. Where possible, insert comments (<!-- html --> , // JavaScript //) to explain the purpose of each line of code.

3 Find out more about the RGB colour system used on web pages by searching for *web safe colours*. What is 'safe' about these colours?

4 What do Adobe® Photoshop® Lightroom®, Angry Birds®, Apache™ Server, Firefox®, MediaWiki® and World of Warcraft® all have in common? Answer: the cross-platform scripting language Lua. Have a look at: www.lua.org/home.html and www.lua.org/demo.html.

Questions

Coding (National 5)

1 What is a scripting language?

2 Name two scripting languages.

3 What is the purpose of JavaScript®?

4 State two advantages of JavaScript®.

5 State two disadvantages of JavaScript®.

6 Explain one difference between JavaScript® and Java™.

7 Explain one difference between JavaScript® and VBScript®.

8 State one feature of AppleScript®.

9 What is a mark-up language?

10 Explain where the term 'mark-up' comes from.

11 What does HTML stand for?

12 What is the purpose of HTML?

13 State the three main elements of an HTML document.

14 What is the purpose of a tag in HTML?

15 State another term for start and end tags.

16 Explain the term nested with respect to tags.

17 State one example which shows how tags may be nested.

18 Expand the term WYSIWYG.

19 Name one application which is WYSIWYG.

20 Which tag is
   a) the anchor tag?
   b) used to display an image?
   c) used to create a paragraph?
   d) used to close an html document?

21 Name two attributes used with the <style> tag.

22 How many values are used in the RGB colour system?

23 What is the maximum RGB value for a single colour?

24 What is the RGB colour code for red?

Key Points

- A scripting language is a programming language that allows the user to carry out or automate tasks.
- Examples of scripting languages include JavaScript®, VBScript® and AppleScript®.
- JavaScript® was invented for use in web browsers.
- The purpose of JavaScript® is to make web pages more dynamic and interactive.
- JavaScript® advantages include:
  - it may be included in the HTML code of a web page
  - the code will operate without an internet connection
  - it can load only the required content of a web page
  - it is a fully-featured programming language.
- JavaScript® disadvantages include:
  - Security: hackers can use JavaScript® to run malware
  - Advertising: JavaScript® may be used to create pop-up windows
  - Layout: the output from JavaScript® may look different on different browsers.
- JavaScript® can be used to write cookies, which are used to identify and track visitors to web pages.
- Java™ is a compiled language used to create stand-alone programs.

- JavaScript® is used with a web browser program and is an interpreted language.
- VBScript® works in a variety of different Microsoft applications and is used in a similar manner to JavaScript®, when used with Internet Explorer.
- AppleScript® is a scripting language which works with the Macintosh Operating System and any scriptable applications.
- A mark-up language is a programming language used for describing how text and other media are presented to the user.
- HyperText Mark-up Language (HTML) is used to create web pages which may be viewed by using a web browser.
- An HTML document has three main elements, the document type declaration, the head and the body.
- Each part or element of an HTML document is separated by a tag.
- Each tag has a start, like this <> and an end tag, like this </>.
- Some tags have attributes, which provide additional information about an element.
- Attributes can contain values and are enclosed in quotes.
- Web pages may be created by using a text editor or web page creation software, which is usually WYSIWYG.

CHAPTER 10 Purpose, features, functionality, users

This chapter gives simple descriptions of the main features and functionality of information systems and also examines:

- description of purpose
- users: expert, novice, age-range.

Simple descriptions of main features and functionality of information systems

What is an information system?

An **information** system is an integrated set of components that enable people to carry out tasks effectively by providing access to information.

Information systems may be manual or computer-based. Manual information systems include your homework diary or planner, telephone directory and shopping catalogues. Computer-based information systems include **databases** and **websites**. This chapter deals with computer-based information systems.

Figure 10.01 Some information systems

What are the main features of an information system?

The main features or components of an information system are **hardware**, **software**, **storage** and **networks/connectivity**.

Hardware

Hardware is the physical parts of a computer system, the parts that you can see and touch. The hardware should be able to store the volume of **data** that is required and provide backup facilities in case of system failures or mistakes. You can read more about hardware in Chapters 11 and 12.

Software

Software is the programs that the hardware of the computer runs. The software should be able to process, **search** and sort the data quickly and efficiently. The software may be a general purpose **package** such as a database or other dedicated information management software, for example for attendance and reporting in schools or stock control in a shop. Databases are structured collections of similar information, which can be searched. You can read more about databases in Chapter 6.

Storage

All information systems have a storage requirement. Typical **storage media** include **hard** and **solid-state disks** and the **cloud**. The quantity of storage required depends upon the amount and type of files to be stored. For instance, images and **video** data will take up more storage space than **text** or numbers.

Networks/connectivity

Networks are sets of computers joined together so that data can be transferred or communicated between them. You can read more about networks in Chapter 13.

What are the main functions of an information system?

The main **functions** of an information system are *collecting*, *organising*, *storing*, *processing* and *outputting* information.

Collecting information means taking it in and gathering it together. Computer systems have variety of **input devices** for this purpose, including **keyboards**, mice and **scanners**.

Organising information means managing it using software such as a **database package** or **web page** creation application.

Storing information is saving information so that it may be used again. It is important that all the information stored on a computer system is regularly copied to backup media. If this is not done, one mistake could mean that all of the information is lost.

Processing information is performing operations on information. For instance, searching, sorting and calculating.

Outputting information is displaying or communicating it in whatever format is required, for example in a printed report or a web page on a **monitor**.

What is the difference between data and information?

Information has a meaning. For example, '21 August 2014' is information, meaning the 21st day of the month of August, in the year 2014. Computers store information as a series of numbers. These numbers are data, which don't mean anything on their own. Only if you know how the computer has organised the information as data, does it mean anything to you. For example, 210814 … is data.

If you know that the computer puts the last two digits of the year as the first two digits of this data, and the number of the month as the third and fourth digits and the day of the month as the last two digits, then you understand that these numbers mean the same as the information in the previous paragraph.

Example

When people apply for a driving licence they are given a personal identification number. This is used to help identify a person's details. Part of this number refers to the person's date of birth – but the figures are arranged differently from the way we normally write a date.

For example, if the person were born on 12 October 1998, this would normally be written as 12.10.98 (where 12 is the day of the month; 10 refers to October as the 10th month and 98 is the year 1998).

On the driving licence the computer records the date as 910128. This is simply a string of digits, or a piece of data, unless you know how to 'decode' the data to make the date. When you can do this, the digits become information.

So we can say that:

> Information (for people) = data (for computers) with structure.

Data becomes information when you understand what it means. Computers process data, people use information.

GIGO

An information system is only of use if the information it contains is *accurate*, *complete* and *up to date*. A computing term, which has been in use for a long time, is 'Garbage In – Garbage Out', which sums up this point very well.

If the data in an information system is **input** incorrectly or in the wrong format it is useless. Most systems will ask the user to input important data, such as **passwords**, twice. This is called verifying the data. We looked at this and other methods of making sure that data is accurate in Chapter 6.

For instance, if you are a student in school, each year you are given a copy of the personal information that is held in the school office. You should check this information carefully and supply any updates that are required.

It is so important that data in an information system is always accurate, complete and up to date that the government has created a law called the **Data Protection Act**. You can read more about the Data Protection Act 1998 later on in this book in Chapter 15.

Figure 10.02

What are the advantages of computer-based information systems?

Computer-based information systems have the following advantages over manual systems:

- The computer can retrieve (or find) the data very quickly, but searching through manual filing systems can take a very long time.
- Manual files take up much more space than computer files to store the same amount of information.
- It is difficult to get a complete set of information when using separate manual filing systems.
- Computers can store large quantities of information on a single storage **medium**.
- Computer-based information systems can be constantly **updated**, so that the information that they contain is always accurate and up to date.
- Databases held by different organisations can be linked in networks, and accessed from anywhere in the world via the **internet**. This improves the flow of information between and within organisations.

Check Your Learning

Now answer questions 1–8 (on page 215) on main features and functionality (National 4).

Users

Who are the users of an information system?

Users of information systems include **experts** and **novices**.

An expert user is a person who is familiar with the features and functions of the information system and can use it to their advantage. An expert user does not need to be provided with detailed instructions on how to get started, but can find their own way around the system and make use of **online help** if required.

A novice user is a person who is unfamiliar with the features and functions of the information system and requires support on how to use the system and how to get the best out of it. A novice user will benefit from being given detailed instructions on how to get started with the system.

Age-range

The **age-range** refers to the ages of the users of the information system. Typical users include: young child, teenager and adult.

Any of these different users may form the **target audience** for an information system. Designers and **programmers** of information systems should take the target audience into account when creating the **user interface** for their systems. We looked at some **user interface requirements** in Chapter 7. These were **visual layout**, **navigation**, **selection**, **consistency**, **interactivity**, **accessibility** and **readability**.

Description of purpose of an information system

What is the purpose of an information system?

The purpose of any information system is to contain information and present it to the user in a form which is useful to them.

An information system which collects, organises, stores, processes and outputs information for the benefit of a company or organisation is called an **organisational information system**. Organisations which use information systems for this purpose include schools, shops, banks and hospitals. Some examples of computer-based information systems are shown in Figures 10.03, 10.04 and 10.05. Their purposes and some of their functions are described here.

Figure 10.03 Computer-based school information system

The *purpose* of a school information system is to take care of all of the administrative tasks in a school. The functions of a school information system include:

- Collecting: gathering registration information and examination marks.
- Organising: sorting students into classes for different lessons.
- Storing: keeping **backup copies** of data in case of system errors or mistakes. The companies which provide these services will store all of the information on their own **file servers**. Each school or education authority will access the information using computers attached to a Wide Area Network. See Chapter 13 for more about networks.
- Processing: putting reports from different teachers together for each student.
- Outputting: printing reports for parents and senior staff, and sending marks to examiners.

The *range of users* of a school information system are students and their parents, the staff in the school, the local authority, examiners and inspectors.

Figure 10.04 Online shop (© 2014 Amazon.com Inc. and its affiliates. All rights reserved.)

The *purpose* of an online shopping information system is to sell items to customers. The functions of an online shopping information system include:

- Collecting: gathering the descriptions and prices of items to be sold and names and addresses of customers.
- Organising: sorting related items into different categories to make it easier for shoppers to find what they are looking for.
- Storing: keeping backup copies of data in case of system errors or mistakes.
- Processing: updating the stock levels when goods arrive and are sold, using payment information from customers to transfer funds, calculating the profit made!
- Outputting: printing packing lists for parcels of goods, and sending invoices to customers.

The *range of users* of an online shopping information system are the customers and staff of the company. The methods of payment required by online shops means that the customers who pay are unlikely to be very young children, but there is no age restriction on who chooses the items!

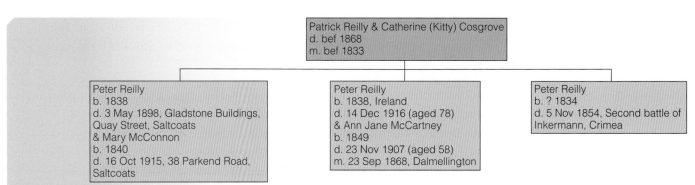

Figure 10.05 Part of a family tree information system

The *purpose* of a family tree is to record details of family members and their lives. The functions of a family tree include:

- Collecting: gathering the names of relations and dates of significant events in their lives such as births, marriages and deaths.
- Organising: sorting relatives into families, searching for names and dates.
- Storing: keeping backup copies of data in case of system errors or mistakes.
- Processing: linking people to show relationships, making sure entries are valid, for example that a person was not born before their parents were.
- Outputting: displaying and printing charts of family trees, and exporting family files to send to relatives.

The *range of users* of a family tree are the members of the families who make up the tree. This includes all age groups. The person who adds information to the family tree would be an expert user in terms of this information system.

Check Your Learning

Now answer questions 9–15 (on page 215) on purpose and users (National 5).

Practical Tasks

1 Make a list of the names of four information systems that you use, for instance Facebook.

2 Using the information given in this chapter as a starting point, complete the following table for one of the information systems that you use.

Name	School information system	
Purpose	School administration	
Users	Students, staff, parents	
Functions	Gathering registration information and examination marks	
Hardware	Teacher computers	
Software	Dedicated database software	
Storage	On company servers	
Connectivity	Wide Area Network accessed from school network	

3 Compare the two websites CBBC
(www.bbc.co.uk/cbbc/) and CBEEBIES
(www.bbc.co.uk/cbeebies/) in terms of
age-range. Make a list of the features
of each web page to help explain
your findings.

4 Find out how to create a 'wordle' and make
one for the features and functions of
information systems that you learned about in
this chapter.

Questions

Main features and functionality (National 4)

1 What is an information system?

2 State one example of a manual information system
and one example of a computer-based information
system.

3 List the four main features of an information system.

4 List the five main functions of an information
system.

5 Explain the difference between data and information
by using an example item of data. Use today's date
as your example.

6 What is GIGO?

7 Why is it so important that an information system is
accurate, complete and up to date?

8 State two advantages of computer-based information
systems compared to manual information systems.

Purpose and users (National 5)

9 What is an expert user?

10 What is a novice user?

11 What does the term age-range mean?

12 Name three typical users throughout the
age-range.

13 What is the purpose of an information system?

14 State one purpose for each of the following
information systems:
a) Family-tree database.
b) Police database.
c) Income Tax database.
d) Home shopping website.
e) National Health Service website.

15 What is an organisational information system?

Key Points

- An information system is an integrated set of components that enable people to carry out tasks effectively by providing access to information.
- Information systems may be manual or computer-based.
- Computer-based information systems include databases and websites.
- The main features or components of an information system are hardware, software, storage and networks/connectivity.
- The main functions of an information system are collecting, organising, storing, processing and outputting information.
- Information has a meaning.
- Computers store information as a series of numbers.
- These numbers are data, which don't mean anything on their own.
- Only if you know how the computer has organised the information as data, does it mean anything to you.
- Information (for people) = data (for computers) with structure.
- Data becomes information when you understand what it means. Computers process data, people use information.
- An information system is only of use if the information it contains is *accurate*, *complete* and *up to date*.
- If the data in an information system is input incorrectly or in the wrong format it is useless.
- Computer-based information systems have the following advantages over manual systems:

  - the computer can find the data very quickly, but searching through manual filing systems can take a very long time
  - manual files take up much more space than computer files
  - it is difficult to get a complete set of information when using manual filing systems
  - computers can store large quantities of information on a single storage medium
  - computer-based information systems can be constantly updated
  - databases held by different organisations can be linked in networks.

- Users of information systems include experts and novices.

  - An expert user is a person who is familiar with the features and functions of the information system and can use it to their advantage.
  - A novice user is a person who is unfamiliar with the features and functions of the information system and requires support on how to use the system and how to get the best out of it.

- The age-range refers to the ages of the users of the information system, for instance: young child, teenager and adult.
- The purpose of any information system is to contain information and present it to the user in a form which is useful to them.
- An information system which collects, organises, stores, processes and outputs information for the benefit of a company or organisation is called an organisational information system.

CHAPTER 11 Hardware and software requirements

This chapter describes a range of input and output devices and their uses. It also provides more information on processors and memory, and describes different computer devices. Operating systems and platforms are also discussed.

Hardware requirements:

- input and output devices
- processor clock speed
- memory (RAM, ROM)
- processor type and speed (Hz)
- device type (including supercomputer, desktop, portable devices [including laptop, tablet, smartphone])

Software requirements:

- operating system platform required
- operating systems
- web browsers
- specific applications and/or utilities

Hardware requirements: input devices

What is an input device?

An **input device** is a **device** which allows **data** to be entered into a computer system. A **peripheral** is any device that may be attached to a computer system for **input**, **output** or **backing storage**.

Keyboard

The input device used most often with a computer system is a **keyboard**. Each key on a keyboard has a switch under it. When you press the key, the switch beneath it sends a signal to the computer. The keyboard is wired so that each key switch sends a different code number into the computer. This code is called the **American Standard Code for Information Interchange** (shortened to **ASCII**). You found out more about ASCII in Chapter 1. The keys on a computer keyboard are normally arranged in the same way as they are on a typewriter, so a standard computer keyboard is sometimes called a QWERTY keyboard (from the top row of a typewriter, where the keys are QWERTYUIOP).

Figure 11.01 A computer keyboard

Many computer keyboards also have function keys, and on some computers you can program these keys. Other keys have built-in functions (like 'print' or 'clear screen'). Some keyboards also have a small keypad to the side of the main keyboard which has numbers on it (it is the **numeric keypad**). This can speed up your work if you have to enter a lot of numbers. Battery-powered **wireless** keyboards are also available.

> ### Checklist for keyboard
>
> ✓ Features: a complete **character set** of keys, plus additional function keys.
> ✓ Functions: entry of **text**.
> ✓ Uses: entry of text to a computer system.

Mouse

Figure 11.02 Microsoft® optical mouse

An **optical mouse** has a light underneath. Any movement is detected by a sensor which picks up the reflected light from the surface under the mouse. All mice have at least one button (or a click function) to allow objects on the **screen** to be selected. Some mice have a small wheel or ball on top to help with **scrolling**. Mice may also be wired or wireless (battery-operated).

Whatever type of **mouse** you're using, when you move the mouse on your desk, a signal is sent back to the computer, giving the position of the mouse and indicating whether you've pressed a button. The computer uses this information to move a **pointer** and to select items on the screen.

> ### Checklist for mouse
>
> ✓ Features: light underneath, buttons, scroll wheel or ball on top.
> ✓ Functions: control of a cursor on screen in a **graphical user interface** (GUI).
> ✓ Uses: selection of items from a **menu**, **navigation** in documents and **web pages**.

Microphone

Figure 11.03 Microphone

A **microphone** is used to allow **sound** to be input to a computer system. Most computer systems have microphones built in, usually above the screen, or have an **interface** where a microphone may be plugged in. The sound **quality** captured by a built-in microphone is low and so would not normally be used for recording music.

Voice recognition

One application which uses a microphone is **voice recognition**. To use this system, the computer must have voice recognition software. Voice recognition is used for controlling devices and also for dictating text into **word-processing** documents. To use voice recognition, the user must speak slowly and clearly. The system usually understands only a limited number of words. The user has to 'teach' the computer to recognise her voice by repeating certain words or phrases, especially when dictating text. Users who may have difficulty operating a mouse or a keyboard to control a computer system can use voice recognition instead.

Voice recognition is also used in applications such as 'hands-free' mobile phones. The Royal Society for the Prevention of Accidents (RoSPA) advises that drivers who use phones are much less aware of what's happening on the road around them and are also four times more likely to crash, injuring or killing themselves or other people.

Checklist for microphone

✓ Features: changes sound into an electrical signal.

✓ Functions: connects to the computer's **sound card** to input sound.

✓ Uses: recording of sound, voice control of devices, dictation of text.

Sound card

Figure 11.04 A sound card

A sound card allows sound to be both input to and output from a computer system. It is therefore both an input *and* an **output device**. The output feature of the sound card is dealt with later on in this chapter.

Sound is **analogue** in nature; it is a continuously varying quantity. Computers work in **digital** quantities. In order to input sound into a computer the sound must be changed from analogue into digital. This process is called **Analogue to Digital Conversion** or **ADC**. A microphone or another sound source is connected to the computer's sound card in order to capture the sound. The sound card carries out the ADC in a process called **sampling**. Sampling is a form of **digitising**. The **sampling rate** is the frequency at which samples of the sound are taken and is usually twice the maximum frequency of the sound being sampled. The sampling resolution is the number of **bits** used for data storage, which is 16 bits for CD-quality sound, with a sampling rate of 44.1 KHz.

When sampling a sound, the analogue signal is *chopped* into a number of slices per second. At each slice, the amplitude (or height) of the signal is measured and rounded to the nearest available digital value. The more *chops per second* (sampling rate) and the finer the values which may be assigned to the amplitude (sampling resolution), the better the digital representation of the original analogue sound. The benefit of sampling is that it reduces the quantity of data that requires to be stored, as compared to the analogue version. We read about sound quality in Chapter 8.

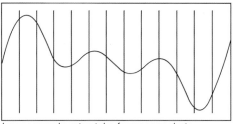

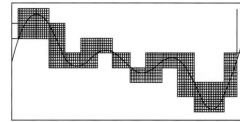

Lower sample rates take fewer snapshots of the waveform ...

resulting in a rough recreation of the waveform.

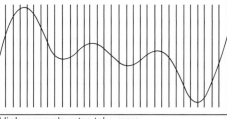

Higher sample rates take more snapshots ...

resulting in a smoother and more detailed recreation of the waveform.

Figure 11.05 Sampling an audio signal

Checklist for sound card (input)

✓ Features: samples sound from a microphone or other input.

✓ Functions: changes the sound signal from analogue to digital.

✓ Uses: creates a digital version of the sound for editing and/or **storage**.

Figure 11.06 A track pad on a laptop computer

Figure 11.07 A wireless track pad

Track pad

A **track pad** is a touch-sensitive plate. Movements of the user's finger over the plate control the movement of the pointer on the screen. If you use a track pad on a **laptop** computer you don't need any extra space on a desk compared to using a mouse.

A wireless track pad is a separate device, which may be used as a replacement for a mouse when using a **desktop computer**. It is made up of a touch-sensitive plate, with buttons or a click function.

Checklist for track pad

✓ Features: touch-sensitive plate, one or more buttons.

✓ Functions: control of a cursor on screen in a graphical user interface (GUI).

✓ Uses: selection of items from a menu, navigation in documents and web pages.

Figure 11.08 A graphics tablet

Graphics tablet

A **graphics tablet** is a flat, pressure-sensitive board used with a pen or a **stylus**.

A graphics tablet is used for **Computer Aided Design (CAD)**, and for artists to be able to draw more freely than a mouse would allow.

Checklist for graphics tablet

✓ Features: a device for drawing more naturally.

✓ Functions: allows users to draw and select items on screen.

✓ Uses: Computer Aided Design (CAD), artwork.

Touch-sensitive screen

Figure 11.09 A touch-sensitive screen

A **touch-sensitive screen** is useful when it is not appropriate to use a mouse. A screen is an output device, so a touch-sensitive screen is both an input and an output device. Screens (**monitors**) are described later in this chapter.

The most common use for touch-sensitive screens is on devices such as mobile phones and **tablets**. Touching a screen with a finger is easy and quick, but for some applications, not very precise. Using a special pen with a plastic nib, called a stylus, can provide more precision. Some users, such as graphic artists, prefer to work in this way, since holding a stylus feels like using a real writing implement or paintbrush.

Checklist for touch-sensitive screen

✓ Features: an input and output device.

✓ Functions: allows users to draw and select items directly on the screen.

✓ Uses: operating mobile phones and tablet computers.

Figure 11.10 A touch-sensitive screen on a tablet computer (an iPad®)

Joystick

A **joystick** is used mainly for computer games, to control the movement of a **character** or **icon** on the screen. Joysticks have one or more buttons which may be programmed for various actions within the game. Sometimes two joysticks are connected to a computer so that two people can play the game at once.

Checklist for joystick

✓ Features: has controls for games.

✓ Functions: allows users to control the movement of a character or icon on screen.

✓ Uses: games, driving, flight simulation.

Figure 11.11 A joystick

Figure 11.12 A selection of different types of memory cards

Figure 11.13 Card reader

Figure 11.14 A digital still camera (Canon PowerShot G1X)

Digital still camera

Digital still cameras are similar to film cameras, in that they both use a lens which focuses reflected light from the subject onto a sensor and the image is then stored for later processing. In a film camera, the film itself is both sensor and **storage medium**. In a digital still camera, the sensor is a postage stamp-sized electronic **chip**, called a **CCD** or **Charge Coupled Device**. The surface of the CCD is full of light-sensitive elements. The greater the number of these elements, then the greater the level of detail, or **resolution**, that may be obtained. The resolution of a digital still camera is measured in **Megapixels**. Once the CCD has been exposed to light, the **information** from these elements is turned into digital data, or digitised, and stored in the camera's **memory**. Unlike film, the stored picture does not need to be developed, and the memory can be reused over and over again. Perhaps the greatest benefit of digital photography is the fact that you can see the pictures that you have just taken, decide whether or not to keep them, copy them to a computer's backing storage, then delete all of the pictures from the camera and start over.

Most digital still cameras store their pictures on removable **memory cards**. The low cost and high **backing storage capacity** of these cards makes it possible to store a large number of high-quality photographs relatively cheaply. The number of photographs that may be stored depends upon the capacity of the card in use and the settings in the camera, such as resolution and **compression**. The resolution at which the photograph is taken and the amount of compression used may be adjusted by the user. You can find out more about resolution in Chapter 1. Compression is a technique used to reduce the size of a **file**. We read about compression in Chapter 8. Many digital cameras store their photographs using **JPEG**, a file format which uses compression. Flash ROM memory cards are described in Chapters 11 and 12.

In order to edit pictures, it is necessary to transfer them to a **graphics package**, whether on a computer system or **online**. A **cable** can be used to connect the camera to one of the computer's interfaces, or a **card reader** may be attached directly to, or be built in as part of a computer system.

Some cameras may also be connected to a TV set to allow the images to be viewed. Most digital cameras incorporate a colour **LCD** screen, which may be used to view an image and check it.

If you own a digital still camera, you can use a computer system and **printer** to store, edit and print out your photographs. However, printers are now available which contain card slots to accommodate the memory cards used by digital cameras. Such printers allow the user to print images directly from the card. Rather than printing your own photographs, you may take the memory card to a shop, or upload the images to an online service, and have the printed pictures sent out to you.

Figure 11.15 Taking a photograph with a mobile phone camera

Many mobile phones have built-in digital still cameras, with typical resolutions of between three and twelve Megapixels. Phones are also able to transfer their photographs to other devices by using wireless communication such as **Bluetooth**®, but it is more common to upload the photographs directly to a **website** for sharing with friends, or to send them as an **email** or multimedia message (MMS).

> ### Checklist for digital still camera
>
> ✓ Features: lens, microphone, CCD, LCD screen, removable memory card, speaker.
> ✓ Functions: capturing and storing images and movies, viewing images and movies on the built-in LCD panel.
> ✓ Uses: taking still photographs and movies.

Digital video camera

Figure 11.16 A digital video camera

A **digital video camera** or camcorder is used for taking **video**. It works on the same principal as a digital still camera, with a CCD which detects the images. Digital video cameras can use a variety of recording media, including **flash ROM**, **hard disk**, **DVD-Recordable** or **magnetic tape**. Current video cameras use high-capacity flash ROM cards. Video cameras have a small colour screen, which may be used as a viewfinder when filming, and also as a monitor when playing back video.

A digital video camera may be connected to a computer system in order to download the video and edit it on screen. A great deal of storage space is required to hold video taken with a digital video camera. For instance, video lasting one hour requires between 11 and 13 **Gigabytes** of backing storage.

Most digital still cameras and phones are also capable of recording video. Many digital still cameras can record video in full HD quality, so it is not always necessary to have a separate video camera for everyday use.

> ### Checklist for digital video camera
>
> ✓ Features: lens, microphone, CCD, LCD screen, removable memory card, speaker.
> ✓ Functions: capturing and storing images and video, viewing images and video on the built-in LCD panel.
> ✓ Uses: taking video and still photographs.

Figure 11.17 A 2-D scanner (top) and a 3-D scanner

Scanner

Using a **scanner** you can input printed drawings, photographs or text directly into a computer. A scanner works like a photocopier: a light is shone on the material and the scanner detects the reflected light. A scanner uses a CCD, like a digital camera. You can use a scanner with **Optical Character Recognition** (OCR) software to input the scanned text into a word-processing package. A scanner may be fitted with a transparency adapter, which allows slide films and negatives to be scanned.

Scanners are often joined to printers to produce a so-called 'all-in-one' or **multi-function device**. These devices have all of the features of both scanners and printers, and, in addition, are capable of producing photocopies and faxing documents via a telephone connection independently of a computer system.

A **3-D scanner** may be used to scan an object and create a **data file** containing its measurements. This data may be used to display an image of the object on screen or be sent to a **3-D printer** to create a physical copy.

Checklist for scanner

✓ Features: (2-D) CCD, glass plate, lid, transparency adapter.

✓ Functions: (2-D) digitises printed documents, photographs; (3-D) scans objects.

✓ Uses: scanning of documents and photographs, OCR (with appropriate software); measuring 3-D objects.

Figure 11.18 A laptop computer with a built-in webcam

Webcam

A **webcam** is a small digital camera, which is normally positioned on or beside the computer's monitor in order to capture images which may be transmitted across a **network**. Many computer monitors and laptop computers have built-in webcams. The main difference between a webcam and a digital camera is that a webcam is not capable of independent storage of images or movies. A webcam must be connected to a computer system or a network in order to have its images recorded or stored.

Webcams make applications like **video conferencing** possible.

Figure 11.19 A webcam and typical output

Figure 11.20 Video conference

Video conferencing

Video conferencing is the use of communications links to conduct meetings between people who are geographically separated. A typical video conferencing set up requires a computer system (including a microphone and **loudspeakers**) and a webcam in each location, together with a network connection between everyone involved. The video conferencing software allows each participant to see and hear the others on their computer screens, and sometimes to interact with a common document in a screen **window**.

Home security

Webcams are often used for home security applications alongside burglar alarms, and may be set to switch on automatically and transmit images to a remote computer system over a network (**video streaming**), or even to your mobile phone.

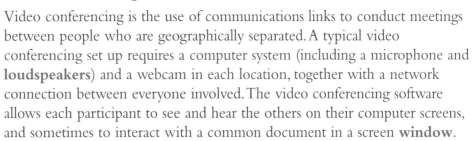

Checklist for webcam

✓ Features: lens, CCD, connection to computer.
✓ Functions: taking photographs, video.
✓ Uses: taking low-resolution still images and video, video conferencing, video streaming, home security.

Figure 11.21 Data glove

Data glove (virtual reality)

Virtual reality is a method of reproducing the outside world digitally within a computer system and displaying it to the user in such a way that it allows them to interact with a wide range of situations. **Data gloves** are used to take part in virtual reality.

Interactive whiteboard

Figure 11.22 Interactive whiteboard

An **interactive whiteboard** is an input device for **multimedia**. Multimedia is the presentation of information by a computer system using graphics, **animation**, sound and text. One mistake which is often made is to regard the whiteboard as an output device because it acts as a screen where the image is projected. However, it is the multimedia projector which is the output device, *not* the board.

Interactive whiteboards may also be used with specialised software and **hardware** which provides many additional functions, making the board much more than a simple input device. Handheld learner response systems, for example, make it possible for students to interact with what is being displayed on the board, such as a multiple-choice quiz.

Check Your Learning

Now answer questions 1–16 (on page 248) on input devices (National 4).

Hardware requirements: output devices

What is an output device?

An output device is a device which allows data to be displayed or passed out of a computer system.

Monitor

A monitor is an output device which accepts a video signal directly from a computer and displays the output on a screen. The screen is the part of a monitor which displays the output.

A monitor gives a higher quality output than would be obtained by connecting the computer to a television set. Monitors are available in **monochrome** (black and white) and colour as well as in different resolutions. A high-resolution monitor will be able to show very fine detail on the screen compared to a low-resolution monitor. It is important to choose a monitor of a suitable resolution to avoid eyestrain, especially when using an application such as a word processor which displays a lot of text on the screen.

Another difference between a monitor and a television set is that a monitor does not usually have a tuner, so, on its own, it cannot receive television broadcasts. However, the opposite is not the case. Many 'smart' televisions have built-in network connections, and can access the web. A monitor may have one or more loudspeakers which can output sound.

The image is made up of **picture elements** or **pixels**. A large number of pixels taken together is used to make up a complete image on the screen.

The quality of the display depends upon the screen resolution, which is the *number of horizontal pixels in a row × the number of vertical rows*.

All current computer monitors are made up of a basic **Liquid Crystal Display**, which consists of a thin layer of fluid sandwiched between two sheets of plastic. Complicated wiring is used to apply voltages to different points, changing the ability of the liquid to reflect or transmit light. So a Liquid Crystal Display is built up of light and dark dots (pixels) of varying intensity. Computer monitors are sometimes also called TFT (**Thin Film Transistor**) displays, because of the type of technology used inside the screen.

The resolution of an **LCD monitor** is fixed when it is manufactured. This is its so-called **native resolution**. Images displayed at other resolutions may appear to be less sharp, because they must be **scaled** to fit. One way around this problem is for an image to be displayed using only part of the LCD panel, just in the same way as a widescreen film looks different on some televisions.

Although all monitors use LCD panels to display the image, the technology used to light up the screen inside the monitor may be different. Basic LCD monitors use a fluorescent tube as a **backlight**. **LED** (Light Emitting Diode) **monitors** use **LEDs** to backlight their screens.

OLED (Organic Light Emitting Diode) displays use an organic chemical compound as their light source, which means that the screens themselves may be flexible. OLED technology is already in use in some phones and tablets.

Figure 11.23 A monitor

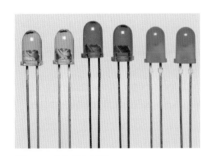

Figure 11.24 LEDs

Figure 11.25 An OLED TV

Table 11.01 compares some features of LCD, LED and OLED screens.

	LCD	LED	OLED
Backlighting	Fluorescent lamp	LED	Organic polymer
Backlit area	Large	Groups of pixels	Individual pixels
Relative manufacturing cost	Cheap	Expensive	Very expensive
Contrast	Medium	High	Very High
Can be flexible?	No	No	Yes
Lifespan (hours)	10–15,000	35–50,000	14,000
Screen thickness (relative)	Thin	Thinner	Thinnest

Table 11.01

Checklist for monitor

✓ Features: LCD, LED, OLED.

✓ Functions: outputs data on screen.

✓ Uses: display of documents, images, videos.

Printers

A printer is a device which is used to produce a printout or a **hard copy** of the output from a computer. Both **laser** and **inkjet printers** are able to produce monochrome (black and white) and colour images. The speed of a printer is measured in **pages per minute**, which refers to how many pages the printer can produce in one minute. Colour printers will have two figures for pages per minute, one for printing pages in colour and one for printing in black and white. The actual speed of printing a document usually differs from the figures quoted by the manufacturer, since it will depend on how much is on each page.

A 3-D printer can produce three-dimensional objects from solid materials such as plastic or resin.

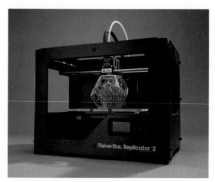

Figure 11.26 An inkjet printer (Canon i850), a laser printer (Canon i-SENSYS) and a 3-D printer (MakerBot Replicator 2)

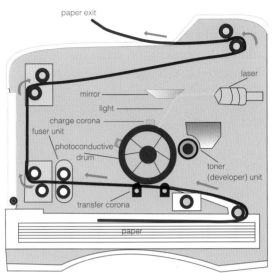

Figure 11.27 The inside of a laser printer

Laser printers

Laser printers use a special powder called **toner** to produce the image on the paper. A laser beam is used to project the image of the page to be printed onto a cylinder known as a drum. The toner sticks to the parts of the drum which have the image on them. The paper is passed over the drum and the toner is transferred to the paper. The paper, now with the toner on it, is then passed between heated rollers, to melt and seal the toner onto the paper. If you have used a laser printer, you will notice that the printouts are warm to the touch. Contrary to popular opinion, a laser beam is *not* used to burn the image on the paper!

A monochrome laser printer uses only black toner. A colour laser printer uses four different colours of toner: cyan, magenta, yellow and black, to produce the different printable colours.

Figure 11.28 Black and colour laser toner cartridges

Inkjet printers

Inkjet printers are quiet in operation and can produce a high-quality printout of both graphics and text. They are particularly good at producing **photographic** printouts and can print on different surfaces, even on CDs.

Figure 11.29 Printing on CD

An inkjet printer works by squirting small droplets of ink onto paper, through tiny holes in the print head. The number of holes in the print head determines the printer's resolution. Some inkjet printers hold two ink cartridges, one with black ink and one containing three different colours, Cyan, Magenta and Yellow. This system can cost more to replace, because not all of the three colours will be used up at the same rate. It is more economical for inkjet printers to have separate colour cartridges, meaning that less ink will be wasted.

Figure 11.30 Black and colour ink cartridges

Figure 11.31 Card slots on an inkjet printer

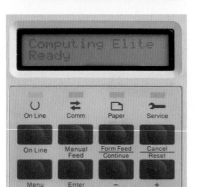

Figure 11.32 Printing directly from a digital still camera and two types of LCD screens used on printers

Photo printing

Apart from printing text, inkjet printers are used mostly to print hard copies of photographs taken by a digital camera and stored in its memory card. To make this task easier, some inkjet printers have memory-card slots so that photographs stored on a card may be printed out without needing to load the photographs first into a computer system.

Alternatively, it is possible to connect a digital camera directly to a printer. Some printers have small LCD screens to help with printing photographs, and to display error messages to the user, such as 'out of paper'.

3-D printers

One type of 3-D printer uses heated plastic which is squirted through a nozzle onto a flat plate called a **build table**. The nozzle can move in two dimensions and the build table moves down after each layer of plastic has been deposited. The 3-D object is complete after all of the successive layers have been deposited on the build table. This type of 3-D printing is known as **Fused Deposition Modelling** (FDM).

Another type of 3-D printing is **Selective Laser Sintering** (SLS). SLS uses a powerful laser beam to fuse together particles of powder to create objects. The types of powder used include plastic, metal, ceramic and glass. SLS has the advantage that the unfused powder acts as a support structure to the object while it is being printed. This allows objects containing moveable parts to be created.

In order to print a 3-D object, it is necessary to have a file containing a description of the object to be printed. This can be created by using a Computer Aided Design (CAD) application or by using a 3-D scanner. 3-D printing services are available on a variety of websites. These provide free software to allow you to design your own 3-D objects which the companies will print and send you the completed work. Have a look at:

- www.shapeways.com
- www.sculpteo.com/en/
- www.mixeelabs.com

Checklist for inkjet and laser printers

✓ Features: liquid ink (inkjet) and toner (laser), print head (inkjet) or drum and heated rollers (laser).

✓ Functions: outputs printed data.

✓ Uses: producing hard copies of documents and photographs, transparencies, labels.

Figure 11.33 Plotter

Plotter

A **plotter** is another device for producing hard copy. One difference between a printer and a plotter is that a plotter can print out onto very large paper sizes. Plotters are capable of producing very accurate drawings and are most often used in Computer Aided Design (CAD).

Checklist for plotter

✓ Features: coloured pens or liquid ink.

✓ Functions: outputs printed data in large format.

✓ Uses: producing hard copies of technical drawings and plans in CAD.

Loudspeakers and headphones

Figure 11.34 Headphones

A loudspeaker is a sound output device. Most computers have built-in loudspeakers or can be connected to one or more loudspeakers. A loudspeaker changes an analogue electrical signal into sound, so that we can hear it. A loudspeaker is connected to a sound card inside the computer. A sound card changes the sound, stored in digital form, into analogue form for the loudspeaker.

Computer systems sold as multimedia computers usually include so-called **active speakers**, which are mains powered and have a built-in amplifier. Active speakers also form the main component of devices such as **MP3** players or iPod® **docks** which allow the music to be played to an audience. Loudspeakers on a computer system are useful if there is only one computer in use, but not otherwise. When sound output is required from a classroom full of computers, then it is much more sensible to use **headphones**. If the computer is being used for developing a multimedia program or sound editing, then headphones will give a better sound quality than loudspeakers.

Figure 11.35 Loudspeakers

Checklist for loudspeakers and headphones

✓ Features: changes analogue electrical signal into sound. May incorporate its own amplifier. May be built in to monitors, LCD panels, all types of **portable** computer and digital cameras.

✓ Functions: outputs **audio** from a computer system or other device.

✓ Uses: to allow sound produced by, or held in a computer system, to be heard by the user. Headphones are personal output devices.

Figure 11.36 An iPod dock

Sound card

Sound cards improve the quality of sound output from games and multimedia applications. Additional bundled software allows users to compose, edit and print music, record and edit digital audio, and play audio and multimedia CDs. You can see a picture of a sound card in Figure 11.04, earlier in this chapter.

Sound is analogue in nature; it is a continuously varying quantity. Computers work in digital quantities. In order to output sound from a computer the sound must be changed from digital to analogue. This process is called **digital-to-analogue conversion**. This is exactly the same process which is used when an audio CD is played in the **CD-ROM drive** of a computer or in a music CD player. Sound cards are capable of outputting a number of sound channels in high-quality formats such as Dolby® Digital.

Checklist for sound card (output)

✓ Features: improves the quality of sound output.
✓ Functions: changes the sound signal from digital to analogue, adds effects to sounds.
✓ Uses: output of a sound signal to loudspeakers or headphones.

Graphics card

Figure 11.37 Graphics card

A **graphics card** is a device which controls the quality of output on a monitor. Another name for a graphics card is a **display adapter**. Graphics cards contain a large quantity of **RAM** to allow them to support high-resolution displays, and have powerful **processors** to improve the graphics performance of the computer, especially when playing games.

Checklist for graphics card

✓ Features: improves the quality of the display signal.
✓ Functions: outputs the signal to a display screen or **multimedia projector**, reduces the workload of the computer's processor.
✓ Uses: enhances graphics, especially in games.

Headset

Virtual reality is a method of reproducing the outside world digitally within a computer system and displaying it to the user in such a way that it allows them to interact with a wide range of situations. To take part in

Figure 11.38 Virtual reality headset

virtual reality, the user wears a **headset** together with special data gloves rather than using a keyboard, mouse and monitor. In this way, the computer controls three of the five senses. A data glove is shown in Figure 11.21, earlier in this chapter.

In addition to feeding sensory input to the user, the devices also monitor the user's actions. The headset, for example, tracks how the head moves and responds accordingly by sending new video to the user. The headset is therefore both an input and an output device.

Checklist for headset

✓ Features: twin screens, **earphones**, connection to computer.
✓ Functions: feeding back user's head movements to computer, lets user know where they are in the virtual reality world.
✓ Uses: control of virtual reality programs.

Figure 11.39 Multimedia projector

Multimedia projector

A multimedia projector connects to a graphics card and displays the contents of the computer screen on a wall or interactive whiteboard. Multimedia projectors are most commonly used for delivering presentations to an audience. One other popular use is as a home cinema display, instead of having a large screen television set.

Checklist for multimedia projector

✓ Features: lens and very bright lamp.
✓ Functions: displaying the contents of a computer screen, a television picture or a video on a large screen.
✓ Uses: classrooms, lecture theatres and cinemas.

Check Your Learning

Now answer questions 17–33 (on pages 248–249) on output devices (National 4).

Processor clock speed (Hz)

You found out about the processor in Chapter 1. The processor can carry out instructions very quickly because it can process several billions of instructions every second.

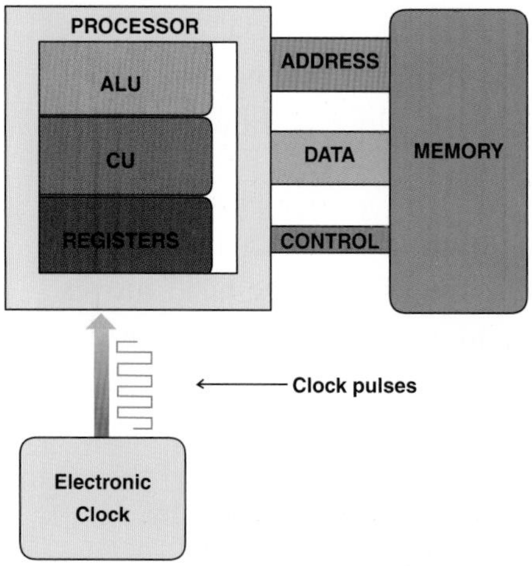

Figure 11.40 Processor clock speed

We can get an idea of how fast the processor is capable of working by looking at the *clock speed*. When we talk about **processor clock speed**, we are not referring to the part of the computer that displays the time of day and the date on the screen. The processor clock is connected to the **control bus**.

The processor clock produces a series of electronic pulses at a very high rate. Everything the processor does is kept precisely in time with the clock, so the faster the clock speed, the faster the processor will operate. A processor clock speed is measured in **Gigahertz (GHz)**. 1 Gigahertz is approximately 1000 million pulses a second.

If we consider two processors, from the *same* manufacturer, one of which has a clock speed of 1 GHz and the other, 2 GHz, which are identical in all other respects, then the 2 GHz processor will process data twice as fast as the 1 GHz processor.

Note that two different processors, which have different clock speeds, *cannot be compared only in this manner* since there may be other differences between them. Increasing the performance of the processor does not mean that other parts of the computer, such as the **buses** or memory, will also be capable of increased performance. This may lead to a so-called 'bottleneck' situation, where the rest of the computer is unable to keep up with the processor.

It is relatively easy to obtain an increase in computer performance by increasing the clock speed of a processor. However, manufacturers have found that this increase cannot go on forever and current processors have a maximum clock speed of around 4 GHz.

Check Your Learning

Now answer questions 34–38 (on page 249) on processor clock speed (National 4).

Processor type and speed (Hz)

Processors may be classified into a variety of different types, for example by the number of cores, the types of instructions which they can carry out (**instruction set**), or the number of functions that they have.

Number of cores

Manufacturers have looked for other ways of increasing the performance of a computer system, and have come up with the idea of increasing the number of processors or 'cores'. The Intel® Core™ 2 Duo processor, for example, is a single chip, or piece of silicon, but the name 'Core 2' means that it contains two processors in one. Similarly, a processor described as 'quad core' has four processors on a single chip.

Instruction set

Reduced Instruction Set Computers (**RISC**) have simpler (not fewer) instructions than **Complex Instruction Set Computers** (**CISC**). These simpler instructions can take less time to execute, for example in a single clock cycle.

Examples of RISC architectures include ARM™ (used in iPhone®, iPad®, RIM and many Android™ phones); MIPS (used in PS®, PS2®, N64®, PSP®); Hitachi SuperH™ (Used in Sega®, Saturn® and Dreamcast®).

The number of functions

A single chip may contain *all* of the components of a computer system. This is known as a **system on chip** (**SOC**). The SOC will contain a processor, memory and peripheral interfaces. SOCs are often used on embedded systems, and typically these include phones, tablet computers, televisions, **DVD** and MP3 players. An **embedded computer** is a special purpose computer system which is designed to perform one or more dedicated functions.

Embedded computers process data in **real-time**. In general, a SOC uses less power and is more reliable than an alternative multi-chip computer system.

"We couldn't afford faster computers, so we just made them *sound* faster."

Figure 11.41 Making computers faster

Name of processor	Cores	Clock speed (GHz)
Intel® Core 2 Duo	2	1–3.5
Intel® Core i5	2–4	1–3.7
Intel® Core i7	4–6	1–3.7
AMD FX	4–8	2.8–4.2
ARM A6X (SOC)	2	1.3

Table 11.02 Computer processors

Check Your Learning

Now answer questions 39–47 (on page 249) on processor type and speed (National 5).

Memory

We first looked at memory in Chapter 1. The memory of a computer system is made up of a set of memory chips. There are two types of memory chip. Each type of memory chip is used for a different purpose in a computer system. These two types of memory chip are **Random Access Memory** (RAM) and **Read Only Memory** (**ROM**).

Random Access Memory (RAM)

RAM is a type of computer memory which holds its data as long as the computer is switched on. RAM can only store programs and data *temporarily* because anything stored in RAM is *lost* when the computer is switched off.

RAM is a **direct-access medium**, because data held in RAM can be read from, or written to by the processor in any order.

The place where an item of data is stored in a computer's memory is important because the processor has to be able to find any given item of data. An item of data is stored in memory in a **storage location** at a specific **address**.

The purpose of RAM is to hold the computer's programs and data while they are being processed. In most microcomputers, RAM is also used to hold the **operating system** program when the computer is on. While using the computer, you should normally save the contents of RAM to a **backing storage medium** such as **hard disk** or flash ROM (see opposite and following) so that your work is not lost when you switch the computer off.

It is a good idea to have plenty of RAM installed in your computer system. Extra RAM improves the performance of the computer because:

- the computer can have more or larger programs loaded in RAM at one time
- it is faster to process files held in RAM because the time it takes to access data held in RAM is about 1000 × faster than hard disk.

You can see that the amount of RAM in a computer system is one of the factors affecting *the relationship between software, hardware and system performance*.

National 5

Figure 11.42 Random Access Memory (RAM) chips

A checklist of the features and uses of RAM

✓ The main use of RAM is to hold programs which are loaded from backing storage.

✓ Stores programs and data temporarily, only when power on.

✓ Data lost when power off.

✓ Data held in RAM may be altered by being written to.

✓ Data held in RAM may be read from or written to in any order/a direct-access medium.

Figure 11.43 Installed RAM

Figure 11.44 Read Only Memory (ROM) chip

Read Only Memory (ROM)

ROM is used to **store programs** and data permanently. The contents of a ROM chip are *not* lost when you switch the computer off. ROM is **permanent memory**. The contents of ROM are fixed when the chip is manufactured.

Data held in ROM can be read by the processor in any order, and ROM is therefore another type of direct-access medium.

ROM chips are used on some computers to store part of the operating system, the **bootstrap loader**, to help the computer start up when it is switched on. The function of the bootstrap loader is to load the rest of the operating system program from disk. In some games machines, software is stored on ROM.

ROM software is also used in embedded computers. (See SOC earlier in this chapter.)

A checklist of the features and uses of ROM

✓ Stores programs and data permanently, even when power off.

✓ Data is NOT lost when power off.

✓ Used to hold part of the operating system.

✓ Data held in ROM cannot be altered.

✓ Data held in ROM may be read from in any order/a direct-access medium.

Figure 11.45 A flash ROM card in use in a digital still camera

Flash ROM

Flash ROM has most of the features of ROM as described on the previous page, but it has an advantage over ROM because it may also be used to save data. Flash ROM is a very popular backing storage medium. Flash ROM is used in **USB flash ROM drives** (USB 'sticks') and **flash memory** cards for use in mobile phones, video and digital still cameras. Flash ROM is also used as the main backing storage medium in some laptops and netbook computers, replacing magnetic **hard disk drives** with **solid-state drives** or **SSDs**.

Quick Tip

Memory size

If you are asked a question about the **total amount of memory** in a computer, you should remember to add the amount of RAM and amount of ROM together to get the answer. For example, a computer with 1 **Gb** of RAM and 96 **Mb** of ROM will have a total memory size of 1024 Mb (1Gb) + 96 Mb = 1120 Mb.

Check Your Learning

Now answer questions 48–55 (on page 249) on memory (RAM and ROM)(National 4).

Check Your Learning

Now answer questions 56–64 (on page 249) on memory (RAM and ROM)(National 5).

Device type

We will look at different types of computer (device) in this section. **Device types** include desktop, **supercomputer**, **mainframe** and portable devices such as laptop, tablet and **smartphone**.

Desktop computer

A desktop computer is so-called because it is normally used whilst sitting at a desk and is mains operated.

A desktop computer has a monitor and a keyboard, usually with cursor keys, function keys and a numeric keypad. The pointing device is a mouse, with one or more buttons and a scroll wheel.

All desktop computers have either a hard disk drive or a solid-state drive, with a typical capacity of between 256 Gb and 2 **Tb**. Many desktop computers have a **DVD-Rewriter drive**, which can read and write to a variety of optical disk formats. Some desktop computers may also have a **Blu-ray™** drive. All desktop computers use a **Network Interface Card** in order to connect to a school's **Local Area Network** or a **router** at home.

All desktop computers have one or more loudspeakers and may also have a microphone for sound input. Other peripheral devices, usually attached to a desktop computer system, are a printer, scanner and webcam, which may be built into the monitor.

Figure 11.46 Two desktop computers

Laptop computer

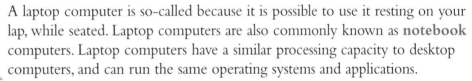

A laptop computer is so-called because it is possible to use it resting on your lap, while seated. Laptop computers are also commonly known as **notebook** computers. Laptop computers have a similar processing capacity to desktop computers, and can run the same operating systems and applications.

Laptop computers use an LCD screen as an output device, and have a large keyboard suitable for word processing. Typical laptop computer screen sizes range from about 11 to 17 inches. Laptop computers use a track pad or a raised button to control the pointer on the screen. Laptop computers are battery operated, with rechargeable power packs. A laptop computer normally has a battery life of between 4 and 8 hours, depending on use.

Like a desktop computer, a laptop computer has either a solid-state drive or a hard disk drive. The current trend is to replace the hard disk drive with a solid-state drive (SSD), which has the advantage of being more robust, since it contains no moving parts, has a fast access time, and also uses less power. Laptop computers may connect to a network using a **Wireless Network Interface Card** and **WiFi** or a wired connector similar to a desktop computer. Laptop computers may also have an optical drive, although some manufacturers are no longer including these. In this case, an external DVD drive may be used if required.

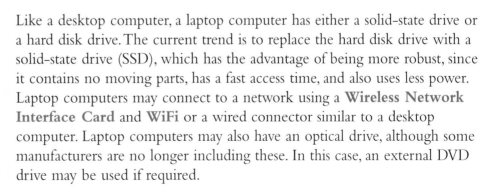

Figure 11.47 Various designs of laptop computer

Tablet computers

Like a laptop, a tablet computer is also battery-operated, although with a longer battery life. A tablet computer has a large, touch-sensitive screen, which is used as its main input and output device. Some tablet computers also have a detachable keyboard for data entry. Current tablet computers have one or more cameras for taking digital photographs, movies and video conferencing. They also have a microphone and one or more loudspeakers.

Figure 11.48 A tablet computer (Microsoft Surface™)

Tablet computers use either the same operating system as a desktop computer, or a mobile version, such as Android, Symbian® or iOS. Tablet computers communicate via Bluetooth®, WiFi or by using the mobile telephone network, and can be used with suitable application software (**apps**) to make phone calls, send **text messages** and take part in video conferencing. Tablet computers are also commonly used for reading books and magazines, playing games and displaying multimedia. Tablet computers are very popular, perhaps because they are very easy to use compared to a laptop or a desktop computer.

Tablet computers are, like smartphones, *always-on* devices, and as such, are in constant communication with **Wide** and **Local Area Networks** in order to send and receive data.

Smartphone

A smartphone is a mobile phone, which has its own operating system and is capable of running a variety of applications. A smartphone shares many of its features with a tablet computer (described earlier), except for its main function of making and receiving telephone calls.

A smartphone is battery-operated and is an *always-on* device, with the longest battery life compared to laptops and tablet computers. Some people use smartphones instead of having any other type of computer.

Like tablets, smartphones can run a wide variety of applications designed to run on their mobile operating systems. The range of applications available for smartphones is vast, from games to office programs, from satellite navigation to shopping.

Figure 11.49 Smartphones

One application which is being developed is the use of a smartphone as a 'digital wallet', which can be used for cashless payments. One example of this technology, already in use in the United States, is Google Wallet™.

Figure 11.50

Mainframe computers

A mainframe computer is a very large computer system, which can process a very large amount of data at high speed. It occupies a whole room and may be connected to hundreds of user **terminals**. It is common to have many simultaneous users on a mainframe computer. This is why a mainframe is a **multi-user** or **multi-access** system. The users of a multi-access system each appear to have individual control of the computer at the same time, although only one program is actually being run at any one time. The mainframe computer also allows **multi-tasking** or **multi-programming** which allows several different tasks or applications to be available at the same time.

A mainframe computer has a number of processors – it is a **multi-processor** machine. There is usually a vast amount of RAM, and many extra peripherals such as tape and disk drives.

A **dumb terminal** has no processor and no **local storage** devices. All that is required is a screen and a keyboard since all of the processing and storage will be done within the mainframe computer.

Figure 11.51 A mainframe computer system occupies a whole room

Mainframe computers have many uses, for example supermarket stock control, online shopping and banking, including the control of automated teller machines (ATMs) and running the National Lottery.

Supercomputers

A mainframe computer is not necessarily the fastest and most powerful type of computer. Instead, this term is reserved for the supercomputer. Supercomputers are used for intensive mathematical calculations such as weather and climate forecasting, car design, aerospace engineering, molecular modelling or the production of high-resolution graphics such as digital animation (CGI) in motion pictures.

Some universities, research establishments and companies have created their own designs of supercomputer by linking together hundreds of ordinary microcomputers to provide a huge amount of processing power. You can check this out on the website www.top500.org, which is updated regularly with the performance data of current supercomputers. The website also provides a table which ranks each machine in order of processing power and performance.

Figure 11.52 The Tianhe-2 supercomputer, ranked fastest in the world in June 2013, has 3 120 000 processing cores, each operating at 1.8 GHz. It occupies 720 square metres.

Check Your Learning

Now answer questions 65–78 (on page 250) on device type (National 5).

Software requirements: operating systems

What is an operating system?

Most people probably don't realise that there is a program running in a computer from the moment it is switched on. This program is called the operating system. The operating system program controls how the computer works and controls any devices attached to the computer.

Examples of operating systems

Figure 11.53 Various Microsoft Windows® logos

Microsoft Windows®

Microsoft Windows® is the most popular operating system, used on the majority of desktop and laptop computers. Vista and XP are two versions of Microsoft Windows®. The latest version of Microsoft Windows® is Windows®8.

Figure 11.54 Oracle Solaris®, Linux®, FreeBSD® and Ubuntu® logos

Unix®

Unix® was originally developed by AT&T at Bell labs. **Commercial** versions of Unix® include BSD/OS®, Oracle Solaris® (Sun), HP-UX®, AIX® (IBM), and **Mac OS X®**. Free versions include Linux®, FreeBSD® and Ubuntu®.

Mac OS X®

Mac OS X® (X stands for the number ten) is produced by Apple® and runs on their range of desktop computers, laptops and **servers**. Snow Leopard® (10.6), Lion® (10.7), Mountain Lion® (10.8) and Mavericks® (10.9) are all versions of Mac OS®. The latest version of Mac OS® is Yosemite® (10.10).

What is the purpose of an operating system program?

The operating system program is needed because the computer cannot work without it. The operating system program provides instructions to run every aspect of the computer.

The operating system is the first program that must be loaded into the computer's memory when the computer is switched on. A program called the bootstrap loader is used to do this. This process of loading the operating system is often referred to as 'booting' or 'boot-up'. Once the operating system has been loaded, then the computer is ready for use. The bootstrap loader was mentioned earlier in this chapter.

Operating system platform required

A **platform** refers to the hardware and software which makes up a particular type of computer system. For instance, an iMac® computer with an Intel® Core i7 processor, running Mac OS X® is commonly referred to as a 'Mac® platform' or an 'Apple® platform'. Similarly, a Dell computer with an AMD processor, running Windows® 8 would be an example of a 'Windows® platform' or a 'PC platform'. Software normally works on a **single platform** and must be specially written for it. Software which is **dual platform** is able to run on two different types of operating system, for instance Windows® and Apple®.

Check Your Learning

Now answer questions 79–91 (on page 250) on operating system platform required (National 4).

Software requirements: operating systems, web browsers, specific applications and/or utilities

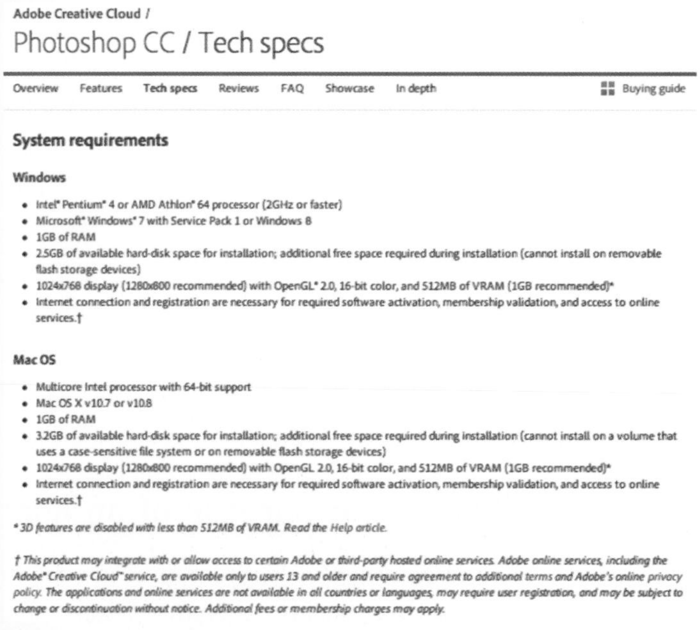

Adobe Creative Cloud /

Photoshop CC / Tech specs

| Overview | Features | **Tech specs** | Reviews | FAQ | Showcase | In depth | | Buying guide |

System requirements

Windows

- Intel® Pentium® 4 or AMD Athlon® 64 processor (2GHz or faster)
- Microsoft® Windows® 7 with Service Pack 1 or Windows 8
- 1GB of RAM
- 2.5GB of available hard-disk space for installation; additional free space required during installation (cannot install on removable flash storage devices)
- 1024x768 display (1280x800 recommended) with OpenGL® 2.0, 16-bit color, and 512MB of VRAM (1GB recommended)*
- Internet connection and registration are necessary for required software activation, membership validation, and access to online services.†

Mac OS

- Multicore Intel processor with 64-bit support
- Mac OS X v10.7 or v10.8
- 1GB of RAM
- 3.2GB of available hard-disk space for installation; additional free space required during installation (cannot install on a volume that uses a case-sensitive file system or on removable flash storage devices)
- 1024x768 display (1280x800 recommended) with OpenGL 2.0, 16-bit color, and 512MB of VRAM (1GB recommended)*
- Internet connection and registration are necessary for required software activation, membership validation, and access to online services.†

*3D features are disabled with less than 512MB of VRAM. Read the Help article.

† This product may integrate with or allow access to certain Adobe or third-party hosted online services. Adobe online services, including the Adobe® Creative Cloud™ service, are available only to users 13 and older and require agreement to additional terms and Adobe's online privacy policy. The applications and online services are not available in all countries or languages, may require user registration, and may be subject to change or discontinuation without notice. Additional fees or membership charges may apply.

Figure 11.55 System requirements for Photoshop® CC

Specific applications and/or utilities

To find out which platform a particular item of software requires, it is necessary to consult the **system requirements**. Note that in this book, system requirements and **software requirements** are the same. Note also that system requirements will change as applications and operating systems are **upgraded** or replaced.

The system requirements for a version of Photoshop® are shown in Figure 11.55. Have a look at the specifications of a computer system you use. Do they match the system requirements shown here in all respects?

Web browsers

A **web browser** is a program that allows the user to browse or surf through the **World Wide Web**. When browsing the World Wide Web, a browser loads web pages from another computer on the **internet** and displays them. You can read more about browsers in Chapter 6.

Browsers include: **Internet Explorer®**, **Firefox®**, **Chrome™**, **Safari®** and **Opera™**. Which of the browsers listed here are *single platform* and which are *dual platform*?

Figure 11.56 Browsers

A **utility program** is a type of systems software designed to perform an everyday task, like making a **backup copy** or protecting a computer system from **viruses**. You can read more about protecting computer systems in Chapter 14. An **emulator** is another example of a utility program.

Emulators

One way around the problem of not being able to run software because it is written for a different platform is to use an emulator. An emulator is a program which allows a computer to run a different operating system. **Parallels Desktop®** for Mac is one example of an emulator which allows Apple® computers to run other operating systems, including versions of Windows®.

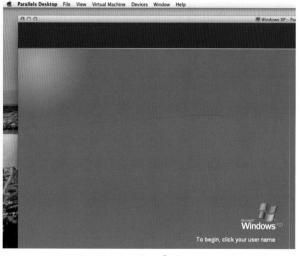

Figure 11.57 Parallels Desktop® for Mac

What does the operating system do?

The operating system:

- manages the reception of data from input devices like the keyboard and mouse
- manages the sending of data to output devices like the screen and the printer
- controls where programs and data are placed in the computer's memory
- manages the filing system
- controls the **security** of the system
- provides a **Human Computer Interface (HCI)** for the user
- lets the user know if any mistakes have occurred.

The operating system in action

Let's look at how the operating system helps a user who is using a word-processing application program on a computer system.

1 The operating system retrieves the word-processing program from backing storage and puts it in the right place in the computer's memory.
2 Each time the user presses a key on the keyboard, the operating system checks to see which key he has pressed and displays that character on the screen.
3 When the document is finished, the operating system asks the user to name the file and then saves the document to backing storage.
4 If the user wants to print the document, the operating system sends the data to the printer.

Figure 11.58 Everyone has their favourite operating system...

Check Your Learning

Now answer questions 92–99 (on page 251) on operating systems (National 5).

Practical Tasks

1. Have a look at www.top500.org.

   a) Which is the current top supercomputer?

   b) How many cores does it have?

   c) What is the clock speed of each core?

   d) How does it compare with the clock speed and number of cores in your

      i) school computer?

      ii) home computer?

2. Look at Table 11.02 on page 235, which shows details of processors, and carry out some research to check if it is still current. If not, use what you have found out to update the table entries.

3. You have £1500 to spend on a

   a) desktop computer system

   b) laptop computer system.

   For each computer, list the name of the processor, clock speed, number of cores, amount of RAM and size and type of backing storage (HDD / SSD), image and cost in a word-processing document.

4. Time how long it takes for the computer to start up from the time it is switched on until it is ready for use. If you have access to a number of different types of computer system, preferably running different operating systems, like PC and Apple® or Vista and XP, make up a comparison table like the one below to record the results.

5. a) Look back at the browsers listed on page 245. Choose one browser and find out its system requirements (software requirements).

   b) Choose another application, for example a game that you play on your computer, and find out its system requirements (software requirements).

Name of computer	Laptop or desktop	Type of backing storage (HDD/SSD)	Name of operating system	Version	Start-up time (seconds)
Dell	desktop	HDD	Windows®	Windows® 8	
Apple®	desktop	SSD	Mac OS®	Mavericks®	
Sony	laptop	SSD	Windows®	XP	

Questions

Input devices (National 4)

1 What is an input device?

2 Name two input devices.

3 List the input devices that are part of the computer system that you use in class.

4 What is
a) a keyboard?
b) a mouse?
c) a microphone?
d) a sound card?
e) a track pad?
f) a graphics tablet?
g) a touch-sensitive screen?
h) a joystick?
i) a digital (still) camera?
j) a digital (video) camera?
k) a scanner?
l) a webcam?
m) a data glove?
n) an interactive whiteboard?

5 Name an input device used to
a) enter text.
b) select from a menu.
c) capture audio.
d) change audio from analogue to digital.
e) capture images.
f) capture text for OCR.
g) capture video.
h) select an icon on the screen
i) play a game.
j) control a pointer on a laptop computer.
k) help teach a class.
l) carry out Computer Aided Design.

6 Why is a keyboard called a QWERTY keyboard?

7 How is it possible for each key on a keyboard to produce a different character?

8 Why don't laptop computers have a mouse?

9 Which device is used for sampling?

10 What is a CCD?

11 Name two devices which contain a CCD.

12 Name two input devices for which resolution is an important feature.

13 What storage medium is used in a digital camera?

14 Name two items that a scanner can be used to scan.

15 A 1200 dpi scanner is used to scan a 10 inch by 8 inch document.
a) What is the total number of bits of data captured by this scan?
b) How many Megabytes would this be?

16 Suggest how a webcam could be used by
a) a security company.
b) a family with relatives in Canada.

Output devices (National 4)

17 What is an output device?

18 Name two output devices.

19 What is
a) a monitor?
b) an inkjet printer?
c) a laser printer?
d) a loudspeaker?
e) a graphics card?
f) a multimedia projector?

20 Name an output device
a) used to view or display a document.
b) used to obtain a hard copy.
c) found on a digital camera.

21 What does LCD stand for?

22 What does LED stand for?

23 How may the screen resolution be calculated?

24 What is a hard copy?

25 How does
a) an inkjet printer work?
b) a laser printer work?

26 What type of printer uses toner?

27 Which type of printer can print on a DVD?

28 What unit is the
a) speed
b) resolution
of a printer measured in?

29 Which three colours are used in colour printing?

30 Why are individual colour cartridges replacing some three-colour cartridges in inkjet printers?

31 What use is the small LCD screen found on some inkjet printers?

32 Why are some inkjet printers fitted with memory-card slots?

33 What is an active speaker?

Processor clock speed (National 4)

34 What is the clock?

35 What is clock speed?

36 What units are used to measure clock speed?

37 What does clock speed tell you about the performance of a computer system?

38 Approximately how fast is 1 Gigahertz?

Processor type and speed (National 5)

39 Mary's computer has a 2.3 Gigahertz Intel® Core 2 Duo processor and Sarah's computer has a 3.2 Gigahertz Pentium processor. Sarah says her computer is faster than Mary's because it has a higher clock speed.

Who do you think is correct? Give a reason for your choice.

40 Explain why it is not a fair test to compare two processors by using their clock speeds.

41 State three different types used to classify processors.

42 State one method of increasing the performance of a computer processor, other than by increasing the clock speed.

43 What is a processor 'core'?

44 What is a RISC?

45 State one advantage of RISC.

46 What is a SOC?

47 State one example of an embedded system.

Memory (RAM and ROM) (National 4)

48 What does the term RAM stand for?

49 State one feature of RAM.

50 State one use of RAM.

51 What does the term ROM stand for?

52 State one feature of ROM.

53 State one use of ROM.

54 State one difference between RAM and ROM.

55 Which type of ROM may be used as a backing storage medium?

Memory (RAM and ROM) (National 5)

56 Why are computer games programs often sold stored in ROM media?

57 Why do computer systems need a memory when programs and data can be loaded from disk?

58 What can you do to stop a program stored in RAM from being lost when you switch your computer off?

59 What is an embedded computer?

60 Why is an embedded computer so called?

61 Explain why embedded computers process data in real-time.

62 Explain why fitting extra RAM improves the performance of a computer system.

63 Explain why both ROM and RAM are direct-access media.

64 Explain how to calculate the total amount of memory in a computer.

Questions *continued*

Device type (National 5)

65 What is a desktop computer?

66 What is a laptop computer?

67 What is a tablet computer?

68 What is a smartphone?

69 What is a mainframe computer?

70 What is a supercomputer?

71 Describe one use for each of the following types of computer:
   a) Desktop.
   b) Laptop.
   c) Tablet.
   d) Smartphone.
   e) Supercomputer.

72 Which of the types of computers named in Question 71 would be *unlikely* to have a
   a) keyboard?
   b) monitor?
   c) mouse?

73 Which of the types of computers named in Question 71 would be *likely* to have
   a) many processors?
   b) a built-in flash ROM storage device?
   c) a built-in optical storage device?
   d) a touchscreen?
   e) a touchpad (track pad)?

74 What device on a tablet computer acts as both an input and an output device?

75 State two ways in which a tablet computer may communicate with other computers.

76 State one difference between a
   a) mainframe computer and a supercomputer.
   b) tablet computer and a smartphone.

77 In addition to a keyboard, what input device would you expect to find on a
   a) desktop computer?
   b) laptop computer?

78 State one reason why tablet computers are so popular.

Operating system platform required (National 4)

79 What is an operating system?

80 Why do computers need an operating system program?

81 a) When does the operating system program run?
   b) Why does it run at this point?
   c) Name the program used to load the operating system program.

82 Name two operating systems.

83 What is a platform?

84 What does single platform mean?

85 What does dual platform mean?

86 Why should a user be concerned about system requirements?

87 Where would you find system requirements?

88 With what must system requirements match?

89 Why do system requirements need to match?

90 Look at the system requirements for Photoshop®, shown in Figure 11.55. Why is a DVD-ROM drive required?

91 Your computer has an Intel® processor running at 2.8 GHz, 2 Gb RAM and 1Gb ROM. The backing storage device is a 500 Gb hard disk drive which is half full. The operating system in use is Windows® 7.

   Look at the table below detailing the four items of software.
   a) Which of the items of software would work on your computer?
   b) Explain your choice in each case.

System requirements	Grabbit	Trappit	Stoppit	Pausit
OS	Windows® XP	Windows® Vista	Windows® 7	Windows® 8
Minimum processor GHz	2.7	2.8 (3.2 preferred)	1.9	2.6
Minimum RAM	4	2	1	3
Storage Gb	25	30	15	40

Operating systems (National 5)

92 State two functions of an operating system.

93 What do the letters HCI stand for?

94 Referring to a computer system with which you are familiar, state one way in which the HCI may be altered.

95 Explain the difference between an operating system and an application program.

96 What is a web browser?

97 What is a utility program?

98 What is an emulator?

99 What problem is an emulator designed to solve?

Key Points

- A single item of hardware is called a device.
- A peripheral is any device that may be attached to a computer system for input, output or backing storage.
- An input device is a device which allows data to be entered into a computer system.
- Examples of input devices are:
  - keyboard
  - mouse
  - microphone
  - sound card
  - track pad
  - graphics tablet
  - touch-sensitive screen
  - joystick
  - digital (still) camera
  - digital (video) camera
  - scanner
  - webcam
  - data glove (virtual reality)
  - interactive whiteboard.
- Each key on a keyboard sends a different code number into the computer in ASCII.
- A mouse controls the movement of a pointer on a screen.
- A mouse has buttons to select items.
- A microphone is used to allow sound to be input to a computer system.
- A microphone may also be used for voice recognition.
- Voice recognition is used for controlling devices and also for dictating text into word-processing documents.

- A sound card allows sound to be both input to and output from a computer system.
- A sound card captures sound in a process called sampling.
- A track pad is a touch-sensitive plate.
- Movements of the user's finger over the plate of a track pad control the movement of the pointer on the screen.
- A graphics tablet is a flat, pressure-sensitive board used with a pen or a stylus.
- A graphics tablet is used for Computer Aided Design (CAD).
- A touch-sensitive screen is useful when it is not appropriate to use a mouse. A screen is an output device, so a touch-sensitive screen is both an input and an output device.
- A joystick is used mainly for computer games, to control the movement of a character or icon on the screen.
- All digital cameras detect images using charge-coupled devices (CCDs).
- Digital still cameras store images on removable memory cards.
- A digital video camera or camcorder is used for taking video.
- Most digital still cameras can also take video.
- A scanner is used to input printed drawings, photographs or text directly into a computer.
- A scanner with optical character recognition (OCR) software may be used to input text into a word-processing package.
- A 3-D scanner may be used to scan an object and create a data file containing its measurements.

- A webcam is a small digital camera, used in order to capture images which may be transmitted across a network.
- A webcam may be used for video conferencing.
- Data gloves are used to take part in virtual reality.
- An interactive whiteboard is an input device for multimedia.
- An output device is a device which allows data to be displayed or passed out of a computer system.
- Examples of output devices are:
  - monitor:
    - LCD
    - LED
    - OLED
  - printer:
    - laser
    - inkjet
    - 3-D
  - plotter
  - loudspeaker/headphones/earphones
  - sound card
  - graphics card
  - headset (virtual reality)
  - multimedia projector.
- A monitor is an output device which accepts a video signal directly from a computer and displays the output on a screen.
- The screen is the part of a monitor, which displays the output.
- All current computer monitors are made up of a basic Liquid Crystal Display, which consists of a thin layer of fluid sandwiched between two sheets of plastic.
- The quality of the display depends upon the screen resolution, which is the number of horizontal pixels in a row x the number of vertical rows.
- Basic LCD monitors use a fluorescent tube as a backlight.
- LED (Light Emitting Diode) monitors use LEDs to backlight their screens.
- OLED (Organic Light Emitting Diode) displays use an organic chemical compound as their light source.

- A printer is a device which is used to produce a printout or a hard copy of the output from a computer.
- Laser printers use a special powder called toner to produce the image on the paper.
- An inkjet printer works by squirting small droplets of ink onto paper, through tiny holes in the print head.
- A 3-D printer can produce three-dimensional objects from solid materials such as plastic or resin.
- A plotter is a device for producing hard copy which can print out onto very large paper sizes.
- A loudspeaker is a sound output device.
- Active speakers are mains powered and have a built-in amplifier.
- A sound card improves the quality of sound output from games and multimedia applications.
- A graphics card is a device which controls the quality of output on a monitor.
- A headset is used to take part in virtual reality.
- A multimedia projector connects to a graphics card and displays the contents of the computer screen on a wall or interactive whiteboard.
- The processor can carry out instructions very quickly because it can process several billions of instructions every second.
- The processor clock produces a series of electronic pulses at a very high rate.
- Everything the processor does is kept in time with the clock, so the faster the clock speed, the faster the processor will operate.
- Processor clock speed is measured in Gigahertz (GHz).
- Increasing clock speed is one way of increasing the performance of a computer system.
- Processors may be classified by the number of cores, the types of instructions which they can carry out (instruction set), or the number of functions that they have.
- An embedded computer is a special purpose computer system which is designed to perform one or more dedicated functions.
- Embedded computers process data in real-time.

- Memory consists of Random Access Memory (RAM) and Read Only Memory (ROM).

- The place where each item is stored in a computer's memory is important because the processor has to be able to find any given item of data.

- An item of data is stored in memory in a storage location at a specific address.

- Features and uses of RAM:
  - the main use of RAM is to hold programs which are loaded from backing storage
  - it stores programs and data temporarily, only when power on
  - data is lost when the power is turned off
  - data held in RAM may be altered by being written to
  - data held in RAM may be read from or written to in any order/a direct-access medium.

- Features and uses of ROM:
  - it stores programs and data permanently, even when the power is off
  - data is *not* lost when the power is turned off
  - it is used to hold part of the operating system when a computer is off
  - data held in ROM cannot be altered
  - data held in ROM may be read from in any order/a direct-access medium.

- ROM chips are used on some computers to store part of the operating system, the 'bootstrap loader', to help the computer start up when it is switched on.

- Flash ROM may be used to save data.

- The total memory in a computer system is RAM + ROM.

- A desktop computer is used whilst sitting at a desk and is mains operated.

- A laptop computer may be used resting on your lap, while seated.

- A tablet computer has a large, touch-sensitive screen, which is used as its main input and output device.

- A smartphone is a mobile phone which has its own operating system and is capable of running a variety of applications.

- A mainframe computer is a very large computer system, which can process a very large amount of data at high speed.

- A supercomputer is the fastest and most powerful type of computer, used for intensive mathematical calculations such as weather forecasting.

- The operating system is a program that controls the entire operation of the computer and any devices which are attached to it.

- The operating system is the first program that must be loaded into the computer's memory when the computer is switched on.

- Examples of operating systems include Microsoft Windows®, Unix® and Mac OS X®.

- A platform refers to the hardware and software which makes up a particular type of computer system.

- To find out which platform a particular item of software requires, it is necessary to consult the system requirements.

- A web browser is a program that allows the user to browse or surf through the World Wide Web.

- A utility program is a type of systems software designed to perform an everyday task.

- An emulator is a program which allows a computer to run a different operating system.

- The operating system carries out the following tasks:
  - checks input devices like the keyboard and mouse
  - manages the sending of data to output devices like the screen and the printer
  - controls where programs and data are placed in the computer's memory
  - manages the filing system
  - controls the security of the system
  - provides a Human Computer Interface (HCI) for the user
  - lets the user know if any mistakes have occurred.

- The operating system controls how the computer works. An application program performs a task, like word processing or a game.

CHAPTER 12

Storage

This chapter examines what storage is and what devices are used for storage.

Storage:

National 5

- capacity, speed
- rewritable, read-only
- local, web, cloud
- capacity (in appropriate units)
- interface type
- data transfer speed

Storage devices:

National 5

- built-in, external, portable
- magnetic, optical
- solid state

Backing storage

What is backing storage?

Backing storage is used to **store programs** and **data** permanently. Computers need backing storage because data held in the **memory** is lost when the computer is switched off. A **backing storage medium** is the substance which holds the data. **Magnetic tape**, **hard disks**, **flash ROM** (N5) are all examples of backing storage media and the **hardware** that uses or holds the media is known as a backing **storage device**. Be careful not to confuse the terms *media* and *software*.

There are three main methods of storage in current use. These are magnetic, **optical** and **solid-state** (N5).

Storage devices may be **built in** to the inside of a computer system or be **external** (connected to the outside). This is **local storage** (N5). External devices are usually **portable**, which means that they can be used for making a **backup copy**. A backup copy is required in case your data, stored on a backing storage **medium**, is lost or damaged. A backup copy should be kept in a safe place, away from the computer.

> **Reminder**
>
> ! Remember: *software* means programs or data not disks!

Backup copies may also be kept on the **World Wide Web** in **cloud storage**. You can read more about local, web and cloud storage later in this chapter.

We will look at the following types of backing storage devices and media in this chapter:

Backing storage devices	Backing storage media
Magnetic	**Magnetic**
Tape drive	Magnetic tape
Hard disk drive	Hard disk
Optical	**Optical**
CD drive	CD-ROM/R/RW
DVD drive	DVD-ROM/R/RW
Blu-ray™ drive	BD-ROM/R/RE
Solid-state	**Solid-state**
USB flash drive	flash ROM
Memory card	
SSD	

Table 12.01 Backing storage devices and media

Storage characteristics

When considering each type of backing storage, we will look at the following characteristics:

Capacity: the quantity of data that can be held on a backing storage medium. This book makes no distinction between *capacity* and *capacity (in appropriate units)*.

Speed: how quickly the device provides access to data held on it.

Two types of access to data are provided by storage devices, They are **serial** (or **sequential**) **access** and **direct** (or **random**) **access**. Serial access means that data may only be read back in the order it was written. Serial access is slow. Magnetic tape provides serial access. Direct access means that data may be accessed directly rather than having to be written to or read back in a particular order. Direct access is fast.

Rewriteable or **read-only**: whether or not data may be saved on the medium contained by the device. A read-only medium may not have data saved to it, nor deleted from it. Magnetic media are rewriteable. Optical media may be rewriteable (RW), write once (R), or read only (**ROM**).

Figure 12.01 An SD card showing a write protect switch

Flash ROM is rewriteable, but some memory cards have a **write protect switch**.

Data transfer speed

The **data transfer speed** is the speed at which the **interface** on the computer can send and receive data to and from the **peripheral** device to which it is attached. The speed of data transfer for all devices depends entirely upon the method of connection, that is, the type of interface used. Examples of interfaces include **USB** and **Firewire**®. Note that **Mbps** is **Megabits per second**. This book makes no distinction between *speed* and *data transfer speed*.

Cost

You should note that the general tendency with cost of media and capacity of media is for cost to go down and capacity to increase. When comparing the cost of different media you should look at the cost per **Gigabyte** of storage.

Magnetic storage

Formatting

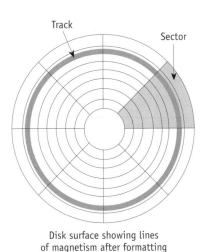

Disk surface showing lines of magnetism after formatting

Figure 12.02 Formatting a magnetic disk. You can't see the tracks on the disk, because they're circles of magnetism.

Before you can use any type of magnetic disk in your computer it must be prepared in a special way. This process is called **formatting**. Formatting produces invisible circles, called **tracks** of magnetism on the surface of the disk. You can see these in Figure 12.02. A disk doesn't look any different after it has been formatted – you can't see the tracks or tell by looking at it. But if you try to use an unformatted disk you won't be able to save any data. By the same token, if you format or **initialise** a disk, which already contains data, then all the data will be lost.

There are many different types of disk formats. If you format a disk on one type of computer system, it may not be readable on another. For example, Apple® computers and PCs have a number of different disk formats. Most magnetic hard disks come pre-formatted for PC, which is also readable on Apple® computers, but the reverse is not always the case.

USB flash drives, solid-state drives and memory cards for cameras must also be formatted before they can be used. They do not use **magnetic storage**, and so they do not contain tracks, but they can be formatted in different ways for different filing systems, so the advice in the previous paragraph still applies.

Hard drive and hard disks

A **hard disk** is a circular metal disk coated with magnetic material. Hard disks are usually sealed inside a hard disk drive and cannot be removed (**internal**), though you can buy external hard drives, which can be easily transported between computers. Hard disks are used because you can store much more data on them and access the data more quickly than any other current backing storage medium.

Figure 12.03 Inside a hard disk drive

How a hard disk works

A hard disk drive normally contains several disks, stacked on top of each other with a gap between them – you can see how in Figure 12.04. The gaps are needed so the read/write heads on the disk drive can move across the disk surface and reach the tracks nearest the centre of the disk.

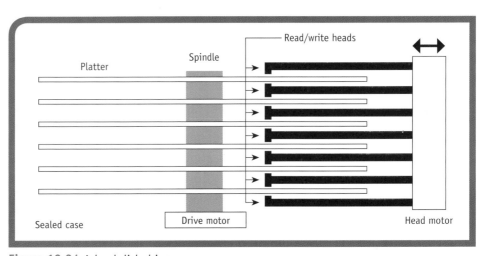

Figure 12.04 A hard disk drive

Hard disks rotate quickly and the gap between the read/write heads and the surface of the metal disk is tiny. If you bump or drop the hard disk drive while it is switched on or switch it off without shutting it down properly the heads could collide with the surface of the disk. This is called **crashing** and it usually results in all the data on the disk being lost. The disk itself could be permanently damaged.

Hard disks can load and save programs faster than optical. It takes a second or two for the optical drive to start spinning the disk around before the read/write head can move to the right track but a hard disk drive is spinning all the time and much faster than an optical disk, so there is only a fraction of a second delay before the **read/write head** can reach the correct track.

Checklist for hard drive

✓ Features: fixed media backing storage device, direct access (fast).
✓ Functions: writes data to, and reads data from a hard disk.
✓ Uses: to store large quantities of data, and retrieve it at high speed.

Magnetic tape drive

Magnetic tape is a backing storage medium, which uses plastic tape, coated on one side with magnetic material. It is many years since audiotape cassettes were the only backing storage medium on home computers, but magnetic tape is now widely used as a backup system for computer data. The system which is most commonly used for this is **Linear Tape-Open™** or **Ultrium™**.

Tape is a sequential access medium, which makes it ideal for routine backups and long-term archiving of data. Loading and saving individual programs on magnetic tape takes much longer than from hard disks, so magnetic tape isn't used where speed of access to data is important.

Capacity depends upon the length of tape being used. Because the backing storage capacity of hard disks is now measured in Gigabytes, tape is one of the few types of media that allows a complete hard disk to be backed up on a single tape. Typical tape capacities range from 400 **Gb** to 1.6 **Tb**. Tape is also relatively inexpensive in terms of capacity, compared to other media. Backups made on tape are often *compressed* to allow more data to fit on a single tape. Restoring a compressed **file** from a backup means that it must be *uncompressed* before use.

Checklist for magnetic tape drive

✓ Features: removable media backing storage device, sequential access (slow).
✓ Functions: writes data to, and reads data from a magnetic tape.
✓ Uses: to store data, especially backups.

Optical storage

CD-ROM (Compact Disk Read Only Memory)

A CD-ROM looks just like an **audio** compact disk. A CD-ROM disk comes with **information** already stored on it so it doesn't need to be formatted. A CD-ROM disk is read only, so you can't erase the data on it. Many software companies distribute their programs on CD-ROM.

A CD-ROM is 120 mm in diameter and 1.2 mm thick. When a CD-ROM is made, the data is moulded into tiny holes called **pits** on the clear plastic disk. The plastic disk is then coated with a reflective metal layer and then a protective lacquer. The pits are arranged in a spiral starting in the centre of the disk. If it were possible to unwind the spiral of data on a CD-ROM and lay it in a straight line, it would stretch for three and a half miles or five and a half kilometres. If you lived at the end of a CD-ROM, you would qualify for free bus travel to school!

The data is read from a CD-ROM by focusing a laser beam through the clear plastic onto the tracks. When the laser light strikes the area between the pits (these areas are called **lands**), it is reflected into a photo-detector and any light which hits a pit is scattered and absorbed. The result is that the series of pits and lands in the surface of the disk are interpreted as a series of corresponding 0s and 1s which make up the data.

CD-ROMs should be treated with care, because scratches on the label side can enable air to penetrate and cause the metal layer to oxidise, making the disk unusable. On the other surface, the laser focuses on a layer within the clear base and small scratches have no effect.

CD-ROM drives must have extensive error correction features. This is not as important in an audio CD where a single **bit** being read incorrectly will be unlikely to be noticed. However, a single bit wrong in a **computer program** or a **data file** could have disastrous results.

Read/write heads on a CD-ROM drive are faster than ordinary CD players. One important difference between an audio CD player and a CD-ROM drive is that the read/write head in a CD-ROM drive *must* move faster than in an audio CD player because the CD-ROM drive must be able to access the different tracks on the CD-ROM in a random fashion. It's not so important when you're playing music to be able to leap randomly from track to track.

Checklist for CD-ROM

✓ Features: read only backing storage medium, direct access, maximum storage capacity 700 **Mb**.

✓ Functions: holds data moulded into it when it is made.

✓ Uses: to store data permanently, such as music and application programs. Cannot be erased.

CD-Recordable and CD-Rewriteable

CD-R and CD-RW disks are the same size and have the same outward appearance as CD-ROMs. Writing data to a CD-R or CD-RW is called **burning** and a drive capable of writing to a CD-R or CD-RW is often called a **CD burner**.

CD-Recordable (CD-R)

The part of a CD-R which stores the data (the recording layer) is a layer of dye. A microscopic reflective layer, either a special silver alloy or gold, is coated over the dye. The colour of the disk depends on the particular combination of metal and dye used. Like a CD-ROM, a CD-R writes data in a spiral pattern, which is formed on the disk when it is manufactured.

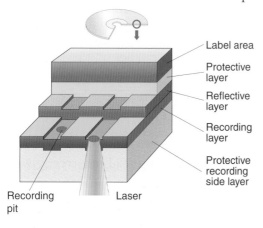

Label area
Protective layer
Reflective layer
Recording layer
Protective recording side layer

Recording pit   Laser

CD-R structural cross-section

Figure 12.05 Recording on a CD-Recordable disk

Data is written to a CD-R by using a high-powered laser beam, which is focused on the layer of dye in the disk. When the laser shines on a tiny area of the dye, the dye is heated and a chemical change takes place. A CD-R's data is represented by changed and unchanged areas, in a similar manner to a CD-ROM's pits and lands. A low-powered laser beam, which does not affect the dye, is used to read the data back from the CD-R. After a CD-R disk has been written to, it can be used in an ordinary CD drive as if it were a CD-ROM. One feature of a CD-R is that the whole disk does not need to be written to at once, instead data may be written in stages called *sessions*. However, once all of the available space on the recording surface has been used up, a CD-R behaves just like a CD-ROM.

CD-R drives are classified according to their speed of recording. CD-R drives are now available which write data at around 50× normal speed. Given that a 74-minute CD-R disk takes 74 minutes to completely fill with data at single speed (1×), these fast recorders are a considerable advance.

Checklist for CD-Recordable (CD-R)

✓ Features: write-once backing storage medium (until full), direct access, maximum storage capacity 700 Mb.

✓ Functions: holds data written to it in a CD writer drive.

✓ Uses: to store data permanently, such as backups. Cannot be erased.

Figure 12.06 CD-Rewriteable disks

CD-Rewriteable (CD-RW)

The fact that CD-R disks cannot be erased and rewritten has given rise to the development of CD-RW. CD-RW allows a user to record over data or to delete individual files.

Like recording data on a CD-R disk, a CD-RW disk works by using a laser beam to change the state of a recording medium. In the case of the CD-R disk, this recording medium is a dye, which is permanently changed by a high-powered laser beam. In the case of a CD-RW disk, if it is to be erasable, then the recording medium must be able to have its change of state reversed. In simple terms, an example of a change of state is when ice (solid state) melts to form water (liquid state), and this may be reversed to form ice again. CD-RW disks use special chemicals for this purpose.

When a CD-RW drive is operating it uses a laser beam set at three different powers: high, medium and low. The high or *write power* is used to record data by changing the state of the recording layer to absorptive. The medium or *erase power* is used to change the state of the recording layer back to reflective. The low or **read power** is not powerful enough to affect the state of the recording layer, so it is used to read the data. Some CD-RW drives are also capable of reading DVD-ROMs. These are called 'combo' drives.

One disadvantage of CD-RW disks is that there is a limit to the number of times CD-RW disks may be rewritten, but this is several thousand times so the restriction is unlikely to become a problem in normal use. CD-RW drives are dual function, capable of handling both CD-R and CD-RW recording, so the user can choose which recordable medium is going to be the best for a particular job. The low cost of CD-R media compared to CD-RW makes CD-R media the most popular choice.

CD-rewriter drives are usually described as having three speeds, such as 48×10×32×. The first speed is the speed at which a CD-R may be written to. The second speed is the speed at which a CD-RW may be written to. The third speed is the speed at which any type of CD may be read. Blank CD-R and CD-RW disks are also rated for different speeds. The drive described above would be able to write to a 52× CD-R at its maximum speed of 48×. However, writing at 48× to a CD-R rated at only 32× may not work and the CD you create may be unreliable, or may only work on your drive and not on another one.

Checklist for CD-Rewritable (CD-RW)

✓ Features: rewritable backing storage medium, direct access, maximum storage capacity 700 Mb, more expensive than CD-R.

✓ Functions: holds data written to it in a CD-rewriter drive.

✓ Uses: to store data temporarily or permanently. May be erased and rewritten.

DVD-ROM

DVD-ROM is a high-capacity data storage medium, with the same overall size as a standard CD-ROM. **DVD** disks can provide from 4.7 up to 17 Gigabytes of **storage** (if a double-layer, double-sided disk is used).

A DVD-ROM can easily be mistaken for a CD-ROM: both are plastic disks 120 mm in diameter and 1.2 mm thick and both use lasers to read data stored in pits in a spiral track. So how is it possible that a DVD can hold so much more data than a CD-ROM?

There are several reasons:

- The tracks on a DVD-ROM are placed closer together and the pits are also a lot smaller than on a CD-ROM.
- DVD-ROMs can have two layers on each side of a disk and DVD-ROMs can also be double-sided, but they need to be taken out of the drive and turned over to read the data on the other side.
- A DVD-ROM has more efficient error correction than a CD-ROM, and this means that more space on the disk is available to hold data.

Checklist for DVD-ROM

✓ Features: read-only backing storage medium, direct access, storage capacity from 4.7 to 17 Gb.

✓ Functions: holds data moulded into it when it is made.

✓ Uses: to store data permanently, such as movies and application programs. Cannot be erased.

DVD-Recordable (DVD-R)

DVD-R is a write-once medium that can contain any type of information normally stored on DVD, such as **video**, audio, images, data files and **multimedia** programs. DVD-R disks may be used on DVD-ROM drives and DVD video players. DVD-R operates in a similar manner to CD-R, with recordable disks containing a layer of dye.

Checklist for DVD-Recordable (DVD-R)

✓ Features: write-once backing storage medium (until full), direct access, maximum storage capacity 8.4 Gb (double layer).

✓ Functions: holds data written to it in a DVD-writer drive.

✓ Uses: to store data permanently, such as home movies and data backups. Cannot be erased.

Figure 12.07 Various types of DVD

DVD-Rewritable (DVD-RW)

DVD-RW uses more complex methods of recording data than the purely optical methods used for CD-R and DVD-R. A special format also allows data to be recorded on both the grooves formed on the disk and in the lands between the grooves.

There are currently several different DVD-Rewriteable standards available, but most current computers have DVD-Rewritable drives, which can use all types of disk.

Checklist for DVD-Rewritable (DVD-RW)

✓ Features: rewritable backing storage medium, direct access, maximum storage capacity 4.7 Gb, more expensive than DVD-R.

✓ Functions: holds data written to it in a DVD-Rewriter drive.

✓ Uses: to store data temporarily or permanently, such as home movies and data backups. May be erased and rewritten.

Blu-ray™

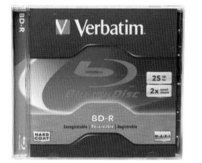

Figure 12.08 A Blu-ray Disc™

Blu-ray Disc™ (BD) is the name of another type of optical disk format. The format was developed to enable recording, rewriting and playback of high-definition video (HD). The format has become a standard for HD movies. Blu-ray Discs™ are available in several varieties, including BD-ROM, BD-R, BD-RE and **BD-XL**.

Despite being the same physical size as a DVD, a Blu-ray Disc™ is able to hold much more data:

- a single-layer disk can hold 25 Gb
- a dual-layer disk can hold 50 Gb
- a BD-XL disk can hold up to 128 Gb.

This increased storage capacity is possible because the laser beam in the drive is coloured blue (hence the name) and produces a narrower beam of light than a red laser on a DVD drive. Blue light has a shorter wavelength than red light.

Checklist for Blu-ray™

✓ Features: backing storage medium, direct access, maximum storage capacity 128 Gb.

✓ Functions: holds data written to it in a Blu-ray™ drive.

✓ Uses: to store HD movies.

National 5

Check Your Learning

Now answer questions 1–39 (on page 274) on storage devices (National 4).

Solid-state storage

USB flash drives

USB stands for **Universal Serial Bus**. USB is a type of computer interface. Many different devices use the USB interface, such as **printers**, **scanners**, external hard disk drives, mice and **keyboards**. USB flash drives are very common. They are *solid-state* devices, because they have no moving parts and the storage media itself is solid. The media contained inside the USB flash drive is called **flash ROM**. Although flash drives contain computer memory **chips**, they are not used instead of **RAM**, but more as a substitute for a disk drive.

One type of USB flash drive has been incorporated into a wristwatch, and another into a penknife. They are much easier to use than a disk drive. Most computers recognise the devices and display the **icon** on the desktop the moment they are plugged in. The USB interface means that the device is compatible with many different computer systems and is easy to connect. Their range of capacities from 1 to 256 Gigabytes makes them suitable for a large number of applications, from storing digital photographs to transporting multimedia presentations and holding movies.

Figure 12.09 A USB flash drive

Memory cards

Memory cards incorporating flash ROM are in widespread use in a variety of cameras and mobile phones. **Secure Digital (SD)** and **CompactFlash (CF)** are two popular memory card formats. MicroSD is the smallest memory-card format, and is used mainly in phones. High-capacity SD formats include **SDHC** and **SDXC**. Some older **digital cameras** may not support these high-capacity formats. A 12-**Megapixel** digital camera can store over 30 000 **JPEG** images on a 128 Gb memory card.

Figure 12.10 A penknife incorporating a USB flash drive

Some memory cards incorporate **WiFi**. Photographs and videos stored on WiFi memory cards may be automatically transferred to any other device, such as a **tablet** or phone, without having to remove the card from the camera.

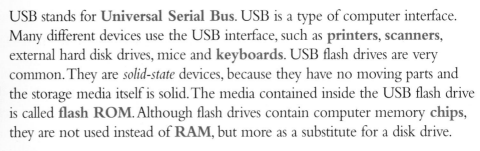
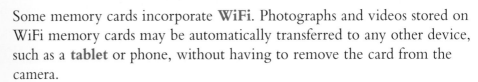

Figure 12.11 Memory cards

Solid-state drives (SSD)

Figure 12.12 A solid-state drive

Solid-state drives are devices with relatively large storage capacities, which are typically used as replacements for hard disks in **laptop** and **desktop computers**. Solid-state drives use flash memory, like USB flash ROM drives and memory cards.

Solid-state drives share many of the features and advantages of USB flash ROM drives and memory cards, in that they are robust devices which provide fast access to data. The storage capacity of solid-state drives is approaching that of hard disk drives, but at a considerable cost.

Many other devices, such as mobile phones, music and video players use flash ROM as a backing storage medium.

Checklist for solid-state storage

✓ Features: USB connects to all current computers, robust, memory cards are small, SSDs have fast access.

✓ Functions: holds data written to it.

✓ Uses: to store data permanently, such as photos and data backups, SSD used as replacement for HDD.

Cloud storage

Cloud storage is online storage which is accessed via a **Wide Area Network**. The media used by the storage provider is unknown to the user, but is typically a **file server** 'farm' containing a vast number of hard disks. Remember not to think of the **cloud** itself as a storage device! You can read more about the cloud later in this chapter.

Check Your Learning

Now answer questions 40–47 (on page 275) on storage devices (National 5).

More about file sizes, backing storage and memory capacities

A file is information held on backing storage or in memory. Files may hold data (your own work which you have saved, like a **text** file) or programs (applications) which you use, or have written yourself using a programming language. The **file size** is the amount of space taken up by a file on backing storage. Backing storage is a system for permanently holding data on media such as disk, tape, CD or DVD. **Backing storage capacity** is the amount of space available on a given medium, such as a hard disk. **Memory capacity** is the amount of space available in a computer system (RAM), used to hold programs and data once they have been loaded.

Quick Tip — Backing storage

It is very common for people to confuse the terms backing storage capacity and memory capacity because they both use the same units, namely Gigabytes. You will not make this mistake if you *only* use the term 'memory' when speaking about RAM, and 'backing storage capacity' when referring to the space available to store data on media such as hard disk or USB flash ROM.

At the time of writing this book, the memory of a microcomputer is measured in Gigabytes, with between two and eight Gigabytes being a typical amount for a normal desktop or laptop computer. The backing storage capacity is measured in Gigabytes, with typical hard disk capacities ranging from 256 to 2048 Gigabytes (two Terabytes).

You will be familiar with Gigabytes as a unit of storage used in many other everyday devices. For instance, your mobile phone, iPod® or other media player may have a backing storage capacity of between 16 and 64 Gigabytes.

Figure 12.13 Dialog boxes showing information on file sizes. The file on the left is an application, and the file on the right is a data file.

Reminders

Converting between units

! Remember: to change:
   - bits to bytes, divide by 8
   - bytes to bits, multiply by 8
   - bytes to Kilobytes, divide by 1024
   - Kilobytes to bytes, multiply by 1024
   - Megabytes to Kilobytes, multiply by 1024
! All larger units are multiples of 1024.

Look at Figure 12.13, which shows the sizes of two different files. The file size of the file on the left is 173.4 Mb. This means that the space required to store that file on backing storage, for example hard disk, is 173.4 **Megabytes**. If this file is loaded into the computer's memory (RAM), it will take up the same amount of space. If you tried to store this size of file on a USB flash ROM drive of 128 Mb capacity, then it would not fit, because the file is too large. If you wished to save this file to a different backing storage medium, for instance a CD-Recordable disk, then it would be possible to save this file, since the storage capacity of a CD-Recordable disk is between 650 and 700 Mb. This file would also fit on a DVD-Recordable disk with a backing storage capacity of between 4.7 and 8.4 Gb (single and double-layered).

The other file on the right-hand side of Figure 12.13 is much larger, at 9.95 Gb. If you wanted to save all of the music that it contains, then you would have to choose an iPod® or other media player with a backing storage capacity of at least 10 Gb. A double-layered DVD-Recordable disk would not have sufficient backing storage capacity at 8.4 Gb.

It is also important to know how much backing storage and memory capacity is present in a computer system when deciding whether a given program will run or not. This is part of the software **system requirements**, and is a good example of *the relationship between software and hardware* in a computer system.

"I hope you don't mind, but the size of the file I just sent you was 198,753 gigs."

Figure 12.14 File size

Media	Capacity range
CD-ROM, CD-R, CD-RW	650–700 Mb
DVD-R	4.7–8.4 Gb
DVD-ROM	4.7–17 Gb
Blu-ray Disc™	25–128 Gb
Memory card	1–256 Gb
USB flash ROM	1–512 Gb
Solid-state disk	64 Gb–1 Tb
Hard disk	100 Gb–6 Tb

Table 12.02 A variety of backing storage capacities

Check Your Learning

Now answer questions 48–51 (on page 275) on capacity (National 4).

Interface type

An interface is the hardware and associated software needed to allow communication between the **processor** and its peripheral devices. A peripheral is a device which may be connected to the outside of a computer system, for input, output or backing storage.

Interfaces also compensate for any differences between the computer and the peripheral, such as data transfer speed and differences in data format. The data transfer speed is the speed at which the interface on the computer can send and receive data to and from the peripheral device to which it is attached. The tables in this section show the maximum data transfer speed for each interface named.

A wide variety of interfaces are used to connect backing storage devices. These include USB, Firewire®, **Thunderbolt**®, **Ethernet** and **wireless**. You read more about interfaces in Chapter 1.

 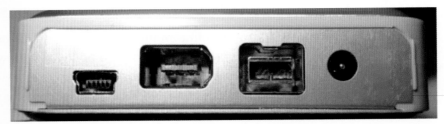

Figure 12.15 Interfaces on external hard drives (left: USB3 and Thunderbolt; right: USB2, Firewire® 400, Firewire® 800)

USB

The Universal Serial Bus (USB) is the most common interface used on current computer systems. USB 3 (**SUPERSPEED**) is the latest version of this interface. Earlier versions include USB 1 and USB 2. All new desktop and laptop computers have at least one USB connector. A wide variety of peripherals, from scanners, printers, cameras and **card readers** to fairy lights and cup warmers all use the USB interface.

Interface type	Version	Maximum data transfer speed
USB	1	12 Megabits/second
USB	2	480 Megabits/second
USB	3	5 Gigabits/second
USB	3.1	10 Gigabits/second (proposed)

Table 12.03 Types of USB interface

The maximum transfer speed is rarely achieved in practice. Factors such as length and type of **cable** and connector can influence this. For example, in my classroom, the **interactive whiteboard** is connected to the teacher's computer by a USB interface with six metres of cable. When it was first installed, the length of cable used was 10 metres, and it was found that communication with the board failed.

Thunderbolt®

Thunderbolt® is an interface for connecting peripheral devices to a computer via an expansion bus. Thunderbolt® was developed by Intel® and brought to market by Apple®.

Interface type	Version	Maximum data transfer speed
Thunderbolt®	1	10 Gigabits/second (two channels)
Thunderbolt®	2	20 Gigabits/second (one channel – bi-directional)

Table 12.04 Thunderbolt® interface

The original idea for Thunderbolt® was to use **optical fibre**, but it was found that the required speed could be obtained by using **copper wire**. Unlike optical fibre, copper wire can also carry power. Thunderbolt® can also carry video signals to a **monitor**.

WiFi (IEEE 802.11)

WiFi allows an electronic device to exchange data wirelessly over a **Local Area Network**, for instance a high-speed **internet** connection.

Interface type	Version	Maximum data transfer speed
802.11	b	11 Megabits/second
802.11	g	54 Megabits/second
802.11	n	600 Megabits/second
802.11	ac	1 Gigabit/second
802.11	ad	7 Gigabits/second (proposed)

Table 12.05 Types of 802.11 interface

A typical house which has a **broadband connection** will contain a WiFi router, usually of at least 802.11n specification. Most routers can also work with signals from slower versions of WiFi.

It is sensible to protect your home WiFi with a hard-to-guess **password**, to prevent other people from using your **bandwidth**. If they do steal bandwidth in this way, they may be liable to prosecution under the law. However, if someone else uses your internet connection to do something illegal, you may well be held responsible unless you can prove otherwise.

You can read more about networking in Chapter 13.

Check Your Learning Now answer questions 52–57 (on page 275) on interface type (National 5).

Local and web/cloud storage

What is cloud computing?

Cloud computing is the use of computing resources (such as hardware and software) that are delivered as a **service** over the internet. The name comes from the use of the cloud symbol to represent the internet or other **networks**. The cloud computing user does not know (or care) about the structure of the network inside the cloud, they only know that when they are connected, they can use the services that the cloud provides. The users benefit because they are able to use, and pay for, the services only when required.

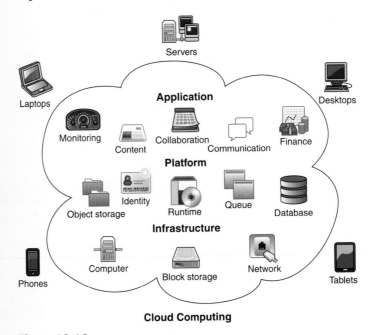

Figure 12.16

Cloud computing services

Three main types of service are provided in the cloud. These are **Infrastructure as a service**, **Platform as a service** and **Software as a service**.

Infrastructure as a service (**Iaas**) provides services which involve hardware, data storage, networking and bandwidth.

Platform as a service (**Paas**) provides software and development tools which help the user to create applications (**apps**).

Software as a service (**Saas**) is a software delivery model in which applications are held on, and run, from the cloud. The user can run much more powerful applications on the cloud than they could on their own computers without having to **upgrade**.

Note that this book makes no distinction between web *and* cloud *as far as storage is concerned.*

Advantages of web/cloud storage

- **Security**: if you lose your data locally, a backup is available in the cloud.
- Storage: virtually unlimited storage is available in the cloud, compared to local.
- Processing: your data is processed in the cloud, meaning that you or your company can save money on hardware costs, initial costs, running costs, upgrades and **maintenance**: however, you should set these savings against what you are charged for the cloud services provided.
- Server: the cloud can provide the services normally associated with a server.
- Scaling: more services can be brought online to meet (temporary) increased demand, for example **Black Friday** (discount) promotion on a company **website**.

Disadvantages of web/cloud storage

- Security: all cloud providers have terms and conditions, which say they will store your data but will not be responsible for any loss or damage that you or your company may sustain as a result of this provision, for example if your data is lost.
- Privacy: if your data is of a sensitive nature, for instance financial information, you may not wish it to be stored by someone else. You are responsible for keeping your cloud access details, such as your password, safe. However, since you are handing over all of your data to the cloud provider, you cannot be absolutely certain that no one else can see your data, for example employees of the cloud computing company.
- Access time: depends upon your internet connection. Most domestic connections are **ADSL**-based, which means that download speeds and upload speeds are different, for example data may be downloaded from the cloud at 20 Mbps but uploaded at only 1 Mbps. Internet connections for businesses may have higher speeds, but at greater cost.
- Cost: while many cloud providers offer a free service for limited amounts of data, these are usually only valid for individuals rather than companies. Cloud storage of data in excess of a few Gigabytes is likely to require a subscription.
- Loss of internet connection: the company will not accept responsibility for this; if it occurs, you may not be able to create (upload) a backup or retrieve (download) data. You must be constantly connected to the internet to use the cloud.

Figure 12.17 Cloudwash

Local storage in comparison to web/cloud storage

Advantages of local storage

- Privacy: only you can see your data, and you can control access to it.
- Availability: no problems accessing data if your connection to the internet is not working or unavailable.

Disadvantages of local storage

- Security: you are responsible for making and keeping backup copies of your data.
- Processing: you must pay all costs (initial, running, upgrade, maintenance), for both hardware and software. If you need new software and new computers to run it, then it can be costly to upgrade. When the next version of the software is released, you may have to upgrade again, and so on.
- Server: you must install, run and maintain the services that you require the server to provide.

Check Your Learning

Now answer questions 58–64 (on page 275) on local and web/cloud storage (National 5).

Practical Tasks

1 Create a table of backing storage media. Find out the cost per Gigabyte for each medium and use this information to complete the table.

Media type	Speed: serial/ direct	Capacity	Cost (per Gb)	Rewritable/ read-only
Magnetic tape	Serial	800Gb–1.6Tb	£25 (3.1p/Gb)	Rewritable
Magnetic hard disk				
CD-ROM/R/RW				
DVD-ROM/R/RW				
BD-ROM/R/RE/XL				
USB flash ROM				
Memory card				
SSD				

2 Find out about the speed of data transfer provided by two interfaces. Choose two interfaces from the list below:

- USB (Universal Serial Bus)
- Firewire®/IEEE 1394
- IDE/ATA (Integrated Drive Electronics/ Advanced Technology Attachment)
- SATA (Serial ATA)
- SCSI (Small Computer System Interface)
- SAS (Serial Attached SCSI)
- FC (Fibre Channel) (note: copper)
- NAS (Network Attached Storage): Ethernet
- Thunderbolt®
- WiFi

a) Write out the full name and abbreviation for each interface.

b) Are the interfaces typically used for

i) internal or external storage?

ii) both hard disks and/or other devices?

c) What is the maximum speed of data transfer for each device?

d) How long would it take to copy a 25Gb movie file on to an external hard disk drive using each of your chosen interfaces?

Example

Universal Serial Bus (version 2.0 – high-speed USB)

Data transfer speed = 480 Megabits/second

Size of file to be copied = 5 Gigabytes

5 Gigabytes = $5 \times 1024 \times 8 = 40\,960$ Megabits

Time taken = $40\,960 \div 480 = $ **85.3 seconds**

Note that in practice, the maximum data transfer speed is rarely available to connected devices. See http://en.wikipedia.org/wiki/List_of_device_bit_rates.

3 Jane is a games programmer. She needs a storage solution to hold her programs, which can be as large as 7Gb. It must also be possible to use the solution on different computers, because she also works at home.

a) Recommend a storage solution that Jane can use for this purpose.

b) Once you have found a suitable storage solution, give a reason for your choice.

Think carefully about why your choice is suitable and why other solutions may be unsuitable.

4 In 2012, one magnetic hard disk manufacturer announced that they had developed a method of filling their drives with helium gas instead of air. Find out the manufacturer's name, and what advantages helium-filled drives have over air-filled drives.

5 Read www.bbc.co.uk/newsbeat/16838342 to see what happens if the cloud 'crashes'.

6 Look at www.bbc.co.uk/news/technology-19982440 to see one example of how the cloud is used to promote illegal file sharing.

7 Read www.wired.com/wiredenterprise/2013/08/memsql-and-amazon/?mbid=social10837774 and find out why some companies have a different view of the cloud.

Questions

Storage devices (National 4)

1 What is backing storage?

2 Why do computers need backing storage?

3 What is a storage device?

4 What is a backing storage medium?

5 Explain the difference between media and software.

6 Name two types of backing storage media.

7 Name two backing storage devices.

8 Name two main methods of storage.

9 What may external storage devices be used for that built-in devices cannot?

10 Why is it a good idea to keep backup copies?

11 Where should backup copies be kept?

12 What is the difference between backing storage and backup?

13 Explain the meaning of the term storage capacity.

14 Name one type of access to data provided by a storage device.

15 State one factor which affects the speed of data transfer for a device.

16 State two features of a read-only medium.

17 What is formatting?

18 What happens when a magnetic disk is formatted?

19 Why is it important to know how a storage medium is formatted?

20 What is 'hard' about a magnetic hard disk?

21 What happens when a hard disk 'crashes'?

22 Explain why hard disks can load programs faster than optical disks.

23 Which storage medium provides only sequential access to data?

24 Why is a sequential access medium slower than a direct-access medium?

25 What is the main use of magnetic tape?

26 Why is data sometimes compressed?

27 Why are some disks called optical disks?

28 Explain how data is stored on a CD-ROM.

29 What effect do scratches have on a CD-ROM?

30 Why does a CD-R drive need to use two different powers of laser?

31 What type of substance forms the recording layer on a CD-R?

32 Why is it important to know the speed rating of CD-R media?

33 In a CD-R, what are 'sessions'?

34 What is the main difference between a CD-R and a CD-RW?

35 What is a 'combo' drive?

36 State one difference between a CD-ROM and a DVD-ROM.

37 If a DVD-ROM and a CD-ROM are the same size, how is it possible for a DVD-ROM to hold so much more data than a CD-ROM?

38 From where does a Blu-ray Disc™ get its name?

39 Explain why a Blu-ray Disc™ can hold much more data than any other type of optical disk.

Storage devices (National 5)

40 What is the term USB short for?

41 What is solid about 'solid-state storage'?

42 What is a USB flash drive?

43 State one advantage of a USB flash drive over a magnetic hard disk drive.

Capacity (National 4)

48 What is the meaning of the term 'backing storage capacity'?

49 What is the meaning of the term 'memory capacity'?

50 Which backing storage device would you choose if you needed
   a) fast access to large quantities of data?

Interface type (National 5)

52 What is an interface?

53 What is a peripheral?

54 Name two interfaces used to connect backing storage devices.

55 State one advantage the USB interface has over all other interfaces.

56 State one advantage of a Thunderbolt® interface over a USB interface.

57 Look at Figure 12.18.
   a) Which two interfaces does this device have?
   b) What is the main advantage of this device over USB flash ROM?

Figure 12.18 Maxell portable wireless reader with powerbank function

44 What do USB flash ROM drives, memory cards and solid-state drives have in common?

45 State two memory-card formats.

46 What is cloud storage?

47 What storage medium is typically used in cloud storage?

   b) compatibility with the maximum number of computers?
   c) to record an HD TV programme?

51 Suggest a storage medium to hold a backup of
   a) 2 Gigabytes of photographs.
   b) 50 Gigabytes of photographs.

Local and web/cloud storage (National 5)

58 What is cloud computing?

59 From where does cloud computing get its name?

60 Why does the cloud computing user not care about the network inside the cloud?

61 Name and describe three main types of cloud computing services.

62 State two advantages of web/cloud over local storage.

63 State two disadvantages of web/cloud compared to local storage.

64 State one advantage of local over web/cloud storage.

Key Points

- Backing storage is used to store programs and data permanently.

- Computers need backing storage because data held in the main memory is lost when the computer is switched off.

- A backing storage medium is the substance which holds the data.

- A backup copy is required in case your data, stored on a backing storage medium, is lost or damaged.

- A backup copy should be kept in a safe place, away from the computer.

- Magnetic tape, hard disks and flash ROM are all examples of backing storage media and the hardware that uses or holds the media is known as a backing storage device.

- Storage devices may be built in to the inside of a computer system or be external.

- Examples of backing storage devices are:
  - Magnetic:
    - tape drive
    - hard disk drive
  - Optical:
    - CD drive
    - DVD drive
  - Blu-ray™ drive
  - Solid-state:
    - USB flash drive
    - memory card
    - SSD.

- Examples of backing storage media are:
  - Magnetic:
    - magnetic tape
    - hard disk
  - Optical:
    - CD-ROM/R/RW
    - DVD-ROM/R/RW
    - BD-ROM/R/RE
  - Solid-state:
    - flash ROM.

- Storage characteristics include: capacity, (data transfer) speed, rewriteable/read-only and cost.

- The capacity of a storage device refers to how much data may be held by the device.

- Magnetic disks and flash ROM media must be formatted before they can be used to store programs.

- Formatting produces invisible tracks and sectors on the surface of a magnetic disk.

- A hard disk is a circular metal disk coated with magnetic material.

- Hard disks are used because you can store much more data on them and access the data more quickly than any other current backing storage medium.

- Disks give you direct access because the data on a disk can be read in any order, not just the order in which it was written.

- Magnetic tape is a backing storage medium which uses plastic tape, coated on one side with magnetic material.

- Magnetic tape gives sequential access to data because the data can only be read in the order it was written.

- CD-ROMs use pits and lands to represent the data.

- A CD-ROM disk doesn't need to be formatted and it can't be accidentally erased since it is a read-only disk.

- Data may be written onto a CD-R or CD-RW using a CD-rewriter drive.

- CD-R/CD-RW disks use dye to record data in place of pits and lands.

- CD-RW allows a user to record over data or to delete individual files.

- A DVD can hold more data than a CD-ROM because:
  - the tracks on a DVD-ROM are placed closer together and the pits are smaller
  - DVD-ROMs can have two layers on each side of a disk and can also be double-sided
  - a DVD-ROM has more efficient error correction than a CD-ROM.

- Data may be written onto a DVD-R or DVD-RW using a DVD-rewriter drive.

- Blu-ray Disc™ (BD) was developed to enable recording, rewriting and playback of high-definition video (HD).
- A Blu-ray Disc™ is able to hold much more data than a DVD because the blue laser produces a narrower beam than a red laser on a DVD drive.
- Solid-state devices have no moving parts, which makes them robust.
- USB flash drives, memory cards and solid-state drives all use flash ROM media.
- A file is information held on backing storage or in memory.
- Files may hold data or programs.
- The file size is the amount of space taken up by a file on backing storage.
- Backing storage capacity is the amount of space available on a given medium, such as a hard disk.
- Memory capacity is the amount of space available in a computer system (RAM), used to hold programs and data.
- An interface is the hardware and associated software needed to allow communication between the processor and its peripheral devices.
- A peripheral is a device which may be connected to the outside of a computer system, for input, output or backing storage.
- Interfaces also compensate for any differences between the computer and the peripheral, such as data transfer speed and differences in data format.
- The data transfer speed is the speed at which the interface on the computer can send and receive data to and from the peripheral device to which it is attached.
- A wide variety of interfaces are used to connect backing storage devices, including USB, Firewire®, Thunderbolt®, Ethernet and Wireless.

- Cloud storage is online storage which is accessed via a Wide Area Network.
- Cloud computing is the use of computing resources (such as hardware and software) that are delivered as a service over the internet.
- Three main types of service are provided in the cloud: infrastructure as a service, platform as a service and software as a service.
- Web/cloud storage has these advantages:
  - security: a backup is available in the cloud
  - storage: virtually unlimited storage is available in the cloud
  - processing: your data is processed in the cloud
  - server: service provided on the cloud
  - scaling: cloud services can be increased or decreased.
- Web/cloud storage has a number of disadvantages:
  - security: cloud providers may lose your data
  - privacy: others may see your data
  - access time: depends upon your internet connection
  - cost: subscription required
  - loss of internet connection: you must be constantly connected to use the cloud.
- Local storage has the following advantages and disadvantages:
  - privacy: only you can see your data
  - security: you make your own backup copies
  - processing: you must pay all costs for both hardware and software.
  - server: you must install and run the server
  - availability: no problems if connection to internet is not working or unavailable.

CHAPTER 13 Networking and connectivity

This chapter examines different types of networks; how they are set up and how they work. It covers the following:

- stand-alone or networked
- LAN/internet
- wired/wireless
- peer-to-peer, client/server
- media: wired, optical, wireless.

What is a network?

A **network** is a linked set of computer systems that are capable of sharing programs and **data**, and sending messages between them.

When a computer is *not* part of a network, it is called a **stand-alone computer**.

There are two main types of network, depending on the distance between the computers making up the network.

Local Area Network (LAN)

A **LAN** covers a small area such as a room or a building and is usually owned by an individual, a single company or an organisation such as a school. The school or centre in which you are studying Computing Science is likely to have a **Local Area Network**.

Figure 13.01 Computers in a Local Area Network

Wide Area Network (WAN)

A **WAN** covers a larger geographical area, such as a country or a continent. The **internet** is the best-known example of a **Wide Area Network** to which the general public has access.

The internet

The internet is a Wide Area Network spanning the globe. It can be thought of as many different, smaller networks connected together. This is why the internet is known as a 'network of networks'. Each connected network may be of any size, use any **hardware** or be situated anywhere in the world. These networks include:

- very large and well-organised networks like those of:
    - governments
    - universities
    - multi-national corporations
- small company networks
- individuals using **Internet Service Providers** (ISPs).

An Internet Service Provider is a company that provides a **host computer**, to which the user can connect. The host computer manages the communications, and also stores data such as electronic mail, **web pages** and **files** for its subscribers. This host computer is connected to the internet and subscribers can communicate with other computers on the internet.

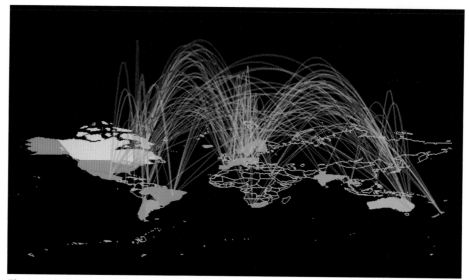

Figure 13.02 An artist's impression of the internet

Connectivity

What is a transmission medium?

A **transmission medium** is the material which carries the data in a network, for example wired (**cable**) or **wireless** (**WiFi**).

Note: Be careful not to confuse transmission media with backing storage media, which we learned about in Chapter 12.

What is bandwidth?

Bandwidth is a measure of the quantity of data which may be carried by a **communications channel** at any one time. The term **data transfer speed** is also used to mean the same as bandwidth when referring to networks. Bandwidth is measured in **Mbps – Megabits per second** – or **Gbps – Gigabits per second**.

LAN: transmission media

Stations on a Local Area Network are relatively close together and can be connected by using wires or wireless technology to transmit data. The transmission media on a Local Area Network are owned by a single organisation.

Figure 13.03 UTP (top) and optical fibre cables

Wired: cables

Computers on a wired network are connected by cables. Two types of cable are commonly used. These are **unshielded twisted pairs** of **copper wire** (**UTP**) and **optical fibre** (N5).

Copper wire carries data using electrical signals that can be subject to interference, unlike optical fibre.

Optical fibres are very fine strands of glass that can transmit data very rapidly by using beams of light. Many strands are put together into a single cable and each strand is capable of carrying more than one data signal.

Optical fibre cable is more expensive than copper, but does not corrode.

Copper cables can be **tapped** but optical fibre cables provide **secure** data transmission. Copper metal is also much heavier than optical fibre. Copper can be used to supply power as well as data signals to **devices**. Optical fibre can carry much more data (has a higher bandwidth) over a much longer distance than copper cable.

National 5

Checklist for copper and optical fibre

	Copper	Optical fibre
Longevity	Corrodes over time	Does not corrode
Security	Can be 'tapped'	Cannot be 'tapped'
Interference	Liable to electrical interference, and can create interference	No electrical interference
Bandwidth	Lower bandwidth	Higher bandwidth (1000×)
Range	Shorter range than fibre	Longer range than copper (100×)
Cost	Cheap	Expensive
Signal	Can carry power and data	Can only carry data
Weight	Heavier	Lighter

Table 13.01 Comparing copper and optical fibre

Figure 13.04 Bluetooth® logo

Figure 13.05 WiFi logo

LAN: bandwidth

Wired bandwidth

A typical Local Area Network has a bandwidth of 1 Gbps (**Gigabit Ethernet**). To give some idea of what such bandwidth is capable of, consider the delivery of a **DVD**-quality, full-length Hollywood movie. At 1 Gbps it could take as few as 30 seconds to download, depending on network conditions, compared with several hours over a typical internet **broadband connection**.

Wireless

Wireless networking covers a range of possible methods of data transmission. These include **Bluetooth®**, WiFi, **microwave transmission** and **satellite links**. Microwave transmission and satellite links are used as the transmission media in Wide Area Networks and you can read about these in the next section.

Bluetooth® can make temporary short-range links between personal devices, such as mobile phones and **headsets, palmtop** and **laptop** computers. Stand-alone Bluetooth® devices have a maximum range of 10 metres, and are able to transfer information at a rate of between 1 and 3 Megabits per second (Mbps). Wireless mice and **keyboards** typically use Bluetooth® transmission.

WiFi is mainly used in laptop computers, wireless routers, mobile phones and some games consoles – See Figures 13.06 and 13.07.

Figure 13.06 A wireless router (BT Home Hub 5 ac Router)

Figure 13.07 A games console (Xbox One)

WiFi (IEEE 802.11)

WiFi allows an electronic device to exchange data wirelessly over a Local Area Network, for instance a high-speed internet connection.

Interface type	Version	Bandwidth (max)	Range inside (max)	Range outside (max)
802.11	b	11 Megabits/second		
802.11	g	54 Megabits/second	30m	95m
802.11	n	600 Megabits/second	60m	200m
802.11	ac	1 Gigabit/second		
802.11	ad	7 Gigabits/second (proposed)		

Table 13.02 WiFi interfaces

A typical house which has a broadband connection will contain a WiFi router, usually of at least 802.11n specification. Most routers can also work with signals from slower versions of WiFi.

It is sensible to protect your home WiFi with a hard-to-guess **password**, to prevent other people from using your bandwidth. If they do steal bandwidth in this way, they may be liable to prosecution under the law. However, if someone else uses your internet connection to do something illegal, you may well be held responsible unless you can prove otherwise.

Network Interface Card

A **Network Interface Card** (**NIC**) is used to connect a computer to a network. Three different types, wired and wireless, are shown in Figure 13.08.

wireless   wired   wireless

Figure 13.08 Network Interface Cards

WAN: transmission media

The transmission media in a WAN may be any combination of copper cable, optical fibre and wireless. The transmission media in a WAN are owned by many different organisations.

WANs use telecommunications links to transmit and receive data. Telecommunications is a general term that describes the communication of **information** over a distance. The telecommunications links used in wide area networks include microwave transmission, satellite links and optical fibre.

Microwave transmission

Microwave transmission is used in the public telephone service. Many organisations use private microwave installations to transmit data between important locations. Microwave systems are highly directional and use dish aerials.

Satellite links

A satellite link is a form of telecommunication link that operates over long distances. Public telephone service providers use satellite links for international communications. Unlike satellite broadcast systems (Sky), these links use highly directional, narrow beam, two-way transmissions. A single satellite channel is capable of carrying a very large number of separate transmissions.

Optical fibre

Optical fibres are described earlier in the cables section. Figure 13.11 shows optical fibre submarine cables also being used as the transmission **medium** in a Wide Area Network.

Figure 13.09 Microwave transmission

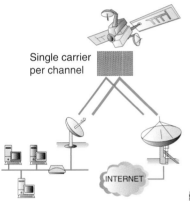

Figure 13.10 A satellite link

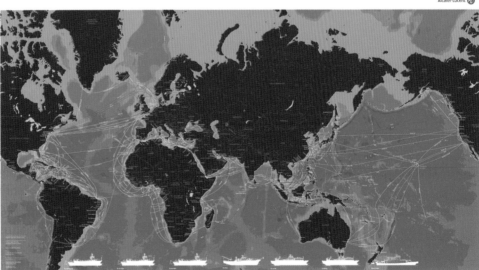

Figure 13.11 Optical fibre submarine cables

283

Sometimes the data in a telecommunications link is accidentally changed or **corrupted** by interference. The less chance there is of interference affecting the telecommunications link, the more **reliable** the data transmission will be. An optical fibre data link is very reliable because it is not affected by electrical interference.

WAN and the internet: bandwidth

A WAN has a low bandwidth compared to a LAN. The most common method of connecting a home computer to the internet is known as **ADSL** or Asymmetric Digital Subscriber Line.

A typical home computer may connect to a WAN such as the internet, at a data transfer speed of 8 Mbps using ADSL via a standard home telephone line. This bandwidth is download (receiving data) only. Sending data (uploading) is at a much slower rate, for example 512 Kbps.

The bandwidth of a WAN connection may be greatly improved if your locality or home has a dedicated **cable** or optical fibre connection, rather than just a standard telephone line. For instance, many urban areas have optical fibre connected to the cabinet in the street (Fibre To The Cabinet: **FTTC**), typically allowing bandwidth of between 40 and 100 Mbps. Higher bandwidth may be expected if your home has a direct optical fibre connection (Fibre To The Home: **FTTH** or Fibre To The Premises: **FTTP**).

Peer-to-peer and client/server networks

What is a peer-to-peer network?

A **peer-to-peer network** is made up of computers, all of which have the same status. Each computer or workstation has its own separate set of application programs and **backing storage devices**, such as a **hard disk** and optical **drives**.

While a user may have to log in to the computer by entering a user name and password, all of the user's data is stored *locally*, on the **hard disk**, for example. This means that the individual user must be responsible for backing up their own data, and that each user must always use the same computer. If they move to a different machine, then their data is no longer easily **accessible**.

Other benefits of networking, such as **resource sharing**, are available to users of a peer-to-peer network.

Resource sharing

The resource which is most often shared on a Local Area Network is a **printer**. It is much cheaper to set up a network of, say, 20 computers with one or two shared printers than it would be if each station had to have its own printer. Sharing a printer is not used on a Wide Area Network – there would be little point in printing out a document on a shared printer if you had to travel some distance to collect it!

Figure 13.12 Select your network printer with care ...

What is a client/server network?

A **client/server** network is a method of organisation in which **client workstations** make use of resources available on one or more **servers**.

What is a client?

A client is the name given to a workstation on a client/server network. **Desktop computers** are the most common type of client on this network. A **Network Interface Card** is required in order to connect to a network.

What is a server?

A **server** is a computer that handles requests for data, **email**, **file transfers** and other network services from other computers.

Types of server

There are a number of different types of server that may be used on a network. Types of **server** include file, printer, **CD-ROM**, **database**, internet, mail and web.

File server

A **file server** provides central disk **storage** for users' programs and data on a network. A file server has a greater amount of **RAM** and much larger **backing storage capacity** than a desktop computer. It is also likely to have a fast **processor**, or multiple processors, so that it can serve many users in as fast a time as possible. In addition, the components used to build a file server (like the hard disk drive) should be of a higher quality than an ordinary desktop computer, because the file server is designed to run constantly 24 hours a day, seven days a week.

Figure 13.13 Two file servers (IBM and Apple®)

File server **software** is also required. The basic function of the file server software is to organise the storage of user data and handle the **security** of the network.

Controlling network security

Before you can use a file server, you have to identify yourself to the file server; this is called logging on. To **log on** you must enter your **user identity** and then a password. When you have done this correctly the file server allows you access to the network; you are now **online** to the network and can load programs or look at your files. When you have finished using the network, you should log off, or go **offline**. This means that the network will no longer accept any of your commands until you log on again.

A server which has to run constantly should be protected from power cuts by an **uninterruptible power supply (UPS)**. The UPS contains a rechargeable battery which can provide enough power to run the server for a short period of time. If the mains power is not restored, then the UPS software can perform a controlled shutdown of the server, preventing any loss of data or **hardware** damage.

A backup device is essential for a file server, especially if the clients have no **local storage**. A **magnetic tape drive** is often used for this. **Magnetic tape** is discussed in Chapter 12.

Printer server

A **printer server** allows all of the client stations to use a printer controlled by it. A printer server will also provide a queuing facility that allows users to receive their printouts in turn. A network printer is designed to work quickly, so that users on the network will not have too long to wait for their printouts!

Current network printers are usually large **monochrome** lasers, although colour **laser printers** are becoming more common. The network printer will have its own processor and a sufficient amount of RAM in order to hold the print data (print jobs) that are sent to it. Sometimes a photocopier may be used as a network printer. This is more economical for organisations because of the lower cost per printed page.

Desktop computers on a network without a printer server usually save data temporarily to their own local hard disk drive. This allows **background printing**.

The benefits of networks

Networks have several benefits over **stand-alone computers**:

- You can *share data and programs* between stations. If you don't have a network connection, you can only share files by copying them to an external hard disk or **flash ROM** drive and carrying the files from one computer to another. This is known as 'sneaker-net'.
- **Data sharing** allows several users to have access to the same data. This can save storage space, for example, since only one copy of the data need be stored on a file server, rather than an individual copy for each user. Data sharing in this manner allows **workgroup computing**, where several users can work on the same document simultaneously.
- An **electronic mailing service** can be operated.
- By using passwords your data can be kept *secure*. Each user must log in to the network to gain access to their files.
- Everyone on the network can **share peripherals** such as printers, which makes the system cheaper to set up than if every station had its own printer. This is called resource sharing.

In addition, a client/server network has these advantages:

- **Flexible access.** A network user may access their files from any computer connected to the network. If the computer you normally use in the network is not working, then you may use any other computer on the network.
- Different users are given *different levels of access*. This prevents unauthorised interference with another user's files.
- Backup is done centrally; the **network manager** is responsible for making **backup copies** of all of the data on the file server. Users do not have to make their own individual backups.

Disadvantages of a client/server network:

- If the file server is not working, then users cannot access their data.
- A client/server network is expensive to set up, because it is necessary to buy a file server and server software.

Checklist for peer-to-peer and client/server

Peer-to-peer	Client/server
All machines same status.	Servers have a higher status than clients.
Users' data stored separately.	Users' data stored centrally.
Users must back up their own data.	Centralised backup is possible.

Check Your Learning

Now answer questions 1–22 (on page 289) on networking and connectivity (National 4).

Check Your Learning

Now answer questions 23–47 (on page 289) on networking and connectivity (National 5).

Practical Tasks

1 Send a copyright-free file via Bluetooth® and the same file via WiFi and Ethernet. Compare the time taken.

2 Create a large file of around 20 Megabytes in size (for example by compressing ('zipping') a folder containing images). Log on to a free cloud storage service, and time how long it takes for you to upload the file. Set the file for sharing, and send a link to another person, and time how long it takes to download the file.

3 Research the current maximum bandwidth (or data transfer rate) for Bluetooth®, WiFi and Ethernet.

4 Find out about the file server(s) used in your school or centre. If possible, make a note of the number of users and the total backing storage available. Find out whether any other servers are used, and describe their function on the school or centre network.

Questions

Networking and connectivity (National 4)

1 What is a network?

2 What is a stand-alone computer?

3 What is a Local Area Network?

4 What is a Wide Area Network?

5 What is the internet?

6 What is an Internet Service Provider (ISP)?

7 What is a transmission medium?

8 State one type of transmission medium suitable for a LAN.

9 What is WiFi?

10 State one use of WiFi.

11 What is Bluetooth®?

12 State one advantage that WiFi has over Bluetooth®.

13 What is bandwidth?

14 Which units are used to measure bandwidth?

15 Which peripheral is most often shared in a LAN?

16 Which type of transmission medium is common to both LANs and WANs?

17 Who owns the transmission medium in a
a) LAN?
b) WAN?

18 State a typical bandwidth for connection to a WAN from home.

19 State one difference between microwave transmission and satellite links.

20 Describe four benefits of networks.

21 Which type of network (LAN or WAN) is likely to have the highest bandwidth?

22 What device is required to connect a computer to a network?

Networking and connectivity (National 5)

23 Which function of a LAN allows workgroup computing to take place?

24 State one type of transmission medium suitable for a WAN.

25 State one type of transmission medium which is very reliable.

26 Why are WANs not used for sharing peripherals?

27 What is ADSL?

28 How may the bandwidth of a home connection to a WAN be improved?

29 State one benefit of copper wire over optical fibre as a data transmission medium.

30 Why is optical fibre cable more secure than copper wire?

31 Suggest two reasons why a wired network in an aeroplane uses more optical fibre than copper.

32 Why is it sensible to protect your home WiFi with a hard-to-guess password?

33 What is a peer-to-peer network?

34 State two features of a peer-to-peer network.

35 What is a client/server network?

36 What is a client?

37 What is a server?

38 What does a client require in order to connect to a network?

39 Name three types of server.

40 Which type of server might use queuing, and what would be in the queue?

41 Explain how security may be controlled on a network.

42 What is the purpose of network security?

43 What is a UPS?

44 Where would you expect to find a UPS being used?

45 Why should the components used to build a file server be of high quality?

46 What does the file server software do?

47 Describe one possible disadvantage of a client/server network.

Key Points

- A network is a linked set of computer systems that are capable of sharing programs and data, and sending messages between them.

- When a computer is not part of a network, it is called a stand-alone computer.

- A Local Area Network (LAN) covers a small area such as a room or a building and is usually owned by an individual, a single company or an organisation such as a school.

- A Wide Area Network (WAN) covers a larger geographical area, such as a country or a continent.

- The transmission media in a Wide Area Network are owned by many different organisations.

- The internet is a WAN spanning the globe.

- An Internet Service Provider is a company that provides a host computer, to which the user can connect, in order to access the internet.

- A transmission medium is the material which carries the data in a network, for example wired (cable) or wireless (WiFi).

- Bandwidth is a measure of the quantity of data which may be carried by a communications channel at any one time.

- Copper wire carries data using electrical signals.

- Optical fibres are very fine strands of glass that can transmit data very rapidly by using beams of light.

- Wireless networking includes Bluetooth®, WiFi, microwave transmission and satellite links.

- Bluetooth® can make temporary short-range links between personal devices.

- WiFi allows an electronic device to exchange data wirelessly over a Local Area Network, for instance a high-speed internet connection.

- A Network Interface Card (NIC) is used to connect a computer to a network.

- The telecommunications links used in Wide Area Networks include microwave transmission, satellite links and optical fibre.

- A WAN has a low bandwidth compared to a LAN.

- A peer-to-peer network is made up of computers, all of which have the same status.

- Users' data on a peer-to-peer network is stored locally.

- A client/server network is a method of organisation in which client workstations make use of resources available on one or more servers.

- A client is the name given to a workstation on a client/server network.

- A server is a computer that handles requests for data, email, file transfers, and other network services from other computers.

- A file server provides central disk storage for users' programs and data on a network.

- A printer server allows all of the client stations to use a printer controlled by it.

- The benefits of networks include:
  - sharing data and programs between stations
  - passwords to keep your data secure
  - workgroup computing
  - resource sharing.

- The benefits of client/server networks include:
  - flexible access
  - different levels of access for users
  - central backup.

- The disadvantages of client/server networks include:
  - if the file server is not working users cannot access their data
  - servers and server software are expensive to buy.

CHAPTER 14 Security risks and precautions

This chapter describes security risks and what may be done to minimise them.

Security risks

- viruses, worms, Trojans
- hacking

- spyware, phishing, keylogging
- online fraud, identity theft
- DOS (Denial of Service) attacks

Security precautions

- anti-virus software
- passwords/encryption
- biometrics
- security protocols and firewalls
- use of security suites

Security risks

Figure 14.01

A computer system is **secure** if it is unable to be accessed by an unauthorised person, and is not affected by malicious software or '**malware**'. Malware is software that has been deliberately created to disrupt the operation of a computer system, or gain illegal access to it in order to gather **information**. Malware includes **viruses**, **worms**, **Trojans**, **spyware**, **adware** and **keylogging** software.

All computer systems should be protected against malicious software by the use of **security precautions**. Security precautions are described later in this chapter. The first part of this chapter will look at different types of malicious software.

Viruses, worms and Trojans

What is a virus?

How does a virus operate?

A virus is a program which can copy or replicate itself and infects other programs or computers.

A virus program must be run in order to infect a computer system. Viruses attach themselves to other programs in order to ensure that this happens.

Figure 14.02 The story of the wooden horse is thousands of years old. The story tells how Greek soldiers hid inside the horse and were able to capture the city of Troy.

What is a worm?

How does a worm operate?

A worm is a stand-alone program which copies or replicates itself in order to spread to other computer systems.

Worms actively transmit copies of themselves to other computer systems by using computer **networks**. Worms use up a great amount of network **bandwidth** in order to spread. Some worms only spread and do nothing else. Other types of worms carry additional malicious software which can damage, or take over control of a computer system. This additional software is called a **payload**.

What is a Trojan?

The term Trojan or Trojan horse, is used to refer to a program that appears to be safe, but hidden inside is usually something harmful, like a worm or a virus. For instance, you may download a game or a picture, but once you run the **file**, the worm or virus gets to work. Sometimes Trojans will only provide a nuisance to the user by displaying a message, but usually a worm or virus hidden inside will cause damage to a computer system. A *backdoor Trojan* may be placed on your computer by a virus. Once in place, the person who sent the Trojan can take control of your computer over the **internet**. One of the most common uses of backdoor Trojans is to make your computer into a source of **spam email messages**.

What is the difference between a virus, a worm and a Trojan?

A virus attaches itself to or 'infects' an existing program. A worm operates on its own, without requiring other programs in order to spread. Like a worm, a Trojan does not infect an existing program.

What distinguishes a worm from a virus is that a worm can make copies of itself and spread between computers without having to be attached to a file, unlike a virus, which infects other *host* files and is distributed along with them. What distinguishes a Trojan from a virus is that a Trojan is disguised as another type of file, in some cases even pretending to be an anti-virus **utility program**.

In spite of these important differences, which you need to know about because you are following a Computing Science course, most people refer to all types of malware as 'viruses'. For instance, few people say, 'My computer has a worm', or 'My computer has malware'.

An example of malware

The 'I Love You' virus is an example of all three types of malware: it's a:

- Trojan because it comes disguised as a 'Love Letter' when it is carrying a harmful program
- virus because it infects files, turning them into new Trojans
- worm because it copies itself by sending itself out to everyone listed in the computer's email address book.

This type of attack is known as a **blended threat** because it uses a variety of techniques to increase the spread and the severity of the infection.

Figure 14.03 The 'I Love You' virus

Virus effects

A virus can lie in wait or watch for a particular action or date before it is activated. The longer the time before activation, the greater the number of computer systems which will be potentially infected. A virus which watches for a date is called a **time bomb**, and a virus which waits for an action to take place is known as a **logic bomb**.

Some of the more serious effects of a virus infection could be:

- the virus causes the **data** stored on the computer's **hard disk** or other **backing storage medium** to be **corrupted** or lost
- the virus program records every key pressed on the user's **keyboard**, and sends the keystrokes, including **passwords**, to the virus writer's computer. You can read more details about keylogging later on in this chapter.

How do you know if a computer system may be infected by a virus?

Common symptoms of virus infection include:

- displaying unwanted messages
- unusual visual or sound effects
- computers rebooting or restarting unexpectedly
- unwanted generation of **emails**.

Displaying unwanted messages

Figure 14.04 shows two examples of a message displayed by a virus.

Figure 14.04 The Phantom 1 virus displays the image of a skull, and the Cascade virus causes letters to 'fall' to the bottom of the screen.

Unusual visual or sound effects

Viruses may cause silly messages to be displayed or **sounds** to be produced. One of the early viruses, 'Cascade', caused the letters to fall down the **screen**. See Figure 14.04.

Computers rebooting or restarting unexpectedly

Some viruses attempt to disable the computer by changing the **operating system** program. This may cause the computer to reboot or restart when the user least expects it.

Unwanted generation of emails

Some viruses can infect a user's email address book, sending messages to all of the email addresses it contains. A virus outbreak which infects many computers in this manner can result in so many email messages being generated that it will cause email **servers** to **crash** or be shut down.

For example, suppose you had 50 of your friends' email addresses in your address book, and each of your friends who were listed had 10 new email addresses that were not in common with each other. After one generation of the virus, 50 computers would become infected to start with, then 50 × 10 new addresses = 500 addresses, total 550 computers. After two generations of the virus there would be the original 550, then 500 × 10 = 5000 addresses, total 5550.

Another type of virus can take over control of your computer and use it to attack other computers by generating spam or overloading a company **website** with data. If this happens to your computer and you do not fix the problem, then at best, your **ISP** will disconnect you from the internet, and at worst, you may be held liable for any damage caused by the attack. These types of attacks are explained further later on in this chapter.

Spreading viruses

The *delivery* of a virus is the method used by the virus in order to enter the computer system and cause the infection.

Infected media and drives

Sharing infected disks, such as CDs and **DVDs**, or external drives among computers can deliver viruses. If a computer which already contains a virus is used to make a **CD-ROM** or **DVD-ROM**, for example by **burning** data to a blank disk, then it is possible for that disk to become infected with the virus. Inserting the disk into an uninfected computer would cause that computer to become infected with the virus.

USB flash ROM drives are commonly used for the storage and transfer of files. These **backing storage devices** may become infected with a virus by being plugged into an infected computer. Once infected, these devices can then spread the virus by copying it to any other computer systems to which they may be connected.

Networks

Viruses may be spread in seconds over all types of networks. In some cases, **security** flaws in the computer's operating system, or failure to take adequate security precautions, can allow viruses to infect your computer through the internet connection, without you having to do anything.

Email attachments

Email is another virus delivery method, along with file sharing, instant messaging, micro-blogging and social networks. If you receive a message from an unknown address, DO NOT OPEN IT – DELETE IT IMMEDIATELY. This advice applies even more to messages which contain attachments. The act of clicking on the message to open it can allow a virus to enter your computer.

Downloads

Some websites and file sharing services containing 'free' versions of **commercial software**, music and **videos** can be sources of virus infection. Users should always ensure that the software that they allow onto their computer comes from a reputable source, to reduce the chance of virus infection.

Example

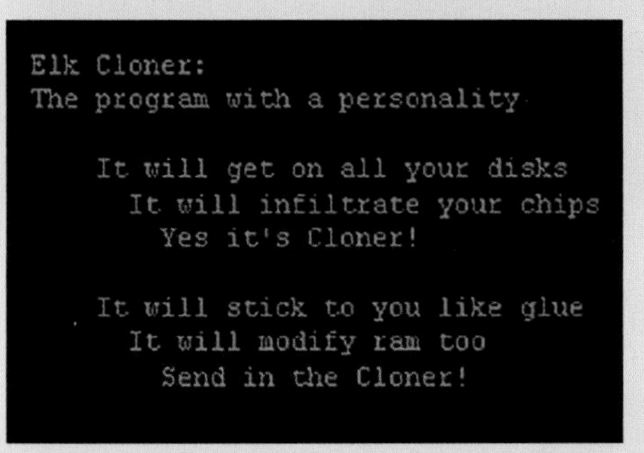

```
Elk Cloner:
The program with a personality

   It will get on all your disks
     It will infiltrate your chips
        Yes it's Cloner!

   It will stick to you like glue
     It will modify ram too
        Send in the Cloner!
```

The first ever virus to infect other computers was called 'Rother J' and was written by Richard Skrenta in 1981, when he was 15 and still at school. Rother J infected the Apple® operating system and was spread by floppy disk. On its 50th use the virus would be activated, infecting the computer and displaying a short poem.

Figure 14.05 Rother J / Elk cloner virus

Hacking

What is hacking?

Hacking is gaining unauthorised access to a computer system and is usually illegal. Hacking is a **crime** under the **Computer Misuse Act**, which applies in the United Kingdom, and similar laws in other countries. The Computer Misuse Act 1990 is explained in more detail in Chapter 15.

White hats and black hats

In the computer security community, a **black hat** is a skilled hacker who uses his or her ability to pursue their interest illegally. They are often economically motivated, or may be representing a political cause. Sometimes, however, it is pure curiosity. The term comes from old Western movies (viewed in black and white), where heroes typically wore white or light-coloured hats and outfits, and the villains wore black outfits with black hats.

Figure 14.06

White hat hackers try to break into systems for legal purposes, for instance, as employees of a computer company, testing the security of their own systems. White hat hackers will find security flaws in a company's system and provide the information to allow the 'loopholes' to be repaired.

Organisations have been set up to combat the activities of black hats. One such organisation is Honeynet (www.honeynet.org). Honeynet constructs its own networks especially in order to trap black hats. Each Honeynet contains one or more **honeypots**. A honeypot is a system which is deliberately left open to attract the activities of black hats, in the same way as bears are attracted to honey. Once a black hat has entered the Honeynet, then the hacking techniques that they use can be monitored in order to provide information to combat their activities.

Figure 14.07 Security software

Check Your Learning Now answer questions 1–18 (on pages 314–315) on security risks (National 4).

Spyware, phishing, keylogging, online fraud and identity theft

What is phishing?

Phishing is an attempt to trick someone into giving away personal information using the internet by pretending to be a well-known company or a bank. Phishing is so called because criminals who carry it out would like to 'hook' as many victims as possible.

Phishing techniques

A variety of techniques are used to try and make people believe that they are dealing with a genuine company, including email, **text messaging**, telephone calls, **social engineering** and theft of documents like bank statements, passports or driving licences. Social engineering ('socialing') is tricking someone into performing an action or giving away confidential information, for example by pretending to be someone else on the phone and persuading them to reset a victim's password. All of these techniques are used to obtain information, such as bank account details, or personal facts that can be used to steal someone's identity. Once your personal details have been stolen, then all of your money can be taken out of your bank account and you may also become the victim of **identity theft**.

Figure 14.08 Mimail.I and Mimail.J are email worms, which disguise themselves as an email from an online payment service and try to steal credit card information. This method of fraud is known as phishing.

How can you detect phishing?

Emails

Look out for:

- bad spelling or grammar, especially if not addressed personally, e.g. 'dear customer'
- requests to re-enter your personal details or 'verify your account'
- threats to close your account if you don't respond.

Texts

Watch for messages which tell you:

- your personal information has been posted on the web
- your account is closed; contact us to re-open
- to call a number.

Phone calls

Hang up immediately if you receive a call from:

- someone who wants to 'fix' your computer
- someone claiming to be from Microsoft® Tech Support or **Windows**® Helpdesk.

How can you protect yourself against phishing emails, texts and phone calls?

Delete all suspicious emails (without opening them) and texts. DO NOT CALL any numbers supplied in these messages. If you have opened a message or clicked on a link in an email, make sure that you check out your computer system. Do not give out any personal information to an unsolicited caller or purchase any services from them.

Figure 14.09 Phishing

What is identity theft?

Identity theft is when someone else pretends to be you, in order to carry out fraud. Criminals whose own identities are well known to banks and other companies are unable to purchase goods and services on credit, so they try to steal another person's details in order to impersonate them.

How can you detect identity theft?

If you notice that you are receiving:

- bills for goods that you have not ordered
- letters from debt collectors

- bank statements for accounts you did not open
- withdrawals on accounts that you have not made

then your identity may have been stolen.

How can you protect yourself against identity theft?

You can protect against identity theft by keeping your personal details safe at all times. It is vital that you do not give away passwords or **PINs**; banks and credit card companies will *never* ask you for these details, since the real banks know this information already.

You can read how one person had their identity stolen at: www.wired.com/gadgetlab/2012/11/ff-mat-honan-password-hacker/all/.

What is spyware?

Spyware is a type of malware which, when installed on a user's computer, collects information about them without their knowledge. Spyware can monitor how a computer is used, and collect all kinds of data, including personal information and passwords. Spyware can record a user's visits to **web pages**, and interfere with the normal operation of a computer by changing a variety of settings, such as disabling **anti-virus software** and **firewalls**. In some cases a computer may be so badly infected with spyware that the only cure is to make a **backup copy** of the user's data, and then wipe the computer completely clean before re-installing the operating system and applications. Keylogging software is one type of spyware.

What is keylogging?

Keystroke logging or keylogging is the process of recording every key that is pressed on a keyboard, without the user being aware that it is being done.

Keylogging may be carried out within the law for a number of different purposes, such as:

- testing how a user is operating a computer and interacting with it (HCI)
- monitoring employees' productivity
- protecting children while they are using the internet
- guarding against illegal use of a public computer, for example in a café or library
- providing evidence to assist police and other authorities with criminal investigations.

Keylogging may be used by criminals to gather user names and passwords, and other sensitive data such account numbers and as PINs.

Keylogging can be carried out by a **computer program** (software-based) or by a **device** (hardware-based).

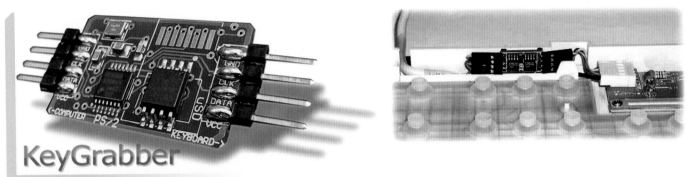

Figure 14.10 A hardware-based keylogger. The device is fitted inside a keyboard to escape detection.

Preventing keylogging

Some software-based keyloggers can be detected and removed by anti-spyware or anti-virus programs, however hardware-based keyloggers must be physically removed or disconnected. Some types of hardware-based keyloggers do not have to be connected to the computer in order to capture keystrokes. These operate by detecting electronic signals from the user's keyboard. Many new keyboards operate using **wireless** technology such as **Bluetooth**®. These types of keyboard use **encryption** to protect against such attacks.

To protect against keyloggers, some systems, such as Microsoft Outlook®, are able to create a single-use code or one-time password. This code allows the user to sign on to the service once only, and it is automatically deleted when they sign out again. The system will send the code to the user's mobile phone. A single-use code is also useful if you are using a public computer, in an internet café or a hotel. Even if a keylogger is present on the system, and records the code, it is impossible to gain access to your account, since the code works only once.

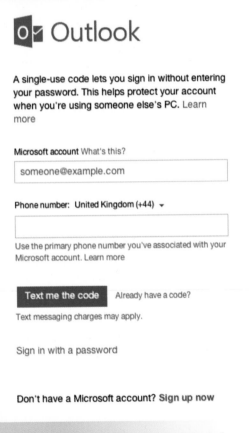

Figure 14.11 Requesting a single-use code from Outlook

Figure 14.12 This anti-virus program has detected spyware in the form of a software-based keylogger

Online fraud

Online fraud or **internet fraud** is the use of services available on the internet to defraud people of money, or to carry out identity theft. There are many different types of online fraud, for example paying for goods that are never received, or supplying bank or personal details to a stranger, usually from a foreign country, who asks for your 'help' in moving money between accounts.

Online fraudsters may advertise brand new goods as part of an online auction, and what the buyer receives is something second-hand, refurbished or even an empty box. The fact that an item was actually 'delivered' to the purchaser makes it possible for the credit card company to pay the supplier, even if the goods are faulty or non-existent. Once the money has been paid, then there is often no way to get it back when the fraud is discovered.

A **money mule** is a person who uses their bank account to transfer stolen money from one account to another. They are often innocent people who earn a commission on each transfer that they make. What they don't know is that they are committing a crime by handling money that has been obtained through fraud. Students are often targeted in this way and lured by false promises of job offers. If a money mule is caught, their bank account may be frozen and they risk being put in prison.

Personal information, which is disclosed to strangers as a result of online fraud, may also be used for identity theft. It is estimated that, in the first three months of 2012, online fraudsters traded 12 million pieces of personal information.

Click fraud is one type of online fraud, which affects businesses and organisations which advertise online. Online advertising networks, such as Yahoo! and Google™, display clickable links on web pages. Each time a potential customer clicks on one of these links, Google™ (for example) charges the advertiser. This is called PPC (Pay Per Click) advertising, and is a useful way of attracting business for the advertiser. However, if a competing business clicks on a link, then the advertiser still has to pay, and so they lose money because they have to pay for every click, whether or not it is fraudulent.

Guarding against online fraud

It is understandable that everyone wants to get good value for their money by making economical purchases, and searching for bargain prices for goods is major use of the internet. However, here is one simple rule which can be followed; 'If it sounds too good to be true, it probably is'. If a website or person is offering goods or services at well below the usual price for such items, then do not purchase them without first checking that the offer is genuine, for example by finding out that you are dealing with a reputable company or organisation.

Example   **Online fraud email**

from: copyright@facebook.com

to: xxxxxxxxx@facebook.com

date: 19 November 2013

Greetings friend

It has come to our attention that there is an issue with your Facebook account. We have discovered this as part of our regular security checks, which we carry out on all members of our system.

Type of issue: Copyright

Date of issue: November 2013

Checker: Ms F.T. Buek

In order to alow us to rectify this issue, we require that you complete the form which you can acess from the link below:

www.facebook.com/copyright_form

Note: You must respond to this request within 3 (three) days otherwise your account will be permanently deleted.

Regards

Fona T. Buek

Facebook Checking Department

Note that the email is not addressed personally: 'Greetings friend'; has spelling mistakes: 'acess', 'alow'; contains a threat: 'your account will be permanently deleted'; and has a link embedded in the email message. All of these features indicate that the message is not genuine and should be deleted, and reported as junk/phishing. If the link is clicked and responded to, then it will lead to a form or a website, which attempts to collect personal information. Often these fake or 'spoofed' websites will appear to be like the real one. If you would like to examine a safe 'spoof' website, then try: www.dhmo.org/.

DOS (Denial of Service) attacks

What is a DOS attack?

A **DOS attack** is a **procedure** which tries to interrupt or suspend the services of a **host computer** which is connected to the internet. A host computer is a physical device which, when connected to a network, provides services to another connected computer. In this case, a host computer could be one which holds a company's website, or **web server**.

A DOS attack involves sending so many requests to a host computer that it is unable to respond to legitimate requests, or slows the host so much that it becomes unusable. In some cases a DOS attack can crash the affected computer, particularly when the attack includes malware.

What is a Distributed Denial of Service (DDOS) attack?

A **DDOS** attack takes place when many different computers carry out a DOS attack on a single host computer. A variety of methods may be used to carry out a DDOS attack. These include:

- a worm such as Mydoom, which attacks a pre-programmed (fixed) target computer

- a Trojan, which takes over a computer and turns it into a **zombie**. A zombie is a computer connected to the internet that is under the control of a hacker and is used to distribute malware, send out spam or steal your private information

- a specific piece of software called a DDOS tool which connects to a **handler** or **master computer**, which, in turn, controls a number of zombie computers, collectively called a **botnet** or **zombie army**. The person in control of a botnet is a **bot herder**. A botnet can be targeted against any computer. The owner of a zombie computer may be completely unaware that their computer has been used in this manner. However, a computer used as a zombie will not operate properly, certainly not to its full efficiency. Some internet security experts believe that botnets are more of a threat to internet security than malware such as viruses.

What is the difference between DOS and DDOS?

The difference between these two types of denial of service attack is that a DOS attack is carried out by a single computer, and a DDOS attack is carried out by many separate (distributed) computers simultaneously. As may be expected, it is much more difficult to defend against a DDOS attack, because of the number of computer systems involved.

Defending against attack

A number of different methods may be used to defend against or limit the effect of a DOS attack, including the use of a firewall. Firewalls are discussed later in this chapter. What the defence is trying to do is to block the attack, which is unwanted traffic, and allow access to genuine internet traffic.

http://news.cnet.com/2100-1017-236728.html shows a simple **animation** of a DOS attack.

Who are the attackers?

Large-scale DDOS attacks do not happen at random. The criminals choose their victims deliberately, whether they have a grudge against them, or to take revenge, or to bully them into giving in to their demands, including extortion of money. The creators of botnets actually rent them out to other criminals in order to carry out attacks.

How is a botnet created?

1 A hacker creates an email with a link to a website containing a hidden virus. This is sent to several home and business computers.
2 A user opens the email and clicks on the link: immediately their computer becomes infected by the virus.
3 The botnet is created: the virus software makes the computers into slave machines or zombies, waiting for commands from the hacker. Each slave machine has the potential to infect many others.

What happens next?

4 **Spammers**, who are trying to sell, for instance, prescription drugs, pay the hacker to send out spam via the botnet.
5 Hackers can also make money by selling data stolen from infected computers, such as identity and bank details, and using them to launch attacks.
6 Hackers extort money from companies by threatening to attack their website using the botnet – a DDOS attack.

Example **DDOS extortion letter**

from: botmaster@net.com

to: xxxxxxxxx@lotsamoneybank.com

date: 22 August 2016

Hello banker

You are welcomed with a command of hackers.

If you want your website to continue to operate you must pay us 20,000 pounds per month. Starting on date XXXXXXX, we attack your site with 5,000 bots and your site will remain unusable until you pay.

If you try stop us, we will increase 50,000 bots and it will cost you a lot more to prevent.

If you do not pay, then you will not be in business for very longer, as you will be constant attack until you are closed down.

You must pay on first day month otherwise money go up every single day you pay late, to 30,000 pounds and then 40,000 pounds and so on.

We offer discount of our generosity: if you want us to attack your enemies, it will only cost you £75 pounds day, not £100. Also, if you pay and they tell us to attack you, we tell them no.

You are free to contact any law you like. We do not care.

We are the one, respect our work.

To see a full explanation of a real-life bot in action, have a look at http://blogs.mcafee.com/mcafee-labs/ngrbot-spreads-via-chat.

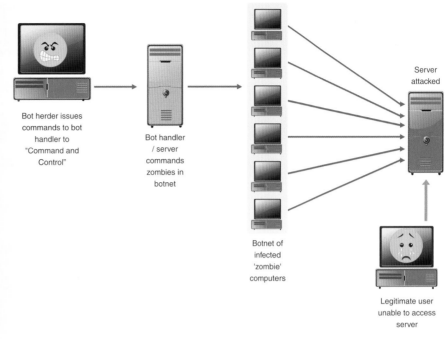

Bot herder issues
commands to bot
handler to
"Command and
Control"

Bot handler
/ server
commands
zombies in
botnet

Botnet of
infected
'zombie'
computers

Server
attacked

Legitimate user
unable to access
server

Figure 14.13 Operating a botnet

Check Your Learning

Now answer questions 19–45 (on page 315) on security
risks (National 5).

Security precautions

All computer systems should be protected against malicious software by the
use of security precautions. Security precautions include: anti-virus software,
passwords/encryption, **biometrics**, **security protocols** and firewalls and
the use of **security suites**.

Anti-virus software

What is anti-virus software?

Anti-virus software is a type of application software which protects a computer
system against attack or infection by viruses and other types of malware.

Why is anti-virus software needed?

Anti-virus software is an essential utility. A virus can be copied from one
computer system to another, either by being carried on removable media, or
through a network via email or file sharing.

Figure 14.14 The use of anti-virus software

Anti-virus software should be able to detect a virus infection and remove it from a computer system. When copying a file from a disk or downloading a file from the internet, the **virus checking** software should also check that the file does not contain a virus.

New viruses are constantly being written; so most companies which produce anti-virus software allow the user to download **updates** to the software from the internet. This ensures that the anti-virus software is always up to date.

Most viruses are specific to a computer's operating system. For example, a computer running the **Unix**® operating system, would be unable to become infected by a virus written for the Windows® operating system. However, if an email attachment contains a virus, then the virus may still be passed on from a Unix®-based computer and infect a Windows®-based computer.

One type of virus, known as a **macro virus**, infects Microsoft application software, such as Excel and Word, because these programs use **macros**. This means that any computer which uses these programs may become infected.

Many thousands of viruses have been written to infect the Windows® operating system, perhaps because this is the most widely used operating system on **desktop** and **laptop computers**. Users of other computer operating systems should not be too complacent, because virus writers are turning their attention to them as they become more popular.

The writing and distribution of viruses is a criminal offence under the Computer Misuse Act 1990. You can read more about the Computer Misuse Act in Chapter 15.

Quick Tip

To protect your computer from viruses and some other types of malware

- Install anti-virus software and keep the subscription up to date.
- Avoid downloading programs from unknown sources.
- Never open an email attachment that:
  - contains an executable file, such as .EXE, because when it runs, you have given it permission to do anything on your machine
  - comes from an unknown email address, since your computer may be infected just by opening or previewing a message.
- Never run macros in a document unless you know what they do.
- Run an alternative operating system like Unix®, because fewer viruses have been written to infect it (so far!).

Password/encryption

Passwords

The use of computers for almost every aspect of life nowadays means that people are constantly being asked to prove their identities when going **online**. The most common means of identifying a person on a computer system is by having them enter a **user identity** and a password. Earlier in this chapter we looked at crimes which can be committed against a person who has their password or other means of identification stolen.

Choosing a password

You should always choose a password that will be difficult for others to guess. One school was told by its local authority to assign students' dates of birth as their passwords for the school network. This was not a very secure idea, as each student had friends who knew their birthdays! Passwords like *retep* or *yram* are too obvious. A mixture of random numbers, upper- and lower-case letters and punctuation marks or special **characters**, is best.

The 'strength' of a password depends on the different characters in it, the length of the password, and the password not being in a dictionary. Criminals will use a variety of methods to crack someone's password, including software which has been specially programmed with a list of common passwords and familiar substitutions, such as p@$$w0rd.

Adding repeated characters, words spelled backwards, or using part of any personal information, like family or pet names, is not recommended.

It is very important to change your password on a regular basis. Many systems are automatically programmed to insist that users do this every few weeks or months. One other condition is that the user is unable to use any previous passwords.

One other piece of advice about passwords: use different passwords for different websites. If you use the same password for all or many of your services, you are just making it easier for a hacker to steal your money or your identity. For instance, imagine if your front and back doors, your bicycle and your school locker, all opened with the same key.

Quick Tip | **Instructions for creating a password**

- The password must be at least eight characters long.
- The password must contain at least:
  - one upper- AND one lower-case character (a–z, A–Z)
  - one number (0–9)
  - one special character, for example: ` ! @ $ % ^ & * ( ) – _ = + [ ] ; : ' " , < . > / ?.
- The password should not contain more than three repeating characters, for instance: 11111 or ordered characters, like 56789.

You can check out the security of a password on a number of websites, such as:

- https://www.microsoft.com/security/pc-security/password-checker.aspx
- www.howsecureismypassword.net
- www.passwordmeter.com

Table 14.01 shows the most common passwords of 2013. Is your password among the top 10?

Password	Position
123456	1
password	2
12345678	3
qwerty	4
abc123	5
123456789	6
111111	7
1234567	8
iloveyou	9
adobe123	10

Table 14.01 Common passwords of 2013

Figure 14.15 Passwords

Password manager software

Password manager software has been developed because of the difficulty of remembering so many different user identities and passwords for each site that you visit. Password manager software works by storing all of your passwords and login details for every site that you use, and automatically logging you in whenever you visit that site. The security of the password manager software itself may be protected by one or more of: a 'token' like a USB **flash ROM**; a password or PIN and finally a user's biometrics. Biometrics is explained later in this chapter.

Some **browser** software contains password management features that will offer to store your login details for a website. It is not recommended that you use this feature if you work on a shared computer.

Encryption

Encryption means putting data into a code to prevent it being seen by unauthorised users. When you type a password to access a network, it is encrypted before it is sent to the **file server** to prevent it from being read en route. One common use of encryption is to protect email messages and files that are sent over a network.

Files may be encrypted by using an **application package**, like Symantec **Drive Encryption**, or by using a security feature built into the computer's operating system, like **FileVault®**. How Drive Encryption is used with some email applications is shown in Figure 14.16. When the encrypted message reaches its destination, then the same encryption software is used to **decrypt** the message and turn it back into readable **text.**

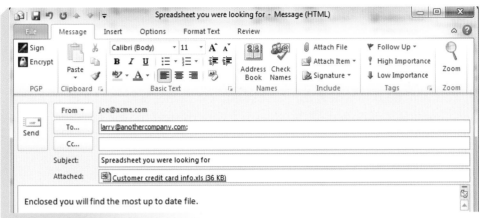

Figure 14.16 Symantec Encryption in email

Other common uses of encryption are to protect storage media such as hard disks and flash ROM. Should the computer containing the media, or the media itself, be stolen, then it will be practically impossible to read the data stored in it without access to the correct password.

Biometrics

What is biometrics?

Biometrics is using a person's physical characteristics in order to provide evidence of their identity. Examples of biometric data which may be used in this manner include facial recognition, fingerprints, retinal scan or voiceprints.

Biometrics may be **physiological** or **behavioural**. Physiological biometrics include a person's face, fingerprints, hands, irises and DNA. Behavioural biometrics include keystrokes, signature and voice.

It may be possible to imitate a person's handwriting and therefore their signature, but it is more difficult to imitate someone's irises or their DNA. A signature biometric may also record the *way* a person writes their signature *while they are doing it*, which will be different from the way a forger will write, although both the genuine and the forged signatures may appear to be identical on paper.

In order to create biometric data, a person must have their physical characteristics scanned into a computer, which adds them to a **database**. The data in the database is normally encrypted. When a person's identity is being verified, then one or more characteristics will be scanned again, and compared with what is held in the database against that person's name. If the details match, then the person is accepted.

Some uses of biometrics in schools include access control, attendance/ registration and school meals systems.

Advantages of biometrics

- More secure than a password or card which can be stolen or lost.
- Difficult to forge some biometrics, for instance, fingerprint as opposed to handwriting.

Figure 14.17 Biometrics

Disadvantages of biometrics

- If someone steals your biometric data, you cannot get new data, for example if someone manages to tamper with or change the biometric of your face, you cannot get a new one!
- You may be in physical danger, like the car owner who had part of his index finger chopped off by thieves trying to steal his car in 2005.

Security protocols and firewalls

What is a protocol?

A **protocol** is a set of rules that determines how something is to be done, for instance, communication protocols are used when sending messages via the internet.

Some examples of communications protocols include: Simple Mail Transfer Protocol (**SMTP**), Post Office Protocol (**POP**), HyperText Transfer Protocol (**HTTP**), Internet Protocol (**IP**), Transmission Control Protocol (TCP), File Transfer Protocol (**FTP**).

What is a security protocol?

A security protocol is a **sequence** of **operations** that makes sure data is protected. Security protocols are often used together with communications protocols, to ensure that sensitive data, such as credit card numbers, is kept private.

Some examples of security protocols include: Transport Layer Security (**TLS**), Secure Sockets Layer (**SSL**).

The HyperText Transfer Protocol Secure (**HTTPS**) is produced by the combination of SSL/TLS and HTTP. Web pages that use HTTPS, have a **padlock icon** somewhere on the page.

Figure 14.18 Example of https

Clicking on the padlock icon on a secure web page should display a **digital certificate**, like the ones in Figure 14.19. Websites which do not have a current or *valid* digital certificate should not be used for secure information such as credit card numbers. A valid digital certificate will be issued by a reputable organisation and not be out of date or expired. Modern web browsers will warn the user if they detect a problem with a certificate. Remember that a website which contains a padlock icon, but does not display any certificate information, may be fraudulent.

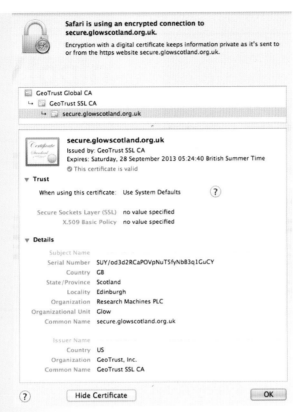

Figure 14.19 Digital certificates

What is a firewall?

A firewall is a system designed to prevent unauthorised access to or from a private network, such as in a school or local authority. The firewall contains rules and conditions which specify what is and is not allowed to pass through. All messages which pass through the firewall are examined to check whether or not they meet these rules and conditions. Those messages which do not, are blocked. The main use of a firewall in a school or home network is to prevent unauthorised (outside) internet users from gaining access to the network.

Firewalls can be created in hardware or software. **Hardware firewalls** are located in the router which connects the network to the internet. A hardware firewall therefore provides protection for the whole network, regardless of the number of computers or other devices connected. A hardware firewall operates independently of the computers, so it has no effect on their performance. **Software firewalls** may use some system resources such as **memory**, storage space and processing and may have an effect on a computer's performance, although less so if the firewall is part of the computer's own operating system. A hardware firewall cannot be easily affected by malware, unlike a software firewall. A software firewall can protect **portable** computers when they are used away from the network, which was protected by the hardware firewall. In practice, it is normal to have both types of firewall installed, in order to provide the maximum possible amount of protection.

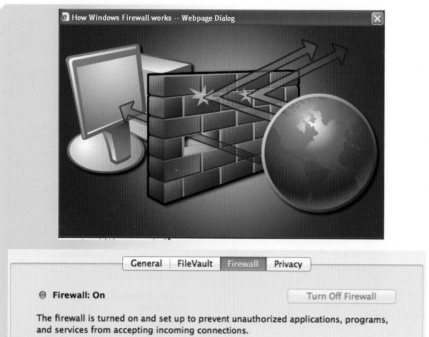

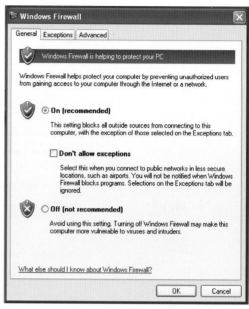

Figure 14.20 Operating system firewall settings

A **web proxy** is often used along with a firewall. A web proxy is a server used to access web pages requested by other computers on a network. This means that the computers outside the network only come into contact with the web proxy and not the computers on the inside of the proxy. A web proxy is often used to control a user's access to web pages by means of **content filtering**. Most schools allow students and staff access to the internet only through such a server, which not only blocks websites deemed to unsuitable, but records the address or **URL** of every page accessed by its users. Some schools and local authorities use a **walled garden**, which only allows access to an approved set of URLs.

The term 'walled garden' is also used to refer to any closed system or **platform**. For instance, the Apple® **app** store only allows applications approved by Apple® to be run on their devices. The Amazon Kindle™ eReader and a wide variety of games consoles operate in the same manner.

Use of security suites

What is a security suite?

A security suite is a collection of software which is sold together as a single **package** and contains programs which protect computers against a variety of malware. A typical security suite may include the following software:

- anti–virus
- firewall
- anti-spam

Figure 14.21 Security suites

- anti-spyware
- parental control
- privacy
- phishing protection.

Additional programs may include features such as password management, online backup and tune-up. Security suites also offer comprehensive online support systems for their users, most importantly a continuous program of software updates which take account of the fact that new malware is constantly being developed and released onto the internet.

Rogue security suites

A number of security suite pro-+grams pretend to be legitimate while installing all sorts of malware on a computer system. These include: 'Security Suite', 'AV Security Suite', 'Antivir Solution Pro', 'Antispyware soft', 'Antivirus Soft' and 'Antivirus suite'. Apart from damaging your computer system and potentially using it to spread malware to other computers, these programs attempt to trick the user into paying for them!

When choosing a security suite, or any other software, you should make sure that it comes from a trusted source. Some examples of reputable security suites are shown in Figure 14.21.

Absolute security

Figure 14.22 Absolute security?

Using all of the methods described on the previous pages will make your data as safe as possible. However, no method is absolutely secure. All that a good security system can do is increase the amount of time it takes for a determined hacker to get your data. If you have a secret that you don't want anyone to know, then don't type it into a computer, especially not one that is connected to any kind of network!

Check Your Learning

Now answer questions 46–80 (on pages 315–316) on security precautions (National 5).

Practical Tasks

1 'A hoax virus does just as much damage as a real virus.'

Find out about hoax viruses and whether there is any evidence to justify this statement. Here are some URLs to get you started:
- www.symantec.com/connect/articles/virus-hoaxes-and-real-dangers-they-pose
- http://rossde.com/frauds_n_hoaxes/virus_warnings.html
- www.giac.org/paper/gsec/2273/virus-hoaxes-cost/103905

2 Take a look at www.skrenta.com/. Scroll down and click on the Archives link and search for elk cloner.

3 Take a look at one of the following websites and test yourself to see if you can spot phishing.

- www.sonicwall.com/furl/phishing/
- www.opendns.com/phishing-quiz/
- http://survey.mailfrontier.com/survey/quiztest.cgi?themailfrontierphishingiqtest

4 Have a look at this website to see how an automated telling machine (ATM) can capture your PIN without you knowing about it: http://gizmodo.com/5725859/this-is-how-cyber+criminals-steal-your-money

5 Use these websites to find out how to protect yourself against identity theft, and write a short report on your findings:

- www.identitytheft.org.uk/
- www.getsafeonline.org/
- www.cifas.org.uk
- www.actionfraud.police.uk/types_of_fraud

6 Read about the world's five biggest cyber threats at www.bbc.co.uk/news/technology-17846185.

7 Some organisations provide free firewall and other types of intrusion tests on your computer. Try the Gibson Research Corporation's Shields UP!! test at www.grc.com/intro.htm.

8 For precautionary social engineering advice, visit www.bbc.co.uk/news/technology-20717773.

9 Consider the number of occasions each day when you are required to use a password or PIN. Make a list of these occasions. *Do not* write down any passwords for this task.

Create a table with two columns: Occasion and Date changed. Enter the occasions and note the most recent date when each password was changed.

10 See a different take on a DDOS attack at http://news.cnet.com/8301-17938_105-57581922-1/see-how-beautiful-a-ddos-attack-can-look/?part=rss&subj=news&tag=title.

11 Read about how some viruses can help others to spread at http://blogs.technet.com – search 'viewing vobfus infections from above'.

Questions

Security risks (National 4)

1 State two features of a secure computer system.

2 What is malware?

3 Name three types of malware.

4 What is a virus?

5 How does a virus operate?

6 What is a worm?

7 How does a worm operate?

8 What is a Trojan?

9 What is the difference between a
a) virus and a worm?
b) virus and a Trojan?

10 State two common symptoms of virus infection.

11 Describe two ways in which viruses may be spread.

12 Explain why the 'I love you' virus was an example of all three types of malware.

13 State two methods of virus activation.

14 Explain how an external drive can cause a computer to become infected with a virus.

Security risks (National 5)

19 What is phishing?

20 State two techniques used in phishing.

21 What can phishing lead to?

22 What is social engineering?

23 State two ways of detecting phishing emails.

24 State two ways of detecting phishing texts.

25 Explain how to protect yourself against phishing
   a) emails
   b) texts.

26 What is identity theft?

27 How can you detect identity theft?

28 How can you protect against identity theft?

29 Describe what can happen to someone who is the victim of identity theft.

30 What is spyware?

31 Describe one method of removing spyware from a computer.

32 What is keylogging?

33 State two methods of keylogging.

34 Which method of keylogging is more difficult to remove from a computer system?

35 Explain one method of preventing a keylogger from finding out your email password.

36 What is online fraud?

37 What is a 'money mule'?

38 What is click fraud?

39 Explain one method of guarding against online fraud.

15 Why is it important to ensure that software comes from a reputable source?

16 What is hacking?

17 What law do hackers break?

18 What is a
   a) black hat?
   b) white hat?
   c) honeypot?

40 What is a DOS attack?

41 What is a DDOS attack?

42 What is a:
   a) zombie?
   b) botnet?
   c) bot herder?

43 State one main difference between DOS and DDOS.

44 Describe one method of carrying out a DDOS attack.

45 Imagine you were in charge of a company threatened with attack, and you had received a letter similar to the one on page 304.
   a) What could you do about the attack?
   b) What would you do?

Security precautions (National 5)

46 Why should computer users bother to take security precautions?

47 Name one security precaution for a computer system.

48 What is anti-virus software?

49 Why is anti-virus software needed?

50 Which type of virus can infect any computer?

51 State three tips which will help protect your computer from viruses and other types of malware.

52 State one common method of identifying a user on a computer system.

53 What is a 'strong' password?

54 Why should you use different passwords for different websites?

55 Follow the instructions for creating a password on page 307, and check the security of your newly created password online.

Questions *continued*

56 Explain why password manager software has been developed.

57 What is encryption?

58 State one common use of encryption.

59 What is biometrics?

60 State one example of a
a) physiological biometric.
b) behavioural biometric.

61 Suppose your school introduced (or already has) a biometric attendance (registration) system. What effect would (or has) this system have (or had) on
a) student attendance?
b) the accuracy of the register?

62 What is a protocol?

63 Name one communications protocol.

64 What is a security protocol?

65 Name two security protocols.

66 The two protocols HTTP and TLS are often used together – why?

67 What is it supposed to mean if you see a padlock icon on a website?

68 How could you tell if the padlock on a website is operational?

69 What is a security certificate?

70 State one important feature of a security certificate.

71 What is a firewall?

72 What does a firewall do?

73 Explain how the use of a software firewall is different from the use of a hardware firewall.

74 What is a web proxy?

75 Explain how it is possible for a user's access to web pages to be controlled.

76 What is a security suite?

77 Make a list of four features of a security suite.

78 What is a rogue security suite likely to do to a user's computer system?

79 'There is no such thing as absolute security.' State your own opinion about absolute security.

80 So-called multi-factor authentication combines 'something you have' with 'something you know' and 'something you are'. State one example for each of these three 'somethings'.

Key Points

- A computer system is secure if it is unable to be accessed by an unauthorised person, and is not affected by malicious software or 'malware'.

- Malware is software that has been deliberately created to disrupt the operation of a computer system, or gain illegal access to it in order to gather information.

- Malware includes viruses, worms, Trojans, spyware and keylogging software.

- All computer systems should be protected against malicious software by the use of security precautions.

- A virus is a program which can copy or replicate itself and infects other programs or computers.

- A worm is a stand-alone program which copies or replicates itself in order to spread to other computer systems.

- The term Trojan or Trojan horse is used to refer to a program that appears to be safe, but hidden inside is usually something harmful, like a worm or a virus.

- Common symptoms of virus infection include:
  - displaying unwanted messages
  - unusual visual or sound effects
  - computers rebooting or restarting unexpectedly
  - unwanted generation of emails.

- Hacking is gaining unauthorised access to a computer system and is usually illegal.
- Phishing is an attempt to trick someone into giving away personal information using the internet by pretending to be a well-known company or a bank.
- Identity theft is when someone else pretends to be you, in order to carry out fraud.
- Spyware is a type of malware which, when installed on a user's computer, collects information about them without their knowledge.
- Keystroke logging or keylogging is the process of recording every key that is pressed on a keyboard, without the user being aware that it is being done.
- Online fraud or internet fraud is the use of services available on the internet to defraud people of money, or to carry out identity theft.
- A DOS attack is a procedure which tries to interrupt or suspend the services of a host computer, which is connected to the internet. A DOS attack involves sending so many requests to a host computer that it is unable to respond to legitimate requests, or slows the host so much that it becomes unusable.
- A host computer is a physical device which, when connected to a network, provides services to another connected computer.
- A DDOS attack takes place when many different computers carry out a DOS attack on a single host computer.
- Security precautions include: anti-virus software, passwords/encryption, biometrics, security protocols and firewalls, and the use of security suites.
- Anti-virus software is a type of application software which protects a computer system against attack or infection by viruses and other types of malware.
- The writing and distribution of viruses is a criminal offence under the Computer Misuse Act 1990.
- The most common means of identifying a person on a computer system is by having them enter a user identity and a password.

- The 'strength' of a password depends on the different characters in it, the length of the password, and the password not being in a dictionary.
- Encryption means putting data into a code to prevent it being seen by unauthorised users.
- When you type a password to access a network, it is encrypted before it is sent to the file server to prevent it from being read en route.
- Biometrics is using a person's physical characteristics in order to provide evidence of their identity.
- Examples of biometric data which may be used in this manner include facial recognition, fingerprints, retinal scan or voiceprints.
- Biometrics may be physiological or behavioural.
- Physiological biometrics include a person's face, fingerprints, hands, irises and DNA.
- Behavioural biometrics include keystrokes, signature and voice.
- A protocol is a set of rules that determine how something is to be done.
- A security protocol is a sequence of operations that makes sure data is protected.
- Clicking on the padlock icon on a secure web page should display a digital certificate.
- https also indicates that a web page uses a security protocol.
- A firewall is a system designed to prevent unauthorised access to or from a private network.
- The firewall contains rules and conditions which specify what is and is not allowed to pass through.
- Firewalls can be created in hardware or software.
- Hardware firewalls are located in the router, which connects the network to the internet.
- A security suite is a collection of software, which is sold together as a single package and contains programs which protect computers against a variety of malware.
- A typical security suite may include anti-virus, firewall, anti-spam, anti-spyware, parental control, privacy and phishing protection.

317

CHAPTER 15

Legal implications

This chapter gives some basic descriptions and examines the implications of the:

- Computer Misuse Act 1990
- Data Protection Act 1998
- Copyright, Designs and Patents Act 1988 (plagiarism)
- Health and safety regulations
- Communications Act 2003.

The **Computer Misuse Act 1990**, the **Data Protection Act 1998**, the **Copyright, Designs and Patents Act 1988** and the **Communications Act 2003** all affect computer users. Since these Acts were passed, individuals may be prosecuted for carrying out certain activities relating to computers which are classified as illegal. Any conviction which is made is a result of the application of these Acts.

Computer Misuse Act 1990

The Computer Misuse Act 1990 makes it a criminal offence to gain unauthorised access:

1 to computer material
2 with intent to commit further offences
3 with intent to impair the operation of a computer.

Therefore, if a person **hacks** a computer system which does not belong to them, or without the owner's permission, they are liable to prosecution. Furthermore, if a person writes or distributes any harmful program, such as any type of **malware**, they are also liable to prosecution.

Remember that malware is **software** which can damage a computer. Malware includes **viruses, worms, Trojans, spyware, keyloggers** and **adware**. We looked at various types of malware in Chapter 14.

These types of **crime** are now widespread because so many computers may be accessed through **networks** such as the **internet**. There is a variety of estimates as to the cost and extent of malware and criminal activities on computers. Kindsight Security Labs is a company which helps to protect consumers and other organisations against malware. It reports that in Autumn 2012, 13 per cent of home networks in the United States were infected with malware.

You can read about some of the examples of prosecutions which took place under the Computer Misuse Act here www.computerevidence.co.uk/Cases/CMA.htm.

Figure 15.01 The difference between authorised and illegal access

Data Protection Act 1998

The widespread use of computerised record-keeping brings dangers. The **information** may be entered wrongly; become out of date or it may be mixed up with information about someone else. The effects can be very serious: people can be refused jobs, housing, benefits or credit, be overcharged for goods or services or even wrongfully arrested.

If an organisation holds any records about you, you have a right of access to **personal data** in order to check that it is accurate. Organisations which hold this type of information are expected to take precautions to ensure that the **data** doesn't get lost, stolen or changed by system failures or mistakes.

The Data Protection Act 1998 covers how personal information may be held and for what purposes.

Specifically, it states that:

- data means information which is being processed or recorded in order to be processed
- **data controller** is the person who determines the purposes for which and the manner in which the personal data are to be processed
- **data processor** means a person (other than an employee of the data controller) who processes the data on behalf of the data controller
- **data subject** means an individual whose personal data is being held
- personal data means data which relates to a living individual who can be identified from that data.

Personal data covers both facts and people's opinions. Facts include: name, date of birth, address, examination results, credit rating and medical history. Opinions include political or religious views.

The Information Commissioner regulates the operation of the Data Protection Act. Organisations which hold personal data must register with the Information Commissioner and must state the purposes for which the personal data is being held. You can find out more about the role of the Information Commissioner at www.ico.gov.uk.

Subject rights

The Data Protection Act gives data subjects a right of access to their personal data, upon payment of a fee.

Data subjects have the right to:

- see data held on themselves within 40 days for payment of a fee
- have any errors in the data corrected
- compensation for distress caused if the Act has been broken
- prevent processing for direct marketing by writing to the data controller
- prevent processing by automated decision-making, that is, when a **computer program** makes a decision about you rather than a person.

Be careful not to confuse **subject rights** with data protection principles, which are described below.

Data protection principles

There are eight data protection principles:

1 Personal data should be fairly and lawfully processed.
2 Personal data should only be used or disclosed for the specified purposes.
3 Personal data should be adequate, relevant and not excessive (for example the Income Tax office (Inland Revenue) does not need to know the name of your goldfish).
4 Personal data should be accurate and kept up to date (for example if you have changed your address).
5 Information should not be kept any longer than necessary (for example the school does not need your emergency contact details after you have left).
6 Data must be processed in accordance with the rights of the data subjects.
7 **Security** measures should prevent unauthorised access or alteration of the data (for example use **passwords**, **encryption** and keep regular **backup copies**).
8 Personal data should not be transferred to countries outside the EU, except to countries with adequate data protection legislation.

Exceptions to right of access

There are **exceptions to the right of access** for government agencies, the police, courts and security services. These exceptions only apply if allowing you to see the data would be likely to, for example, prevent the police from catching a criminal.

You may not see information about you if it is kept in order to:

- safeguard national security
- prevent and detect crime
- collect taxes.

You do not need to register under the Data Protection Act if the information is:

- used in journalism for historical and statistical purposes
- personal data relating to your own family or household affairs, for instance if you have a copy of your family tree on your computer.

The Data Protection Act 1998 places limits on the storage and use of personal information. Many individuals and companies need to store information about us in order to provide goods and services such as healthcare. Computers make it easy to store this information and should make companies more efficient in their service provision. While we may not like to give out personal information, most people agree that it is necessary in some cases. You may well resent a 'cold caller' knowing your telephone number, but perhaps not be so upset if a doctor's computer held the statement *allergic to penicillin*.

Users of commercial **websites** should not be surprised if the type of on-screen advertisements which appear when they are using the service gradually changes to reflect the types of **search** that they have been carrying out and the pages they have browsed. This harvesting and use of personal information is valuable to companies and they argue that targeted advertising is of benefit to the individuals concerned.

The use of networks makes it easy to pass information between organisations, and this means that it is possible to build up a more or less complete picture of an individual when a series of separate data items is gathered together and combined in a **database**.

Identity theft is one activity that has been made easier for criminals because of the use of networks. According to the UK Fraud Prevention Agency, CIFAS, it is estimated that identity fraud is responsible for a criminal cash flow of around £10m per day. It can cost a victim of identity theft up to £8,000 and over 200 hours of their time to restore their reputation in extreme cases.

Copyright, Designs and Patents Act 1988

The Copyright, Designs and Patents Act 1988 covers breaches of **copyright**, such as illegal copying of software, music and movies.

What is copyright?

Copyright is the right to prevent others from copying someone else's work. To see how this might work in practice, let's look at two examples.

Example 1

Some of the information on the internet is free to use but much of it is not. Suppose you are looking for information for a school project and find a graphic of a laser printer, which you download and save to backing storage. You then use an application package to paste the image of the printer into your report, print it, and hand it in. This type of use of the graphic would be classified as research and private study (so-called *'fair dealing'*) and there should be no copyright implications of using the image in this way, providing that your report acknowledges the source of the image.

Example 2

Now, imagine you are writing a computing textbook and you download and save the same graphic of the laser printer for use in your new book. It would be *illegal* to use the image in the book, which is a commercial publication, without first seeking the permission of, and perhaps paying a fee to, the copyright owner.

Commercial software, such as Microsoft Office®, is not free and should be paid for. There are considerable restrictions upon its use. When you purchase commercial software you are only allowed to use it on one computer system and are not allowed to make copies of it, or distribute it in any way.

If you wish to use a piece of software on more than one computer system, you should purchase *one* of the following:

- a sufficient number of single copies to match the number of computer systems required
- a limited licence for the specific number of machines required
- a site licence, which allows you to use the software on all computer systems at a single location, such as a school.

While it is perfectly legal to sell or give away a music CD or a DVD film that you have bought, making a copy of the music or movie is illegal. What is not well understood is that it is also illegal to make **digital** copies of copyrighted materials such as music, movies, games and e-books for personal use, even if you have already paid for a single copy. Some movies sold on **DVD** also contain a digital copy for which permission is granted to copy it to another **device** such as a **laptop** or phone, but this is not the case for the majority.

Piracy

Computer networks with **broadband connections** make it easier for software and movies to be stolen from their legitimate copyright owners. A variety of compressed file formats, such as **MP3** and AAC, can reduce the time it takes to download a single musical track to seconds. These downloads may be legal, for example in the case of Amazon™ or the iTunes® music store, but many are from illegal sources.

The size of a typical movie file makes it a substantial download, even with a broadband connection. To reduce excessive downloading and file sharing, many **Internet Service Providers** (**ISPs**) have introduced a monthly limit. A figure of between 15 and 30 **Gigabytes** is a typical 'cap'. So-called 'unlimited' download accounts are still subject to what the Internet Service Provider calls 'fair use'. If the account is used excessively then it will be closed.

The Digital Economy Act 2010 contains sections related to digital piracy, including illegal file sharing. However, there have been problems with its implementation and at the time of writing, it has not yet been fully enforced.

Many people justify their actions in buying pirated copies of movies by referring to the profits made by film companies. What these individuals may not realise is that the profits from piracy are going straight into the pockets of organised criminals and are used to fund other criminal acts such as the distribution of drugs.

You can find out more about copyright from these two websites:

- www.cla.co.uk
- www.copyrightservice.co.uk

What is plagiarism?

Plagiarism is copying work which has been created by another person and passing it off as your own. Unlike copyright, plagiarism is not in itself illegal (unless it involves copyrighted work), but it is immoral. Plagiarism and accusations of plagiarism can be avoided simply by quoting the author or the source of the material which is being used.

The wide availability of written material on the internet has made the act of plagiarism much easier. Students who copy work for use in essays, without the correct acknowledgement of their sources, are guilty of plagiarism.

Many educational institutions regularly check students' work for plagiarism. This is made much easier if the work is submitted in electronic form. It is easy to check for plagiarism by using a **search engine**: **insert** the sentence to be checked into the search box and check the **hits**. Some universities insist that students carry out plagiarism checking before they submit any work to be marked.

A variety of websites now offer plagiarism-checking services. These allow differing amounts of **text** to be checked, from a few words to whole documents. Some of these services are free to use but some require payment. Several of the websites will actually save your work **online**, which would normally be considered an advantage, but should you revise your writing and recheck for plagiarism, then you may find that the website will report that you have plagiarised yourself!

The Scottish Qualifications Authority regulations current at the time this book was written, state that anyone cheating may have all of their examinations cancelled, not just the one they were caught in.

Communications Act 2003

The Communications Act 2003 set up the Office of Communications, known as Ofcom, which is responsible for regulating communications in the UK. You can find out more about the work of Ofcom by looking at www.ofcom.org.uk.

The Communications Act 2003 includes provisions which regulate:

- electronic communications networks and services
- the use of the electromagnetic spectrum (which frequencies are to be used for different purposes)
- broadcasting including television and radio
- media companies such as newspapers and other enterprises.

Note that the Communications Act has 411 different sections, so this book describes only a small part of the Act which is particularly relevant to networks.

The Communications Act has specific provisions regarding offences relating to networks and services. These include:

- dishonestly obtaining electronic communications services (Section 125)
- possession or supply of apparatus for contravening Section 125 (Section 126)
- improper use of [a] public electronic communications network (Section 127).

With respect to dishonestly obtaining services, Section 125 of the Communications Act states:

(1) A person who—

    (a) dishonestly obtains an electronic communications service, and

    (b) does so with intent to avoid payment of a charge applicable to the provision of that service,

is guilty of an offence.

With respect to improper use, Section 127 of the Communications Act states:

(1) A person is guilty of an offence if he—

 (a) sends by means of a public electronic communications network a message or other matter that is grossly offensive or of an indecent, obscene or menacing character; or

 (b) causes any such message or matter to be so sent.

(2) A person is guilty of an offence if, for the purpose of causing annoyance, inconvenience or needless anxiety to another, he—

 (a) sends by means of a public electronic communications network, a message that he knows to be false,

 (b) causes such a message to be sent; or

 (c) persistently makes use of a public electronic communications network.

http://news.bbc.co.uk/2/hi/technology/4721723.stm describes one example of a prosecution under Section 125 of the Communications Act.

Section 127 of the Communications Act applies to what has become known as 'trolling' on the internet. An internet 'troll' is a person who sets out to deliberately upset people by making comments online.

You can read more about trolling on www.bbc.co.uk/news/magazine-14898564.

Trolling is a form of **cyberbullying** and as such should be dealt with appropriately. The **Child Exploitation and Online Protection Centre (CEOP)** provides information and advice about cyberbullying on its website www.thinkuknow.co.uk/11_16/report/cyberbullying/.

Figure 15.02 CEOP reporting button

Checklist of main features of the Acts

✓ Computer Misuse Act 1990: prevents hacking and planting viruses.

✓ Data Protection Act 1998: controls how personal information may be held and for what purposes.

✓ Copyright, Designs and Patents Act 1988: prevents illegal copying of software, music and movies.

✓ Communications Act 2003: regulates the provision and use of electronic communications.

Health and safety regulations

Effects of computers on health

Computer systems themselves can affect your general **health**, depending on the amount of time that you spend using them.

- The glare from a computer **screen** can damage your eyesight if you look at it for long. You can cut down the glare by fitting an anti-glare filter in front of the computer screen or by wearing specially coated spectacles.
- The continual use of a **keyboard** and **mouse** can cause upper limb disorders such as **repetitive strain injury (RSI)**. Use of wrist supports and adjusting the height of the chair so that the forearms are level with the keyboard is advised. Taking regular breaks from prolonged periods of typing is also recommended. Special ergonomic keyboards have been developed in order to reduce RSI – see Figure 15.03.
- Radiation from some older (CRT) computer screens is also thought to be unhealthy, although this does not apply to modern flat screens (**LCD**).

Regulations have been developed which apply to the health and safety of business users of computers. They cover all aspects of the use of computers, from the lighting in the office to the design of the chair that the operator uses. These regulations do not apply to students and teachers in schools, although some of them have been taken into account by education authorities.

Figure 15.03 Ergonomic keyboard

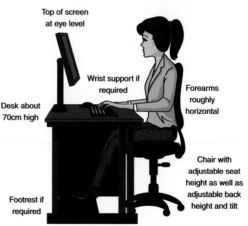

Top of screen at eye level

Wrist support if required

Desk about 70cm high

Forearms roughly horizontal

Chair with adjustable seat height as well as adjustable back height and tilt

Footrest if required

Figure 15.04 Workstation recommendations

The main set of regulations which cover the use of computers in the work place is **The Health and Safety (Display Screen Equipment) Regulations 1992**. The regulations require that users of display screen equipment must be provided with:

- fully adjustable chairs and footrests
- tilting screens which do not flicker and have anti-glare filters
- suitable lighting and window blinds
- eyesight checks (but not free glasses unless normal ones cannot be used).

You can find out more here: www.hse.gov.uk/pubns/indg36.pdf.

Physical hazards

The application of common sense can help to prevent accidents involving the use of computers.

Electrocution risk

Desktop computers, which are fitted with a mains electrical plug, should be treated with the same care that applies to any other piece of electrical equipment. For instance, they should be switched off and unplugged from the mains before carrying out any work which may involve opening the case, such as fitting additional memory **chips**, **graphics** or **sound cards**.

Under no circumstances should any work be carried out on a computer's power supply even when the computer is unplugged, since the components can hold lethal voltages even after being disconnected.

Have a look at this tragic story http://news.cnet.com/8301-17852_3-57528853-71/teen-electrocuted-while-working-on-unplugged-computer/.

Fire hazards

- Keep drinks away from computers; water and electricity do not mix well.
- Carry out regular checks on **cables** for any damage.
- Avoid overloading power sockets with adapters; use a trailing multi-block instead.

Transport

Take special care when moving or lifting computers.

Check Your Learning

Now answer questions 1–26 (on page 328) on legal implications (National 5).

Practical Tasks

1 Carry out some research using a search engine and make a note of the current threat level of malware. These websites are a good starting point:
- www.sophos.com/en-us/threat-center/threat-monitoring/malware-dashboard.aspx
- www.symanteccloud.com/en/gb/globalthreats/

2 If your school or centre has provided you with access to a secure online environment such as GLOW, set up a Wiki on the subject of downloading music and movies.

3 Look back at the regulations covering display screen equipment in the workplace. How well does the provision for students using computers in your school compare with the regulations?

Questions

Legal implications (National 5)

1 Name three Acts which affect computer users.

2 State two illegal activities covered by the Computer Misuse Act.

3 Why are crimes against the Computer Misuse Act so widespread?

4 Describe what may happen when computerised record-keeping goes wrong.

5 Which law covers the holding of personal information?

6 What name is given to the person
   a) who decides the purposes for which personal data is held?
   b) whose personal data is being held?

7 What is personal data?

8 What is the first step that must be taken by an organisation which wishes to hold personal data?

9 State two rights of data subjects.

10 State two data protection principles.

11 Which data protection principle is being broken if
   a) your bank still sends letters to your previous address?
   b) the credit card company asks if you like asparagus?
   c) the utility company loses your record of payments?
   d) the insurance company sells your email address?

12 Name two organisations that do not have to show you what information they may hold about you.

13 State one type of information you may hold on your home computer without registering it.

14 Which law covers illegal copying of software, music and movies?

15 What is copyright?

16 State one example of 'fair dealing'.

17 Explain why you may be required to purchase a site licence for software.

18 What are you allowed to do with a DVD movie that is against the law with a downloaded film?

19 State one method used by Internet Service Providers to reduce file sharing.

20 What happens to money raised from the sale of pirated movies?

21 What is plagiarism?

22 If you wish to quote from another person's work in an essay, what should you do?

23 State two network activities which are liable to prosecution under the Communications Act.

24 What is an internet troll?

25 a) State two effects of computers on health.
   b) State one precaution which will help to prevent each of the effects you mentioned in part a).

26 State two physical hazards when using computers.

Key Points

- The laws which affect computer users include the Computer Misuse Act 1990, the Data Protection Act 1998, the Copyright, Designs and Patents Act 1988 and the Communications Act 2003.

- The Computer Misuse Act is concerned with:
  - gaining unauthorised access to, or hacking into a computer system
  - writing and distributing any type of harmful program such as malware.

- The Data Protection Act controls how personal information may be held and for what purposes.

- The data controller is the person who determines the purposes for which and the manner in which the personal data are to be processed.

- Data subject means an individual whose personal data is being held.

- Personal data means data which relates to a living individual who can be identified from that data.

- Organisations which hold personal data must register with the Information Commissioner.
- The Data Protection Act gives data subjects a right of access to their personal data and to have it amended if it is incorrect.
- The eight data protection principles state that:
  - Personal data should be fairly and lawfully processed.
  - Personal data should only be used or disclosed for the specified purposes.
  - Personal data should be adequate, relevant and not excessive.
  - Personal data should be accurate and kept up to date.
  - Information should not be kept any longer than necessary.
  - Data must be processed in accordance with the rights of the data subjects.
  - Security measures should prevent unauthorised access or alteration of the data.
  - Personal data should not be transferred to countries outside the EU except to countries with adequate data protection legislation.
- You may not see information about you if it is kept in order to safeguard national security, prevent and detect crime or collect taxes.
- You do not need to register as a data controller if, for example, you are storing your own family's data on computer.
- The Copyright, Designs and Patents Act covers breaches of copyright, such as illegal copying of software, music and movies.
  - Copyright is the right to prevent others copying someone else's work.

- Most works of whatever kind cannot be copied without obtaining permission from the copyright holder and perhaps paying a fee.
- Plagiarism is copying work which has been created by another person and passing it off as your own.
- Plagiarism is not illegal unless it involves copyrighted work.
- Plagiarism can be avoided by quoting the source of the material being used.
- The internet makes plagiarism easier.
- The internet makes checking a work for plagiarism easier.
- The Communications Act covers:
  - electronic communications networks and services
    - dishonestly obtaining services
    - sending offensive messages
  - the use of the electromagnetic spectrum
  - broadcasting including television and radio
  - media companies such as newspapers and other enterprises.
- An internet troll is a person who deliberately tries to upset others by sending online messages.
- Computer systems can affect your health, depending on the amount of time that you use them.
  - Glare from a computer screen can damage your eyesight.
  - Continual use of a keyboard and mouse can cause limb disorders.
- The Health and Safety (Display Screen Equipment) Regulations covers the use of computers in the workplace.
- Physical hazards from computers include electrocution and fire risks.

CHAPTER 16

Environmental impact

This chapter looks at the environmental impact of manufacturing, using and disposing of computers. It examines:

- energy use
- disposal of IT equipment
- carbon footprint.

Computers and computing **devices** are becoming simpler for people to use, but they are not simple to create. They contain many complex components, some containing substances which are harmful to the environment both when they are manufactured and when they are disposed of at the end of their use.

Regardless of the size of the device, all computers **use energy** while they are switched on, whether or not they are actually being used to do any work. Generating energy for computers and other devices has an **impact on the environment**.

Computer manufacturers and users are now beginning to take into account the **carbon footprint** arising from their choice, use and **disposal of computer equipment**.

Manufacture of IT equipment

The factory where your computer is assembled is just the last stage in a long journey for the components that are used to create it. The raw materials required in its manufacture pass through many stages, including excavation, refining and smelting, before they are used to make the components of a computer. For example, the copper in the **circuit board** may be mined as ore in the USA and then shipped to China. Gold to coat the sockets or make connections between the processor **chips** may come from Australia or South Africa.

In 2011, the Bingham Canyon Open Pit Copper Mine in Utah produced 215,000 tonnes of copper, 10.75 tonnes of gold, 90.7 tonnes of silver, 13,607 tonnes of molybdenum and 796,780 tonnes of sulphuric acid (source: www.kennecott.com/economy#acc-head-1).

Figure 16.01 Bingham Canyon Open Pit Copper Mine, Utah, USA

Studies show that approximately 80 per cent of the energy used over a computer's lifetime is used in its manufacture and 20 per cent is used in its operation. The main reason for this is because of the extremely fine detail required in microchips. A typical **microprocessor** used in **desktop** and **laptop computers** now contains between 1 000 000 000 and 3 000 000 000 transistors. A great deal of energy is required to produce such complex circuits and to make sure that not one single speck of dust contaminates the process.

Energy use

The amount of energy used by electrical equipment is measured in watts. One Kilowatt is 1 000 watts. Electrical energy is sold in kilowatt-hours (kWh) and costs around 14 pence per unit.

The amount of energy used by some types of computer equipment is shown in Table 16.01. The values in the table were taken from *Powering the Nation* – a report on household electricity-using habits in the UK, published by the Energy Saving Trust in June 2012. You can see that a laptop computer uses much less energy than a desktop computer.

Computing appliance	Average consumption (kWh)	Annual running cost rounded (£)
Desktop	166	24
Laptop	29	4
Fax/printer	160	23
Modem	62	9
Monitor	42	6
Multi-functional printer	26	4
Printer	21	3
Router	58	8
Scanner	20	3

Table 16.01 Energy use and costs of home computer equipment (*Powering the Nation* 2012)

However, the total amount of energy used will depend on how long the equipment is switched on and the task that is being carried out. Intensive use, such as a fast-paced game in 3-D, where there is a greater demand on the computer's processing power, will use more energy than, for instance, **word processing**.

Computers which are not being used but are left switched on will enter standby or power-saving mode, according to how they are programmed in the computer's settings. Some of these settings are shown in Figure 16.02.

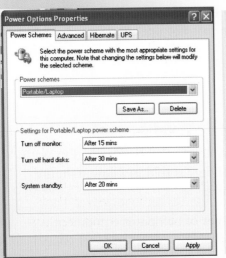

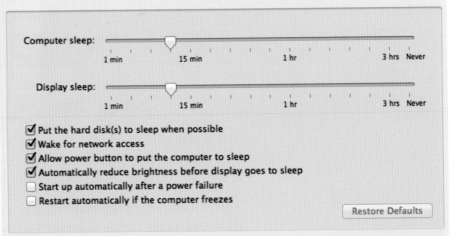

Figure 16.02 Power-saving settings

The settings which save most energy reduce the power to the **screen** and the **hard disk drive**. If the computer is still running programs and has to be left on for this purpose, then these settings can save energy. Running a screensaver program does not save energy; in fact it uses more energy since the screen is not dimmed. The best method of saving energy is to turn the computer off.

Figure 16.03 Energy Star logo

ENERGY STAR

ENERGY STAR is a US Environmental Protection Agency (EPA) voluntary program that provides a certification system for consumer products, including computers. Products which carry the logo are expected to meet or exceed the ENERGY STAR energy efficiency requirements. These requirements for computers include the efficiency of the internal power supply (for example 82 per cent minimum efficiency at 20 per cent and 100 per cent of rated output) and the computer should enter sleep mode after no more than 30 minutes of user inactivity.

epeat

epeat is a searchable **database** of products which meet certain environmental criteria, for instance:

- reduction/elimination of environmentally sensitive materials
- material selection
- design for end of life
- product longevity/life extension
- energy conservation
- end-of-life management
- corporate performance
- packaging.

You can use the epeat database at www.epeat.net/ to search for products which meet, or exceed the criteria.

Figure 16.04 epeat logo

Manufacturers know that consumers are concerned about the environment, and are keen to have their products certified as meeting the epeat criteria.

Disposal of IT equipment

Computers contain substances which are harmful to the environment and can cause a great deal of pollution if they are just thrown away with ordinary household waste. Elements such as cadmium, lead and mercury (so-called heavy metals) together with antimony, arsenic, chromium, cobalt, mercury, selenium and substances such as BFR (Brominated Flame Retardant, found in plastics) and beryllium oxide are all hazardous to health. It is vital that unwanted computers are recycled or disposed of in the correct manner to avoid these hazardous chemicals from polluting our environment.

WEEED

The **Waste Electrical and Electronic Equipment (WEEE) Directive** became European Law in 2003, and UK law from 2007.

Figure 16.05 WEEE logo

The current aim of this directive for the EU member states is to recycle at least 85 per cent of electrical and electronics waste by 2016. The WEEE directive puts the responsibility for collecting and recycling onto the manufacturers and distributors of the equipment sold after 2005. What they are obliged to do is to set up a system for the free return of the equipment at the end of its use. Manufacturers pay for the recovery of waste equipment from household waste recycling centres.

There is a variety of options for your computer when you are finished with it. These include:

- give it to someone who doesn't have a computer, a friend or to charity
- sell it, for example on an online auction site
- part-exchange it for a new computer
- give it to the company that you are buying a replacement from, for recycling.

Precautions when giving away or selling a computer

A survey in 2009, by New York firm Kessler International (www. investigation.com/press/press75.htm), found that more than 40 per cent of the **hard drives** listed for sale on eBay still contained personal, private and sensitive **information**, otherwise thought to have been erased. It is very important to completely wipe the hard disk drive, so that none of your **data** is recoverable. *Make a backup copy of your data* before you do this. Simply **formatting a disk** is not enough, since data can still be recovered by **software**. If this happens, you may become the victim of **identity theft.** It is recommended that you use a specialist program to completely wipe all data. Alternatively, you can remove the original hard disk drive and replace it.

You are allowed to give away or sell original 'boxed' software on CD or **DVD**, providing you have not retained a copy for yourself. This does not apply to software downloads, which must be deleted.

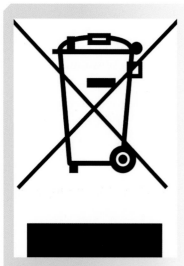

Figure 16.06 The crossed-out wheelie bin. Electrical and electronic equipment that was produced after 13 August 2005 should display this symbol on the packaging or product. A similar symbol without the bar at the bottom is used to identify batteries that can be recycled.

Carbon footprint

Some sunlight that hits the earth is reflected. Some becomes heat.

CO_2 and other gases in the atmosphere trap heat, keeping the earth warm.

ATMOSPHERE

Figure 16.07 The Greenhouse Effect

The carbon footprint is the amount of **greenhouse gases** (including carbon dioxide and methane) produced by people or a particular activity.

Greenhouse gases have an **environmental impact** because they absorb heat and can therefore cause **global warming**.

Reducing the carbon footprint

There is a variety of actions that may be taken by individuals to reduce the carbon footprint. These include:

- walking or cycling instead of driving to school or work
- making more use of **video conferencing** for meetings and working from home
- improving home insulation and turning down thermostats to reduce heating requirements
- making use of reusable instead of disposable items, for example shopping bags instead of plastic carrier bags
- recycling more and throwing away less.

As far as the use of computers is concerned:

- switch off computers and associated equipment, like printers, when not in use, instead of leaving them on standby
- use the energy saving settings on the equipment where possible (see **energy use**, earlier in this chapter)
- do not take unnecessary printouts; send drafts of essays to the teacher by **email** and only print work which is needed as examination evidence
- when you do print, use both sides of the paper
- recycle used printer ink and **toner** cartridges, instead of disposing of them
- purchase remanufactured printer ink and toner cartridges to encourage recycling.

Check Your Learning

Now answer questions 1–17 (on page 336) on environmental impact (National 5).

Practical Tasks

1 Carry out some research about protecting your personal information on a computer you intend to recycle. You can start by looking at this website: http://articles.latimes.com/2012/mar/29/business/la-fi-tech-savvy-protecting-identity-20120329.

2 Find out about how the WEEED is enforced in the UK at www.dft.gov.uk/vca/enforcement/weee-enforcement.asp.

3 Find out about recycling in your local area at www.recycle-more.co.uk/.

4 Have a look at some commercial recycling organisations:
- www.cclnorth.com/

- www.belmont-trading.com/Datec-Technologies.aspx
- www.lowmac.co.uk/

5 Find out how much energy is used by your home computer system, either by looking at the label on it or by looking up the manufacturer's specifications. Think about the number of hours the computer is switched on for each day. Calculate the number of Kilowatt hours of energy used by the computer in one week and one year. How much does this energy cost? How does the energy used by your computer compare to the average figures shown in Table 16.01?

6 Find out why it costs so much in terms of energy use to manufacture computers and other

electronic equipment. This website is a good place to start: www.lowtechmagazine.com/2009/06/embodied-energy-of-digital-technology.html.

7 Find out which elements are used in computer production and what countries they are mined in. Fill in the rest of this table.

Element	Symbol	Country
Aluminium	Al	Australia, China
Cobalt	Co	Congo, Zambia
Copper	Cu	Chile, Peru
Gold	Au	China, Australia
Selenium	Se	Japan, Germany
Silver	Ag	Peru, Mexico
Tantalum	Ta	Rwanda, Mozambique
Tin		

Table 16.02 Elements used in computer production

8 Some mining companies now explore the ocean beds as a source of valuable minerals. Carry out some research into which minerals are being searched for and note whether any of them are used in computer production. You may find the International Seabed Authority's website a useful place to begin: www.isa.org.jm/en/home.

Questions

Environmental impact (National 5)

1 State three ways in which computers have an impact on the environment.

2 Explain how the amount of electricity used by a computer is measured and sold.

3 Which type of computer system has the least environmental impact in terms of energy use?

4 Look at Table 16.01, which shows the average energy consumption for a monitor. By comparing this figure with others in the table, explain how it would be reasonable to say that this figure was for a CRT, rather than an LCD, monitor.

5 Describe a situation in which a desktop computer would use less energy than normal.

6 State two features of a computer's standby mode.

7 Explain why a computer running a screensaver program is not energy efficient.

8 What is the best method of saving energy when you are not using a computer?

9 What is
a) epeat?
b) ENERGY STAR?

10 Name two heavy metals present in computer equipment.

11 What can happen if computers are not disposed of in the correct manner?

12 Name two environmentally friendly options for disposing of a computer.

13 State one danger of giving away a computer to someone else.

14 What is the carbon footprint?

15 What effect are greenhouse gases thought to have?

16 State two actions that people may take to reduce the carbon footprint which do not involve computers.

17 State two actions involving computers which may be taken to reduce the carbon footprint.

Key Points

- All computers use energy when they are switched on.

- The amount of energy used by electrical equipment is measured in watts.

- A typical desktop computer uses six times the amount of energy compared to a laptop.

- The total amount of energy used will depend on how long the equipment is switched on and the task that is being carried out.

- Computers which are not being used but are left switched on will enter standby mode according to how they are programmed.

- Running a screensaver program does not save energy.

- The best method of saving energy is to turn the computer off.

- ENERGY STAR is a certification system for consumer products.

- epeat is a database of products which meet certain environmental criteria.

- Computers contain substances such as cadmium, lead and mercury, which are harmful to the environment when they are disposed of.

- It is vital that unwanted computers are recycled or disposed of in the correct manner to avoid hazardous chemicals from polluting our environment.

- The Waste Electrical and Electronic Equipment (WEEE) Directive aims to recycle at least 85 per cent of electrical and electronics waste by 2016.

- Manufacturers are obliged to set up a system for the free return of the equipment at the end of its use.

- When you are finished with your computer, you can give it away, sell it, part exchange it for a new computer, recycle it back to the manufacturer.

- You should take precautions when disposing of an old computer to prevent identity theft.

- The carbon footprint is the amount of greenhouse gases produced by people or a particular activity.

- Greenhouse gases have an environmental impact because they absorb heat and can cause global warming.

- The carbon footprint of computers may be reduced by switching them off when not in use, using the energy saving settings, taking fewer printouts, recycling used ink and toner cartridges.

Glossary

& The symbol used for string concatenation in some languages. + is also used.

1-D array Arrays which have one number as their subscript are called one-dimensional arrays.

2-D scanner Can input printed drawings, photographs or text directly into a computer.

3-D printer Can produce three-dimensional objects from solid materials such as plastic or resin.

3-D scanner May be used to scan an object and create a data file containing its measurements.

3-D webcam Has two cameras in order to produce 3-D images.

absolute addressing If the URL points to an external website, then the URL is said to be absolute (absolute addressing).

absolute security There is no such thing as absolute security where computers are involved.

accessible An information system is accessible when it is usable by everyone, including people with disabilities.

active speakers Mains-powered speakers with a built-in amplifier.

ADC Analogue to Digital Conversion.

address A binary number used to identify a storage location in main memory.

address bar Part of a web browser which contains the URL of the page being loaded or displayed.

address bus A set of wires which carries the address information from the processor to the memory.

addressability A method of identifying storage locations in main memory using a number called an address.

ADSL Asymmetric Digital Subscriber Line. A means of allowing broadband access over a normal telephone line.

advanced search Allows the user to refine their search. Most search engines allow the use of AND, OR and NOT in an advanced search.

adware Software which provides adverts to the user in order to generate revenue for the author.

age-range (of users) The ages of the users of the information system, for instance: young child, teenager and adult.

algorithm A series of steps to solve a problem.

Alice A high-level computer language.

alt An HTML tag.

ALU See 'Arithmetic and Logic Unit'.

American Standard Code for Information Interchange (ASCII) A seven-bit code which can represent 128 characters.

analogue A signal which changes continuously rather than in steps, such as temperature and speed.

Analogue to Digital Conversion (ADC) Changing an analogue signal into a digital signal takes place in an interface.

analysis Looking at and understanding a problem.

anchor An HTML tag.

AND (logical operator) Used to combine two conditions.

animation Data made up of moving graphics.

anti-virus software A type of application software which protects a computer system against attack or infection by viruses and other types of malware.

AppleScript® A scripting language which works with the Macintosh Operating System and any scriptable applications.

application package (app) Software which performs a particular task.

architecture The structure of a computer system.

arithmetic and logic unit (ALU) Carries out the calculations (arithmetic) and makes the decisions.

arithmetical operations Calculations involving numeric data. The set of arithmetical operators includes add (+), subtract (-), multiply (*), divide (/), exponent (^) and modulus (MOD).

array A set of data items of the same type grouped together using a single variable name.

artefact A flaw in a digital image produced as a result of data compression.

ASCII American Standard Code for Information Interchange.

assignment statement Used to give a value to a variable.

attribute (HTML) Some tags have attributes which provide additional information about an element. Attributes can contain values and are enclosed in quotes.

audio A type of data made up of music or any sound produced by a computer.

audio quality Increasing the sampling rate of an audio file will improve the quality and also increase the file size, since more data must be stored.

Audio Video Interleave (AVI) The standard movie format for Windows®.

automate tasks One function of a program written in a scripting language, e.g. a macro, is to automate tasks for the user.

automatic form-filling (auto-complete) A setting on a browser which automatically enters previously saved data into a form.

background printing A type of background job, which is a secondary task or program which runs in a computer system at the same time as another program being run by the user.

backing storage Used to store programs and data permanently.

backing storage capacity How much data may be held by the device.

backing storage medium An object upon which software and data may be held, such as a CD-ROM.

backlight The part of a monitor which lights up the screen from behind.

backup (copy) A copy of a program or data made in case the original is lost or destroyed.

backward button A button on a web browser which returns the user to a previously visited page.

bandwidth A measure of the quantity of data which may be carried by a communications channel atany one time.

base The number of different digits which may be used at each place value, including 0. Base 2 has two digits, 1 and 0. Base 10 has ten digits, 0 to 9.

basic search Allows the user to enter one or more keywords.

BD-ROM/R/RE/XL Types of Blu-ray Disc™.

behavioural biometrics Include keystrokes, signature and voice.

binary (machine code) Machine code is the computer's own language, written in binary using only 1s and 0s.

binary (system) The binary number system uses two numbers: 0 and 1.

biometrics Using a person's physical characteristics to provide evidence of their identity, e.g. fingerprints or retinal scan.

bit A single unit in binary, either 1 or 0, is called a bit.

bit depth The number of bits used to represent a pixel in bit-mapped graphics.

bit-mapped graphics Bit-mapped packages paint pictures by changing the colour of the pixels which make up the screen display.

Black Friday A day when online retailers discount their products.

black hat A type of hacker.

blended threat More than one type of malware joined together in a single attack.

Bluetooth® The IEEE 802.15.1 wireless standard, with a range of up to 10 metres and a bandwidth of 1 Mbps.

Blu-ray™ A type of optical data storage using a blue coloured laser beam. Used for the storage of movies in HD and 3-D.

BMP A bit-mapped image file format used on Windows® systems.

body (HTML) An HTML tag.

bookmark A method of recording a URL in a web browser.

Boolean (field type or variable) A Boolean variable contains only two values, e.g. true or false, 1 or 0, yes or no.

bootstrap loader Loads the operating system from disk when the computer is switched on.

bot herder A hacker who controls a botnet.

botnet A group of zombie computers used in a DDOS attack.

breadcrumbs A navigation method used in websites.

Brendan Eich The creator of the JavaScript® programming language.

broadband connection A high-speed connection to the internet, e.g. 8 Mbps.

browser A program that allows the user to browse or surf through the World Wide Web.

browser history A list of previously visited web pages.

buffer An area of memory used for the transfer of the data between the computer and a peripheral. Provides temporary storage of data and is an essential component of any interface.

build table The part of a 3-D printer where the object is created.

built-in storage devices Storage devices may be built in to the inside of a computer system or be external.

burning Writing data to an optical disk.

buses A group of wires which connects the processor to the other parts of the computer, such as the memory.

byte A byte has eight bits.

C A high-level programming language.

cable A medium for the transmission of data, including copper wires or optical fibre.

CAD Computer Aided Design.

calculated (field type) Carries out a calculation on another field or fields and gives you an answer, like a formula in a spreadsheet.

calculation of file size for audio The size of an audio file may be calculated by using the formula: Storage requirements = sampling rate (Hz) × sampling depth (bits) × time in seconds × number of channels (2 for stereo).

calculation of file size for colour bit map The file size of a colour bit-mapped image may be calculated by using the formula: Storage requirements = total number of pixels used in the image × number of bits used to represent colours or shades of grey for each pixel.

calculation of file size for video The file size of a video may be calculated by using the formula: Storage requirements = total number of pixels used in each frame × number of bits used to represent colours or shades of grey for each pixel (colour depth) × number of frames per second × time in seconds.

capacity of storage devices The quantity of data that can be held on a backing storage medium, such as CD-ROM.

carbon footprint The amount of greenhouse gases (including carbon dioxide and methane) produced by people or a particular activity.

card reader A device used to connect a flash ROM memory card to a computer system.

Cascading Style Sheets (CSS) A language used to describe the appearance of a web page.

CAT(egory) 6 A type of cable used for data transmission in a Local Area Network.

CCD Charge-coupled device.

CD burner A compact disk drive capable of writing data to CD-Recordable and CD-Rewritable disks.

CD drive Compact disk drive.

CD-Recordable (CD-R) A CD which can be written to until it is full.

CD-Rewriteable (CD-RW) A CD which can be written to and erased over and over again.

CD-ROM Compact Disk Read Only Memory. An optical disk which can hold 600 or 700 Mb of data.

CD-ROM server A computer which allows users on a client/server network access to CD-ROMs.

central processing unit (CPU) The part of a mainframe computer which processes the information.

CEOP Child Exploitation and Online Protection Centre.

character A letter, number or symbol on the computer keyboard.

character set A list of all the characters, symbols and numbers which can be produced by a keyboard.

characters, storage of See 'ASCII and Unicode'.

charge-coupled device (CCD) A chip used in a digital camera to detect images.

chip A small piece of silicon used to make an integrated circuit.

Chrome™ A web-browser application.

circuit board A thin board onto which chips and other components are fixed by solder.

CISC Complex Instruction Set Computer.

client The name given to a workstation on a client/server network.

client (person) The person or company for whom the program is to be written.

client/server A network in which client workstations make use of resources available on one or more servers.

clock speed (Hz) See 'processor clock speed'.

cloud computing The use of computing resources (such as hardware and software) that are delivered as a service over the internet.

cloud computing services Three main types of service are provided in the cloud: infrastructure as a service, platform as a service and software as a service.

cloud storage Cloud storage is online storage, which is accessed via a Wide Area Network.

coding Changing a program design into a program in a high-level language.

color (HTML) An HTML tag.

colour depth The number of bits used to represent colours or shades of grey used in a graphic.

colour wheel A chart used to help choose complementary colours for a web page.

COMAL® A high-level computer language used to teach programming.

commercial software Software which is not free and must be paid for. It is also subject to restrictions as to how it may be used.

Communications Act 2003 The Act covers: electronic communications networks and services; the use of the electromagnetic spectrum; broadcasting, including television and radio; media companies, such as newspapers and other enterprises.

communications channel The medium through which information is transmitted from a sender (or transmitter) to a receiver, e.g. a cable.

CompactFlash (CF) card A form of solid-state storage used in digital still cameras.

compiled language A computer language which is normally translated by using a compiler.

compiler A program that can translate a high-level language program into machine code in a single operation. Translates the source code into machine code, the object code.

complex conditional statement A condition consisting of two or more simple conditions, joined together by AND, OR or NOT.

complex search A search using more than one condition in a database.

compression The process of reducing the size of a file.

computational constructs The parts of a programming language which are used to create a computer program.

computational thinking Thinking of a problem in such a way that makes it possible to solve it by using a computer system.

computed field A field containing a calculation involving one or more other fields.

Computer Aided Design (CAD) Using a computer to design an item.

computer architecture See 'architecture'.

computer crime Using a computer for criminal purposes. Hacking is a computer crime.

Computer Misuse Act 1990 The Act is concerned with gaining unauthorised access to, or hacking into, a computer system, and writing and distributing any type of harmful program such as malware.

computer program The set of instructions that controls how a computer works.

concatenation Joining of two or more strings.

conditional loop There are two types of conditional loop: test at start and test at end. Test at start may never be run if the condition is not met. Test at end is always run at least once.

conditional statement: IF See 'IF (conditional statement)'.

connectivity The ability to make and maintain a connection, e.g. between computers in a network.

consistency An information system is consistent if each page looks similar.

container file A file which contains more than one type of data.

content filtering Controlling a user's access to certain web pages, normally by using a web proxy server.

context-sensitive help system A system which provides a different type of help depending upon what it assumes the user is trying to do.

context-sensitive navigation Hiding those navigation features which are not needed and only displaying those required at a particular time.

control bus Made up of a number of separate wires or lines, each with its own function.

control characters Control certain operations of the computer system.

control structure The three basic control structures used in procedural languages are sequence, selection and repetition/iteration.

control unit Controls all the other parts of the processor and makes sure that the program instructions of the computer are carried out in the correct order.

cookies Used to identify and track visitors to web pages by storing data on the user's computer.

copper wire A Local Area Network transmission medium.

copyright The right to prevent others from copying someone else's work.

Copyright, Designs and Patents Act 1988 (plagiarism) The Act covers breaches of copyright, such as illegal copying of software, music and movies.

corrupt To a file damage so that it cannot be read. This why you should always keep a backup copy!

crashing A hard disk crashes when the head comes into direct contact with the surface of the magnetic disk and damages it.

crop To reduce the size of a graphic by cutting parts from the edges of it.

cross-platform Software which works on more than one platform, e.g. Windows® and Mac®.

CSS Cascading Style Sheets. A language used to describe the appearance of a web page.

cyberbullying Bullying which takes place via a network, e.g. by email.

data A general term for numbers, characters, symbols, graphics and sound which are accepted and processed by a computer system.

data bus Carries data to and from the processor, memory and any other devices attached to it.

data controller The person who determines the purposes for which and the manner in which the personal data are to be processed.

data conversion Involves changing the data received from the peripheral into a form that the processor can understand, and vice versa. One of the functions of an interface.

data duplication error Where two entries are the same; data in a relational database should only be entered and stored once.

data file A file containing data on backing storage or in memory. May be organised as a set of records.

data glove Used to take part in virtual reality.

data modification error An error in a database caused by inserting the wrong information.

data processor A person (other than an employee of the data controller) who processes the data on behalf of the data controller.

Data Protection Act 1998 The Act controls how personal information may be held and for what purposes.

data sharing The ability of users on a network to share data.

data subject An individual whose personal data is being held.

data transfer speed (of storage devices) The speed of data transferred between devices, normally measured in bits per second.

data types The data types stored by a program include numbers, strings and arrays.

database A structured collection of similar information which can be searched through.

database management system Software for creating and managing a database.

database package Software for creating and managing a database.

database structure A database is made up of fields, records and files – its structure.

date (field type) Can only contain dates.

DDOS Distributed Denial of Service.

debugging The process of finding and correcting errors in a program.

declare (a variable) To assign a type and a value to a variable at the start of a program.

declare (an array) To assign a type and a size to an array at the start of a program.

decrypt To remove encryption and return to plain text.

delete (modification error) An error caused by removing data from a database.

Denial of Service (DOS) attack A procedure which tries to interrupt or suspend the services of a host computer which is connected to the internet. Involves a single computer sending so many requests to a host computer that the host is unable to respond to legitimate requests, or slows it so much that it becomes unusable.

design Working out a series of steps to solve a problem.

design notation (graphical) Using diagrams to describe the design of a program.

design notation (pseudocode) Using normal or everyday language to describe the design of a program.

desktop computer Used whilst sitting at a desk and is mains operated.

device A single item of computer hardware.

device driver A program which is an add-on to the operating system in a computer, to allow the computer to operate a particular device which is attached to it.

device type A type of computer such as a supercomputer, desktop or portable devices (including laptops, tablets, smartphones).

digital A signal which changes in steps and not continuously like an analogue signal.

digital (still) camera A digital camera mainly used for taking still photographs.

digital (video) camera A digital camera mainly used for taking video.

digital certificate An attachment to an electronic message used for security purposes, e.g. to indicate that a website is secure.

Digital Rights Management (DRM) A method of protecting digital media against illegal copying.

Digital to Analogue Conversion (DAC) Changing a digital signal into an analogue signal.

digitising Converting an analogue quantity into a digital one.

direct access Being able to locate a data item straight away, wherever it is stored on disk or in main memory. See 'random access'.

directory An area on backing storage where files may be stored (also called a folder on some systems).

display adapter Another name for a graphics card.

disposal of computer equipment What happens to IT equipment when it is no longer of use to the owner.

Distributed Denial of Service attack (DDOS attack) Takes place when many different computers carry out a DOS attack on a single host computer.

division by zero An execution or run-time error.

dock A device where a portable computer may be connected to another device, such as a monitor or loudspeakers.

documenting solutions Documentation is a description of what each part of the program does. May include a user guide and a technical guide.

domain name Part of a URL.

DOS attack Denial of Service attack.

draw package (vector) Vector packages work by drawing objects on the screen.

Drive Encryption A commercial encryption program.

DRM Digital Rights Management.

dual platform Software which is capable of working on two different platforms.

dumb terminal Has no processor and no local storage devices, just a screen and a keyboard.

DVD (Digital Versatile Disk) An optical storage medium, similar to CD-ROM, which can hold video (TV programmes or films).

DVD drive Digital Versatile Disk drive.

DVD-Recordable (DVD-R) A write-once medium, with recordable disks containing a layer of dye.

DVD-Rewriteable (DVD-RW) Similar to DVD-R, but can be written to and erased many times over.

DVD-ROM An optical storage medium, similar to CD-ROM, but with a higher backing storage capacity.

earphones A personal sound output device.

electronic mailing service (email) Sending messages from one computer to another over a network.

electronic signature A method of signing a digital document.

element Each part of an array is called an element.

email Sending messages from one computer to another over a network.

email filter A program which redirects email to specific folders or blocks email according to pre-set rules.

embedded computer A special-purpose computer system which is designed to perform one or more dedicated functions. A tiny computer inside another, larger piece of equipment, like a washing machine, a car or a mobile phone.

empty (null) field A field which has no contents.

emulator A program which allows a computer to run a different operating system.

encryption Putting data into a code to prevent it being seen by unauthorised users.

ENERGY STAR A certification system for consumer products.

energy use All computers use energy when they are switched on. The total amount of energy used will depend on how long the equipment is switched on and the task that is being carried out.

environmental impact What can happen to the environment as a result of the manufacture, use and disposal of computers.

epeat A database of products which meet certain environmental criteria.

error reporting the communication and explanation of errors in the software to the user.

Ethernet The most widely used network interface.

evaluation Involves reviewing your solution against suitable criteria, such as does your program solve the problem?

exceptional test data Data which is invalid and should be rejected by the program under test.

exceptions to the right of access You can not see information about you if it is kept in order to safeguard national security, prevent and detect crime or collect taxes.

execution errors (Also called run-time errors) errors which show up during program execution. Include overflow, rounding, truncation and division by zero.

execution of lines of code in sequence The order in which things are done.

expert user An experienced user of an information system.

exponent Part of a floating point number which contains the power to which the base must be raised.

extended ASCII An eight-bit code which can represent 256 characters.

external hyperlink Takes the user to a different website, either on the same server or on a different server.

external storage devices A drive which is attached to the outside of a computer system.

extreme test data Data which is at the ends of the acceptable range of data, on the limit(s) or boundaries of the problem.

faceted navigation Filters containing different options are displayed and the user makes a selection which narrows the search.

favourites See 'bookmark'.

FC Fibre Channel.

FDM Fused Deposition Modelling. A method of 3-D printing.

field A single item of data stored in a record.

field (database structure) An area on a record which contains an individual piece of data.

field length (validation) Ensures the correct number of numbers or characters have been entered.

field type The type of data which is to be stored in a field. Field types include text, number, date, time, graphics, object, calculated, link and Boolean.

field type (Boolean) See 'Boolean (field type or variable)'.

field type (calculated) See 'calculated (field type)'.

field type (date) See 'date (field type)'.

field type (graphic) See 'graphic (field type)'.

field type (link) See 'link (field type)'.

field type (number) See 'number (field type)'.

field type (numeric, text, graphic, date, time) The type of data which is to be stored in a field. You set up the field types when you create a new database.

field type (object) See 'object (field type)'.

field type (text) See 'text (field type)'.

field type (time) See 'time (field type)'.

field type check (validation) Ensures the correct type of data is entered.

file Information held on backing storage or in memory. Files may hold data or programs.

file (database structure) A collection of structured data on a particular topic.

file server Provides central disk storage for users' programs and data on a network.

file size The amount of space taken up by a file when it is being held on a backing storage medium such as hard disk or flash ROM. The factors which affect file size and quality are resolution, colour depth and sampling rate.

file transfer (attachment) Sending a file over the internet alongside an email message.

File Vault® The name given to one method of encrypting backing storage.

FileMaker™ Pro A commercial database package.

Firefox® A web browser application.

firewall A system (hardware or software) designed to prevent unauthorised access to or from a private network. Contains rules and conditions which specify what is and is not allowed to pass through.

Firewire® IEEE 1394 – a serial connection with maximum data transfer rates of 400 and 800 Mbps. Also called i.Link™.

fixed loops The purpose of a fixed loop is to repeat a set of program statements a predetermined number of times.

flash ROM A solid-state storage medium used in flash cards.

flat file (database structure) A database which is contained in a single table.

flexible access The ability to access a user's files from any computer on a network.

floating point representation A method of representing real numbers by using a mantissa and an exponent.

flow chart A diagram made up of differently shaped boxes connected with arrows to show each step in a program.

folder An area on backing storage where files may be stored (also called a directory on some systems).

font-family An HTML tag.

font-size An HTML tag.

foreign key (database structure) A field in a table which links to the primary key in a related table.

formatting (a disk) Produces invisible tracks and sectors on the surface of a magnetic disk. Other types of storage media may also be formatted to prepare them for use. See 'initialise'.

forward button A button on a web browser which takes the user to the next page. Only works as intended if the user has first selected the backward button.

frame rate The number of frames of a video displayed per second.

freeware Free software which you may use on any number of computer systems without paying any money.

FTP File Transfer Protocol.

FTTC Fibre To The Cabinet.

FTTH Fibre To The Home.

FTTP Fibre To The Premises.

function (pre-defined) Similar to a procedure, but returns a single value to a program.

Fused Deposition Modelling (FDM) A method of 3-D printing.

Gb Gigabyte

GDN Graphical Design Notation.

GIF Graphics Interchange Format.

Gigabit Ethernet Ethernet with a data transmission speed of 1 Gbps.

Gigabits per second (Gbps) A measure of data transfer speed across a network or via an interface.

Gigabyte (Gb) 1024 Megabytes (1024 × 1024 × 1024 bytes).

Gigahertz (GHz) A processor's clock speed is measured in Gigahertz (GHz).

GIGO Garbage In Garbage Out: if a mistake is made with input to a computer system, the output will also have mistakes.

global warming When the temperature of the earth's atmosphere increases, e.g. due to greenhouse gases.

graphic Includes diagrams, photographs and any other images.

graphic (field type) A field which holds a picture.

graphical design notation (GDN) A design notation which uses lines and boxes to show the structure of a program, e.g. a structure diagram.

graphical object An image which is displayed on the screen as part of a computer program. Another name for a graphical object is a sprite.

Graphical User Interface (GUI) An interface which enables the user to work with icons and a mouse, e.g. a WIMP interface.

graphics card A device which controls the quality of output on a monitor.

Graphics Interchange Format (GIF) A standard file format for storing images, with a maximum of 256 colours.

graphics package A piece of software used for the production of, or editing, graphics.

graphics resolution The quality of the picture is determined by the resolution of the graphics available.

graphics tablet A flat, pressure-sensitive board used with a pen or a stylus, used for Computer Aided Design (CAD).

Greenfoot A high-level programming language.

greenhouse gases Have an environmental impact because they absorb heat and can cause global warming.

guided navigation See 'faceted navigation'.

hacking Gaining unauthorised access to a computer system; usually illegal.

handler A master computer which controls a number of zombie computers.

handwriting recognition A system for computer input which involves writing on a touch-sensitive screen using a pen or stylus.

hard copy A printed copy of your work, usually on paper.

hard disk A circular metal disk coated with magnetic material.

hard disk drive A storage device which holds a magnetic hard disk.

hardware The physical parts or devices which make up a computer system.

hardware firewall An electronic circuit in a router which prevents unauthorised access to a network from the outside.

hardware platform A particular combination of processor and operating system.

HCI Human Computer Interface.

head An HTML tag.

header An area at the top of every page of a document. A book header may show the chapter number.

headphones A personal sound output device.

headset Used to take part in virtual reality.

health Computer systems can affect your health, depending on the amount of time that you spend using them.

Health and Safety Regulations   The Health and Safety (Display Screen Equipment) Regulations 1992 cover the use of computers in the workplace.

hertz (Hz)   Clock speed. A measure of processor speed.

hexadecimal   A number system which uses base 16.

hierarchical filing system   A filing system which has a top level or root directory and one or more sub-directories.

hierarchical navigation   A method of web page navigation.

high-level program code (language)   A computer language that uses normal or everyday language is called a high-level language.

history (browser)   A list of previously visited web pages.

hit   The results of a successful search, e.g. using a database program or a search engine.

home button   A button on a browser which loads the home page.

home page   The first page on a website or the URL which is loaded when a browser application is first opened.

honeypot   A website designed to attract and trap hackers.

host computer   A physical device which, when connected to a network, provides services to another connected computer.

hotspot (web page)   A special area on a web page which is normally invisible when viewed in a browser; the mouse pointer changes shape when it is moved over a hotspot.

hotspot (wireless)   A hotspot is an area where wireless network signals may be received, and a computer may connect to the network.

href   An HTML tag.

HTML   HyperText Mark-up Language.

HTTP   HyperText Transfer Protocol.

HTTPS   HyperText Transfer Protocol Secure.

Human Computer Interface (HCI)   The way in which the computer and the user communicate.

hyperlink   Link between World Wide Web pages, documents or files. Activated by clicking on text which acts as a button, or on a particular area of the screen like a graphic.

HyperText Mark-up Language (HTML)   Used to create web pages which may be viewed by using a web browser.

Hz   (Hertz) Clock speed. See 'hertz'.

icon   Symbol or picture on a screen; part of a graphical user interface.

identity theft   When someone pretends to be someone else in order to carry out fraud.

IEEE 1394   The Firewire® standard.

IEEE 802.11   The WiFi standard.

IF (conditional statement)   The IF structure is suitable for use when a single selection (or a limited number of selections) is to be made.

image quality   Increasing the resolution and colour depth of an image will improve the quality and also increase the file size, since more data must be stored.

img   An HTML tag.

impact on the environment   See 'environmental impact'.

implementation   Changing the program design into instructions that the computer can understand and the production of internal documentation.

inconsistent (database)   A database which contains data duplication or other errors.

indentation   A structured listing is a program listing which uses indentations (formatting) to show some of the structure of the program.

index (search engine)   Searches the internet for different words and builds up an index of these words and where they can be found. This allows users to search for particular words in their indexes.

index/element number A number which identifies a single element of an array.

information Data with structure.

Infrastructure as a service (Iaas) Provides services which involve hardware, data storage, networking and bandwidth.

initialise To format a backing storage device before use.

inkjet printer Works by squirting small droplets of ink onto paper, through tiny holes in the print head.

input To enter data into a computer system.

input device A device which allows data to be entered into a computer system.

input validation An algorithm used to check that data input is within a certain (acceptable) range.

input–process–output The sequence of operations carried out in a computer system.

insert To put in new information.

insert (modification error) An error in a database caused by inserting the wrong information.

instruction set Instructions built into a processor.

interactive whiteboard An input device for multimedia.

interactivity (user requirements) The 'feel' of a web page, e.g. the feedback that is received from selection.

interface Part of a computer system that allows different devices to communicate with the processor by compensating for any differences in their operation. Interface functions include temporary data storage; compensating for differences in speed between the CPU and peripherals; and data conversion.

interlacing When a low-quality version of an image is displayed while the rest of the data is still being downloaded.

internal commentary (documentation) So called because it is contained inside the program itself, as part of the language statements. Internal commentary has no effect on the running of a program. Helps to explain what the code is doing throughout the program.

internal documentation See 'internal commentary'.

internal hard disk drive A disk drive which is inside a computer system.

internal hyperlink Takes the user to another page within the same website.

internet A Wide Area Network spanning the globe. It can be thought of as many different, smaller networks connected together.

Internet Explorer® A web-browser application.

internet fraud (online fraud) The use of services available on the internet to defraud people of money, or to carry out identity theft.

Internet Service Provider (ISP) A company that provides a host computer to which the user can connect in order to access the internet.

interpreted language A language which is translated and run one instruction at a time.

interpreter Changes one line of a high-level language program into machine code and then executes it before moving on to the next line, each time the program is run.

IP Internet Protocol.

ISP Internet Service Provider.

iteration Repeating a section of code contained in a loop.

Java™ A compiled language used to create stand-alone programs.

JavaScript® Makes web pages more dynamic and interactive.

Joint Photographic Expert Group (JPEG) A standard file format for the storage of graphic images. 24-bit graphic format which allows 16.7 million colours and uses lossy compression.

joystick Used mainly for computer games, to control the movement of a character or icon on the screen.

JPEG Joint Photographic Expert Group.

Kb Kilobyte.

key field Used to uniquely identify a record in a database.

keyboard An input device consisting of a set of buttons or keys marked with characters.

keyboard shortcuts A combination of keys that can be used instead of having to select an item from a menu.

keylogging (keystroke logging) The process of recording every key that is pressed on a keyboard without the user being aware that it is being done.

keyword A word which is used to search for an item in a database.

Kilobyte (Kb) One Kilobyte has 1024 bytes.

LAN Local Area Network.

lands Areas between pits on a CD-ROM.

laptop A portable computer which folds and has an LCD screen and keyboard in a single unit. It is powered from batteries and may be operated while travelling.

laser printer Uses a special powder called toner to produce the image on the paper.

LCD Liquid Crystal Display.

LCD monitor An output device which accepts a video signal directly from a computer and displays the output on a screen. Basic LCD monitors use a fluorescent tube as a backlight.

least significant bit The rightmost bit in a binary number.

LED Light Emitting Diode.

LED (Light Emitting Diode) monitor An output device which accepts a video signal directly from a computer and displays the output on a screen; uses LEDs to backlight its screen.

linear navigation A method of web page navigation.

Linear Tape-Open™ (Ultrium™) A type of tape backup system.

link (field type) A field which contains a hyperlink or URL.

linked tables (database structure) Tables in a relational database may be linked by using key fields.

Liquid Crystal Display (LCD) A type of flat-screen display which is used in calculators and palmtop and laptop computers because of its low power consumption and light weight.

LiveCode® A high-level programming language.

Local Area Network (LAN) Covers a small area such as a room or a building and is usually owned by an individual, a single company or an organisation such as a school.

local storage Backing storage which is part of the computer system in use as opposed to network or cloud storage.

log on The way of identifying the user to a computer system (or to a network).

logic bomb A virus which waits to be triggered by a particular action.

logic(al) errors Mistakes in the design of a program.

logical operation The set of logical operators includes AND, OR and NOT. They are used to link two or more conditions to create a complex condition.

loop/iteration/repetition A programming construct used to allow a process to take place over and over again.

loop counter Part of a loop which determines how many times it will repeat.

lossless compression Compression which does not lose any data from the original.

lossy compression Compression which throws away some of the original data.

loudspeaker A sound output device.

Mac OS X® A type of operating system program.

machine code The computer's own language. It is written in binary (1 and 0).

macro A set of keystrokes and instructions that are recorded, saved and assigned to a single key or a combination of keys. When the key code is typed, the recorded keystrokes and instructions are carried out.

macro virus A virus which can infect applications such as Microsoft Word or Excel which allow the creation of macros.

magnetic storage device Uses magnetism to store data; devices include disks and tapes.

magnetic tape A backing storage medium which uses plastic tape, coated on one side with magnetic material.

magnetic tape drive Uses magnetic tape.

main memory Consists of a number of storage locations, each with a unique address. Made up of Random Access Memory (RAM) and Read Only Memory (ROM).

main memory capacity The number of storage locations available in a computer system.

main steps The main steps in an algorithm become the main program and the refinements of each sub-problem become the code in the procedures.

mainframe A very large computer system which can process a very large amount of data at high speed.

maintainability How easy it is to correct or update the software in future.

maintenance Involves making changes in the form of corrections or updates to the program at some time in the future and is made easier by good practice in software development.

malware (malicious software) Software that has been deliberately created to disrupt the operation of a computer system or to gain illegal access to it in order to gather information. Includes viruses, worms, Trojans, spyware and keylogging software.

mantissa In a floating point number, the mantissa holds the digits of a number, and the size of the mantissa determines the precision of the number.

manual testing Testing a program by hand without using a computer system.

margin-left An HTML tag.

mark-up language (including HTML) A programming language used for describing how text and other media are presented to the user.

master computer A computer which controls a zombie.

Mb Megabyte.

Mbps Megabits per second.

meaningful identifier A name used for any part of a program, such as the name of a subprogram or sub-routine (procedure or function) and not just limited to variable names.

meaningful variable name Contains one or more words which describe it. Using meaningful variable names is a good way of improving the readability of a program.

media types Include graphics, sound, text and video.

media types (sound) See 'sound (media type)'.

media types (text) See 'text (media type)'.

media types (video) See 'video (media type)'.

medium An object upon which software and data may be held, such as a CD-ROM.

Megabits per second (Mbps) A measure of data transfer speed across a network or via an interface.

Megabyte (Mb) One Megabyte has 1024 Kilobytes.

Megapixels 1024 × 1024 pixels (approximately 1 million).

memory The part of a computer where the data is held while it is being processed and the programs are held while they are being run.

memory address A binary number used to identify a storage location in main memory.

memory capacity The amount of data that may be held.

memory card Contains flash ROM storage medium–used in cameras and other devices such as phones.

menu A list on screen from which choices may be made by the user.

microphone Used to allow sound to be input to a computer system.

microprocessor The processor of a microcomputer.

Microsoft Access® A commercial database program.

Microsoft Windows® A type of operating system program.

microwave transmission A telecommunications method.

MOD (MODULUS) Returns the remainder when the first number is divided by the second.

modem A device used to connect a computer system to a telephone line. Short for MODulator–DEModulator.

modification error Modification errors include insert, delete and update.

MODULO (MODULUS) See 'MOD'.

money mule A person who uses a bank account to transfer funds illegally.

monitor An output device which accepts a video signal directly from a computer and displays the output on a screen.

monochrome Black and white (display or printer).

most significant bit The leftmost bit in a binary number.

Motion Picture Expert Group (MPEG) Video file format. MPEG-1, MPEG-2 and MPEG-4 (MP4) are all standards used to store video.

mouse Controls the movement of a pointer on a screen.

MP3 (MPEG-1 Audio Layer-3) File format which is compressed to around one tenth of the size of the original file, yet preserves the quality.

MPEG Motion Picture Expert Group.

MPEG-4 (MP4) A compressed video format.

multi-access Many users online at the same time.

multi-function device A printer combined with a scanner.

multimedia The presentation of information by a computer system using graphics, animation, sound and text.

multimedia projector Connects to a graphics card and displays the contents of the computer screen on a wall or interactive whiteboard.

multi-processor A computer containing more than one processor.

multi-programming Many programs in use at the same time.

multi-tasking See 'multi-programming'.

multi-user Many users online at the same time.

nanosecond 10^{-9} seconds.

NAS Network Attached Storage.

native resolution The resolution of an LCD monitor is fixed when it is manufactured.

natural language queries A normal sentence entered into a search engine, instead of separate keywords.

navigation How the user finds their way around the information system.

navigation methods Include browser features, menus, searching, hyperlinks, context-sensitive navigation, breadcrumbs, guided navigation, tag clouds and site maps.

navigation structure   The way in which the pages or screens in the information system are arranged.

nested loops   Loops which are contained inside other loops.

netiquette   A way of behaving when connected to the internet or sending email messages.

network   A linked set of computer systems that are capable of sharing programs and data and sending messages between them.

Network Interface Card (NIC)   A small circuit board that is fitted inside a computer system to allow it to communicate with a computer network.

network manager   The person in charge of the network. He or she will be responsible for all of the computer systems attached to the company network.

networked computer   When a computer is part of a network.

NIC   Network Interface Card.

normal test data   Data which is within the limits that a program should be able to deal with.

NOT (logical operator)   Combines two conditions.

notebook   Another name for a laptop computer.

novice user   A beginner.

number (field type)   Only stores numbers.

numeric keypad   A small keyboard used to speed the entry of numeric data.

numeric variable   A variable which can hold a number that may have a fractional part.

object   The item of data which is involved in a process.

object attributes   Numbers used to define the features of a vector graphic image.

object code   A machine code program produced as the result of translation by a compiler.

object (field type)   May contain a variety of different types of data, such as a presentation, video, spreadsheet or a bit-mapped graphic file.

OCR   Optical Character Recognition.

offline   Not connected to a remote computer system or a network.

OLED   Organic Light Emitting Diode.

one-dimensional array   An array with only one subscript.

online   Connected to a remote computer system or a network.

online fraud   (internet fraud) The use of services available on the internet to defraud people of money, or to carry out identity theft.

online help   Help which is available in the form of information screens when using a computer program.

online tutorial   A series of guided lessons on how to use a computer program.

operating system   A program that controls the entire operation of the computer and any devices which are attached to it.

operation   A process which is carried out on an item of data.

Opera™   A web-browser application.

optical   Using light.

Optical Character Recognition (OCR)   Characters can be read in automatically from a page of text. A scanner with OCR software may be used to input text into a word-processing package.

optical fibre   A communications medium which is made of thin strands of glass. It is capable of a very high data-transfer rate and is immune to interference from electrical signals.

optical mouse   A mouse with a light and a detector underneath it.

optical storage   A form of non-magnetic storage, e.g. CD-ROM, which uses tiny holes called pits.

optical storage device A backing storage device which can use optical media such as CD/DVD/Blu-ray Discs™.

OR (logical operator) Combines two conditions.

Organic Light Emitting Diode (OLED) Uses an organic chemical compound as its light source.

organisational information system An information system which collects, organises, stores, processes and outputs information for the benefit of a company or organisation.

OS compatibility A program is said to be OS compatible when it is capable of running under a particular operating system.

output Data passed out of a computer system.

output device A device which allows data to be displayed or passed out of a computer system.

overflow When a number is too large to fit in a storage location.

package A computer program and its associated documentation.

padlock icon Clicking on the padlock icon on a secure web page should display a digital certificate.

page See 'web page'.

pages per minute (ppm) A measure of how fast a printer can print.

paint package (bit-mapped) Bit-mapped packages paint pictures by changing the colour of the pixels which make up the screen display.

palmtop A hand-held computer with a touchscreen or a small keyboard.

parallel data transmission Sends each bit which makes up a character simultaneously along separate data lines.

parallel interface An interface which uses parallel data transmission, sending each bit which makes up a character simultaneously along separate data lines.

Parallels Desktop® An emulator program.

parameter Information about a data item being supplied to a subprogram when it is called into use.

partial transparency Not completely transparent. PNG images may be partially transparent.

password A secret code that you use to gain access to private information on a computer system or to log on to a network.

pathname A name used to identify a file or a web page in a hierarchical directory structure or in a URL.

payload The part of the malware that infects the computer system.

Pb Petabyte.

PDF Portable Document Format.

peer-to-peer network Made up of computers, all of which have the same status. Users' data on a peer-to-peer network is stored locally.

peripheral Any device that may be attached to a computer system for input, output or backing storage.

permanent memory Another name for ROM (Read Only Memory).

personal data Data which relates to a living individual who can be identified from that data.

Petabyte (Pb) One Petabyte has 1024 Terabytes.

phishing An attempt to trick someone into giving away personal information using the internet by pretending to be a well-known company or a bank.

photographic A type of data produced by a digital still camera. A bit-mapped graphic image.

phrases A group of terms enclosed in quotes and entered into a search engine.

physical hazards Include electrocution and fire risks.

physiological biometrics Include a person's face, fingerprints, hands, irises and DNA.

picture element Pixel. A tiny dot used to make up a picture on a screen.

PIN Personal Identification Number.

pits The holes in a CD or DVD which, along with lands, help to store the data.

pixel Picture element. A tiny dot used to make up a picture on a screen.

pixelation When an image is enlarged so that the pixels become visible.

plagiarism Copying work which, has been created by another person and passing it off as your own.

platform Refers to the hardware and software which make up a particular type of computer system.

Platform as a service (Paas) Provides software and development tools which help the user to create applications (apps).

plotter A device for producing hard copy which can print out onto very large paper sizes.

PNG Portable Network Graphics.

podcast A sound track, video or other digital media designed to be played on a mobile player, usually consisting of a series of episodes.

pointer A shape displayed on screen which is used to select from a menu. Usually controlled by a mouse or track pad.

POP Post Office Protocol.

portability of software When programs written on one computer system may be used on a different computer system with minimal alteration.

portable devices Laptop computers and smartphones that may be operated while on the move.

Portable Document Format (PDF) A file format developed by Adobe® Systems Inc. in order to exchange complete documents between different computer platforms, including Windows, Mac OS® and mobile. PDF files may contain text, graphics, video, audio and clickable hyperlinks.

Portable Network Graphic (PNG) Incorporates the advantages of GIF files, without the limitations, i.e. more than 256 colours may be represented.

precautions when giving away or selling a computer You should take precautions when disposing of an old computer to prevent identity theft.

pre-defined function (with parameters) A function that has already been created and is part of or built in to a programming language. See 'parameters'.

presence check (validation) Checks to make sure that a field has not been left empty.

primary key (database structure) A field used to uniquely identify a record in a database.

printer A device used to produce a printout or a hard copy of the output from a computer.

printer buffer An area of memory used for the transfer of the data between the computer and a peripheral, in this case a printer.

printer driver A program which takes the codes in a document and translates them into the appropriate code for the printer in use. A type of device driver.

printer server A server which allows all of the client stations to use a printer controlled by it.

problem description The problem you are given to solve, described in your own words.

procedure Produces an effect in a program.

processor The main part of the computer. It is made up of the control unit, the arithmetic and logic unit (ALU) and the registers. The processor is the part of the computer where all the sorting, searching, calculating and decision-making goes on.

processor clock Produces a series of electronic pulses at a very high rate.

processor clock speed (Hz) Measured in Gigahertz (GHz).

program See 'computer program'.

program design The process of planning a solution to a problem.

program listing A printout or hard copy of the program code.

program maintenance Changing a program, often some time after it has been written.

programmer A person who writes computer programs.

protocol A set of rules that determines how something is to be done.

pseudocode (design notation) Uses normal or everyday language to describe the design of a program.

quality How closely a file matches when compared to the original.

RAM Random Access Memory.

random access Being able to locate a data item straight away, wherever it is stored on disk or in main memory.

Random Access Memory (RAM) A set of microchips that stores data temporarily. The data is lost when the computer is switched off.

range (validation) A range check keeps the data within given limits.

Read Only Memory (ROM) One or more microchips that stores data permanently. The data is not lost when the computer is switched off.

read power The power of the laser beam is reduced when reading a CD or DVD Recordable.

readability (user requirements) An information system is readable when it is easy to read and understand. May be tested by looking at the level of difficulty of the language used.

readability of code How easy it is for another person to understand your program code. See 'internal commentary'.

read/write head Part of the hard disk drive which reads and writes the data to and from the surface of the disk.

real numbers, storage of See 'floating point representation'.

real variable (data type) A variable which can hold a number that may have a fractional part.

real-time A system which responds immediately to input.

record (database structure) A collection of structured data on a particular person or thing, containing one or more fields.

refinements The main steps in the algorithm become the main program and the refinements of each sub-problem become the code in the procedures.

registers Used to hold data being processed, program instructions being run and memory addresses to be accessed.

relational database When a database contains links between tables, it is referred to as a relational database.

relational operations Use relational operators to compare data and produce an answer of true or false. The set of arithmetical operators includes add (+), subtract (-), multiply (*), divide (/), exponent (^) and modulus (MOD).

relative URL addressing If the URL points to a page within the same website (i.e. internal), then it is known as a relative URL (relative addressing).

reliable data link A data link is reliable if it is not likely to be affected by interference which may change the signal.

repetition Doing something over again, e.g. in a loop, either conditional or fixed.

repetitive strain injury (RSI) Continual use of a keyboard and mouse can cause limb disorders.

resolution The amount of detail which can be shown on a screen or on a printout.

resolution dependence When the resolution of an image is fixed in a bit-mapped package and cannot be scaled up without losing quality. See 'pixelation'.

resolution independence In a vector graphics package, the resolution of the screen has no effect on the resolution of the printout.

resource sharing A benefit of a LAN is that resources such as printers may be shared between all of the machines.

restricted choice (validation) Gives users a list of options to choose from and so limits the input to pre-approved answers.

RGB (Red Green Blue) colour system Used in a monitor and in HTML for the colours on a web page.

Rich Text Format (RTF) Holds information about the alignment, typefaces, sizes, colour and styles used in the document.

RISC Reduced Instruction Set Computer.

rogue security suite Software which pretends to be a security suite but actually installs malware on a computer system.

ROM Read Only Memory.

ROM software Software which is distributed or stored on Read Only Memory.

Rother J The first ever virus to infect other computers.

RSI Repetitive strain injury.

RTF Rich Text Format.

Safari® A web-browser application.

sample run A hard copy or a screen display of the (input and) output from a computer program.

sampling Taking measurements of a sound in order to convert it from analogue to digital.

sampling depth The number of bits that are used for each measurement.

sampling rate The number of times in one second that measurements of the sound are taken.

satellite links See 'microwave transmission'.

Scalable Vector Graphics (SVG) Scalable Vector Graphics is one method of representing vector graphics on a computer system.

scale graphic Changing the size of a graphic by enlarging or reducing it.

scanner Used to input printed drawings, photographs or text directly into a computer. A 3-D scanner may be used to scan an object and create a data file containing its measurements.

Scratch® A high-level language program which uses graphical objects.

screen The part of a monitor which displays the output.

script A program written in a scripting language.

scripting language A programming language that allows the user to carry out or automate tasks. Examples include JavaScript®, VBScript® and AppleScript®.

scroll Moving the display on the screen by using the cursor keys, mouse or track pad.

SCSI Small Computer Systems Interface.

SDHC A type of flash ROM storage used in cameras and other devices such as phones.

SDXC A type of flash ROM storage used in cameras and other devices such as phones.

search Allows you to look for specific information in a database or on the World Wide Web.

search engine A website which is designed to help you to find information on the World Wide Web.

search string A keyword or words used in a search.

searching Looking for an item using a database program or a search engine and perhaps one or more keywords.

searching on a field A simple search performed on only one field with a single condition.

searching on multiple fields A complex search searching on multiple fields or using multiple conditions.

secure A computer system is secure if it is unable to be accessed by an unauthorised person, and is not affected by malware.

Secure Digital (SD) card A type of flash ROM storage used in cameras and other devices such as phones.

security A method of making sure that data is private or that only authorised people can see the data, e.g. using passwords, encryption and physical security.

security precautions Include anti-virus software, passwords, encryption, biometrics, security protocols and firewalls, and the use of security suites.

security protocols A sequence of operations that makes sure data is protected.

security suites A collection of software which is sold together as a single package and contains programs which protect computers against a variety of malware. May include anti-virus, firewall, anti-spam, anti-spyware, parental control, privacy and phishing protection.

selection Making a choice or deciding something. Based on one or more conditions, used together with a control structure such as IF.

selection construct An IF statement in a high-level programming language is an example of a selection construct.

Selective Laser Sintering (SLS) A method of 3-D printing.

semantics The semantics of a particular instruction is its meaning or its effect.

sentinel (terminating) value Often used to end a conditional loop.

sequence The order in which a set of instructions is carried out or the order in which a set of data is stored on backing storage.

sequential access Access to data which can only be read in the order it was written.

sequential navigation (linear) Useful for processes that may be followed in a set order, like reading a story or making a purchase.

serial access See 'sequential access'.

serial data transmission Sends the bits for each character in the data one after another along the same data line.

server A computer that handles requests for data, email, file transfers and other network services from other computers.

simple condition A condition made using only one relational operator, for example age=18, average_temperature < 15.

single platform Software which is capable of working on only one platform.

site map One navigation method for a website.

SLS Selective Laser Sintering.

smartphone A mobile phone which has its own operating system and is capable of running a variety of applications.

SMTP Simple Mail Transfer Protocol.

SOC System On Chip.

social engineering Tricking someone into performing an action or giving away confidential information.

software The programs run by the hardware of the computer.

Software as a service (Saas) A software delivery model in which applications are held on, and run, from the cloud.

software development process A series of seven stages for the development of software: analysis, design, implementation, testing, documentation, evaluation and maintenance.

software firewall Contains rules and conditions which specify what is and is not allowed to pass through.

software requirements See 'system requirements'.

software specification A precise description of the problem.

solid-state storage device Contains no moving parts. Example: USB flash ROM drive.

sort on more than one field A complex sort.

sort on one field A simple sort.

sorting Allows the user to arrange the records in a database into a certain alphabetic or numeric order, such as: ascending order (a $\rightarrow$ z or 0$\rightarrow$ 9) or descending order (z $\rightarrow$ a or 9 $\rightarrow$ 0).

sound (media type) Includes music or any other noise produced by a computer.

sound card Allows sound to be both input to and output from a computer system. A sound card captures sound in a process called sampling. Also improves the quality of sound output from games and multimedia applications.

sound card (input) In order to input sound into a computer the sound must be changed from analogue into digital. The sound card carries out the analogue-to-digital conversion in a process called sampling.

sound card (output) In order to output sound from a computer the sound must be changed from digital to analogue. The sound card carries out the digital-to-analogue conversion.

source code The original high-level language program is called the source code and the machine code program produced by the translation is called the object code.

spam email messages Unsolicited electronic mail.

spammer An individual who sends out unsolicited email messages.

speech recognition Software which can recognise speech input by the user via a microphone.

speed (ppm) The rate at which a printer can print, measured in pages per minute.

sprite See 'graphical objects'.

spyware A type of malware which, when installed on a user's computer, collects information about them without their knowledge.

src An HTML tag.

SSD Solid-state drive.

SSL Secure Sockets Layer.

stand-alone computer When a computer is not part of a network.

standard algorithm Includes input validation, linear search, counting occurrences and finding minimum and maximum.

standard file format A way of storing data so that it can be understood by and transferred between different application packages.

storage The three methods of storage in a computer system are magnetic, optical and solid state.

storage device A device which holds a backing storage medium. Storage devices may be built in to the inside of a computer system or be external.

storage location A place in a computer's memory where an item of data may be held.

storage medium The substance which holds the data.

stored program A set of instructions which is held in a computer's memory.

storyboards A series of still drawings that maps out a proposed story over a number of separate panels.

string variable A variable which holds one or more characters.

structure diagram A diagram made up of different-shaped boxes containing text and linked by lines. It is usually used to explain the structure of a computer program.

structured listing A program listing which uses indentations (formatting) to show some of the structure of the program.

stylus A pen for use with a touchscreen or graphics tablet.

subject rights The Data Protection Act 1998 gives data subjects a right of access to their personal data and to have it amended if it is incorrect.

subscript Each element in an array is identified by the variable name and a subscript.

substrings String operations include joining strings, known as concatenation, and selecting parts of strings, known as substrings.

supercomputer The fastest and most powerful type of computer, used for intensive mathematical calculations such as weather forecasting.

SUPERSPEED USB USB version 3.

SVG Scalable Vector Graphics.

syntax The way in which you give instructions to the computer.

syntax error Occur when the syntax, or rules of the programming language, are broken. A mistake in a programming instruction, e.g. PTRIN instead of PRINT.

system on chip (SOC) A single chip which contains all of the components of a computer system.

system requirements To find out which platform a particular item of software requires, it is necessary to consult the system requirements.

tabbed browsing A method of opening several web pages in a single window.

table (database) A set of data items organised in rows and columns like a spreadsheet.

table (test data) Test data is used to test a program.

tablet computer A flat computer with a large touch-sensitive LCD screen as the main input and output device. It is powered from batteries and may be operated while travelling.

tag Each part of an HTML document is separated by a tag. Each tag has a start like this <> and an end tag like this </>.

tag clouds A list of terms, either displayed with numbers or in differently sized typefaces to show popularity.

Tagged Image File Format (TIFF) A standard file format for the storage of bit-mapped images.

tap Making a connection in order to intercept data being transmitted between sender and receiver.

tape drive A backing storage device which uses magnetic tape as the backing storage medium.

target audience The people who will use an information system.

Tb Terabyte.

TDN Textual Design Notation.

technical guide Explains how to install the software on to a computer system. Lists the type of computer system(s) upon which the software will run, and the installation requirements.

telecommunications link A data transmission medium for a Wide Area Network.

teleworking Working from home and communicating with your employer or workplace by using email.

template A readymade blank document, with placeholders for items like text and graphics. Using a template can speed up the creation of a document, because much of the page layout has already been done for you.

Terabyte (Tb) One Terabyte has 1024 Gigabytes.

terminal A piece of hardware consisting of a keyboard and a screen. A 'dumb' terminal does not have a processor.

terminating (sentinel) value Often used to end a conditional loop.

test data Used to test that a program works. There are three different types of test data: normal, extreme and exceptional.

testing Ensures that a computer program does not contain any mistakes and that it works as intended.

text Characters or symbols displayed on a screen or printed as hard copy on a printer.

text (media type) Any character which appears on a computer keyboard is text. The most common file format used for storing text is ASCII.

text editor Allows source code to be entered and edited.

text (field type) Used to hold letters, numbers and symbols.

text messaging A method of electronic communication using a mobile phone.

Textual Design Notation (TDN) Pseudocode is an example of a textual design notation.

Thin Film Transistor (TFT) A type of liquid crystal display screen used for high-quality output.

Thunderbolt® interface An interface which provides fast data transfer between computer and peripherals.

TIFF Tagged Image File Format.

time (field type) Can hold hours, minutes and seconds.

time bomb Malware that activates at a pre-set date and time.

title An HTML tag.

TLS Transport Layer Security.

toner Powder used in laser printers to create the image on paper.

total amount of memory RAM + ROM.

touch-sensitive screen / touchscreen Useful when it is not appropriate to use a mouse. A screen is an output device, so a touch-sensitive screen is both an input and an output device.

track pad / touchpad A flat touch-sensitive area used instead of a mouse to control a pointer. Movements of the user's finger over the plate control the movement of the pointer on the screen.

translation of high-level program code to binary (machine code) Converting a computer program from one language to another, e.g. from a high-level language to machine code.

translator program A computer program used to convert program code from one language to another, e.g. compiler, interpreter.

transmission medium The material which carries the data in a network, e.g. wired (cable) or wireless (WiFi).

tree navigation (hierarchical) The user requirements are visual layout, navigation, selection, consistency, interactivity, readability and accessibility.

Trojan A program that appears to be safe, but hidden inside is usually something harmful, like a worm or a virus.

True BASIC® A high-level programming language.

truncation Shortening a number by removing part of it.

two's complement A method of representing negative numbers in binary.

two-state machine A computer system is known as a two-state machine because the processing and storage devices in a computer system have one feature in common: they have two states only. These two states are 'on' and 'off' and are represented using the digits 1 for 'on' and 0 for 'off'.

Ultrium™ (Linear Tape-Open™) A type of tape backup system.

UML Unified Modelling Language.

Unicode (Universal Character Set) Designed to represent the writing schemes of all of the world's major languages.

Unified Modelling Language (UML) A general-purpose modelling language used to describe complete systems and not just software design.

Uniform Resource Locator (URL) A unique address for a specific file available on the internet (web address).

uninterruptible power supply (UPS) A battery which provides power to a computer in the event of a cut.

unique value A primary key has a unique value which identifies individual records in a database.

units of storage A quantity of data. The smallest unit of storage is a bit (1 or 0). Other units include: byte, Kb, Mb, Gb, Tb, Pb.

Universal Serial Bus (USB) A type of computer interface.

Unix® A type of operating system program.

unshielded twisted pair (UTP) A type of cabling used in a Local Area Network.

update For example, adding new data to a file.

update (modification error) An error caused by updating data in a database.

upgrade Obtaining a more recent version of software by downloading or installing from disk.

UPS Uninterruptible power supply.

URL Uniform Resource Locator.

usability (design) How easy it is to use and learn about an item.

USB Universal Serial Bus.

USB flash memory The media contained within a USB flash ROM drive.

USB flash ROM drive A solid-state storage device containing flash ROM. It connects to the computer via the USB interface.

use energy See 'energy use'.

user friendliness Programs that are easy to learn to use and help you understand as you are using them are called user-friendly programs.

user guide Explains how to operate the software once it is installed.

user identity Your name or a code which identifies you to a network. Usually used with a password.

user interface The way in which the computer and the user communicate.

user interface requirements Visual layout, navigation, selection, consistency, interactivity, readability and accessibility.

utility program A type of systems software designed to perform an everyday task, like formatting a disk.

UTP Unshielded Twisted Pair.

validation A check to make sure that an item of data is sensible and allowable. A range check is one way of validating data.

variable The name that a programmer uses to identify the contents of a storage location.

VBScript® Works in a variety of different Microsoft applications and is used in a similar manner to JavaScript®, when used with Internet Explorer®.

vector graphics Vector packages work by drawing objects on the screen. Vector graphics are stored as list of attributes, rather than a bit map.

video (media type) Data made up of a sequence of moving or 'live' action images.

video conferencing The use of communications links to conduct meetings between people who are geographically separated.

video quality Increasing the resolution and colour depth of a video image (or the sampling rate of an audio file) will improve the quality and also increase the file size, since more data must be stored.

video streaming Video being transmitted over a network and played as it is being received without downloading or saving.

virtual reality Reproducing the outside world digitally within a computer system. The user interacts with the virtual reality by wearing a headset and gloves.

virus A program which can copy or replicate itself and infect other programs or computers.

virus checker An anti-virus program.

Visual Basic® A high-level programming language.

visual layout The way a program looks on a monitor screen.

visual display unit (VDU) Made up of a monitor and a keyboard. The screen is the part of a monitor or VDU which displays the output. May be used as a terminal.

voice output Speech produced by a computer system usually by special software and a loudspeaker.

voice recognition Recognising speech input by the user via a microphone. Used for controlling devices and also for dictating text into word-processing documents.

volatile memory Memory whose contents are erased when the power is switched off, e.g. RAM.

VRAM Video Random Access Memory.

VRML Virtual Reality Modelling Language.

walled garden A closed system where the service provider has total control over content, e.g. phone apps.

WAN Wide Area Network.

Waste Electrical and Electronic Equipment (WEEE) Directive Aims to recycle at least 85 per cent of electrical and electronics waste by 2016.

WAV WAVeform audio file format (WAV) is the native sound format for Windows®.

web address See '(URL) Uniform Resource Locator'.

web browser A program that allows the user to browse or surf through the World Wide Web.

web filter A program which prevents access to specific web sites or pages.

web navigation A type of navigation through an information system.

web page A single page of information on a website.

web proxy A server used to access web pages requested by other computers on a network.

web safe colours A set of colours for web pages which will show up correctly in a web browser.

web server A computer that provides World Wide Web services to a network.

webcam A small digital camera used to capture images which may be transmitted across a network. A webcam may be used for video conferencing.

website A collection of related web pages that may be accessed from a single home page.

white hat A type of hacker.

white space The empty part of a screen or web page. Helps to focus the reader's attention upon what is important.

Wide Area Network (WAN) Covers a large geographical area, such as a country or a continent.

WiFi The Wireless Fidelity Alliance standard for wireless networking.

wildcard character The wildcard operator* represents any information. This allows users to search for results with similar information, such as names beginning with Jo*.

WIMP environment A type of human computer interface which uses Windows, Icons, Menus and Pointers.

windows Areas of the screen set aside for a particular purposes, such as displaying files or documents.

wireframe A diagram or sketch used to represent the appearance and function of a website.

wireless A method or a way of transmitting data without using a physical connection, e.g. radio waves or infrared.

wireless hotspot An area where wireless network signals may be received and a computer may connect to a network.

Wireless Network Interface Card Most laptop computers are fitted with Wireless Network Interface Cards in order to access networks without a physical connection.

WLAN A wireless Local Area Network.

word processor A program used for writing and editing text.

wordle A graphic formed from words, the size of each word being determined by its importance.

workgroup computing A type of computing in which more than one user may edit the same document.

World Wide Web (WWW) A collection of information held in multimedia form on the internet.

worm A stand-alone program which copies or replicates itself in order to spread to other computer systems.

write protect switch A switch on a flash ROM memory card or other backing storage media which protects against accidental deletion.

WYSIWYG 'What You See Is What You Get'. What you see on a screen is exactly the same as the way it will be printed.

XGA (eXtended Graphics Array) 1024×768 pixels.

zombie A computer used to carry out a DOS and DDOS attack.

zombie army A group of zombie computers.

Index

Answers

1 Because the components of the processing and storage devices only have two states.

2 a) 2 (0,1)
  b) 10 (0–9)

3 a) A single binary digit: 1 or 0.
  b) A group of eight bits.

4 a) 1111 1111
  b) 255

5 a) 11
  c) 170
  e) 85
  g) 51
  i) 228

  b) 159
  d) 254
  f) 204
  h) 153
  j) 155

6 a) 0111 1010
  c) 1111 1111
  e) 0000 1110
  g) 0111 1111
  i) 1011 0011

  b) 1100 0001
  d) 0011 1000
  f) 0100 1110
  h) 1111 1010
  j) 0111 0000

7 Student's own answer

8 Student's own answer

9 a) 11.23
  b) If all the lights were on, the numbers would be too large to give the correct time, for example 15 hours on a 12-hour watch.

10 a) 128 64 32 16 8 4 2 1
   b) By using powers of two or by doubling each place value starting from one.

11 a) A whole number with no fractional part.
   b) Any number, which may or may not have a fractional part.

12 By using a mantissa, which holds the digits of the number, and an exponent, which holds the power.

13 a) The digits of the number.
   b) The power.

14 a) Mantissa 1110001 exponent 11.
   b) Mantissa 10000101 exponent 111.

15 Two's complement.

16 a) +6 = 0000 0110   −6 = 1111 1010
   b) +25 = 0001 1001 −25 = 1110 0111
   c) +92 = 0101 1100 −92 = 1010 0100
   d) +120 = 0111 1000 −120 = 1000 1000

17 Petabyte, Terabyte, Gigabyte, Megabyte, Kilobyte, byte, bit

18 a) 8
   b) 1024
   c) 1024
   d) 8 388 608

19 a) 1 Kilobyte
   b) 1 Gigabyte

20 a) Gigabytes or Terabytes
   b) Gigabytes

21 a) A letter, number or symbol on the computer keyboard.
   b) A list of all the characters, symbols and numbers which can be produced by a keyboard.

22 a) American Standard Code for Information Interchange.
   b) 128
   c) ASCII is a seven-bit code, so two to the power seven (2^7) gives 128.
   d) i) 69
      ii) 101

23 Student's own answer.

24 WELCOME TO COMPUTING SCIENCE!

25 Unicode can represent many more characters than ASCII.

26 ASCII takes up less space than Unicode in the computer's memory and in backing storage.

27 A set of instructions that a computer can understand.

28 A computer language.

29 Java and Basic.

30 Machine code.

31 0 and 1 (binary)

32 It is just made up of 1s and 0s and nothing else.

33 A high-level language.

34 There is a direct relationship between the contents of the computer's memory (1 or 0) and the screen display.

35 A tiny dot on the screen – short for *picture element*.

36 Vector.

37 The amount of detail which can be shown on a screen or on a printout.

38 a) Bit-mapped.
   b) Zoom in to edit pixels, and try to separate overlapping parts of the image.

39 a) 8 bytes
   b) 1 byte
   c) ASCII

40

41 a) 37.5 Kilobytes
   b) 563.5 Kilobytes
   c) 219.7 Kilobytes
   d) 48.06 Megabytes
   e) 300 Kilobytes
   f) 13.2 Megabytes
   g) 3.4 Megabytes
   h) 192.3 Megabytes

42 4.88 Kilobytes

43 a) Data describing vector graphic objects.
   b) centre x, centre y, radius, fill.

44

Object	SVG code
Rectangle	`<rect x="90" y="80" width="75" height="65" stroke="red" stroke-width="5" fill="purple"/>`
Circle	`<circle cx="300" cy="76" r="90" stroke="black" stroke-width="1" fill="blue"/>`
Ellipse	`<ellipse cx="300" cy="150" rx="200" ry="80" fill="red"/>`
Line	`<line x1="77" y1="77" x2="300" y2="300" fill="black"/>`
Polygon	`<polygon points="220,100 300,210 170,250" fill="green"/>`
Text	`<text x="10" y="20">Here is some text</text>`

45 Each character in the code for vector graphics only requires one byte of storage, whereas a single pixel in a bit-mapped graphic may require as much as three bytes (24 bits).

46 Visual Basic® – learning programming
   HTML – creating web pages

47 A computer program used to convert program code from one language to another.

48 Compiler and interpreter.

49 The computer's processor can only understand programs written in machine code.

50 a) A translator program which changes one line of a high-level language program into machine code, and then executes it, before moving on to the next line.
   b) A program that can translate a high-level language program into machine code in a single operation.
   c) The original high-level language program.
   d) The machine code program produced by the translation.

51 An interpreter.

52 The interpreter must translate each instruction every time the program is run.

53 a) Machine code.
   b) High-level.

54 A compiler.

55 The source code is required if the program is to be maintained in the future.

56 The structure of a computer system.

57 All the physical parts of a computer system.

58 A single item of hardware.

59 Computer programs.

60 A computer cannot think for itself. It can only carry out instructions programmed into it.

61 The processor; memory; input, output and storage devices.

62 The processor.

63 The program.

64 Intel®.

65 Core i7 Haswell.

66 a) To store programs and data.
   b) Memory chips.

67 Two types of memory chip are RAM and ROM.

68 Computer buses are made of wires.

69 Computer buses link the processor to the other parts inside the computer system.

70 Three computer buses are address, data and control.

71 ALU, CU and Registers.

72 ALU (Arithmetic and Logic Unit).

73 CU (Control Unit).

74 Register.

75 The hardware and software which allow the processor to communicate with its peripheral devices.

76 A device connected to the outside of a computer system for input, output or backing storage.

77 Universal Serial Bus (USB).

78 Audio, USB, memory card, Ethernet.

79

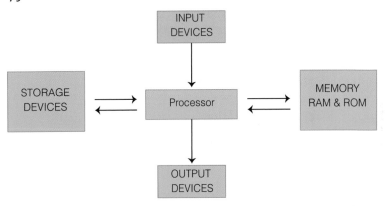

80 A processor and memory.

81 Silicon.

82 Computers cannot think for themselves – they must be programmed with instructions for them to be able to do anything.

83 a) Yes.
   b) To enable him to connect the camera to the computer.
   c) Firewire® or USB.

CHAPTER 2 Answers

1 The set of instructions that controls how a computer works.

2 Machine code and high-level.

3 The parts of a programming language which are used to create a computer program.

4 Thinking of a problem in such a way that makes it possible to solve it by using a computer system.

5 A series of steps to solve a problem.

6 a) Analysis.
  b) Design.
  c) Implementation.
  d) Testing.
  e) Documentation.
  f) Pseudocode.

7 The name that a programmer uses to identify the contents of a storage location.

8 Numbers and strings.

9 A list of characters, e.g. a word in a sentence.

10 Whole numbers.

11 A symbol, letter or number on the computer keyboard.

12 All numbers, both whole and fractional.

13 Data which has only two possible values – true or false.

14 An image which is displayed on the screen as part of a computer program.

15 Scratch.

16 `INPUT name`
`PRINT name`
`ask and wait`
`say name for 5 seconds`

17 To give a value to a variable.

18 Student's own answer, e.g: name$ = "Mark"
  age = 16

19 a) A process which is carried out on an item of data.
  b) The item of data which is involved in the process.

20 Arithmetical and relational.

21 Boolean.

22 Logical.

23 Arithmetical.

24 Equals and does not equal.

25 a) IF word = test
  b) IF mark >= 20
  c) IF counter = 0

26 Joining strings.

27 Substrings.

28 a) 38
  b) 1820

29 Sequence, selection, iteration/repetition/looping.

30 a) Sequence.
  b) Selection.
  c) Iteration/repetition/looping.

31 Student's own answer, e.g: IF age >= 17 THEN I can drive

32 a) Student's own answer, e.g: IF mark > = 12 THEN pass
  b) Student's own answer, e.g: IF mark < 0 or mark >20 then display message 'mark is outwith range'

33 Selection means making a choice – the control structure permits the number of choices and the condition decides which choice is to be made.

34 A loop.

35 Conditional.

36 Fixed.

37 To repeat a set of program statements a pre-determined number of times.

38 By using a loop counter, e.g:

```
FOR times = 1 TO 5 DO
```

39 To change the number of times that a fixed loop repeats.

40 Nested loop.

41 To manage the situation where the number of times repetition must take place is not known in advance.

42 The amount of data to be processed need not be known in advance.

43 The program statements following a conditional loop with test at start need not be run at all if the condition is not met. The program statements inside a conditional loop with test at end are always run at least once.

44 a) To end a conditional loop.
   b) Student's own answer, e.g:

```
REPEAT
SEND "Please enter a word" TO DISPLAY
RECEIVE word FROM KEYBOARD
UNTIL word = "stop"
```

45 A list of data items *of the same type* grouped together using a single variable name.

46 By the variable name and a subscript.

47 If it has a single number as its subscript.

48 So that the computer may set aside the correct amount of memory space for the array.

49 A section of a program.

50 Procedure and function.

51 A procedure produces an effect and a function returns a single value.

52 A calculation which is built in to a programming language.

53 SQR, LEN, INT

54 Information about a data item being supplied to a subprogram (function or procedure) when it is called into use.

1 To make sure that it solves the problem it is supposed to.

2 By using test data.

3 It would take too long to test a program with all possible sets of test data.

4 Normal, extreme and exceptional.

5 Calculate the expected results.

6 a) Normal and extreme.
  b) Exceptional.

7 Plan and record the results of testing a program.

8 An error which occurs when the rules of the programming language are broken.

9 Mis-spelling a keyword.

10 a) When the line containing the mistake is entered.
   b) When the program is about to be compiled.

11 During program execution.

12 Overflow, rounding, truncation, division by zero.

13 Logical errors.

14 Student's own answer, e.g:
```
counter:= 0
REPEAT
counter:= counter+1
UNTIL counter = 0
```

15 Documentation which is contained inside the program.

16 If your or someone else has to look back at the program in the future.

17 The name that a program uses to identify a storage location in the computer's memory.

18 A name that contains one or more words which describe it.

19 Meaningful variable names improve the readability of a program, and a programmer who uses meaningful variable names is less likely to make mistakes.

20 A variable name applies only to variables but an identifier may be used to name any part of a program.

21 To highlight program control structures.

22 A structured listing.

23 You can see at a glance where each of the program control structures begins and ends. You are more likely to be able to spot mistakes in the program.

CHAPTER 4

Answers

1 Design.

2 A conditional loop structure does not have a fixed number of times. You do not know how many 'goes' the user will need before they enter an answer within the range.

3 a) Pseudocode.
  b) Each line of pseudocode equals one line of code.

4 Student's own answer – depends on algorithm chosen.

1 The process of planning the solution.

2 A set of instructions used to solve a problem.

3 The way of representing the design of a program.

4 Student's own answer.

5 A Graphical Design Notation uses shapes to describe a design.

6 a) Structure diagram
  b) i)

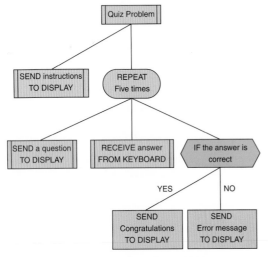

Figure 5.09 Answer to Question 6 b) i)

ii)

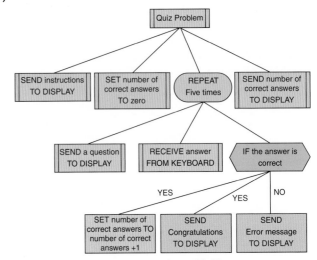

Figure 5.10 Answer to Question 6 b) ii)

7 A series of still drawings that maps out a proposed story over a number of separate panels.

8 I would choose a storyboard because it gives the potential users a better idea of how the completed software will look. OR I will choose a structure diagram because it relates more directly to the coding required.

9 A diagram or sketch used to represent the appearance and function of a website.

10 The position of each element of the page content, such as placeholders for text and graphics, navigation buttons or hyperlinks.

11 The language used to define problems and sub-problems before they are changed into code in a high-level computer language.

12 Ordinary English.

13 Pseudocode fits in neatly with the structure of the code, with each step representing a line of code.

14 a) INTEGER
   b) BOOLEAN
   c) STRING

d) IF ... THEN ...
   ELSE ...
   END IF
e) WHILE ... DO ... END WHILE
f) REPEAT ... UNTIL
g) FOR ... FROM ... TO ... DO ... END FOR
h) RECEIVE ... FROM ... KEYBOARD
i) SET ... TO ...

15 Unified Modelling Language.

16 Structural (class) and behavioural (use case).

1 A structured collection of similar information which you can search through.

2 Fields, records and files.

3 An area on a record which contains an individual piece of data.

4 A collection of structured data on a particular person or thing, made up of one or more fields.

5 A collection of structured data on a particular topic, made up of records.

6 a) Field.
 b) Record.
 c) File.

7 Text, number, date, time, graphics, calculated.

8 a) Text.
 b) Number.
 c) Graphics.
 d) Calculated.

9 Search and sort.

10 Simple search.

11 <, <=, >, >=, =, ≠ (or <>)

12 number > 10

13 * is the wildcard operator. It is used to represent any information, e.g. Sar*.

14

Data	Field type
129.67	number
August	text
27 August 2015	date
	graphic / object
www.waddle.com	hyperlink
True / False	Boolean
net price = price + vat	calculated

15 AND, OR, NOT.

16 Complex sort.

17 On the pay field in ascending order and on the name field in ascending order.

18 Occupation, Surname and First name.

19 A set of data items organised in rows and columns.

20 field, record, table, file

21 A flat file database.

22 A relational database.

23 To link tables in a database.

24 Has a unique value. Must contain an entry.

25 A field in a table which links to the primary key in a related table.

26 a) Class.
   b) The key field is used in the pupil table as the foreign key. The key field is used in the guidance teacher table as the primary key.

27 a) There is data duplication.
   b) Split the database into two tables – one for movies and one for customers.
   c) It would remove the data duplication, reduce the storage space required and reduce the chances of data modification errors.

28 A check to make sure that an item of data is sensible and allowable.

29 Presence check, restricted choice, field length and range.

30 When inserting, deleting or updating a database.

31 a) If my name and address took up 50 characters, then $300 \times 50 = 15\,000$ bytes.
   b) Taking a telephone number as 11 characters, $300 \times 11 = 3\,300$ bytes. Add $15\,000$ giving a total of $18\,300$ bytes.

32 A collection of information held in multimedia form on the internet.

33 At locations called websites in the form of web pages.

34 Links between World Wide Web pages, documents or files.

35 By clicking on text which acts as a button, or on a particular area of the screen like a graphic.

36 A special language called HTML or HyperText Mark-up Language.

37 Uniform Resource Locator.

38 protocol://domain name/pathname

39 By entering its URL into a web browser.

40 An internal hyperlink takes the user to another page within the same website. An external hyperlink takes the user to a different website, either on the same server or on a different server.

41 a) External.
   b) Internal.

42 How the user finds their way around the information system.

43 A program that allows the user to browse or surf through the World Wide Web.

44 Student's own answer.

45 When you bookmark a page, the web address of the page is stored. Clicking on a bookmark or selecting from a menu will cause the page to be found and displayed.

46 Accesses a specific web page.

47 The history remembers all of the web pages visited, so you can return to a previously visited web page without having to create a bookmark or favourite.

48 Tabbed browsing allows many different web pages to be easily accessed from a single screen window by using a tabbed document interface.

49 A search engine.

50 Search engines work by:
   1 searching the internet for different words
   2 building up an index of these words, and where they can be found
   3 allowing users to search for particular words in their indexes
   4 providing hyperlinks to where these words may be found on the internet.

51 A keyword.

52 A successful search using a search engine will result in several matches. Each match is called a hit.

53 *pool NOT swimming*

54 Breadcrumbs, guided navigation, tag clouds, site maps.

55 How easy it is to use and learn about an item.

56 An information system is accessible when it is usable by everyone, including people with disabilities.

57 Links and navigation, and matches user interface design.

58 a) 1508
   b) main colour of flower = red
   c) Internal.

1 The way in which the computer and the user communicate.

2 Human Computer Interface.

3 If a user interface is poor, then no matter how effective the software, no one will want to use it.

4 Keyboard, mouse.

5 Monitor, loudspeaker.

6 The people who will use an information system.

7 They can ensure that the user interface is suitable for the skills and abilities of the target audience.

8 The features of the user interface which should be taken into account by the designer and the programmer of the information system.

9 Visual layout, navigation, selection, consistency, interactivity, readability and accessibility.

10 The appearance of the information system on the screen.

11

User	Visual layout
Young child	Bright and colourful screen which captures and holds the user's attention
Shopper	Clear descriptions of the items displayed on the page
Person with sensory impairment	Large typeface or read aloud / text to speech
Expert	Essential information only, uncluttered
Novice	Step-by-step instructions on how to use the website

12 The part of the screen which does not contain any content.

13 It helps to focus the reader's attention upon what is important on the page.

14 How the user finds their way around the information system.

15 Student's own answer.

16 a) Allows fast movement between pages.
   b) Useful for processes that may be followed in a set order, like purchasing.

17 Back, forward, home.

18 The pointer changes to a hand.

19 a) Hiding those navigation features which are not needed and only displaying those required at a particular time.
   b) A sequence of terms which show you where you are in a website.
   c) Filters containing different options are displayed and the user makes a selection which narrows the search.
   d) A tag cloud has a list of terms, either displayed with numbers or in differently sized typefaces to show popularity.

20 Making a choice.

21 Menu selection, form fill, radio button, hotspot.

22 Being similar.

23 Text style, font, colour.

24 The feel of the system when it is being used.

25 Leading the user through a process by highlighting the next step.

26 When an information system is easy to read and understand.

27 By measuring the reading age of the text on the website.

28 The degree to which an information system is usable by everyone.

29 Magnifying the screen, reading text aloud.

30 a) Bird finder; goose, duck, medium/large, grey & white, coast, estuaries; tap matching birds button

b) Simple interface aids navigation; large on-screen icons/buttons for touch-screen use; clear uncluttered layout.

CHAPTER 8

Answers

1 Sound, graphics, video and text.

2 a) Sound.
  b) Graphics.
  c) Video.
  d) Text.

3 All different types of data are stored as numbers inside a computer system.

4 A way of storing data so that it can be understood by and transferred between different application packages.

5 Users can increase their productivity if it is possible to save files and data so that they may be transferred easily between different applications.

6 a) TXT, RTF
  b) WAV, MP3
  c) JPEG, BMP, GIF, PNG
  d) MPEG, AVI

7 PDF

8 By right-clicking and choosing Open with.

9 The American Standard Code for Information Interchange.

10 Text.

11 Each character has its own code number, e.g. A=65.

12 RTF preserves the formatting information in a piece of text.

13 WAVeform audio file format.

14 They are normally uncompressed.

15 MPEG-1 Audio Layer-3

16 3 Megabytes

17 The Joint Photographic Expert Group.

18 Natural, real-life images.

19 They are normally uncompressed.

20 Graphics Interchange Format.

21 A sequence of images is stored in a single file.

22 Line drawings and pictures with solid blocks of colour.

23 256

24 Portable Network Graphics.

25 1,2,4

26 a) MPEG-2
  b) MPEG-1
  c) MP4 (MPEG-4)

27 Motion Picture Expert Group.

28 Microsoft®.

29 Audio Video Interleave(d).

30 Portable Document Format.

31 Acrobat Reader® or an equivalent, such as Preview.

32 Resolution, colour depth and sampling rate.

33 The amount of space taken up by a file when it is being held on a backing storage medium such as hard disk or flash ROM.

34 How closely the file matches when compared to the original.

35 The amount of detail which can be shown on a screen or on a printout.

36 The number of bits used to represent colours or shades of grey in a graphic.

37 The number of times in one second that measurements of the sound are taken.

38 Increasing the resolution and increasing the colour depth.

39 Increasing the sampling rate.

40 The file size increases because more data must be stored.

41 Storage requirements = total number of pixels used in the image × number of bits used to represent colours or shades of grey for each pixel.

42 The process of reducing the size of a file.

43 To save backing storage space or to reduce the time taken to transmit a file across a network.

44 Lossy compression reduces the size of a file by throwing away some of the data. Lossless compression also reduces the file size, but no data is lost in the process.

CHAPTER 9

Answers

1 A programming language that allows the user to carry out or automate tasks.

2 JavaScript® and VBScript®.

3 To make web pages more dynamic and interactive.

4 May be included in the code of a web page. A fully-featured language.

5 May be used to run malicious code on a user's computer. The output may look different on different browsers.

6 Java® is a compiled language and JavaScript® is an interpreted language.

7 JavaScript® works on a variety of browsers. VBScript® only works with Internet Explorer®.

8 AppleScript® works with the Macintosh Operating System.

9 A programming language used for describing how text and other media are presented to the user.

10 The notations made on a paper manuscript which is being edited and prepared for publication.

11 HyperText Mark-up Language.

12 To create web pages.

13 The document type declaration, the head and the body.

14 To separate each part of an HTML document into elements.

15 Opening and closing tags.

16 Tags which are surrounded by or contained between other tags.

17 Student's own answer, e.g: <head> <title> My first web page </title> </head>

18 What You See Is What You Get.

19 Dreamweaver®.

20 a) <a>
   b) <img>
   c) <p>
   d) </html>

21 Color and font-family.

22 3

23 255

24 (255,0,0)

Answer to VBScript question on page 201:

Bristol Fighter

Gumpert Apollo

Isdera Commendatore

Answer to AppleScript® question on page 202:

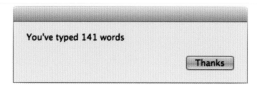

You've typed 141 words

Thanks

1 An integrated set of components that enables people to carry out tasks effectively by providing access to information.

2 Manual: telephone directory; computer-based: database.

3 Hardware, software, storage and networks/connectivity.

4 Collecting, organising, storing, processing and outputting.

5 When a date is written as numbers, for instance 4413, then it is data, because this number could mean anything. When it is written as 4/4/13, then it is recognisable as a date, and so becomes information.

6 Garbage In, Garbage Out.

7 If the data is not accurate, complete and up to date then it is of no use to the user.

8 It is much faster to search and sort information when it is stored on computer. Information stored on computer takes up much less storage space than manual files.

9 A person who is familiar with the features and functions of the information system and can use it to their advantage.

10 A person who is unfamiliar with the features and functions of the information system and requires support on how to use the system and how to get the best out of it.

11 The ages of the users of the information system.

12 Young child, teenager and adult.

13 To contain information and present it to the user in a form which is useful to them.

14 a) Stores family details.
   b) Stores details of crimes committed.
   c) Collects tax.
   d) Sells and delivers items to customers.
   e) Helps you when you are unwell.

15 An information system which collects, organises, stores, processes and outputs information for the benefit of a company or organisation.

CHAPTER 11

Answers

1 A device which allows data to be entered into a computer system.

2 Keyboard, mouse, microphone, sound card, track pad, graphics tablet, touch-sensitive screen, joystick, digital still camera, digital video camera, scanner, webcam, data glove, interactive whiteboard.

3 Student's own answer.

4 a) An input device consisting of a set of buttons or keys marked with characters, for entering text and numeric data and commands into a computer.
  b) An input device which has a light underneath it and one or more switches on top, used to control a pointer on screen.
  c) An input device which allows sound to be input into a computer system.
  d) A device which allows sound to be both input to and output from a computer system.
  e) An input device consisting of a pressure-sensitive plate and one or more switches, used to control a pointer on screen.
  f) An input device used for Computer Aided Design or drawing with a stylus.
  g) An input device which is also an output device, and is operated by pressing on the display with one or more fingers.
  h) An input device used to control the movement of a character or icon in a game.
  i) An input device used to capture images (photographs) and store them on flash ROM.
  j) An input device used for taking movies.
  k) An input device used to input printed material, such as images or text into a computer system.
  l) An input device like a small digital camera but without onboard storage of images.
  m) An input device used to take part in virtual reality.
  n) An input device used to write on a board, used with a computer and multimedia projector.

5 a) Keyboard.
  b) Mouse, track pad.
  c) Microphone.
  d) Sound card.
  e) Digital camera, webcam, scanner.
  f) Scanner.
  g) Digital video camera.
  h) Mouse, track pad.
  i) Joystick.
  j) Track pad.
  k) Interactive whiteboard.
  l) Graphics tablet.

6 Because of the order of characters in the top row.

7 Each key transmits a different number, which is related to the character code in ASCII.

8 There is no room to use a mouse on someone's lap.

9 A sound card.

10 A Charge Coupled Device, used as a light sensor in a camera.

11 Digital camera, scanner, webcam.

12 Digital camera, scanner.

13 A memory card (flash ROM).

14 Text and images.

15 a) 115 200,000 bits
   b) 13.7 Megabytes

16 a) To remotely monitor premises over the internet.
   b) To video conference over the internet.

17 A device which allows data to be output from a computer system.

18 Monitor, laser printer, inkjet printer, plotter, loudspeaker, headphones, earphones, sound card, graphics card, headset, multimedia projector.

19 a) An output device which displays images and text.
   b) An output device which produces a hard copy by squirting ink onto paper.

c) An output device which produces a hard copy by melting toner onto paper.

d) An output device which outputs sound.

e) Controls the quality of output on a monitor.

f) Connects to a graphics card and displays the contents of the computer screen on a wall or interactive whiteboard.

20 a) Monitor.

b) Inkjet or laser printer.

c) LCD panel, loudspeaker.

21 Liquid Crystal Display.

22 Light Emitting Diode.

23 By multiplying the number of horizontal pixels by the vertical pixels.

24 A printout.

25 a) By squirting small droplets of ink onto paper, through tiny holes in the print head.

b) A laser beam is used to project the image of the page to be printed onto a drum and transferring the image onto the paper using toner.

26 A laser printer.

27 An inkjet printer.

28 a) Pages per minute.

b) Dots per inch.

29 Cyan, magenta and yellow.

30 To save money by not having to replace a cartridge which is not completely empty.

31 To preview photographs when printing from a card or directly from a digital still camera.

32 To save having to load the photographs into the computer first – the photo may be printed directly from the card.

33 A speaker which contains its own amplifier and power supply.

34 A device which generates pulses at a very fast rate to keep the processor in time.

35 The rate at which the clock generates pulses.

36 Gigahertz (Ghz)

37 How fast the processor is operating.

38 1000 million pulses a second.

39 Sarah, because the clock speed of her computer is higher. OR Mary, because her processor has two cores.

40 There may be other differences between them.

41 Number of cores, instruction set, number of functions.

42 Increase the number of cores.

43 An individual processor on a chip containing two or more cores.

44 Reduced Instruction Set Computer.

45 Individual instructions may take fewer clock cycles and so less time to run.

46 System On Chip – a whole computer on a single piece of silicon.

47 A computer inside a television set.

48 Random Access Memory.

49 The data held in RAM is lost when the power is off.

50 To hold data and instructions while they are being processed.

51 Read Only Memory.

52 The data held in ROM is not lost when the power is off.

53 To hold programs permanently.

54 When the power is off, the data held in RAM is lost and the data held in ROM is not lost.

55 Flash ROM.

56 To prevent the program from being changed or erased accidentally.

57 The access time of hard disk is too slow compared to RAM.

58 Save the program to backing storage.

59 A small computer inside another, larger piece of equipment.

60 Because it is inside and part of another piece of equipment.

61 Real-time processing takes place instantly. Embedded computers in cars, for example, need to operate straight away without delay.

62 The computer can have more or larger programs loaded in RAM at one time.

63 Data held in them may be accessed in any order.

64 Add the amount of RAM and amount of ROM together.

65 A computer which is normally operated while it is sitting on a desk.

66 A computer which is normally operated on a person's lap, whilst seated.

67 A computer which has a large touch-sensitive screen as its main input and output device.

68 A mobile phone which has its own operating system and is capable of running a variety of applications.

69 A very large computer system which can process a very large amount of data at high speed.

70 The fastest and most powerful type of computer, used for intensive mathematical calculations.

71 a) Writing a computer program.
   b) Word processing while on a train.
   c) Playing a game.
   d) Sending email.
   e) Weather forecasting.

72 a) A tablet.
   b) A tablet, a smartphone.
   c) A laptop, a tablet, a smartphone.

73 a) A supercomputer.
   b) A tablet, a smartphone, a laptop.
   c) A desktop.
   d) A tablet, a smartphone.
   e) A laptop.

74 The screen.

75 Cable or wireless.

76 a) A supercomputer has much more processing power.
   b) A tablet computer is not normally used for making phone calls.

77 a) A mouse.
   b) A trackpad.

78 Easy to use with its touch-sensitive screen, and it can run a wide variety of applications.

79 A program which controls how the computer works.

80 The computer cannot work without it.

81 a) When the computer is switched on.
   b) The operating system program must be the first to load in order to control the computer.
   c) Bootstrap loader.

82 Windows® and Unix®.

83 The hardware and software that makes up a computer system.

84 That software will only run on one type of machine, for instance either Windows® or Apple®.

85 That software will run on two types of machine, for instance both Windows® and Apple®.

86 The system requirements tell the user which particular platform a particular item of software requires.

87 On the software manufacturer's or retailer's website, or printed on the box that the software comes in.

88 The platform.

89 To allow the software to install and run correctly.

90 To install the software from disk.

91 Grabbit would not work because it requires 4GB RAM and your computer only has 2 Gb.

   Trappit would work because it meets the minimum requirements, although the processor is slower than recommended, Windows® 7 is newer than Windows® Vista (assuming backwards compatibility).

   Stoppit would work because all the system requirements are met or exceeded.

   Pausit would not work because it requires Windows® 8 and your computer only has Windows® 7.

92 Any two from:

   Managing the reception of data from input devices like the keyboard and mouse.

   Managing the sending of data to output devices like the screen and the printer.

   Controlling where programs and data are placed in the computer's memory.

   Managing the filing system.

   Controlling the security of the system.

   Providing a Human Computer Interface (HCI) for the user.

   Letting the user know if any mistakes have occurred.

93 Human Computer Interface.

94 Changing the background or wallpaper using the control panel or system preferences.

95 The operating system controls how the computer works. An application program performs a task, like word processing or a game.

96 A program that allows the user to browse or surf through the World Wide Web.

97 A type of systems software designed to perform an everyday task.

98 A program which allows a computer to run a different operating system.

99 The problem of not being able to run software because it is written for a different platform.

CHAPTER 12

Answers

1 Used to store programs and data permanently.

2 Because data held in the memory is lost when the computer is switched off.

3 A device used to store data on a storage medium.

4 The substance which holds the data.

5 Media holds the data (for example hard disk), but software is the data which is held (e.g. a word-processing file).

6 Magnetic tape and hard disk.

7 Magnetic tape drive and hard disk drive.

8 Magnetic and optical.

9 Keeping backup copies.

10 In case the original copy is lost or damaged.

11 In a safe place, away from the computer.

12 Backing storage holds programs and data; backup is an extra copy in case the original is lost or damaged.

13 How much data may be held by the device.

14 Serial or sequential, direct or random access.

15 The method of connection or interface.

16 May not have data saved to it, nor deleted from it.

17 Preparing a storage medium to hold data.

18 Invisible circles of magnetism, called tracks, are created on the surface of the disk.

19 Different computer systems use different formats, and they may not always be interchangeable.

20 The disk is made of metal.

21 The read/write head makes contact with the spinning metal disk and the disk may be damaged.

22 It takes a second or two for the optical drive to start spinning the disk around before the read/write head can move to the right track, but a hard disk drive is spinning all the time and much faster than an optical disk, so there is only a fraction of a second's delay before the read/write head can reach the correct track.

23 Magnetic tape.

24 To find a program by using sequential access, you have to look through all of the tape from the beginning. Using direct access you can go straight to the program required.

25 Routine backups and long-term archiving of data.

26 To allow more data to be stored on a storage medium of fixed size.

27 Because they use laser beams to read the data stored on them.

28 Data is stored on a CD-ROM using pits and lands and the pits and lands are read by a laser beam.

29 Scratches on the label side may cause oxidation of the metal layer.

30 One power to record the data and another, lower, power to read the data.

31 Dye.

32 To ensure that a CD-R is not written to at too high a speed, which may result in failure or an unreliable copy.

33 Different occasions on which a disk is written to.

34 CD-RW may be erased and rewritten; CD-R may be written to until it is full.

35 A drive which can read and write CD-Rs and CD-RWs and read DVD-ROMs.

36 A CD-ROM has a lower backing storage capacity than a DVD-ROM.

37 The pits on a DVD-ROM are smaller than the pits on a CD-ROM; the tracks are closer together on a DVD-ROM; DVD-ROMs may be double layered and double sided; more efficient error correction means that there is more space to hold data on a DVD-ROM.

38 From the blue colour of the laser used to read it.

39 The laser beam in the drive is coloured blue and produces a narrower beam of light than a red laser on a DVD drive. Blue light has a shorter wavelength than red light.

40 Universal Serial Bus.

41 Solid-state storage has no moving parts and the storage media itself is solid.

42 A device containing a flash ROM medium which uses the USB interface.

43 A USB flash drive is more robust (less easily damaged) than a hard disk drive because it has no moving parts – it is solid state.

44 They all use flash ROM as their backing storage medium.

45 Secure Digital (SD) and Compact Flash (CF).

46 Online storage which is accessed via a Wide Area Network.

47 Magnetic hard disks.

48 The amount of space available on a given medium.

49 The amount of space available in a computer system (RAM), used to hold programs and data once they have been loaded.

50 a) Hard disk drive.
   b) USB flash ROM drive.
   c) Blu-ray Disc™ drive.

51 a) flash ROM or DVD-R.
   b) flash ROM or BD-R.

52 The hardware and associated software needed to allow communication between the processor and its peripheral devices.

53 A device which may be connected to the outside of a computer system, for input, output or backing storage.

54 USB and Firewire®.

55 All current desktop and laptop computers also have USB interfaces.

56 Thunderbolt® can also carry a video signal.

57 a) USB, wireless and SD card.
   b) Wireless allows data to be transmitted to devices without requiring a physical connection.

58 The use of computing resources (such as hardware and software) that are delivered as a service over the internet.

59 From the use of the cloud symbol to represent the internet or other networks.

60 They only have to be able to access their data® they do not care how it is stored.

61 Platform as a service provides software and development tools which help the user to create applications. Software as a service is a software delivery model in which applications are held on, and run from, the cloud. Infrastructure as a service provides services which involve hardware, data storage, networking and bandwidth.

62 Security – if you lose your data locally, a backup is available in the cloud. Scaling – services may be increased or decreased on demand.

63 Security – the cloud company may lose your data. Privacy – your data may not be kept private.

64 Privacy – only you can see your data.

CHAPTER 13

1 A linked set of computer systems that are capable of sharing programs and data, and sending messages between them.

2 A computer which is not connected to a network.

3 A Local Area Network (LAN) covers a small area such as a room or a building.

4 A Wide Area Network (WAN) covers a larger geographical area, such as a country or a continent.

5 A Wide Area Network spanning the globe. It can be thought of as many different, smaller networks connected together.

6 A company that provides a host computer to which the user can connect.

7 The material which carries the data in a network, e.g. copper cable or optical fibre.

8 Cable.

9 A high-speed method of wireless data transmission.

10 Using a laptop, tablet or phone to access the World Wide Web.

11 A short-range wireless standard.

12 WiFi has a greater range of data transmission than Bluetooth®.

13 A measure of the quantity of data which may be carried by a communications channel at any one time.

14 Megabits/second or Gigabits/second.

15 A printer.

16 Optical fibre.

17 a) One company or organisation.
   b) Many different organisations.

18 2–8 Mbps

19 Microwave transmission is highly directional and has a shorter range than satellite.

20 Sharing data and programs between stations; an electronic mail service may be operated; each user's data may be kept secure; flexible access enables users to access their files from any station; workgroup computing; resource/peripheral sharing.

21 LAN.

22 Network Interface Card (NIC).

23 Data sharing.

24 Telecommunications links, e.g. microwave transmission, satellite links and optical fibre.

25 Optical fibre.

26 A printer may be some distance from the user.

27 Asymmetric Digital Subscriber Line – a method of broadband access to a WAN.

28 By installing a dedicated cable connection.

29 Copper wire is less expensive than optical fibre.

30 Optical fibre cannot be tapped.

31 Optical fibre is lighter and optical fibre cables do not produce electrical interference, which may affect the operation of other systems on the aeroplane.

32 To prevent unauthorised users from gaining access.

33 A peer-to-peer network is made up of computers, all of which have the same status.

34 Data is stored locally; users must back up their own data; resource sharing.

35 A method of organisation in which client workstations make use of resources available on one or more servers.

36 The name given to a workstation on a client/server network.

37 A computer that handles requests for data, email, file transfers and other network services from other computers.

38 A Network Interface Card (NIC).

39 File, print, web.

40 A printer server; print jobs would be in the queue.

41 By making use of user identities and passwords.

42 To prevent unauthorised users from looking at files belonging to others.

43 An uninterruptible power supply.

44 On a server.

45 Because the server has to run constantly (24/7).

46 Organise the storage of user data and handle the security of the network.

47 If the file server is not working, then users cannot access their data.

CHAPTER 12

1 It is unable to be accessed by an unauthorised person and is not affected by malware.

2 Software that has been deliberately created to disrupt the operation of a computer system, or gain illegal access to it in order to gather information.

3 Virus, worm, Trojan.

4 A program which can copy or replicate itself and infect other programs or computers.

5 Viruses attach themselves to other programs in order to ensure that they are run and can infect programs.

6 A stand-alone program which copies or replicates itself in order to spread to other computer systems.

7 Worms actively transmit copies of themselves to other computer systems by using computer networks.

8 A program that appears to be safe, but hidden inside is usually something harmful, like a worm or a virus.

9 a) A virus attaches itself to or 'infects' an existing program. A worm operates on its own, without requiring other programs in order to spread.
   b) A Trojan is disguised as another type of file; a virus is not.

10 Displaying unwanted messages; unusual visual or sound effects; computers rebooting or restarting unexpectedly; unwanted generation of emails.

11 By sharing infected media and drives between computers, downloading from websites and through email attachments.

12 It's a Trojan because it came disguised; it's a virus because it infected files; it's a worm because it copied itself.

13 Watching for a date or an action.

14 If the drive is first plugged into an infected computer, then it can infect other computers by being attached to them.

15 Illegal copies of software often contain viruses.

16 Gaining unauthorised access to a computer system.

17 The Computer Misuse Act.

18 a) A skilled hacker who uses his or her ability to pursue their interest illegally.
   b) Someone who tries to break into systems for legal purposes, as employees testing the security of their own systems.
   c) A system which is deliberately left open to attract the activities of black hats.

19 Attempting to trick someone into giving away personal information using the internet.

20 Pretending to be someone else on the telephone and stealing personal documents.

21 Identity theft.

22 Tricking someone into performing an action or giving away confidential information.

23 Bad spelling or grammar and a request to verify your account.

24 Stating that your account is closed, or your personal information has been posted on the web.

25 a) Delete suspicious emails.
   b) Do not call any supplied numbers.

26 When someone pretends to be someone else in order to carry out fraud.

27 You receive bills for unordered goods and/or letters from debt collectors.

28 Keeping your personal details safe at all times.

29 Their whole life can be destroyed by receiving a bad credit rating, losing all of their money and becoming bankrupt.

30 A type of malware which collects information about a user without their knowledge.

31 Make a backup, wipe the computer clean and re-install.

32 Recording every keystroke on a computer without the user's knowledge.

33 Using a software program or a hardware device.

34 Hardware, especially if it is hidden inside the computer.

35 Use a single-use code or one-time password.

36 The use of services available on the internet to defraud people of money, or to carry out identity theft.

37 A person who uses their bank account to transfer stolen money from one account to another.

38 Clicking on an advertising link to cause the advertiser to be charged.

39 Check that offers are genuine.

40 Denial of Service – interrupting the services of a host computer, such as a company website, in order to make it unusable, by making multiple requests for access.

41 Distributed Denial of Service® – when many computers carry out a DOS attack on a single computer.

42 a) A computer that has been taken over by malware/a Trojan.
   b) A collection of zombie computers.
   c) The person in control of a botnet.

43 DOS is carried out by a single computer; DDOS by many computers.

44 A DDOS tool connects to a master computer which controls a botnet. The botnet is then targeted against a single computer hosting a website.

45 Student's own answer.

46 To prevent their computers from becoming infected with malware.

47 Use of anti-virus software.

48 Application software which protects a computer system against attack or infection by malware.

49 To detect a virus infection and remove it from a computer system.

50 A macro virus.

51 Install anti-virus software, avoid downloading programs from unknown sources, never open an email attachment containing an executable file.

52 Using a user identity and password.

53 One which is difficult to guess and has a variety of characters including numbers, letters and special characters.

54 To reduce the risk if one of your passwords is discovered.

55 Student's own answer.

56 Users find it difficult to remember a large number of user identities and passwords.

57 Putting data into a code to prevent it from being seen by unauthorised users.

58 To protect emails and files sent over a network.

59 Using a person's physical characteristics to provide evidence of their identity.

60 a) A fingerprint.
   b) A signature.

61 a) Increase.
   b) Increase.

62 A set of rules that determines how something is to be done.

63 TCP.

64 A sequence of operations that makes sure data is protected.

65 TLS and SSL.

66 To make secure web pages – https.

67 The site is secure.

68 Click on it and it should link to a certificate.

69 A valid document that indicates whether a website is secure.

70 Date/expiry date.

71 A system designed to prevent unauthorised access to or from a private network.

72 Controls what is blocked or let through according to the rules.

73 A software firewall protects a single computer. A hardware firewall protects all computers connected to a router.

74 A server used to access web pages requested by other computers on a network.

75 By means of content filtering, e.g. blocking access to unsuitable sites.

76 A collection of software which is sold together as a single package and contains programs which protect computers against a variety of malware.

77 Anti-virus, firewall, anti-spam, anti-spyware.

78 Infect it with malware.

79 Student's own answer.

80 Smart card, password and fingerprint.

1 Computer Misuse Act 1990, Data Protection Act 1998 and Copyright, Designs and Patents Act 1988.

2 Gaining unauthorised access (hacking) and writing and distribution of harmful software (malware).

3 So many computers may be accessed through networks.

4 People may be refused jobs, housing, benefits or credit, be overcharged for goods or services or be wrongfully arrested.

5 Data Protection Act 1998.

6 a) Data controller.
  b) Data subject.

7 Data which relates to a living individual who can be identified from that data.

8 Register with the Information Commissioner.

9 See their own data, correct errors, compensation, no direct marketing, no automated decision-making.

10 Any two from the eight listed:

  1 Personal data should be fairly and lawfully processed.

  2 Personal data should only be used or disclosed for the specified purposes.

  3 Personal data should be adequate, relevant and not excessive (e.g. the Inland Revenue does not need to know the name of your goldfish).

  4 Personal data should be accurate and kept up to date (e.g. if you have changed your address).

  5 Information should not be kept any longer than necessary (e.g. the school does not need your emergency contact details after you have left).

  6 Data must be processed in accordance with the rights of the data subjects.

  7 Security measures should prevent unauthorised access or alteration of the data (e.g. use passwords, encryption and keep regular backup copies).

8 Personal data should not be transferred to countries outside the EU except to countries with adequate data-protection legislation.

11 a) Keep data accurate and up to date
   b) Data should be adequate, relevant and not excessive.
   c) Data should be kept secure.
   d) Data should only be disclosed for the specified purpose.

12 Police, Inland Revenue.

13 Your family tree.

14 Copyright, Designs and Patents Act 1998.

15 The right to prevent others from copying someone else's work.

16 Using a downloaded image in a school report for which you acknowledge the source.

17 In order to use the software on all the computers in your school.

18 Sell it or give it away.

19 Placing a 'cap' or monthly download limit on an account.

20 It goes to fund organised crime.

21 Copying work created by another person and pretending it is yours.

22 Acknowledge the source.

23 Dishonestly obtaining an electronic communications service and sending an offensive message.

24 A person who deliberately tries to upset others by sending online messages.

25 a) Glare: eyesight; keyboard: upper limb disorders.
   b) Use of anti-glare screens; correct height of chairs.

26 Electrocution and fire.

CHAPTER 16

Answers

1 Energy use, disposal of IT equipment and carbon footprint.

2 Watts, Kilowatt hours/price per unit.

3 Laptop.

4 The laptop (which has an LCD) figure is 29 kWh and the monitor is 42 kWh.

5 If the computer was carrying out a less processor-intensive task, such as word processing, rather than gaming.

6 Monitor/display sleep and hard disk sleep.

7 The monitor is constantly displaying an image at full power.

8 Switch the computer off.

9 a) A searchable database of products which meet certain environmental criteria.
  b) A product rating system for home electrical goods.

10 Lead and mercury.

11 Hazardous chemicals can pollute the environment.

12 Give the computer to someone who needs it. Part-exchange it for a new one.

13 If the computer's hard disk is not completely wiped, then there is a danger that your personal information may be retrieved, and could get into the wrong hands.

14 The amount of greenhouse gases (including carbon dioxide and methane) produced by people or a particular activity.

15 They absorb heat and can cause global warming.

16 Walking or cycling instead of driving. Improve home insulation and turn down thermostats.

17 Switch off computers and associated equipment, such as printers, when not in use, instead of leaving them on standby. Do not take unnecessary printouts.